MW00616545

The Russian Army
in the Great War

The Russian Army in the Great War

The Eastern Front, 1914–1917

David R. Stone

*Jim —
Best wishes, + thanks
for your interest in World war I
All the best,
DR Stone*

 University Press of Kansas

Published by the University Press of Kansas (Lawrence, Kansas 66045), which was
organized by the Kansas Board of Regents and is operated and funded by Emporia State
University, Fort Hays State University, Kansas State University, Pittsburg State
University, the University of Kansas, and Wichita State University

Library of Congress Cataloging-in-Publication Data

Stone, David R., 1968–
The Russian Army in the Great War : the Eastern Front, 1914–1917 / David R. Stone.
    pages cm. — (Modern war studies)
Includes bibliographical references and index.
ISBN 978-0-7006-2095-1 (cloth : alk. paper)
1. World War, 1914–1918—Campaigns—Eastern Front. 2. Russkaia Armiia—History—
World War, 1914–1918. 3. World War, 1914–1918—Soviet Union. I. Title.
D550.S75 2015
940.4'1247—dc23

                          2014040565

British Library Cataloguing-in-Publication Data is available.

Printed in the United States of America

10 9 8 7 6 5 4 3

The paper used in this publication is recycled and contains 30 percent postconsumer
waste. It is acid free and meets the minimum requirements of the American National
Standard for Permanence of Paper for Printed Library Materials Z39.48-1992.

Contents

(A photo section appears following page 196.)

Acknowledgments

I am grateful for the financial support of Frank and Elizabeth Burke, whose endowment of the Richard A. and Greta Bauer Pickett Chair supported the research and writing of this book. The generosity of Mark Chapman underwrote the maps in this book, prepared by Darin Grauberger. Illustrations are courtesy of the Library of Congress, the Russian Information Agency Novosti, and the Imperial War Museum.

Introduction

The dominant picture of World War I in the West is, quite naturally, the trenches of the Western Front: immobile, pointless, static. Expanding our focus to the war on the Eastern Front, and particularly to Russia's role in that war, changes the picture fundamentally. The front lines in the east advanced and retreated for hundreds of miles, putting over one hundred thousand square miles of territory under foreign occupation. For all its slaughter, the war altered the landscape of Eastern Europe irrevocably. In the West, those who went through the war could legitimately say that millions had died, but that nothing had changed. In the East, no one could make that claim. Millions had perished, but *everything* had changed. The war on the Eastern Front, and particularly Russia's experience, is the focus of this book.

By the end of 1914, four empires were at war in Eastern Europe: the Austro-Hungarian, the Ottoman, the German, and the Russian. Austria-Hungary, the Ottoman Empire, and Germany made up the Central Powers; Russia alongside Britain, France, and much smaller Belgium and Serbia made up the Allies. Though distinct in many ways, those four eastern empires had much in common. None was fully democratic. Though electoral institutions existed, enormous power still lay in the hands of hereditary monarchs and the men they personally chose to administer their realms. All had been built up over centuries by a lengthy process of conquest, and that accretion left its marks on their internal structure. Each had groups or regions within it that enjoyed different legal standing than others, and were marked by ethnic and religious divisions. Germany was the most homogenous of the four, but it had substantial confessional tensions between Protestants and Catholics, sharp social conflicts, and a significant Polish minority in its eastern territories. Austria-Hungary was proverbial for its polyglot society of a dozen national groups and sharp division between its Austrian and Hungarian halves. The Habsburg monarch ruled Austria as emperor and Hungary as king, and the combined army was accordingly referred to as "imperial and royal." The Ottoman Empire was divided by ethnicity and religion, and those divisions exploded into violence during the war.

As for Russia itself, it possessed all the characteristics of empire under its ruling Romanov dynasty: authoritarian government, varied political structures, and a heterogeneous population. Russia enjoyed an elected legislature, the Duma, as result of its 1905 revolution, but electoral rules guaranteed that the Duma was dominated by conservative social elites, and enormous powers were still reserved to the tsar himself. Nicholas II regarded himself as an autocrat, answering to God for the exercise of his powers, and never fully accepted the constitutional restrictions that had been forced on him in 1905. The Russian state divided its citizens any number of ways, and included substantially different legal regimes. Finland, for example, was largely autonomous, and Central Asian Muslims were exempt from conscription into the army. Only about 40 percent of Russia's population was ethnically Russian. Even if closely related Belarusians and Ukrainians are included, these East Slavic peoples still only made up 70 percent of the population. In addition to the numerically dominant Orthodox Christians, Russia included important populations of Catholics on its western frontier, Lutherans around the Baltic Sea, Jews scattered throughout Russia, and Muslims in Central Asia and the Caucasus.

Of those four empires, none survived. The four emperors ruling in 1914 were out of power by the time World War I ended on 11 November 1918, and only one lived to see the end of the conflict. Austro-Hungarian emperor Franz Joseph died on 21 November 1916 after nearly sixty-eight years on the throne. Ottoman sultan Mehmed V had taken the throne in 1909 but never enjoyed real power, since the sultanate had been stripped of authority by the Young Turk revolution of 1908. He died on 3 July 1918. Two weeks after that, on the night of 16–17 July, Tsar Nicholas II was murdered along with his entire family by his former subjects. Germany's Kaiser Wilhelm II lasted the longest, but the end of the war found him fleeing into the neutral Netherlands to escape the victor's justice and the wrath of his own newly revolutionary people.

The empires those men ruled did scarcely better. Nicholas had outlived his empire by a year, which had become first a ramshackle democracy in March 1917 and then, after the Bolshevik Revolution of November 1917, a communist dictatorship. Franz Joseph's successor and grand-nephew Karl ruled barely long enough to preside over the dissolution of the Habsburg Empire into new national states at the end of the war. Mehmed VI succeeded his brother as Ottoman sultan, and suffered through a four-year term over a rump empire. From March 1920, the Ottoman capital of Constantinople and Mehmed himself lived under Allied occupation. A nascent Turkish nationalist movement obliterated even that attenuated sovereignty. The new Turkish Grand National Assembly declared Mehmed's government null and void and abolished the sultanate on 1 November 1922; Mehmed himself went into exile. And in Germany, even before the end of the war, Wilhelm's regime in October 1918 abolished many of the prerogatives of empire by transforming itself into a constitutional monarchy in hopes of winning a better peace from the victorious Allies. By November, revolution spread through Germany, and the politicians of Germany's moderate left proclaimed a new German republic in hopes of staving off social revolution.

As that litany shows, Russia's descent into anarchy, revolution, and civil war was hardly unique.[1] Russia's experience of the war is often seen as one of unrelieved catastrophe culminating in ignominious collapse. While that story is correct in its broad outlines, a deeper understanding of the war in the east suggests something different. While the Russian Empire and its ruling Romanov dynasty both disintegrated as a result of the First World War, the other empires and dynasties of Central and Eastern Europe did no better. As a result, Russia's fall and the creation of a fundamentally new Soviet regime needs to be seen in comparative context. Russia did have specific political, social, and economic weaknesses that shaped the way it fell apart and then ultimately returned as a new communist Soviet Union under the rule of Vladimir Lenin's Bolshevik Party. The same is true of all Europe's empires: they all fell in ways that reflected the particular strains on their social fabric and their individual experience during the war. While the Russian Empire failed in ways uniquely Russian, war brought with it burdens that none of the other eastern empires could sustain either. None of this is to argue that in any sense Russia won World War I, or even that it did not lose. The point is that Russia's failures must be seen in context. Russia's struggles to meet the challenge of industrial warfare were different in degree, not in kind, from those faced by every other major power. Russia was not the only great power to collapse under the strains of war; it was only the first.

Russia's war, on both the front lines and the home front, had much in common with the other European powers. It had many incompetent generals, particularly early in the war, who sent soldiers across open ground against machine guns and quick-firing artillery to be slaughtered, but the same was true of all the powers. Casualty rates across Europe in 1914, when the true nature of modern war had not yet become clear, far outpaced those of later years. Though tactically and operationally Russia was always unable to match its German opponent, it performed quite respectably against Austria-Hungary and the Ottoman Empire. The test of equaling German performance on the battlefield was a difficult one. The Germans found their own allies unable to meet it. As John Schindler remarked, this was "a test which all other armies of the Great War would have failed in some respects,"[2] and Britain and France never outfought Germany man-for-man. Russia ran desperately short of munitions and supplies, proving at times unable to provide its soldiers with rifles and uniforms, and a crippling shell shortage in 1915 left Russian troops unable to defend against a major German offensive. All the powers, though, found their prewar stocks of munitions utterly inadequate. Every European government had to fundamentally restructure its economy in order to cope with the demands of war.

On the home front, Russia was not the only power to face both military and popular discontent. The 1916 Easter Rising in Ireland and its suppression by the British government crippled recruitment there. The crisis provoked by the German spring offensives in 1918 produced an effort by the British government to extend conscription to the Irish. Only a paltry 5,000 recruits total, all volunteers and a fraction of the daily British casualty count in March 1918, came out of Ireland.[3] By 1917, soldiers on all sides were tired of the war, resentful of profiteering industrialists and distant generals, and unwilling to waste their lives in pointless military actions. To the degree that patterns can be teased out from the mass of open and more subtle indications of discontent, the soldiers of the Central Powers (like their populations) suffered more from material deprivation than did the Allies, primarily as a result of the Allied blockade. British and French soldiers were, at least, better provisioned. Even Russian soldiers ate reasonably well, though high food prices in Russian cities proved fatal to the tsarist regime. On the other hand, by late in the war the Central Powers were largely on the defensive, so it was Allied soldiers who bore the burden of sacrificing their lives in attacks. The spring 1917 offensives of French commander Robert Nivelle destroyed the morale of the French army. Beginning with minor disturbances in April 1917, mutinies reached a crisis point by late May and left half the French army facing some form of collective disobedience.[4] Domestic unrest and serious discontent was thus by no means unique to Russia. Indeed, in some ways, Russia was better prepared for the privations of war. The daily life of Russian industrial workers and peasants was one of hardship and toil, with sudden death a routine part of daily existence. Ian Beckett remarked that "the peoples of Europe were conditioned by their ordinary expectations to endure the kind of ordeal that was soon to confront them."[5] If that was the case for the relatively developed societies of Western Europe, it was even more so for Russian peasants.

One key way in which Russia did *not* share the experience of other powers was fateful: its failure to systematically and comprehensively reorganize its society for war. In the wake of the forced and improvised modernization and mobilization of the first year of the war, the three westernmost powers all embarked on substantial programs of total mobilization for the needs of the war effort. In Britain, David Lloyd George, first as minister of munitions and then as prime minister, presided over an overhaul of economic life to provide material for the conduct of war. The elderly but ferociously energetic Georges Clemenceau took office as French prime minister in 1917 with a single-minded determination to commit all resources to the war. The Hindenburg Program of August 1916, instituted by Germany's de facto military dictators Paul von Hindenburg and Erich Ludendorff to devote maximum resources to munitions, had deleterious effects on food production but nonetheless demonstrated a commitment to total war. By contrast, imperial Russia never found a way to integrate state power and private enterprise into a cohesive war effort. Tsar Nicholas's government always mistrusted initiatives and institutions outside the reach of the state. Even when forced by circumstances to accept a role for civil society, as with the large portion of medical services run by Russian city and local government or the war-industry committees that retooled production, the Russian government resisted full popular participation.

Context is also vital to understanding the particular rhythm of the war in the east. Though World War I lasted from 1914 to 1918, only this book's last three chapters deal with campaigns from 1916 on. That division is deliberate, and results from the necessary connections between the Eastern Front and the Western Front. The first eighteen months of war were marked by an almost uninterrupted sequence of campaigns in the east. At the very beginning of the war, Russia attempted to achieve rapid victory with whirlwind operations in East Prussia and Galicia. By the autumn of 1914, the German high command responded to the failure of its initial attack on France with a series of efforts to win overall victory by driving Russia from the war. These key campaigns in late 1914 and 1915 were an enormous test for the Russian Empire, but also demonstrated that Russia's resources of population and space made German victory difficult to achieve. By 1916, Russian exhaustion and German conviction of the difficulty of final victory in the east meant that the balance of German effort shifted back to the Western Front. From 1916 on, the Eastern Front became for Germany a place for economy of force: countering Russian actions and engaging in limited attacks to achieve the maximum results from the minimum expenditure of men and supplies.

Emphasizing the common fate of Europe's multinational empires, and then the particular circumstances and events that shaped their experience of the war, affects how we think about the war and its meaning. The eastern empires' race toward collapse underlines the importance of *contingency*. By contingency, I have in mind the impact of specific events and individual choices, as opposed to long-term social and economic structures. Contingency is the idea that things could have happened very differently, that individual events and choices had an enormous impact on history's direction. It is a central theme of this book. War is of course profoundly influenced by the societies that wage it and the economies that sustain those societies. This is even more true of World War I, the first industrial war. Nonetheless, war is also the quintessential theater of contingency, where the decisions of soldiers and diplomats, and the chaos and friction of the battlefield, determine events. It mattered a great deal that the final collapse of Russia's war effort came in November 1917, and not in November 1916 or November 1918. Precisely when and how Russia lost the war was influenced by the structural strengths and weaknesses of its social and economic system, but also by the outcome of events on the battlefield. This book will focus on those events.

The importance of contingency is easiest to see when looking at the outbreak of war. The event that precipitated war, in a Europe already fraught with tension, was the assassination of Archduke Franz Ferdinand, heir to the Austro-Hungarian throne. But the actual killing was a comedy of errors. Young student and Serbian nationalist Gavrilo Princip, along with his coconspirators, missed several chances to kill Franz Ferdinand. He and his wife fell victim only because their motorcade took a wrong turn in Sarajevo. The archduke's car stopped to reverse direction in front of Princip, who had been wandering the city aimlessly. This random event allowed Princip to step to the archduke's automobile and shoot him and his wife. The spark that brought the war might not have happened at all. Of course, the long-standing stresses in European politics might well have brought war eventually, but the fact that the war started in 1914, and not in 1915 or 1916, made an enormous difference. The outbreak of war caught the Russian Empire in the midst of a massive program of rearmament, as well as long-term improvement in its railroad network. Both those facts meant that with every year that passed, the Russian military would predictably and reliably improve and German vulnerability increase.

Once fighting began, contingency continued to be extremely important. One of the recurring patterns of World War I in Eastern Europe was the way in which whole armies fell apart when the strain of war became too great, or when faint prospects of victory seemed to disappear entirely. At the October–November 1917 battle of Caporetto, for example, 300,000 Italian troops marched into Austrian captivity as three armies collapsed. The Italian war effort survived this debacle, but just barely and with substantial British and French assistance. The Italians managed to return the favor a year later. As Austria-Hungary itself was disintegrating in October–November 1918, the Italians captured 300,000 Austrians who no longer saw a point in fighting in a lost war. On the Macedonian Front, a largely Bulgarian force managed to bottle up the British and French troops at Thessaloniki for three years. In September 1918, however, an Allied offensive finally broke Bulgarian resistance and forced the Bulgarian government to sue for peace in a matter of weeks. Even the German army, rightly noted for its discipline and operational effectiveness, lost its cohesion in the late summer of 1918. After the German spring offensives failed, German troops recognized that the weight of men and material on the Western Front was inexorably against them and that there was little point in continued resistance. Erich Ludendorff called 8 August 1918, the first day of the Battle of Amiens, the "black day of the German Army" because of the clear failure of German morale.

Armies in the First World War did not just reach defeat gradually and incrementally, but in the face of disaster could fail suddenly and catastrophically. As John Keegan has remarked, "The sensation of defeat . . . is unmistakeable and often uncontrollable. . . . When the germ of defeat takes a hold, even very large armies can fall apart with epidemic rapidity."[6] At a number of points during the war, the Russian war effort could easily have suffered such a sudden collapse, or produced a unprecedented triumph. The Russian invasion of East Prussia at the outbreak of war was handled with astounding clumsiness. In more skilled hands, it might easily have produced a real political crisis for the German government. In November 1914, the German attack on Łódź came very close to encircling and annihilating two full Russian armies, at a point when Russia's ready reserves had been fully mobilized and few resources remained for the defense of Russian Poland. Even more seriously, in the summer of 1915 an offensive by the Central Powers expelled Russian troops from Poland altogether and pushed the front lines hundreds of miles to the east. Though the Russian army suffered terribly, it remained intact, capable of effective defense, and generally disciplined and under control. In the other direction, the Brusilov offensive of summer 1916 inflicted terrible losses on the Austro-Hungarian army, pushing it to the point of collapse. In all those cases, it is easy to imagine how the war might have turned out quite differently. If the Russian defense at Łódź in 1914 had been just a little less tenacious, if the Russian withdrawal from Poland in 1915 had gone just a little worse, or if Brusilov's offensive in 1916 had been managed with just a little more creativity and skill, World War I would have ended very differently. Russia might have had to sue for peace in 1914 or 1915, or Austria-Hungary might have been driven from the war in 1916.

All this is, of course, counterfactual reasoning—it extrapolates consequences from choices and events that did not happen, in order to see differences from the actual historical events. This sort of thinking tends to make historians very uneasy. Historians are trained to analyze what actually happened, and speculation that runs down other paths can, if taken too far, verge on fantasy. But counterfactual reasoning, if only in a disguised form, is something that all historians do. To make the claim that a particular decision was wise is necessarily to make a simultaneous claim, either implicit or explicit, that some *other* decision would have produced a worse outcome. To condemn a policy as foolish or short-sighted requires a claim that some *other* policy would have produced better results.

The easily imaginable ways in which Russia's First World War could have come to a very different conclusion are not important simply in themselves, but for their profound impact on Russia's subsequent development. Any of the four potential turning points mentioned above—a successful Russian invasion of East Prussia, successful German encirclement of Łódź, Russian collapse during the Great Retreat of 1915, or Austrian collapse as the result of the Brusilov offensive—would have made Russian history after the war very different. For example, a victory for the Entente in 1914, or a Russian loss in 1914 or 1915, or an Austrian collapse in 1916, would have brought the war to a close with the Russian state and the ruling Romanov dynasty in far better condition than they actually were when the collapse did come in 1917. By 1917, Russia had suffered through three full years of growing inflation, casualties at the front, deteriorating support for the monarchy, and burgeoning class antagonism. While the regime might well have been fundamentally altered by a war that ended earlier, it is difficult to imagine such a complete and devastating political collapse as the one that happened in 1917 without the embittering experience of three years of war.

That the war could easily have ended differently means that Russia's subsequent history could have been different as well. The concrete experience of imperial Russia at war matters not only because of its inherent interest, but because of what came after: the revolutions of 1917 and the creation of a new Soviet Russia. Historians are always wary of teleology, the short-sightedness that reads historical events exclusively in terms of where we know the story will end, and thereby neglecting how things might have turned out differently. It would naturally be foolish to neglect the Russian Revolution in thinking about Russian experience of the war, but reading Russia's prerevolutionary history as leading inevitably to revolution would be a mistake. Had Austria-Hungary, say, broken under the stresses of war before Russia, the history of the twentieth century would look very different. If Russia had left the war before Nicholas's regime had lost all legitimacy, it is easy to imagine Nicholas remaining as tsar, or the Romanov dynasty's continuing through Nicholas's son Aleksei, his brother Mikhail, or the Grand Duke Nikolai Nikolaevich. The fact that Russia collapsed before Austria is the result of the contingencies of war. Understanding them requires careful attention to the military history of the war: the plans and campaigns that determined its outcome, and that is where this book will focus.

While comparative context and contingency are worth exploring, my primary goal in this book is simpler: to present a clear and brief synthesis of scholarly research on Russia's experience in fighting the First World War. The book is not really intended for my fellow specialists on Russian military history, who are themselves familiar with much of the literature that I draw upon. While I have done archival work on the Brusilov offensive of 1916, most of what I present here is based on the careful research of dozens of scholars, beginning with the generals of Russia's imperial army who digested their own experience in a series of histories written immediately after the end of the war, and continuing with Russian and Western scholars who are mining the archives now. My debt to all of them is great.

My emphasis is primarily military and operational, though I include discussion of society, politics, economics, and diplomacy in order to make that primary military narrative comprehensible. My motivation for emphasizing military institutions and operations is that this book is, after all, telling the story of a war, and wars are fundamentally about the organized application of large-scale violence in pursuit of political aims. Militaries and battlefields are integral to that story. Finally, good work already exists in English on the Russian home front at war. Peter Gatrell's *Russia's First World War*, for example, fully incorporates recent scholarship on the important social and economic developments of wartime Russia, but has almost no coverage of military matters.[7] Histories of the war in the east date back to 1931 and one of Winston Churchill's lesser-known works: *The Unknown War*.[8] A number of more recent brief, popular accounts rely heavily on English-language sources, and the story of the war in the east is told primarily from the German point-of-view as a result of the relative predominance of accessible sources covering the German side.[9] Two older works give comprehensive accounts of the Eastern Front from the Russian point of view: Norman Stone's 1975 *The Eastern Front* and W. Bruce Lincoln's 1986 *Passage through Armageddon*.[10] Each is the product of a knowledgeable scholar and skilled writer. They have suffered, however, from the passage of time: written when the Cold War and the Soviet Union were still going concerns, before a flood of recent archivally based scholarship. There is thus room for a clear and readable military history of Russia in World War I that incorporates the research of recent decades. In addition to those broader works, recent detailed campaign studies have covered important parts of the campaign in the east for an English-speaking audience, and I have found them invaluable. As a group, though, they do not use a great deal of Russian-language sources or scholarship, and as a result describe events from the point of view of Germany, Austria-Hungary, or Romania.[11] There was another side to the war in the east, and this book tries to bring that story across.

Finally, some technical notes. This book will not put a great deal of emphasis on numbers. Even given the modern, bureaucratic states waging war from 1914 to 1918, the most basic statistics on the size and scope of the war effort, particularly on the Eastern Front, are difficult to obtain. This is particularly true for Russia, where sources agree on the rough size of the Russian army at the outbreak of war (1.3–1.4 million) and the approximate number of soldiers added through immediate mobilization (3 million), but more precision than that seems impossible. Even such a well-defined and manageable group as the Russian officer corps admits to only a figure of 40,000–50,000, but little agreement beyond that. Part of the problem is conceptual: Russia had (then as now) large militarized groups such as the uniformed gendarmes that could in some ways be reasonably counted as part of military manpower. Part is practical: Russia began fighting in 1914 before all mobilized troops had arrived at the front, so careful recordkeeping was necessarily sacrificed to the exigencies of war. Casualty figures are even more problematic than manpower. Most combat deaths were the result of artillery, and high explosives could bury or obliterate those whom it killed, leaving no trace for military bureaucrats to track. When troops failed to make roll call after a battle, they might be dead, have been captured, or simply have deserted to go home. In Russia, where space was vast, government thin, and the population still largely illiterate, records were difficult to maintain. It was even more difficult for the powers at war to assess their opponents' losses. Accounts from the time judge military success in ground captured, prisoners taken, and artillery pieces seized. These were not necessarily bad measures of military success, but they were the only measures available.[12]

Though all powers, the Russians included, attempted to monitor their losses in killed, wounded, captured, and missing, the strains of the war made precise recordkeeping impossible. On the Western Front, universal literacy and relatively static lines meant that records were more reliable and the number of prisoners taken relatively small, at least until the last few months of the war. Even so, major offensives overwhelmed the statistical machinery on both sides, leaving casualties in dispute during the war and ever since. In France, *half* of all corpses went unidentified.[13] Things were worse in the east. For example, spring 1916 reports from the Russian Eighth Army for the two weeks *prior* to the major Brusilov offensive record 62 officers sick, 25 wounded, none "missing or left on the field," and 2 killed for total officer losses of 89, only 27 of which were combat losses. For lower ranks, the figures were 5,571 sick, 1,725 wounded, 9 missing, and 188 killed, for a total of 7,493 losses, 1,922 of which were from combat. For the next two weeks, the beginning of the offensive, casualties rose to 48 officers sick, 410 wounded, 8 missing, and 188 killed for 654 casualties—a 2200 percent increase in combat losses. Lower ranks lost 6,568 sick, 37,222 wounded, 2,094 missing, and 6,035 killed, for 51,919 casualties, 45,351 in battle. That meant a 2350 percent increase in combat losses. This was only one of four Russian armies participating in the Brusilov offensive. Casualties on that scale necessarily overwhelmed the feeble administrative machinery in place to track them. The rise from 9 missing to 2,102 is particularly noteworthy. Since this was a period of unqualified Russian success, few Russians were taken prisoner and few bodies were abandoned in a retreat. Nonetheless, the Eighth Army simply lost track of more than 2,000 men. Periods of active combat produced an enormous leap in the human toll of the war, and deceptively precise figures in official records can be only an approximate guide.[14]

Names, dates, and places are fraught with peril. I have presented Russians by their first and last names, not including their patronymics. My reasoning is that those who know what patronymics are and wish to find them can do so easily enough, and readers who do not would find them off-putting. During the period covered by this book, Russia still used the Julian calendar instead of the Gregorian calendar employed in the West. As a result, a particular day was dated thirteen days earlier in Russia than in the rest of Europe. The German declaration of war on Russia took place on 1 August 1914 for the Germans, but on 19 July 1914 for the Russians. Russia's 1917 February Revolution took place, from the Western point of view, in March, and its October Revolution in November. At the beginning of 1918, Lenin's government switched Russia to the Gregorian calendar, to the enormous relief of historians of Russia and the Soviet Union. The discrepancy caused great headaches for diplomats and generals of the time, and does for scholars and readers now. Since this book is intended for general readers, likely to be far more familiar with events in the West, I have rendered all dates according to the Western Gregorian calendar (New Style) rather than the Russian Julian calendar (Old Style).

Place names in the part of the world covered by this book are notoriously difficult. The city of L'viv in present-day Ukraine has been also known as L'vov (Russian), Lwów (Polish), and Lemberg (German). Sibiu in Romania has also been called Hermannstadt (German) and Nagyszeben (Hungarian). I have generally used the present-day name of a particular place, except where that would be blatantly anachronistic. In cases where the English name of a place is well established, I have used that instead (Warsaw instead of Warszawa). My use of place names is not intended to imply any judgment on the validity of territorial claims by any group or government; the index indicates alternative names.

Finally, some military terminology. The hierarchy of increasingly larger military units, from platoon to company to battalion to regiment to brigade to division to corps, is relatively uncomplicated. "Army" is an ambiguous term. It can mean the armed forces of a state generally, as "the Russian army" or "the German army," but also a specific subunit of a country's armed forces comprising two or more corps, as "the Russian Second Army" or "the German Eleventh Army." For levels above that, the Germans used the term *Heeresgruppe*, "Army Group," to refer to the largest formation of more than one army. The Russians used the term "Front" to express the same idea. Thus, the Russians opened World War I with two Fronts: the Northwestern and Southwestern, each comprised of several numbered armies. The Germans also used the term *Armeegruppe* for an ad hoc organization assembled for a particular mission and often referred to by its commander's name, as for example *Armeegruppe* Gallwitz.

1

The Origins of Russia's First World War

Although this book will focus on Russia's military experience in World War I, the war's origins are important to establish necessary context. Library shelves bend under the weight of books on the causes of the First World War. During the war, governments published selections from their diplomatic archives to demonstrate that the fault lay with their enemies, and the struggle over assigning blame has never ceased. For many years after the war, the predominant attitude among historians was to blame all participants (which, in effect, blamed no participants) for the creation of an international system pregnant with the danger of war, for their clumsy handling of prewar crises, and for underestimating the devastation war would bring: the war was a mistake, rather than deliberate policy. All along, though, a substantial minority of scholars saw primary responsibility as lying with Germany. During the 1960s, the pioneering West German historian Fritz Fischer argued in a pair of books that Germany had indeed engineered war in 1914. Ever since Fischer, a basic consensus among historians has agreed that all the powers regarded war as a legitimate feature of the international system, but that in 1914 only Germany and Austria-Hungary were willing to provoke a limited war and risk a general war to achieve their ends. No other great power wanted war in 1914: Great Britain was satisfied, France was too uncertain of its prospects against Germany, and Russia saw its military potential growing with every year that passed. Austria-Hungary, on the other hand, was conscious of the danger it faced from Slavic nationalism in the Balkans, and saw a war to crush Serbia as

14

preferable to disintegration, even if that risked general war. Every year made Austria's relative position worse, and immediate war as a solution more attractive. Germany likewise saw the passage of time increasing Russian power and closing the window within which Germany might achieve European domination.[1]

This book accepts the consensus that Germany and Austria-Hungary bore primary responsibility for the war, but the way the world looked from St. Petersburg is worth reviewing: how it was that Russia came to fight in 1914. The quest for roots of the First World War can be pushed back endlessly into the past, but discussion here will focus on three key elements: the alliance system that structured international relations in 1914, the concrete grievances and policy goals that fueled international rivalries, and finally the 1914 July crisis that brought war.[2]

ALLIANCE SYSTEMS

European politics in 1914 were structured but not determined by two competing alliance systems. The older and more formal was the Triple Alliance. When Prussian chancellor (i.e., prime minister) Otto von Bismarck engineered the wars of German unification—against Denmark in 1864, Austria-Hungary in 1867, and finally France in 1870–1871—his policies forged the fragmented petty states of Germany into one empire under Prussian leadership, but guaranteed enduring Franco-German hostility. Relatively mild terms for Austria-Hungary meant that the Habsburgs became German allies in short order after their 1867 defeat. After Bismarck won the Franco-Prussian War of 1870–1871, however, the peace he imposed on France provided grounds for forty years of enmity by seizure of the provinces of Alsace and Lorraine.[3]

Once Germany was unified, Bismarck regarded his state as a satisfied power, and his priority was to prevent France from finding allies to undo the settlement of 1871. Bismarck's lack of colonial or naval ambitions meant that the British had no cause for opposition to Germany. Bismarck used shared commitment to political conservatism to bind Russia and Austria-Hungary to Germany as well. This ideological consensus became formal in 1873 as the Three Emperors' League, a vague commitment to solidarity among monarchies. Bismarck moved to establish more lasting connections with Austria and Russia to lock out the French. Prior to serving as chancellor, Bismarck had been ambassador to Russia and so had a well-developed sense of Russia's potential power. He played on Habsburg fear of Russia to win Austria-Hungary to a Dual Alliance in 1879, expanding this into the Triple Alliance with the addition of Italy in 1882. As soon as Bismarck attached Germany to Austria, however, he took steps to reassure Russia and prevent any opening for a Russo-French alliance. Bismarck engineered a renewed Three Emperors' League in 1881 among the conservative Great Powers, again binding Russia to Germany and Austria. The treaty committed its members to very little: neutrality in the event of war with a fourth power, maintaining the status quo in the Balkans, and keeping the Turkish straits closed to warships. For Germany, this closed off the possibility of a Russo-French alliance and kept Germany from needing to choose between the Austrians and the Russians. In 1887, Bismarck went still further with the Reinsurance Treaty, promising Russia that Germany would maintain neutrality unless Russia attacked Austria-Hungary, providing St. Petersburg some protection against the nightmare of fighting alone against Germany and Austria. By staving off any temptation for Russia to ally with France, Bismarck had created a system that provided Germany with remarkable security, but it depended on his skillful management, limited objectives, and keen perception of the limitations of power. Without Bismarck in command, German foreign policy could go awry quickly.

The Triple Alliance lacked any rival for a decade, until a German blunder created one. The aged German kaiser Wilhelm I had been tractable and content to let Bismarck determine policy, but he died in March 1888. His son, the liberal Frederick III, was already dying of cancer when he took the throne, and survived only ninety-nine days. The throne then passed to Frederick's eldest son, Wilhelm II, who proved a disaster. Impulsive, shallow, and blustering, Wilhelm was not content to entrust governing to Bismarck nor leave intact Bismarck's intricate system. Bismarck remarked in 1888 that "the young lord wants war with Russia, and would like to draw his sword straight away if he could. I shall not be a party to it."[4] By March 1890, Wilhelm II had compelled Bismarck's resignation, replacing him as chancellor with a series of mediocrities. None had anything close to Bismarck's force of personality or sense for international politics. Bismarck had created a system that lacked the resilience to continue without him.

Wilhelm refused to renew the Reinsurance Treaty in 1890, compelling the Russians to look for security elsewhere.

Bismarck had inadvertently started France and Russia down the path toward alliance by his efforts to prevent Russo-German financial entanglement. He had barred the use of Russian government bonds as collateral for German state loans to Russia. Though ostensibly quite narrow in scope, this policy's political significance was clear: Bismarck's government disapproved of financial ties with Russia, and German lending to Russia dried up. German bondholders sold Russian securities; many were snapped up by the French. At the same time, Russian restrictions on foreign ownership of property alarmed German investors. The result was that Russian finance shifted to France. From 1888 to 1890, a series of major Russian bond issues were underwritten in Paris. This suggested official sympathy in both directions and committed the French investing classes to Russian political and military security *before* the creation of formal political ties.[5] With financial and diplomatic incentives both pushing for alliance, the result was the emergence from 1891 to 1894 of the Russo-French alliance. In a series of stages, the relationship deepened from consultation through a military convention to a full treaty in 1894. Both parties committed to attack Germany if the other was attacked. Both agreed to mobilize if any of the Triple Alliance mobilized, with France committing 1.3 million men and Russia 800,000 to fight against Germany in the event of war.

For a decade after the creation of the Franco-Russian alliance, Europe's political structure remained relatively stable. But just as German blundering had driven France and Russia to cooperation, further German missteps pushed Britain to overcome its colonial and imperial rivalries with France and Russia. In 1898, Britain and France had nearly gone to war in the Fashoda crisis over influence on the Upper Nile, but the French government recognized that it needed British cooperation against Germany. France backed down and negotiated a settlement of its African colonial disputes with Britain, opening the door for future cooperation. At the same time, Germany alienated Britain by asserting its own right to colonies and building a substantial battleship fleet, policies that could only be directed against British interests.

Britain and Russia had engaged in a long cold war for influence in Central Asia, a cold war that threatened to become hot at several points over the nineteenth century. At the beginning of the twentieth, however, both sides came under increasing pressure to settle their differences and concentrate on more pressing threats. For the British, the vulnerabilities of their far-flung empire, when combined with the growing German threat to the balance of power in Europe, made a settlement with Russia attractive. For Russia, the twin disasters of defeat in the 1904–1905 Russo-Japanese War and the resulting 1905 revolution likewise compelled a reevaluation of foreign policy. Even in 1903, the British government had proposed talks with the Russians. In addition, France, seeing an opportunity to strengthen its own position by reconciling its two allies, brokered initial steps toward an Anglo-Russian settlement. In March 1906, British foreign secretary Edward Grey formally proposed an entente to the Russians, seeing Anglo-French-Russian cooperation as a guarantee against German aggression. Immediately thereafter, Aleksandr Izvol'skii took over as Russian foreign minister, replacing the pro-German Vladimir Lamsdorf and clearing the way for the more Anglophile Izvol'skii to pursue closer relations with Britain. Britain had signed an alliance with Japan in 1902, so defusing the threat of an Anglo-Japanese coalition against Russia was attractive to Russian military planners. Negotiations culminated in a 31 August 1907 Convention of Mutual Cordiality committing both sides to maintenance of the status quo across their arc of conflict in Afghanistan and Tibet while defining spheres of influence for each side in Iran.[6]

While the Anglo-Russian Convention focused on resolving conflicts in Asia, it did remove an important stumbling block to a de facto Anglo-French-Russian alliance in Europe. The underlying imperial tensions between Britain and Russia never went away, and pro-German and right-wing elements in Russia never accepted the convention. Nonetheless, Anglo-Russian tensions were reduced just enough for cooperation in Europe to last through the outbreak of war in 1914. After 1907, the British, French, and Russians—the Triple Entente—saw themselves as having a common interest in restraining German power.

EUROPEAN RIVALRIES

While the Triple Alliance and the much looser Triple Entente provided some basic structure for European politics, they did not determine the course of events. Indeed, when war broke out in 1914, Italy did not regard the conditions of the Triple Alliance as being met and refused to honor the alliance. Russia remained on remarkably good terms with Germany and Austria-Hungary for much of the period prior to 1914. Both Austria and Russia saw the Balkans as their natural sphere of interest, and were certainly rivals for influence among the new states emerging from the slow retreat of the Ottoman Empire. Russia had ethnic and religious ties to the population of the Balkans, and an abiding interest in the Turkish straits. Russia had, for example, subsidized the Montenegrin military since 1895 in amounts running to several hundred thousand rubles each year.[7] Nonetheless, in May 1897, Austria and Russia formally agreed to accept the existing state of affairs in the Balkans, removing the most significant possible cause of conflict between them and, by implication, between Russia and Germany.

Russian relations with Germany were also reasonably good, though much depended on the vicissitudes of German domestic politics. In 1894, the German government reversed Bismarck's policy of estrangement from Russian markets. The tariff on Russian grain, the most important export to Germany, was reduced despite strenuous objections from the landed *Junker* nobility of East Prussia. In 1894 and 1896, Germany again encouraged the purchase of Russian bonds, fearful of growing French domination of Russian finance. By 1904, though, a new Russo-German trade treaty raised German tariffs on Russian imports, while the intensification of German agriculture made German food competitive with Russian exports in European markets. Russian public opinion generally pushed for a harder line on German trade as World War I approached. These trade disputes had little effect on the basic fact that the Russian and German economies were highly complementary: Russia produced the raw materials Germany's burgeoning industrial cities demanded; German industrial goods were essential to Russia's economic growth. On the eve of war Germany accounted for almost 40 percent of Russian foreign trade; Russia accounted for 12–13 percent of Germany's much larger trade.[8] Conservative elements in the Russian government often preferred semi-authoritarian Germany to republican France, and veteran statesmen Pyotr Durnovo and Sergei Witte were unabashedly pro-German. In 1910–1911, the new foreign minister, Sergei Sazonov, negotiated an accommodation with Germany permitting a Russian sphere of influence in northern Iran in return for Russian acceptance of German railroad construction in the Ottoman Empire. German hostility toward Russia came remarkably late—indeed, German popular fear and animosity toward Russia seems to have developed only in spring 1914 as a result of a jingoistic press campaign.[9]

The moment at which Russia's relations with the Central Powers took a stark turn for the worse can be dated precisely: on 6 October 1908, Austria-Hungary declared its formal annexation of the former Ottoman provinces of Bosnia and Herzegovina. This not only destroyed any Russian agreement with the Austrians on the status quo in the Balkans, but demonstrated to the Russian government that the Austrians could not be trusted to cooperate in defending their mutual interests. The German-dominated Triple Alliance became far more threatening. The annexation of Bosnia-Herzegovina had a long and complex history. The Habsburg Empire had occupied but not formally annexed Bosnia-Herzegovina in the 1870s as a result of the crisis unleashed by a rebellion of the Christian peasants of the Balkans against Ottoman rule in 1875. Joint European efforts to resolve the crisis by forcing the Ottoman Turks to reform went nowhere. The tiny states of Montenegro and Serbia declared war on the Ottomans in June 1876 and were promptly defeated. Russian public sentiment in favor of these Orthodox Balkan Slavs grew steadily, to the point where even the autocratic tsar had to be mindful of his people's wishes. In order to guarantee that war against the Ottomans could proceed without outside interference, Russian foreign minister Aleksandr Gorchakov cut a deal with Austria-Hungary: In return for benevolent neutrality, he promised the Habsburgs freedom to occupy Bosnia and Herzegovina. Thus provided with diplomatic cover, Russia declared war on the Ottoman Empire in April 1877. After a short but successful war, Russia had to accept limited gains in a settlement brokered by the 1878 Congress of Berlin. Though Russia had done the fighting, Austria-Hungary for little expenditure of blood or treasure got what it had been promised: occupation of Bosnia-Herzegovina. This half-measure—Austrian administration of territory still formally part of the Ottoman Empire—proved remarkably durable.

It could not last forever. The 1877–1878 Russo-Turkish War had been part of a long Ottoman decline, and the decay of Ottoman power in the Balkans created a series of small national states—Greece, Montenegro, Serbia, Bulgaria, and Romania. Serbia in particular served as a focus of nationalist sentiment for the South Slavs under Austrian rule. By the 1900s, the Austrian government was looking for some way to demonstrate its power and cut burgeoning Balkan nationalism down to size. Franz Conrad von Hötzen-dorf, Austrian chief of staff since 1906, was viscerally anti-Serbian and desperate to counter nationalist pressure on the Habsburg Empire. The new foreign minister, Alois von Aehrenthal, was equally desperate to find some signal victory. In Russia, Foreign Minister Izvol'skii also wanted a diplomatic triumph. In summer 1908, Izvol'skii and Aehrenthal devised a scheme to satisfy them both: Russia would support Austria-Hungary's formal annexation of Bosnia-Herzegovina. In return, Austria-Hungary would support a Russian initiative to force the Ottoman Empire to allow Russian warships to pass through the Turkish straits. Izvol'skii overlooked a key point: Austria-Hungary already held physical possession of Bosnia-Herzegovina, and so could present Russia and the rest of Europe's powers with a fait accompli.[10]

Thus Austria-Hungary's 1908 declaration that it had formally annexed Bosnia-Herzegovina left Izvol'skii in a terrible position. Russia needed cooperation of the European powers to change the legal regime at the Turkish straits, and no power was willing to exert itself on Russia's behalf. Austria already had what it wanted, and no reason to fulfill its promise to support the Russians. His own government and public were deeply unhappy with his game, so Izvol'skii's protests against Austria's preemptive annexation could go nowhere. Russian defeat in the Russo-Japanese War of 1904–1905 meant that his government was in no position to threaten war. By spring 1909, Izvol'skii had no choice but give in to a German ultimatum threatening war unless Russia accepted Austrian annexation of Bosnia-Herzegovina and ended the ongoing crisis. Izvol'skii's grand bargain with Austria had netted Russia nothing. Russian-Austrian hostility had come roaring back, and Germany's heavy-handed backing of its alliance partner had renewed the Triple Entente's concern with Kaiser Wilhelm's ultimate aims.[11]

After Bosnia-Herzegovina, European politics were wrenched by a series of successive crises. Not all involved Russia directly, but all worsened the political atmosphere and made war increasingly thinkable as a means of resolving the ongoing tension. France moved troops into Morocco in 1911 as a result of antiforeign demonstrations. Germany protested by sending the gunboat *Panther* to Agadir, again alarming Britain and France about German intentions. Russia was not so disturbed, as the matter was quite distant from its own interests, and the new foreign minister, Sazonov, had just negotiated his agreement with the Germans on spheres of interest in the Near East. The most important follow-on effects with regard to Russia were indirect: the British were now squarely in agreement with the French over alarming German designs. Confident in this backing, the French themselves took a more forthright line against the Triple Alliance.[12]

The Moroccan crisis was followed by a series of developments that had a far more direct effect on Russia. On 29 September 1911, Italy declared war on Ottoman Turkey and attacked Ottoman territory in North Africa. Subsequently, direct Italian attacks on Ottoman islands just outside the Turkish straits led the Ottoman government to close the straits, doing substantial damage to Russian commerce. Taking advantage of Ottoman distress, the small states of the Balkans attacked the remaining Ottoman possessions in Europe in October 1912 in the First Balkan War (discussed in greater detail in chapter 8). Both these conflicts showed that the complete disintegration of the Ottoman Empire might take place in the very near term. Russia could not afford to let other powers seize control of Ottoman territories in the Caucasus and astride the straits. While Russia could live with a weak Ottoman government, the prospect of another great power throttling Russia's commercial lifeline was completely unacceptable. When in November 1912 it seemed as though the Ottoman Empire was indeed on the verge of complete destruction, the Austrians began military preparations and got promises of support from Germany if they found themselves compelled to step in to limit Serbian and Bulgarian gains. Tsar Nicholas was likewise ready to fight, keeping soldiers under arms instead of discharging conscripts at the end of their term. Nicholas's generals were eager to test their strength, but the civilian members of his government insisted that Russia could take no such steps without consulting France, the ally whose assistance Russia needed for war with Germany and Austria.[13] Against this background, Kaiser Wilhelm held an infamous war council on 8 December 1912. Wilhelm met with his army and navy heads: Helmuth von Moltke and Alfred von Tirpitz. Wilhelm declared his sense that European war was inevitable, but his commanders demurred, arguing that the German military was not yet ready. It is difficult to know what to make of this meeting; Wilhelm's chancellor, Theobald von Bethmann Hollweg, was not present, and there was little concrete follow-through on the preparations discussed. In retrospect, it seems typical of Wilhelm's belligerent declarations unmatched by actual action. It does show, however, how war had become an active subject of German consideration.[14]

Though war seemed near at the end of 1912, an international conference in London brought a halt to the First Balkan War in a settlement generally acceptable to the European powers, and an Anglo-German naval agreement removed some of the tension from international affairs. Europe's continental powers, however, continued to expand their preparations for war: a summer 1913 German army bill provided for the expansion of Germany's peacetime army by 120,000 men to 800,000. France extended conscript service from two years to three in August 1913. The Habsburgs instituted a modest increase in their forces in October 1913. In late summer, a French military mission led by Joseph Joffre visited Russia, and was impressed by what it encountered. In the event of war, the French promised an offensive by the eleventh day of mobilization; General Yakov Zhilinskii, speaking for the Russians, made an extravagant promise of 800,000 men on the German frontier by the fifteenth day of mobilization. Both sides were clear on the importance of each taking the offensive against Germany to prevent the Germans from concentrating on either one individually.[15]

THE JULY CRISIS

The steadily growing European tension finally exploded into war in summer 1914. In order to understand the precise nature of the July Crisis, and why Germany and Austria were so frantic to force it toward either war or acceptance of German dominance, it is necessary first to look at German and Austrian war planning, and the implications of that planning for diplomacy. In keeping with this book's theme of contingency, it is too easy to see Germany's Schlieffen Plan as dictated by remorseless logic: that, supposedly, Germany had to destroy one of its continental enemies to avoid a two-front war. Since geography made France more liable to rapid destruction, and Russia was slow to mobilize, all available German forces had to be thrown against France in a furious offensive. While this logic seems compelling, it was not self-evident to the planners of the Triple Alliance. Helmuth von Moltke the Elder, chief of the German General Staff until 1888, and his Austrian counterpart Friedrich von Beck had planned that Germany would stay on the defensive against France in the west, counterattacking there as opportunity presented. At the same time, Austria and Germany would cooperate in a joint offensive against Russia. Although

Moltke's thinking did fluctuate over time, his basic principles remained the same: Germany was incapable of defending the eastern frontier against Russia and simultaneously concentrating the force necessary for victory against France. Concentrating against Russia and remaining on the defensive against France offered, he believed, the best chance of success. His concept was a giant pincer attack, launched from German East Prussia and Austrian Galicia to cut off the Polish salient and all Russian troops deployed there.[16]

Unfortunately for German-Austrian coordination, Moltke and Beck's excellent working relationship was not maintained. German strategic thinking fundamentally changed after Moltke's retirement in 1888; Austria's did not. After a brief interval under Alfred von Waldersee, Alfred von Schlieffen became chief of the German General Staff in 1891, and he held that office until 1906. Even after retirement, the force of his personality dominated German military thinking. His successor, Helmuth von Moltke the Younger (nephew of the elder Moltke) maintained Schlieffen's basic conceptions about the fundamentals of German strategy, though details necessarily changed with time and circumstances. Schlieffen engineered a strategic vision fundamentally opposed to his predecessor's conception. Believing a concentration against Russia to be a doomed push into unending space with little hope of quick victory, Schlieffen instead planned a rapid wheeling attack on France, leaving the Alsace-Lorraine frontier thinly guarded in order to allow a massive German force to move through Belgium and descend on Paris and the French armies from the north. A vigorous scholarly debate, albeit too often mired in technicalities, has emerged around the precise nature of the Schlieffen Plan, but the general outlines of Schlieffen's thinking are clear. His successive war plans shifted the focus of Germany's war effort to the west and reduced German commitment to the east. Schlieffen's final *Denkschrift* of December 1905 envisaged seven German armies fighting on the Western Front, five of which would pass through Belgium, then turn south to descend on Paris from the north and pin France's armies against the German frontier. While successive iterations of the German plan altered Schlieffen's conception in points of detail—how far west to swing in driving south to Paris, whether the westernmost German armies should pass west or east of Paris, whether to use Dutch territory for the passage of German troops, the relative balance of strength between the German forces passing through Belgium and those holding the German frontier—

Schlieffen's 1905 conception matched in its essentials what German armies actually did in 1914.[17]

Schlieffen's plan, and the younger Moltke's preparations to carry it out, had a number of fundamental flaws. In order to provide the necessary space for the German forces to push west before moving south, the plan required the violation of Belgian territory, regardless of whether Belgium was a party to any Franco-German war. It placed enormous time pressure on German policymakers. Statesmen could not afford to temporize in a crisis, since the plan's success depended on Germany's advantage in speed of mobilization over Russia. German troops on the Western Front would have little margin for error. Should Russia mobilize and deploy troops to Germany's eastern frontier before the start of hostilities, Germany would be defenseless. Confusion, exhaustion, or delay would mean failure at Paris and result in the two-front war that German planners dreaded. The Schlieffen Plan presumed Russian weakness and passivity: a reasonable assumption in 1905 as a result of the Russo-Japanese War, but not in 1913. Despite the undoubted fact of improving Russian mobilization performance, the German response was not to rethink Schlieffen's strategy, but instead to reemphasize speed. In April 1913, the German military abandoned its secondary plans for an attack on Russia instead of France and committed wholeheartedly to a western attack: the German plan in 1913–1914 sent seventy divisions against France and nine against Russia.[18]

The more fundamental issue for German policy and planning was the lack of effective coordination. Within the army, the General Staff created war plans, but the War Ministry built the forces to implement that plan. The navy was its own institution entirely, and the chancellor, the head of government, had authority over neither. The sole mechanism for coordination of military, naval, and foreign policy lay with the German emperor, Kaiser Wilhelm II, but he was utterly incapable of playing that role. Mercurial, hysterical, convinced of his own military talents but incapable of deep thinking, he lacked the maturity and judgment necessary to bring together the various strands of German policy and formulate a rational grand strategy that balanced German ends and means.

Considered from the point of view of the Eastern Front, the Schlieffen Plan's chief flaw was that its details were deliberately hidden from the Austrian government. Schlieffen and Beck got on badly at their first meeting in 1891, and matters went downhill from there. The two allied governments conducted no serious staff talks from 1896 to 1909. Misled in part by Schlieffen's deliberate obfuscation and in part by wishful thinking, Austria continued to count on a substantial German offensive out of East Prussia to complement its own offensive from Galicia. When Conrad and Moltke the Younger became Austrian and German chiefs of staff in 1906, relations got no better. Conrad and Moltke finally resumed an exchange of information in early 1909, but Moltke deliberately misled Conrad into thinking that Germany planned a commitment of forty-five divisions to its eastern frontier and an early offensive into Russia, a far cry from the skeleton force screening East Prussia that Moltke actually envisaged. Moltke needed an Austrian offensive to help protect a weakly defended East Prussia, and lying to Conrad about a German offensive was the best way to achieve that. Conrad did little better, suggesting to Moltke that Austria's priority was an offensive against Russia and concealing Conrad's actual prioritization of the fight against Serbia.[19]

On 28 June 1914, amid growing tension and expanding militaries, Archduke Franz Ferdinand, heir to the Habsburg throne, was shot to death in Sarajevo along with his wife by Gavrilo Princip, a young Serbian nationalist.[20] The event was highly symbolic: Sarajevo was the heart of Bosnia-Herzegovina, inhabited almost entirely by Slavs (whether Orthodox Serbs, Catholic Croats, or Muslims). The 1908 annexation had put a substantial population of South Slavs under the rule of the German and Hungarian-dominated Habsburg Empire. The small but ambitious state of Serbia saw itself as the natural leader of the Slavs of the Balkans, and Franz Ferdinand's visit took place on the anniversary of the 1389 battle of Kosovo Field, which had destroyed the medieval Serbian kingdom. The Austrian investigation quickly uncovered connections between Princip, his fellow conspirators, and ultranationalists in the Serbian government and army.

The Austro-Hungarian government's response to the assassination was carefully calculated. Franz Ferdinand had been an abrupt and harsh man, whose most attractive characteristic had been his affection for the wife who died with him. He had not been personally popular with the Austrian and Hungarian ruling classes, who found his manner off-putting and his interest in improving the status of the Habsburg Empire's Slavs to be dangerous. His uncle, the Emperor Franz Joseph, had not liked him. Still, his assassination could not go unpunished, particularly when the event could be used to cut the troublesome Serbian kingdom down to size. The governing elites of Austria-Hungary were almost entirely united on the need to discipline Serbia, with István Tisza, prime minister of the Hungarian half of the empire, the only prominent voice for restraint. For the rest, the universal European horror at the killings made the moment especially opportune. Chief of Staff Conrad was especially vociferous in pushing for war. The only question was how precisely to act. A short glorious war against Serbia would be ideal. Quick action might humiliate Serbia, wreck its prestige, and end its appeal as a nucleus for Slav nationalism in the Balkans, thereby reinvigorating the moribund Habsburg Empire, but quick action was impossible. Though the Serbian army was tough and experienced, the Austrians could feel confident in their ability to gain victory in a one-on-one struggle. The Serbian capital, Belgrade, lay just across the Danube River, in reach of Austrian artillery, and the Serbian army was dwarfed by the Austrian.

Serbia was unlikely to fight alone, however, so Austria needed assistance. Though Serbia was separated from Russia by 600 kilometers of Austrian territory, Austria had an 800-kilometer frontier with Russia. Russia shared both ethnic (Slavic heritage) and religious (Orthodox Christian) connections with Serbia, as well as geopolitical interests. The Russian Empire saw the Balkans as its natural sphere of influence, and any increase in Austrian power and prestige was necessarily damaging to Russia. For any hope of victory, therefore, Austria needed German backing. German support might overawe the Russians and thereby prevent a wider war, keeping any conflict localized to Austrian disciplinary action against Serbia. If a larger war came nonetheless, an Austro-German coalition should easily deal with Russia. The Austrians were, however, unaware that Germany had no plan for a war against Russia alone; for Germany, war automatically meant war against Russia and France.

An Austrian delegation presented the case for harsh measures to Germany on 5 July. Kaiser Wilhelm here displayed the unstable personality that made him such a pernicious influence. Though he would waver at the moment of actual bloodshed, he was a great supporter of war in the abstract. He enthusiastically endorsed the Austrian plan, and gave his absolute commitment to stand by the Habsburg Empire. Wilhelm's affection for dramatic gestures meant that he neglected to think through the implications of Germany's France-centered war plan, and the necessary two-front war that would accompany it. Wilhelm did stress the importance of quick action, something the hidebound Habsburg government was utterly incapable of managing. Though Wilhelm was not thinking things through, his military and political elites were. They saw a local war as clearly positive, and were willing to risk a more general war. German chances were reasonably good, particularly if Britain remained aloof.[21]

Only on 23 July, more than two weeks after Germany's assurances of unconditional support, did the Austrian ambassador finally present Serbia a list of demands deliberately designed to be unacceptable. It took that long to convert waverers inside Austria-Hungary, allow soldiers on leave for the harvest to return to their units, and wait on France's President Raymond Poincaré and Prime Minister René Viviani to end a state visit to St. Petersburg. Their return to France by ship would make effective Russo-French consultation more difficult. Not least, Conrad, who had been eager for war for years, found he needed time to prepare for mobilization. While all Austria's reasons for delay were rational, they meant almost a month had passed after the assassination, allowing passions to cool and sympathy for Austria to ebb away. The passage of time had led European governments to consider that danger had passed. Generals, diplomats, and monarchs left on their summer vacations. Indeed, Radomir Putnik, the Serbian army's chief of staff, spent the month of July at an Austrian spa.

The Austrian ultimatum, requiring complete acceptance within forty-eight hours, included demands for the dissolution of Serbian nationalist organizations, arrest of individuals connected with the assassination, a halt to anti-Austrian propaganda, and the participation of Austrian investigators on Serbian soil. Sazonov, on reading it, declared "this means European war," and correctly saw it as formulated in collaboration with Germany. Tsar Nicholas was less exercised, trusting in German good will and remaining largely detached. The Russian Council of Ministers met on 24 and 25 July, and agreed to back Serbia. As the ministers saw it, Germany and Austria clearly intended to shut Russia out of the Balkans, and Russian public opinion would abide neither Russian weakness nor abandonment of the Serbs. Vladimir Kokovtsov, generally an advocate for peace, had been dismissed as prime minister in early 1914 and was no longer present to counsel restraint. On 25 July, after private Serbian conversations with the Russian government, and a Russian declaration that it would not remain indifferent to Serbia's fate, the Serbs mobilized their army and at the same time tried to parry the Austrian ultimatum by accepting most of its demands. Serbia's carefully calculated response agreed to most Austrian conditions, but rejected the most intrusive violations of Serbian sovereignty. Austria wanted either full submission or war, and so rejected the Serbian response and broke relations on 25 July, declaring war on 28 July. A local war had now begun; general war in Europe was imminent.

The prospect of general war finally produced frantic efforts to contain the conflict. Britain, distant from continental disputes, tried to broker a settlement. Kaiser Wilhelm, who had stoked the fires of European conflict with belligerent rhetoric, was now troubled by doubts and second thoughts. Germany attempted to urge restraint on Austria with the option of a "halt in Belgrade" that would limit the scale of the conflict, but that effort was doomed. Austrian war plans massed troops on Serbia's western border, not on the northern frontier opposite Belgrade. The option of capturing Belgrade alone was thus a nonstarter. Confused responses to the Austrian ultimatum and subsequent declaration of war made the situation even worse. Britain and Russia, for example, were working at cross-purposes: Britain was attempting to broker a settlement short of European war, but Sazonov wanted the British to be more confrontational with the Germans to warn Berlin away from war. Others, including Moltke and Conrad, desperately wanted a war and did all they could to accelerate it. Moltke declared on 26 July 1914 that "we shall never again strike as well as we do now."[22]

After Austria-Hungary declared war on Serbia on 28 July and bombarded its capital, Belgrade, the next day, the key decisions now lay with Russia: acquiesce in an Austrian war against Serbia, or mobilize to protect Serbia and risk a wider war with Germany. For reasons of both national prestige and domestic politics, Russia's policymakers believed they could not stand aside. As early as 6 July, Foreign Minister Sazonov had warned the Austrians and Germans alike that Russia had an interest in Serbia's fate. Tsar Nicholas responded to the Austrian ultimatum by ordering preparations for mobilization, but not yet mobilization itself. Though committed to the defense of Serbia, Nicholas believed that it might yet be possible to avoid a wider war. He approved general Russian mobilization, then reconsidered and canceled mobilization based in part on advice from Sazonov and in part from a plea from his cousin Kaiser Wilhelm. Nicholas then ordered a *partial* mobilization starting the morning of 29 July, but only for those military districts facing Austria. Nicholas hoped that this self-limitation would encourage in return German restraint by making it clear that Nicholas saw the crisis as a local Balkan matter. By this logic, Austria would find itself standing alone against Russia and moderate its position, and if not, would fight Russia alone and lose.

Nicholas, though a decent man and devoted to his family and his sense of duty, has a well-earned reputation for fecklessness. His actions here demonstrate his profound lack of understanding of international politics. Purely on technical grounds, Russia's mobilization experts were aghast at the thought of partial mobilization. Russia had only one plan for mobilization. Anything less would hopelessly disrupt Russian preparations and leave Russia helpless in the event of war with Germany. More significantly, a Russian war against Austria alone could not resolve Germany's essential problem. If Austria-Hungary backed down, its internal political problems and the growth of South Slav nationalism would quickly become entirely unmanageable. If instead Austria-Hungary fought Russia alone, it would lose and face the same fate. In either case, Germany would be left alone against the Franco-Russian alliance and have to accept a permanent end to its goal of European hegemony. As a result, any Russian mobilization put the German government in a difficult position. Whether Russian mobilization was full or partial, Germany had no choice but either to fight or to accept second-class status in Europe. On 30 July, Nicholas was subjected to sustained arguments from Foreign Minister Sazonov, War Minister Vladimir Sukhomlinov, and the army chief of staff Nikolai Yanushkevich, all of whom agreed he had no choice but to proceed to full mobilization. By that afternoon, Nicholas was finally convinced and agreed. Orders to begin mobilization the next day went out immediately; Sazonov joked that Yanushkevich should smash his telephone to prevent the tsar from changing his mind yet again.

This was a fateful and momentous step, immediately posing a number of key questions for the Germans and Austrians. With their war plans contingent on their time advantage over slow Russian mobilization, each passing day that Russian peasants gathered at their assembly points and boarded trains to the frontier whittled away at the Central Powers' already precarious military advantage. German plans left Germany's eastern border essentially undefended. If fighting began with 5 million Russian soldiers already on the frontier, Berlin would come under immediate threat with the bulk of the German army embroiled in Belgium and France. Germany's only hope was immediate war.

The remaining steps unfolded almost automatically, since the nature of German war plans required war as soon as serious danger arose. On 31 July, the Austrians moved to full mobilization and Germany demanded Russia cease all military preparations. Berlin likewise demanded that France promise neutrality in the coming conflict. The French were bound by alliance to Russia, and in any event saw little appeal in a Europe where they stood by while Germany and Austria-Hungary crushed their most important ally. France proceeded with mobilization. The German war plan, dependent on time, required swift action. German troops moved into Luxembourg on the night of August 1 to seize necessary railroads, and that same evening the German ambassador presented a declaration of war in St. Petersburg. German troops crossed the French border on 2 August, and Britain declared war on Germany on 4 August. The First World War had begun.

2

The Russian Army

The Russian army that marched to war looked much like the armies of the other continental powers. They were all based on conscripting large numbers of young men for relatively short service before discharging them into reserves to be mobilized back into the army in the event of war. As a result, peacetime strength grew by three to five times when war began and reservists were called up. Their organization—from small platoons and companies up through larger formations of battalions, regiments, divisions, corps, and finally armies—was essentially the same. The basic fighting formation was the infantry division of 15–20,000 men, dominated by riflemen, whose firepower was supplemented by grenades, machine guns, mortars, and artillery in increasing quantity over the war. Precise figures for total peacetime strength and wartime mobilized strength vary for all the combatants, depending on how such paramilitary forces as border guards or militarized police are counted. In approximate terms, though, the relative strength of the European powers is clear. France and Germany were approximately equal in peacetime strength at about 800,000 men each. At mobilization, the French army amounted to a little under 4 million men, the German to a little over. Austria-Hungary had a peacetime army of 450,000, expanding to 2.5–3 million on mobilization. The British army was an outlier. A volunteer, long-service professional force, it benefited from regular experience in colonial warfare and excellent rifle marksmanship, but was short on artillery and machine guns and smaller than other European armies, sending only six divisions to the continent at the outbreak of war.[1]

The Russian army differed in two key ways from its European counterparts: it had much more cavalry, and it was by far the largest peacetime
army in Europe: 1.4 million men and over 40,000 officers. At mobilization,
it grew to 4.5 million men and doubled the size of its officer corps. European military thinking prior to World War I had focused on the implications of the Russian steamroller: the capacity of Russia's reserves of manpower to crush all potential resistance. As measured crudely by peacetime
strength, there was some justice to this: Russia's 1.4 million men outnumbered Germany's 800,000 and Austria's 450,000 *combined*, even leaving
aside Russia's ally France. Russia's 170 million people dwarfed Germany
(68 million) and Austria-Hungary (51 million). These raw figures concealed, however, factors that meant Russia's real advantage was not nearly
so impressive. Russia's high peacetime strength reflected the need for substantial domestic policing, as well as the country's extended frontiers. This
mandated a substantial military presence in the Caucasus against the Ottoman Empire and the Far East against Japan. Russia's vast internal distances and sparse railroad network compelled a greater commitment to
standing forces instead of reserves.

In terms of its basic element—the individual rifleman—the Russian Empire was blessed and cursed by its reliance on the Russian peasant. When
historians look at Russian soldiers, they are almost compelled to see them
as a mass, not as individuals. Eighty-five percent of them were peasants,
in keeping with their share of the Russian population, and as a result many
were illiterate. Even those who could read and write often did so at a rudimentary level. A third of the 1913 call-up and as much as 61 percent of the
wartime draft were illiterate, compared to less than 1 percent in the German army. While the Russian army did much to teach basic literacy to its
soldiers, these efforts could only partly rectify the deep lack of familiarity
with modern, mechanized life that those levels of literacy represented. The
Russian army had long experience in teaching illiterate recruits to march
and shoot, but the new warfare of artillery, machine guns, radios, and railroads put a premium on an educated soldiery. Rushed wartime training
provided relatively little time to acculturate peasants to military norms.
Peasant soldiers swung their bayonets like pitchforks, instead of thrust-
ing with them, and were particularly horrified by war's technological aspects, including artillery bombardment and airplanes. They died in the millions, and those who survived were not literate enough to record their

experiences. Those who could have done so found that postwar Russian society, caught up in the creation of a new communist state, had little interest in their accounts of the war.[2]

The damage caused by low levels of education went beyond technical competence. Universal primary education in Western Europe had inculcated a common sense of national identity. While continuing class, regional, and religious differences might weaken that identity, the sense of common purpose was far beyond what Russia could manage. Russia was a multinational empire, not a nation-state, and Russian peasants had less sense of national identity. They had some awareness of events on a national scale, not simply local developments, and their loyalty to the Romanov dynasty and the Russian state was real, at least early in the war. This sense of belonging, however, and in particular the motivation to translate it into action, was far weaker than in Western Europe and would prove insufficient to overcome the burdens imposed by defeat after defeat.[3]

Russians made their way into the army through an extensive system of conscription. It had originated in the Great Reforms of Tsar Alexander II, who ruled from 1855 to 1881. Prior to Alexander, the Russian army had been manned primarily by peasants pulled from their villages for essentially lifetime service. In other words, a small proportion of men did long-term service. The rigors of army life meant that survival through a typical twenty-five-year term was hardly assured. This system had real drawbacks: with most soldiers serving for decades, Russia lacked a large pool of trained reservists who could be pulled back into uniform in the event of war. It was thus expensive and inflexible. Implemented by War Minister Dmitrii Miliutin in 1874, Russia's new system entailed a large proportion of men doing short-term service. The term of active service was initially set at six years, though deferments and exemptions generally cut that substantially. In 1906, army service for conscripts was set at three years active duty and fifteen years in the reserves for infantry and field artillery, and four years active and thirteen years reserve for other branches. Upon discharge, those veterans formed a reserve of trained manpower that could be mobilized in the event of war, divided into two groups—younger, more fit veterans as a reserve for frontline units and a second reserve of older veterans for service outside the front lines. A final group, the militia (*opolchenie*) consisted of those aged twenty-one to forty-three who had either avoided active service through deferments or older veterans who had completed their term in the reserves. This militia was not much better suited for wartime service than entirely raw recruits, and was intended at best for rear-area garrison duties.[4]

In principle, the 1874 conscription system aimed at a universal obligation, but in practice huge numbers of young men were excused from active duty. Russia's administrative and economic lag behind the more-developed powers meant that a smaller fraction of Russian manpower could be extracted from society, trained to fight, and sent to the front. Though all continental powers ostensibly practiced universal service, a host of exemptions and deferrals undermined this principle. Only some fraction of the cohort of young men reaching service age in any particular year were called to active duty and thereafter to reserve service and potential wartime call-up. Russia had neither the capacity nor the desire to employ its full yearly cohort of young men reaching age twenty-one. The state's budget could not afford to feed and clothe them all, and the army lacked the infrastructure to train and manage them. While other European states primarily provided for exemptions on health grounds, Russia instead was quite liberal in releasing men from service as a result of family circumstances, such as being the sole able-bodied male. Almost half the yearly cohort was excused from service on grounds of family circumstance. On the eve of war, the Russian Empire attempted to extract more manpower. A law of 6 July 1912 narrowed the scope of exemptions and deferments on family and professional grounds, and increased the annual call-up to 450,000 men.[5]

Ethnicity also excused young men from the draft. The many nationalities of Russia's southern and eastern frontiers, far from St. Petersburg and Moscow in geographic, religious, and cultural terms, fit poorly into universal service and required substantial flexibility from the Russian state. Finns, in keeping with Finland's autonomous status, did not serve as conscripts in the Russian Army but in their own small formations. Mennonites, whose ancestors had immigrated from Germany under Catherine the Great, enjoyed a grant of perpetual immunity from conscription. Jews were not exempted from service but faced substantial restrictions on their responsibilities and possibilities for promotion. More significantly, the nomadic Muslim populations of Central Asia were not drafted, unlike other Russian Muslims, who were hailed for their martial qualities. As a result, Muslims served in numbers far below their proportion in the population.[6]

Russia's complex ethnic geography, with less than half the population of the empire ethnically Russian, dictated a complex system of nonterritorial service. The regime simply could not risk letting soldiers serve in large numbers close to their homes, since ethnic Russians lived far from the borders, and the borderlands were populated by peoples of dubious political reliability. In addition, the ever-present threat of rebellion made it essential that soldiers garrisoned in a particular region not feel affinity with the local population. Soldiers generally served with other conscripts from their home district, but in a far distant region. Particular units would year after year draw their soldiers from specific feeder provinces. Typically, a formation would draw from a number of different regions to ensure that non-Russian minorities were diluted by a sufficient number of recruits from East Slavic populations. The 128th Starooskol'skii infantry regiment on Russia's southwestern border, for example, pulled its recruits from Kursk, Orenburg, Poltava, and Warsaw. As a rule, military units in the late tsarist empire were at least 75 percent East Slavs (Russians, Ukrainians, or Belarusians). In Russia's Polish provinces, military units were overwhelmingly Russian, while Polish conscripts were not to exceed 20 percent of the manpower in the units outside Poland to which they were sent. In the politically restive Warsaw military district, over 99 percent of recruits did their service elsewhere. Though in 1910 the system was adjusted to increase the number of recruits serving near their home, its overall principles remained the same.[7]

The social and national exemptions, combined with Russia's relative inability to track and catalog its vast population, meant the Russian state was far less efficient in extracting military manpower than its European rivals. In France, obsessed with Germany's larger population, the proportion of eligible youth inducted reached 84 percent in 1913. In Germany, by contrast, it was 53 percent, 29 percent in Austria, and only 20 percent in Russia. Russia's peacetime army contained just under 2 percent of its male population, roughly half the norm for France or Germany. Russia's large and illiterate population, in combination with underdeveloped administration in the countryside, meant that *opolchenie* who had been altogether excused from military service at age twenty-one were difficult to find and conscript when the regime needed additional manpower. This had fateful consequences during the war.[8]

Once in the army, Russian soldiers were well-equipped and -fed. At the most fundamental level, they ate better as soldiers than they had as peasants. The average Russian peasant ate perhaps a half-pound of meat a week, while Russian soldiers received well over two pounds. Forty percent of new conscripts reported that their first regular consumption of meat came upon joining the army. During the war, Germans and Austrians found Russian prisoners generally in good shape, and soldiers had enough food to send excess to their families at home. The fundamental dynamic over the war, though, was the steady reduction of meat, and the gradual replacement of fresh meat by salted. The relatively large meat ration meant that when massive numbers of peasants were inducted into the army, military demands swelled to unsustainable levels. By 1915, the army's consumption of meat amounted to 60 percent of Russia's total prewar consumption. In 1916, demand was 3.6 million pounds of meat per day.[9]

Russian soldiers also possessed quality equipment. Their rifle, the 7.62mm Mosin-Nagant (1891 model) was certainly up to European standards. The basic machine gun was the venerable Maxim gun in its 1910 variant, and Russia went to war with about 4,000 machine guns in its arsenal. The Russian army also had fine artillery. The basic field gun was a 76mm 1902 model, only slightly inferior in rate of fire to the French 75mm gun that set the world standard. Russia's arsenal included a 1910 Schneider 107mm field gun, a 1909 Krupp 122mm howitzer, a 1910 Schneider 122mm field gun, and a 1910 Schneider 152mm howitzer. The Soviet Union continued to use all those systems through the interwar period and in some cases through the Second World War. The Russian army did still have some outdated systems lacking gun shields or mechanisms to minimize recoil, including a trio of 1877 Krupp designs. In comparative terms, though, the Russian army's problem was not the quality of the systems it used, but their quantity and particularly their type: at the outbreak of war, it had 6,200 76mm field guns, suitable for use against troops in open ground. It was less well supplied with mortars and heavy artillery, systems better suited to trench warfare and the destruction of fortifications and entrenchments. Frontline units had only 750 107mm, 122mm, and 152mm guns in 1914. All the warring powers were short on howitzers and heavy artillery for trench warfare, but Russia adapted more slowly than its opponents once the need for specialized artillery became apparent.[10]

The Russian army fought in 1914 with tactics and training that were also in line with the standards of the time, and even gave some regard to the menace of modern firepower. No other European great power matched

Russia's experience in the Russo-Japanese War of maneuvering large formations in an environment dominated by machine guns and artillery. In the wake of the Russo-Japanese War, the Russian military recognized that its doctrine had to change. Even with this experience, though, the Russians had not yet fully grasped the lethality of the modern battlefield. Ongoing debate meant that a new field service manual was not available until spring 1912. This new manual emphasized the importance of offensive action and frontal assault, despite the growth in firepower that had made the battles in Manchuria so deadly. The model of infantry battle in the 1912 manual was of infantry moving forward in small groups under the cover of artillery, machine gun, and rifle fire to assemble at a final assault line 150 meters from the enemy position. After sufficient fire by supporting units, an infantry assault with the bayonet would take the objective. That said, the manual was not blindly subservient to the frontal assault. Russian doctrine emphasized the need for fire and movement, combining frontal attacks to fix an enemy in place with simultaneous envelopments or flanking maneuvers to complete the destruction of the enemy. The manual instructed commanders to respect the power of modern weaponry, minimizing troop movement in the open and maximizing the use of suppressive fire by artillery, machine guns, and rifles, while taking maximum advantage of dispersion and terrain to reduce losses from defensive fire. Indeed, the Russian high command held before World War I that "attack against a well-organized defensive position is hopeless."[11]

The 1912 field manual was supplemented on the eve of war by a February 1914 "Instruction for Infantry Action in Battle." Continuing the emphasis on suppressing enemy positions by fire before storming them with the bayonet, the manual also emphasized initiative, flexibility, and individual judgment by small-unit commanders. Infantry attacks were to be carried out not by dense columns of infantry, but instead by what the Russians termed "chains," with individual infantrymen separated by two to five paces. Frontal assaults on defensive positions had to accompanied by flank attacks, and units had to remain dispersed. The 1914 manual, for example, set the frontage of a divisional attack at 6–9 kilometers, compared to a much narrower (and hence more dense) 3-kilometer frontage in the 1912 manual. Like earlier Russian manuals, this final 1914 instruction envisaged a battle divided into stages: an approach march to contact with the enemy, the gradual achievement of fire superiority over the enemy by accumulating a mass of riflemen, and a final attack with the bayonet to break enemy resistance, followed by pursuit assisted by cavalry to complete the victory. This emphasis on the bayonet continued despite its utter irrelevance to modern warfare: one Russian survey found that only 0.6 percent of wounds came from sabers or bayonets.[12]

All this was similar to the doctrine of Russia's European counterparts, with minor differences in the relative emphasis on fire, bayonet charge, offensive frontage, and pace of attack. The Germans, for example, had abandoned attacking in neat lines, based on the heavy casualties the British took from defensive fire in the Boer War. After experimenting with open order attack but fearing the inability of officers to maintain control, the Germans decided on concentration. Like the Russians, the German army planned on dispersing for the advance, assembling advancing troops on a firing line several hundred yards away from the enemy, then charging. They also stressed outflanking and encircling enemy positions as the most reliable path to victory. Certainly Russian doctrine had flaws, but in overestimating the ability of infantry to cover open ground and deliver a close assault, the Russians had ample company.[13]

Russian training had a regular yearly rhythm. New recruits spent their first winter practicing the individual tasks of soldiering: mastering their weapons, drill, and the basic skills of fieldcraft. They were taught predominantly by senior soldiers and noncommissioned officers, though the War Ministry did try to increase officer participation before the war. By summer, soldiers proceeded to training in small-unit tactics, and, finally, large formations. Training put a great deal of emphasis on aimed rifle fire at a distance, a practice that inflicted severe casualties in the early stages of the war on enemy infantry moving in the open. Summer training concluded with substantial maneuvers involving the forces of multiple military districts. While Russian training was certainly adequate when carried out as designed, troops suffered from constant distractions. Inadequate barracks and poor funding meant that soldiers spent limited days of good weather on construction or as hired agricultural labor.[14]

The Russian army at its lowest levels was organized around a square structure: four squads (*otdelenie*) made up a platoon (*vzvod*); four platoons formed a company (*rot*) of 226 men; four companies a battalion (*batal'on*) of around 1,000 soldiers. Four battalions made up a regiment (*polk*) of 4,000 men and 80 officers. The regiment also possessed more specialized formations, including an intelligence section, a machine gun company, and communications personnel. A division (*diviziia*) contained four regiments along with the addition of an integral artillery brigade. Altogether, a Russian infantry division on paper contained some 21,000 men, making it somewhat larger than its German or French counterparts. During the war, casualties and illness meant that units were substantially smaller. Multiple divisions made up a corps, and multiple corps an army. Prior to and during the Russo-Japanese War of 1904–1905, the Russian army had a highly complex structure with a bewildering variety of unit types, but a set of reforms beginning in 1907 had simplified its organization.[15]

The Russian army was commanded and led by its officer corps, a group of over 40,000 men. This group was going through a fundamental transformation prior to the First World War. By comparison to other powers, Russia relied less on its noncommissioned officers to provide low-level leadership, a pattern that persisted into the Soviet Union and post-Soviet Russia. Russia's relatively simple social structure, with fewer lower-middle and middle-class families to provide a pool of literate and educated manpower, proved ill-suited to generating sufficient candidates for platoon leaders and company sergeants. Instead, leadership was more the responsibility of commissioned officers, who retained much of their noble ethos even as the share of actual nobles declined. While the Russian nobility had traditionally identified itself with the officer corps, and the officer corps with the nobility, changes in the Russian army since the Great Reforms had substantially altered the social makeup of the officer corps. While the traditional nobility still dominated the upper ranks of the prerevolutionary army, half of Russia's officers were nonnoble by 1911. The fundamental mechanism of this transformation prior to World War I was education. Traditionally, officers had come through a number of cadet corps or through the more aristocratic imperial Corps of Pages. By the start of World War I, they came instead from a network of two- or three-year military schools.[16] The war itself naturally produced a new flood of nonnobles into the officer ranks. In addition to the social transformation from noble to commoner, the political outlook of the officer corps had been shaken by the Russo-Japanese War and subsequent 1905 revolution. The experience of military defeat at the hands of a non-European power previously deemed racially inferior proved deeply traumatic for Russia's officer corps. In April 1906, the Higher Attestation Commission began to review the suitability of officers for high command. It purged the officer corps of superannuated or incompetent personnel, cashiering 4,300 officers, including 337 generals, by 1908. In addition, the revolution's political disruption shook even the holy of holies of the Russian elites: the guards regiments. The Preobrazhenskii regiment, dating back to Peter the Great, mutinied on 2 July 1906 and demanded redistribution of agricultural land in favor of the peasantry. To a significant degree, the tsarist regime had taken its officer corps for granted, presuming that dynastic ties, regimental solidarity, and the aristocratic core of the officers would guarantee loyalty. That presumption proved mistaken.[17]

Building new sources of loyalty and cohesion was problematic. Russia was an empire, with the Romanov dynasty as its uniting principle. Nationalism was thus flawed as a means of strengthening the empire's unity, given its enormous ethnic diversity. Only a minority of Russia's population was ethnically Russian, and so a purely ethnic identity was fraught with peril. Making the Russian people themselves central to the empire and what it meant inevitably raised the question of whether those people ought to govern themselves. Ethnicity was not the foremost concern of the Russian state, which generally viewed its population in social and religious terms rather than ethnic. Orthodox Christianity was an important part of officer education, but Orthodox faith and Russian nationality were *not* necessary for full acceptance into the officer corps. Lutheran Baltic Germans, for example, were a presence among the officer corps far out of proportion to their share of the population. Catholic Poles, on the other hand, faced systematic discrimination, with quotas limiting their number and a requirement for special attestations of loyalty; Jews were essentially barred from the officer corps altogether. The prewar officer corps did included a substantial number of Muslims from Russia's traditionally Muslim regions in the Caucasus and Central Asia, totaling around 400 (with perhaps 30 generals). This group was not particularly Islamic in its outlook, as a career spent in tsarist military schools and military service alongside Orthodox Christians and Baltic German Lutherans produced a general de-emphasis on personal religion in service life. Most prominent among Muslim officers was the khan of Nakhichevan, who served with notable lack of success as cavalry commander during the First Army's invasion of East Prussia in 1914.[18]

The officers of European armies on the eve of World War I were generally characterized by relative lack of intellectual engagement. Historically aristocratic, the officer corps tended to acculturate those from other social classes into its anti-intellectual ethos, with some exceptions in the more technically demanding engineering and artillery branches. In Russia, the officer corps saw itself as a conservative and apolitical body whose engagement with politics was limited to uncritical support for the Romanov dynasty. Seniority and political connections trumped education and competence. The serious intellectual study of war was largely limited to General Staff officers, a small, self-conscious minority of the officer corps. Even the training of this intellectual elite at the Nikolaev General Staff Academy emphasized ancient history over the study of Russia's recent conflicts. Under Mikhail Dragomirov, director of the Nikolaev Academy from 1879 to 1889, the curriculum stressed the importance of morale over technology. Though subsequent directors did much to improve and modernize the curriculum, the inherent conservatism of the Romanov dynasty and its officer corps proved a formidable deterrent to real change.[19]

Supreme command over Russia's armed forces lay, as it always had, with the tsar himself. Lacking a tradition of collective government, Russia was ruled through ministers who held office at the pleasure of the tsar and were individually responsible for their particular sphere. This had a pernicious influence on the making of policy, notably in the lack of coordination between the ministries of finance, foreign affairs, war, and the navy. Policies were coherent only to the extent that individual ministers engaged in mutual consultation and, particularly, that the tsar imposed coherence. Tsar Nicholas II—intelligent, kind-hearted, but weak and indecisive—was poorly suited to such a role. Strong coordination was the exception, not the rule, despite efforts at instituting more centralized government after the 1905 revolution. Throughout the period before World War I, rationalization and efficient organization were consistently at odds with traditionalism, factionalism, and the whims of the tsar. All of Europe's militaries, as particularly tradition-bound organizations, faced this problem, but the clash between modernity and tradition was particularly acute in Russia.

The difficulty of rational policy was particularly clear in the ongoing struggle (still unresolved in the Soviet Union and, indeed, Russia today) between the relative power and authority of the war minister and the General Staff. Russia's model was similar to Germany's: that is, the War Ministry was responsible for day-to-day administration of the routine business of the army, including drafting, training, and feeding soldiers, procuring equipment, and handling all the paperwork generated by millions of men. The General Staff, by contrast, was much smaller but had a role equally important: the systematic planning in peacetime for the eventuality of war, including plans for mobilizing soldiers from the civilian population, assembling them into units, deploying them to the front, and deciding what they should do once they got there. The basic principle of dividing responsibility was relatively clear, but making it work in practice was extremely complex. For example, plans for the next war, the purview of the General Staff, should certainly be reflected in levels of manpower, procurement of equipment, and troop training, all of which typically fell under the war minister. How could policies be best coordinated, and who should dictate policy to whom? One concrete and surprisingly difficult question was whether the chief of the General Staff reported and answered directly to the tsar, as in the German system, or was instead subordinate to the war minister? Whatever precise form the division of responsibilities took, the inevitable outcome was two separate and competing authorities inside the army. If the chief of the General Staff was powerful (the German practice), he tended to dominate. If he was not, the war minister's authority hindered the chief of staff's effective preparation for war. When the war minister and chief of the General Staff were both competent and worked well together, the arrangement was manageable. The War Ministry handled conscription, procurement, and general matters of day-to-day administration, while the General Staff focused on war planning. In practice, the two spheres necessarily impinged on one another.

The period between the Russo-Japanese War and the First World War was marked by repeated overhauls of Russian military administration. In the immediate aftermath of the Russo-Japanese War, a new Main Directorate of the General Staff was split off from Russia's existing Main Staff to handle war plans. While this made some sense, administrative rationality was soon trumped by bureaucratic politics. Vladimir Sukhomlinov became chief of staff at the end of 1908 and then war minister in early 1909, replacing Aleksandr Rediger. Sukhomlinov's talents lay primarily in the good-humored glad-handing of court politics, making him an easy scapegoat for more general problems of military administration. Sukhomlinov shuffled through five chiefs of staff in six years, thereby assuring the weakness of the General Staff and his own ascendancy as war minister. Sukhom-

linov dominated the Russian army before World War I, but his evident political ambition and striking venality alienated the bulk of his subordinates,
who systematically destroyed his reputation after the war. Though
Sukhomlinov certainly had weaknesses and made mistakes, he did preside
over the systematic expansion of the Russian military, an expansion that
deeply alarmed Germany and Austria-Hungary.[20]

RUSSIAN WAR PLANS

Sukhomlinov's positive influence on Russian military capacity was evident
in the changing nature of Russian plans for the next war.[21] In the late 1800s,
Russian war plans had been fundamentally defensive. During the Great Reforms, Miliutin had been cautious, anxious to avoid war while engaged in
root and branch reorganization. Russia was in no position to open the next
war with an offensive against Germany or Austria-Hungary, so war plans
were fundamentally reactive. In the wake of the creation of the Dual, then
the Triple, Alliance, with the predominant force and greater speed of concentration that Germany and Austria-Hungary would enjoy, Russia had no
choice but to deploy its troops well back from its borders and develop a system of fortresses. A series of assessments of Russian defenses and corre-
sponding war plans in 1880, 1883, 1887, and 1890 all came to essentially this
same conclusion. Nikolai Obruchev, chief of the main staff from 1881 to
1897, accepted that the initial Russian stance must be defensive, though he
yearned for some way of seizing the initiative. As a result, Russian planning
was never entirely passive, since it always incorporated an eventual move
to offensive action. Nonetheless, plans all began with Russian forces awaiting attack rather than attacking. Russian planners generally anticipated concentrating against Austria-Hungary. Not only was the Habsburg army ob-
jectively weaker than the German, but the forests and swamps in the
northern sector of the front opposite the Germans would simplify a Russian
defense. This defensive mindset required fixed fortifications to defend
Poland, particularly against the Germans. Warsaw was shielded by its own
fortifications as well as major fortress complexes to the northwest at Modlin and southeast at Dęblin. In addition, the Russians screened the East
Prussian frontier by a line of fortresses along the Biebrza and Narew rivers.[22]

Russian thinking changed very slowly. In 1899, War Minister Aleksei

Kuropatkin informed Nicholas II that Russian railroads were so far behind the German and Austrian that Russia's potential foes could begin military operations while the Russians were still in the midst of transporting troops to the front (the Germans after twelve days of mobilization, the Austrians after sixteen). Russia also faced terrible uncertainty in not knowing whether German intent was to send its troops east against Russia or west against France. The result was constant tension between pulling troops back into Russia's interior for security against the faster-mobilizing Germans and Austrians and needing forward deployment to assist Russia's ally France. Dragomirov was the chief partisan of a more aggressive stance against Germany, but lacked backing from the rest of the high command. In late 1902 and early 1903, the Main Staff prepared a new war plan, Schedule 18, that put the weight of Russian forces squarely against Austria-Hungary, but still maintained a conservative approach. The Northwestern Front's two armies, the First and Second, were supported on their left flank by the troops of the Warsaw garrison and had a primarily defensive mission, counterattacking only if a German offensive into Russia offered such an opportunity, or if German concentration against France left the German eastern border unprotected. Under Schedule 18, the Southwestern Front had three armies, the Third, Fourth, and Fifth, but was nonetheless similarly intended for initial defensive operations, and a turn to the offensive only if opportunity offered itself. Two additional armies, the Sixth and Seventh, protected the Baltic coast and St. Petersburg.[23]

War with Japan took this considered choice of a passive, defensive strategy in the west and made it a necessity. Russian war plans, never aggressive, were even more conservative after the Russo-Japanese War. Of the 1,500 battalions intended for war in the west, a fifth were transferred to the Far East. The toll on Russian stocks of ammunition was even greater. Until Russia's armed forces were in better condition, any European war would therefore require a defensive posture. In early 1909, Nicholas II approved a new variant of Schedule 18. It remained conservative, planning for Russian forces along the western frontier (five armies and a separate corps at Odessa) to observe and absorb any German and Austrian movements, delaying offensive action until well after the outbreak of hostilities once the precise nature of Austro-German plans had become clear.[24] Real reform after the Russo-Japanese War was slow. At the end of 1906, War Minister Aleksandr Rediger proposed an overhaul of Russia's military, reducing peacetime manpower but improving quality through better training and preparation. The expense of the measures (2,000 million rubles in one-time expenses and 144 million annually after that), combined with Russia's empty treasury, ensured the proposal went nowhere, along with a series of other unfunded reforms. In summer 1908, Chief of Staff Fyodor Palitsyn and his subordinate Mikhail Alekseev produced a massive "Report on Measures for Defense of the State." The report was long on recommendations for expanding and improving fortresses, building roads and railroads, and adding artillery and machine guns throughout the Russian army, but short on detailing the concrete financial realities of those commitments. Indeed, they declared that "it would be mistaken to derive our planned measures from available monies and financial considerations."[25]

Prospects were, however, improving after 1908. Humiliation during the Bosnian crisis had underlined the importance of military reform. Aleksandr Guchkov, leader of the moderately conservative Octobrist Party in the Duma, saw military reform as an issue that could mobilize and unite popular opinion and reconcile Russian society with the tsarist regime, though at the cost of pointed criticism of the failings of the military reconstruction in the wake of the Russo-Japanese War. Guchkov saw military power as an essential element of any foreign policy worthy of the name. He could also rely on the tacit support of substantial reforming elements in the Russian army itself, dissatisfied like he was with official neglect of military reform. On 9 June 1908, in response to the Russian government proposal of a military budget, Guchkov lambasted the tsar's regime for its utter failure to think through the needs of Russian defense. Russia's powerlessness in the wake of Austria's annexation of Bosnia-Herzegovina only confirmed Guchkov's attack. Austrian reticence alone had prevented a crushing defeat of Serbia and with it all Russian hopes for influence in the Balkans.[26]

The change in Russian military capability did not result primarily from dramatic increases in spending, but instead from general economic growth and more efficient use of available resources. Russian military spending from 1907 through 1913 ranged between 4.0 and 5.4 percent of net national product. This expenditure, while high in absolute terms, was far below the European average in both per capita terms, given Russia's large population, and spending per soldier, given Russia's heavier reliance on its standing army as opposed to reserves mobilized in wartime. The problem was worsened by Nicholas II's irrational insistence on prioritizing the replacement of the capital ships lost in the Russo-Japanese War, diverting scarce resources from the service of Russia's real security needs. The result was that Russia's soldiers had fewer guns and less ammunition than their rivals in the years before the war and went to fight in 1914 with serious shortages of equipment. Even so, Russian capabilities and the railroad network that sustained mobilization were improving steadily.[27]

As Russian military capability recovered from the Russo-Japanese War, and the German danger in the west outweighed the Japanese danger in the east, Russian plans became more aggressive. Nicholas approved Sukhomlinov's new Schedule 19 in July 1910, increasing the armies on the Western Front from five to seven, by upgrading corps and garrison troops dedicated to defense of the far north (St. Petersburg) and far south (Odessa) to the status of full armies. It allowed for more initiative and clearly emphasized war against Germany (four armies) as opposed to Austria-Hungary (only one). These plans were supported by a reorganization that split officers and men from existing regiments to form the core of new reserve regiments, providing approximately 500 additional battalions at mobilization. The move to more aggressive planning remained limited: strategy was more ambitious but deployments were more cautious. Russian formations mobilized to locations substantially further east than under Schedule 18. Much of the Polish salient was left undefended, as Russian plans foresaw allowing the fortress complexes of central Poland to bear the burden of defense. In 1910, the Duma allocated over 700 million rubles in extraordinary expenditures on defense, well over half of which went toward the improvement of fortresses in Poland: fixed positions and immovable artillery that would prove almost entirely useless during the war. This raised an important question at the time: why devote four armies against Germany when those four armies would mobilize and deploy well behind the Polish salient and in no position to undertake meaningful offensive action against Germany, while at the same time investing heavily in static defenses? Part of the answer is a general overestimation of the value of fortifications among European military thinkers. Sukhomlinov tried with only mixed success to reduce Russian dependence on fortifications at the expense of field forces, but Russia was not alone in devoting a staggering amount of money and artillery to fortifications. From 1907 to 1909, 47 percent of extraordinary credits voted in Italy went toward fortifications, to which Austria responded with an ambitious building program of its own in 1911. The French in 1914 devoted over 30 percent of their army budget to fortification, and even the offensive-minded Germans on the eve of war spent 21 percent.[28]

In keeping with this book's general emphasis on contingency, it is worth emphasizing the late and sudden Russian switch to an offensive war plan. Had it begun at any point between 1880 and 1912, European war would have seen Russian troops deploying well back from the frontier and awaiting events, not making the aggressive incursion into East Prussia that actually took place in 1914. While military capability was improving, the political implications of Schedule 19—its conservative deployments that abandoned the defense of Russia's borderlands—were disturbing to many in Russia's high command, who wanted a more aggressive stance. Given Poland's history of rebellion against Russian rule, abandoning sections of Poland without a fight might make it impossible to bring those territories under control again. Alliance politics played a key role as well. In a summer 1911 visit to Russia, the French chief of staff, Auguste Dubail, pressured the Russians to commit to a major offensive against Germany as quickly as possible on the outbreak of war to divert German forces that might otherwise be pushing toward Paris. The Russians had to admit an offensive was still beyond their capability. A year later, in summer 1912, Chief of Staff Yakov Zhilinskii could assure the French of a Russian advance into Germany fifteen days after the start of mobilization. The *promise* of such an action was not a particularly new development: the 1892 Franco-Russian military convention had committed Russia, in the event of an attack on France, to attack Germany with "all available forces," specified in the Russian case as 700–800,000 men, with such speed as to ensure that Germany would have to fight simultaneously on both fronts. Zhilinskii's declaration in 1912 put a more specific timetable on the Russian commitment, but did not change its essence. What was new was that Russian plans and improving rail network could make that commitment a reality.[29]

In 1912, Russian planning shifted to become predominantly offensive for the first time in decades. A number of proposals for revisions of Russian war plans were circulating within the army, and at the start of 1912, under pressure from military district commanders who wished to take advantage of the geographical advantage offered by the Polish salient, Quartermaster-General Danilov argued for a reorientation of Russian war plans to move quickly to the offensive against Germany and Austria-Hungary.

The relationship with Britain and France seemed stronger, and the re-building of the Russian army after the Russo-Japanese War gave the high command increasing confidence. Germany's westward orientation would leave a short but invaluable window of opportunity for the Russian army to attack an undefended German eastern border. This would require push-ing Russian units over the frontier before mobilization was complete, but for Danilov this risk was worth taking. Alekseev, now stationed at Kiev, saw Russia's chief interests as lying in the Balkans, and the terrain of Gali-cia as more favorable for action. Accordingly, he argued for an offensive focus on Austria.[30]

The result was a major conference on 21 February 1912 by the chiefs of staff of Russia's military districts to resolve the debate over Russia's main effort in the event of war. On whether to direct Russia's limited resources against Austria or Germany, the answer was "both." As assembled by the General Staff in spring 1912, Russia's war plan included two variants. Under the more likely case of a German push west into France, the new de-fault Schedule 19A (for "Austria") projected sending two armies against German East Prussia and three armies, later expanded to four armies, into Austrian Galicia. Despite the letter "A" indicating its primary direction against Austria, the war plan nonetheless envisaged the Northwestern Front crossing the German border to occupy East Prussia. The variant schedule 19G (for "Germany"), never fully developed, allocated the North-western Front three armies for the invasion of East Prussia, while the Southwestern would have two defending against Austria in Galicia.[31] Though Schedule 19A was a violation of the military principle of massing effort at the most important point, and Russia would possess only a slight advantage in each theater and a decisive advantage nowhere, there was logic behind the Russian policy. For strategic reasons Russia had no choice but to engage in some offensive action against Germany. A clash between Germany and France without any outside intervention would likely lead to French defeat, and Russia could not hope to stand against the combined forces of Germany and Austria alone. Second, Russia's concrete foreign pol-icy aims had far more to do with Austria's position in the Balkans than with any German territory.

On the very eve of war, the Russian state committed itself to a "Great Program" intended to further strengthen the Russian army. As early as the end of 1912, the General Staff had been developing plans for expansion

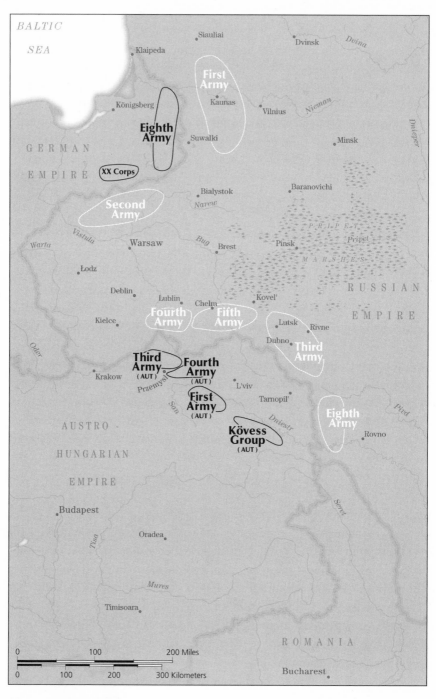

Map 1. 1914 Deployments

over the period 1914–1917. These were given additional impetus by the adoption of 1912 and 1913 German army laws that expanded German forces. After lengthy political jockeying between Sukhomlinov, the Duma, and Prime Minister Kokovtsov, the program finally became law after Nicholas' approval on 7 July 1914. Under its terms, the Russian peacetime army was set to grow by over a third with the addition of 480,000 officers and men. Roughly 40 percent of the new manpower would go toward new formations, including two new corps and substantial expansion of fortress garrisons in Poland. The remaining 60 percent of the increase would fill out existing formations. The program also created new brigades, divisions, and corps on Russia's threatened frontiers. Russia's cavalry was expanded by the provision of standing cavalry attached to corps and divisions, in place of newly mobilized units intended to join them in wartime. Artillery was improved by the plan to break up Russia's unwieldy eight-gun batteries into more manageable six-gun units. At the same time, it substantially expanded the heavy artillery attached to each corps, including a battery of 152mm howitzers and two batteries of 107mm guns. On full implementation, Russia's field artillery would reach 8,358 guns. Engineering, aviation, and railroad troops were also slated for reorganization and expansion. Sadly, the delay in implementation of the law gave Russia the worst of both worlds. Extended discussion of military expansion further alarmed Germany and Austria-Hungary and increased their willingness to wage preventive war; delayed implementation meant that Russia went to war without the appreciable benefits the program might have brought. To be sure, the army did not wait on formal legislative approval to begin the Great Program, but nonetheless only a small fraction of its provisions were in place on the outbreak of war.[32]

THE GERMANS AND THE AUSTRIANS

The German army at the outbreak of war was built on a pattern roughly similar to the Russian, though with some minor differences. A platoon of 80 men was the smallest independent unit. Three such platoons along with support and command staff made a company of 259 men. Two twelve-company regiments of 3,000 men each made a brigade, two brigades (along with a cavalry regiment of 600–700 men) made a division, and two divisions a corps. Together with its supporting elements, the corps included some 40,000 men. The corps was a standing formation, with its divisions serving under it over long periods of time, and included reconnaissance aviation and a sixteen-gun battalion of 150mm howitzers. A typical German division had seventy-two artillery pieces: fifty-four of the antiquated FK 96 n.A and eighteen of a superb 105mm howitzer. Each regiment also had a thirteenth machine gun company.[33] The German system also differed from the Russian system in that its reserve units were regarded as independent formations, assumed to be able to act on the same basis as others. This was quite different from the Russian or Austrian approach, which saw reserves as inherently less effective, intended for use on secondary fronts, as garrison troops, as replacements for losses, or to fill out and expand larger units alongside a core of regular troops.[34]

The Germans' greatest advantage was in training and organization. Its officer corps, though not particularly gifted at grand strategy, was superb at operations and tactics. Well-trained and encouraged to use their independent judgment, officers combined discipline and flexibility. Essentially universal literacy and linguistic homogeneity gave the German army a key advantage by comparison to the Austrians or the Russians. High levels of education and a well-developed industrial economy also meant that Germany had a large population of men with experience of low-level management and leadership to form an effective corps of noncommissioned officers. Throughout the war on the Eastern Front, the German army was able to act and react to changing circumstances far faster than its Russian counterpart.

The Habsburg military was substantially more complex, reflecting the nature of the multinational Austro-Hungarian Empire itself. Its army was faced by a substantial array of handicaps in its efforts to fight a modern war effectively. The Habsburg federal system, with a whole range of institutions divided between its Austrian and Hungarian halves, hindered the effective coordination of policy. Most specifically, the Habsburg army actually consisted of three separate forces. As part of a far-reaching 1867 compromise between the two halves of the empire, a new structure for the armed forces was established in 1868: the regular army was the "imperial and royal army" (*k.u.k. Armee*) reflecting the Habsburg monarch's dual status as emperor of Austria and king of Hungary. This was supplemented by two separate reserve or militia forces: the Austrian *Landwehr* and the Hungarian

Honvéd. The Habsburg high command was not happy with the resulting division, but the empire's delicate ethnic balance meant that politics trumped military efficiency. Decades of chronic underfunding, and an emphasis on static fortifications over artillery modernization, meant that Austria-Hungary had an artillery park that was smaller and older than any other Great Power. Poor funding meant not only that equipment was skimped on, but also that each annual intake of conscripts could take in only a fraction of the available manpower for training. In the early 1900s this amounted to only 100,000 men, increased in 1910 to 126,000 and in 1912 to 181,000.[35]

Ethnic tensions also played a role in Habsburg inability to fight a major war, though this is easy to overstate. In the wake of the military defeat and political disintegration of 1918, German-speaking elites had a clear incentive to point to Hungarian and Slav disloyalty as the Habsburg Empire's downfall. Conversely, once Austria-Hungary had disintegrated into a host of national states, new nationalist elites had a similar incentive to downplay prior loyalty to the dynasty, though those sentiments had clearly existed. Ironically, while the South Slavs were the heart of resistance to conscription in the first decades after the compromise, it was the West Slavs (particularly Czechs) who were perceived during the war itself as disloyal, liable to surrender or desert to the Russians. The command and control difficulties introduced by a dozen nationalities and languages were real and severe, as were the political fights over language of command in ethnically mixed units. Ethnic Germans made up three-quarters of the officer corps, but only one-quarter of the soldiers were competent in German. That said, active efforts to destroy and break up the Habsburg Empire arose only quite late in World War I, and it is easy to overstate the impact of ethnic factors on Habsburg effectiveness. While Hungarian nationalist sensibilities had been a constant source of tension before the war, eventually turning the *Honvéd* from a militia into something more like a Hungarian national army, during the war itself the *Honvéd* fought loyally, acquitting itself as well as any section of the army. Just as in Russia in 1914, Austrian mobilization went well, with draft dodging and nationalist resistance to the war remaining limited within quite acceptable bounds. There were, however, cases of mass disloyalty: in April 1915, a Czech regiment deserted en masse to the Russians.[36]

3

The Opening Campaigns: East Prussia, 1914

The war on the Eastern Front began with two massive clashes in separate theaters. In the northern theater, two Russian armies—the First and Second—invaded East Prussia against a defense conducted by the German Eighth Army. In the southern theater, four Russian armies—the Fourth, Fifth, Third, and Eighth—collided in a vast meeting engagement with three Austro-Hungarian armies—the Fourth, First, and Third, supported by two additional task forces—across the open plains of Galicia. Each army and corps attempted to outflank and encircle its opponent. Two additional Russian armies, the Sixth and Seventh, protected the newly renamed Russian capital Petrograd and the Black Sea coast at Odessa in the south. Judged by the number of troops involved, Galicia was by far the more significant theater. Austria-Hungary was the foe with which Russia had the greatest clash of interests: in effect, the enemy Russia wanted to fight. Nevertheless, Russia's initial victory in Galicia has been eclipsed by its initial defeat in East Prussia. Part of this is deliberate propaganda: Paul von Hindenburg and Erich Ludendorff, who obtained near total control of the German war effort by war's end, established their reputations as ostensible military geniuses in the battle for East Prussia, and assiduously promoted their achievements during the war and after. In addition, East Prussia had more significance to the broader war outside the Eastern Front itself. The battle for Galicia, whether decisive Russian victory or catastrophic defeat, was unlikely to affect the immediate course of war elsewhere. East Prussia, by contrast, had everything to do with what happened in the west. Ger-

54

many needed every man it could spare for the drive on Paris, and its effort to destroy the French army before Russian mobilization was complete; rapid Russian victory in East Prussia would mean failure at Paris and doom Germany to a two-front war; quick Russian defeat might allow Germany's gamble to succeed.

The campaigns of 1914 differed substantially from those of later years. First, their tempo was more rapid. Six months of war witnessed Russian invasions of East Prussia and Galicia, an Austro-Hungarian attack out of Galicia, two autumn German offensives against Warsaw, an Austro-Hungarian offensive in the Carpathians, and a German winter offensive in Masuria, all in quick succession. Since unit density—the number of men per mile of front—was lower than in the west, the fronts moved with great speed. Neither side could sustain this pace, though, and the tempo of events in subsequent years was more restrained. Second, the battles in the east in 1914 were operationally distinct from later years as a result of limited manpower in a large space. The low unit density that made fronts mobile was a product in part of the unalterable vastness in the east, but also of the nature of mobilization. Because of its slow mobilization, the Russian army began fighting with many of its troops still making their way to the front. Nicholas had approved full mobilization on 31 July, but by the time the first serious clashes took place in mid-August, only a fraction of Russia's available forces had been moved to the front. Russia could deploy only a third of the force to frontier zones after fifteen days and another third by thirty days, forcing the Russian generals in East Prussia and Galicia to go to war before their full complement of men was available.[1] At the same time, bungling by Conrad, the Austrian chief of staff, forced his troops to spend much of the first month of the war shuttling between the Balkans and Galicia. Finally, commanders were still thinking of war in Napoleonic terms, with formations marching independently, then concentrating for battle as compact masses. The fronts in 1914 were *not* continuous. Corps and armies moved and fought as discrete and separate units, certainly by comparison to later in the war. This is, of course, relative. No Napoleonic army fought on a front of 100 kilometers, as armies in the east routinely did. Nonetheless, commanders allowed substantial gaps between their divisions and their neighbors, with the spaces between covered by cavalry or not at all. Huge sections of the Eastern Front were essentially unmanned in the early days of the war—the western border of the Polish salient, for example. The fighting of 1914 thus took a unique shape, with commanders on both sides constantly striving to find and turn their opponents' open flanks or move into gaps between separated enemy formations. Razgonov, a colonel of the General Staff, wrote that "contemporary battle consists almost entirely of the struggle for flanks."[2] That was true in 1914, but by 1915 those open flanks had disappeared.

Russian mobilization went unexpectedly smoothly. The experience of the 1905 Revolution had led many to expect draft dodging and general disorder. Instead, reservists were somber and subdued but compliant. There were some draft riots, provoked either by mass consumption of alcohol as a last hurrah or by soldiers' breaking into liquor stores—one particularly serious riot in Barnaul took more than a hundred lives. Like Western Europe, Russia witnessed outbursts of patriotic enthusiasm from middle- and upper-class urban citizens, particularly large rallies in Palace Square in Petrograd. Russia's War Ministry was surprised by substantial numbers of volunteers driven by patriotic enthusiasm, and the tsar had to specifically approve such unorthodox recruits. Despite the best efforts of Soviet historians to find a nascent anti-war movement among Russian workers, what labor disturbances did take place seem to have been drunken farewells rather than protest against the war. Strikes abruptly ended with the announcement of mobilization. What strikes did take place were sometimes motivated by patriotism, as when locomotive workers in Kharkov struck in August 1914, demanding the dismissal of German and Austrian shop foremen. That enthusiasm had a much darker side: newly mobilized soldiers engaged in isolated pogroms against ethnic Germans or Jews. On balance, though, Russia's conscripts marched to their assembly points in good order with surprisingly little desertion. The Russian rail system moved with remarkable efficiency to get those soldiers to the front lines, in accordance with detailed schemes for the first two weeks of mobilization.[3]

The war required an overhaul of the machinery of Russian military command. Grand Duke Nikolai Nikolaevich, the son of Nicholas's great uncle, became the army's supreme commander. Twelve years older than the tsar and immensely tall, towering over his contemporaries, he fully looked the part of a commander in chief. Prewar thinking had generally presumed that the tsar, or perhaps the war minister, would step into this role.

Nicholas, in yet another example of the indecisiveness and malleability that marred his character, abandoned his prewar intent to command, convinced by his ministers to avoid the direct responsibility for battlefield failure that being commander in chief would entail. A long-time professional soldier, the grand duke had a full military education and career that the tsar himself lacked. He was adored by his soldiers and the Russian peasantry, who developed legends of his personal heroism in foiling German plots. This acclaim created an unhealthy dynamic between the grand duke and the tsar's inner circle. Though Nikolai Nikolaevich was loyal to the regime, his popularity raised suspicions, and the tsar himself had an uneasy relationship with his elder but nominal inferior. In addition, Nikolai Nikolaevich had real weaknesses as a commander. The grand duke lacked the work ethic to manage the massive flow of information into and out of the high command. As result, much of the actual business of the war fell to his rather limited subordinates. Chief of Staff Nikolai Yanushkevich (a vicious anti-Semite) had served exclusively in administrative roles and lacked field experience. Quartermaster-General Yurii Danilov, responsible for planning military operations, was more effective, taciturn but hard-working. Also, despite the grand duke's heroic image, he lacked physical and moral courage, keeping himself away from the front lines and from wounded soldiers. Prone to nervousness and anxiety, he was ill-suited for the mental strains of his position. He also suffered from poor relations with War Minister Sukhomlinov, hindering coordination of the overall war effort. Tsar Nicholas might have overcome this difficulty by an active role in enforcing unified policy on his generals and ministers, but this was entirely outside of the tsar's character.[4]

As supreme commander, Nikolai Nikolaevich worked with and through *Stavka*, the administrative and bureaucratic machine that controlled strategy and operations. Once war began, the supreme commander and *Stavka* established a command post in railroad cars at the junction town of Baranovichi in order to ease the burden of communications and reduce the distraction of Petrograd society. The war minister and the War Ministry, stripped of much of their personnel and authority, remained in Petrograd to handle administrative tasks and supply the material needs of the front. The War Ministry's Main Directorate of the General Staff was gutted to provide the human material for *Stavka*. Yanushkevich, the prewar chief of the General Staff, went to *Stavka* to head the grand duke's staff. A substantial portion of the quartermaster-general section under Danilov went to *Stavka* as well. The hollow shell of the General Staff, headed by the newly appointed Mikhail Beliaev, stayed in Petrograd and lost its planning responsibilities, serving as a supply bureaucracy. It also handled the business of conscription, training, and organizing troops into new formations. As the colossal logistic demands of the war became clear, the separation of operational control at *Stavka* from supply management in Petrograd became increasingly untenable. *Stavka* acquired greater control over supply with time, growing to encompass major questions of the war economy in addition to the operational-strategic tasks that occupied it early in the war. Despite its responsibilities, *Stavka* remained remarkably small. Particularly under Grand Duke Nikolai Nikolaevich, it was not marked by particular urgency in its day-to-day work, and only numbered about sixty staffers to command Russia's war effort. It suffered from rudimentary communications facilities as well. By 1917, *Stavka* had grown to sixteen directorates and three chancelleries, with 250 personnel (still remarkably small for the demands on it). Even from the first days of the war, *Stavka* and the high command in general bore a huge responsibility for administration. Russian law gave the military authority over civil government in a belt of territory behind the front lines, burdening Russia's operational commands still further. Russian officers, inexperienced in civil affairs, did not work well with their civilian counterparts. In one case, a reserve *praporshchik*, the lowest officer rank in the army, threatened to shoot the governor of Lifland for objecting to the requisition of property.[5]

Though Nikolai Nikolaevich held command, Tsar Nicholas believed it his duty to be close to the front, and so he joined *Stavka* at Baranovichi in early autumn 1914 and spent much time there over the next year. Nicholas was intensely psychologically dependent on his wife, Alexandra, and his physical distance from her was a constant strain. Though he returned home between his stints at *Stavka,* his absences meant he lacked a direct sense of politics in the capital and of the growing resentment and disgust at the political and social antics of the Siberian holy man Grigorii Rasputin, who had convinced Nicholas and Alexandra alike of his mystical powers. With Alexandra alone in Petrograd, public suspicion of her German birth grew steadily in conjunction with failures at the front. The very real war work done by the royal daughters as nurses tending to wounded soldiers did nothing to alleviate the burgeoning sense that treachery reached into the tsar's household itself.[6]

Two Fronts served as the next link in the chain of command underneath *Stavka*. Based on experience of the Russo-Japanese War, the Russian government recognized that modern warfare required a new link in the hierarchy of military units, one that would fall between the individual armies that made up the Russian army and *Stavka* at the center. This intermediate formation, the Front, controlled two or more individual armies, up to a half-dozen, depending on time and circumstance. In 1914, the Warsaw Military District became the core of the Northwestern Front under Yakov Zhilinskii, the Kiev Military District the core of the Southwestern Front under Nikolai Ivanov. The headquarters of Russia's internal military districts became the headquarters of armies boarding trains to the front.[7]

EAST PRUSSIA: SETTING THE STAGE

Strategic calculations in the invasion of East Prussia were relatively clear to both sides. Since German efforts would be focused in the west, East Prussia would be defended by relatively small forces, intended not to defeat the Russians but to delay Russian advance, counterattacking where possible, in order to allow time for German victory in the west. The Russians invaded East Prussia with two armies. The First Army under the command of Pavel von Rennenkampf had three corps: the III, IV, and IX, along with a substantial force of cavalry. The Second Army under Aleksandr Samsonov had six corps: I, II, VI, XIII, XV, and XXIII, and a smaller cavalry force. Both armies belonged to Zhilinskii's overarching Northwestern Front. Zhilinskii's ostensible purpose was to provide the necessary coordination for his two subordinate armies, though he proved quite incapable of that task: stilted, formal, and devoid of leadership qualities. The mission was clear: since Germany had sent the bulk of its forces west against France, Russia had a moral and strategic obligation to its ally to move against weak German defenses in the east as quickly as possible. Yanushkevich explained to Zhilinskii that his Northwestern Front would enjoy a manpower advantage of at least two to one. "Bearing in mind," Yanushkevich wrote, "that Germany declared war first against us and that France as an ally considered it her duty to support us against Germany, it is naturally necessary under the same obligations of alliance, to support the French when the main German blow is directed against them. That support must be expressed by our quickest possible offensive against those German forces remaining in East Prussia."[8]

The defense of East Prussia lay with the German Eighth Army under Max von Prittwitz. Prittwitz had four corps: the I, XVII, XX, and I Reserve, plus a single cavalry division and a motley mixture of militia and garrison troops. Though precise figures are disputed, the Russians mustered eighteen or nineteen infantry divisions, eight or nine cavalry divisions, and 1,100–1,200 guns between their two armies, with the Second Army substantially larger. By all quantitative measures, the German Eighth Army was smaller than the Russian formations it faced, possessing fourteen infantry divisions and 1,100 guns, though many were relatively immobile and committed to fortifications. The Russians could thus expect an advantage of a little less than 3:2 in East Prussia.[9] As a result, the Russians had a substantial but not overwhelming advantage, but only if the First and Second Armies could coordinate their actions effectively. The moral and political imperative to defend German soil made it likely that Prittwitz would have to split his forces to confront both Russian armies; Samsonov and Rennenkampf thus had to stay close enough to provide mutual support, but not so close that Prittwitz could keep his forces concentrated. Since Prittwitz could not hope to defeat either Russian army without concentrating, Samsonov and Rennenkampf needed to avoid being drawn into decisive battle, instead fighting only to engage and entangle German forces to allow time for the other army to move behind the Eighth Army and thereby crush it between them.

On 13 August, Zhilinskii outlined his plan of campaign. Rennenkampf's First Army would skirt the Masurian Lakes on their northern side, engage elements of the German Eighth Army, cut them off from the fortress-city of Königsberg to the west, and pin them in place. Samsonov's Second Army would push into East Prussia from the south, west of the Masurian Lakes, and cut off the Eighth Army from escape to safety west of the Vistula. Zhilinskii's idea was that the Second Army would skirt closely around the western edge of the Masurian Lakes, remaining close to Rennenkampf's First Army. Samsonov altered the plan to be more aggressive, shifting his main blow west. This sacrificed mutual assistance with Rennenkampf in favor of a deeper and more complete encirclement of the German Eighth Army, cutting off retreat across the Vistula. It was an audacious gamble, but one that carried with it the seeds of disaster. Zhilinskii's strategy required a balance between caution and speed, not allowing the Germans to win a decisive victory against one army by operational superiority but moving quickly to catch Prittwitz's Eighth Army between the Russians. Unfortunately for the Russians, neither geography, personality, nor technology worked in their favor.[10]

The inherent weakness in the Russian plan was geographic. The Masurian Lakes, lying at the hinge of the East Prussian border, divided the frontier into an eastern and a southern sector, and imposed substantial distance between the two Russian armies. The armies took up too much space for both to concentrate in the same sector, which would in any event allow Prittwitz to keep his own army concentrated. As a result, Rennenkampf and Samsonov were separated by the Masurian Lakes and the substantial fortified district the Germans had emplaced around them. The two armies could offer each other mutual support only after penetrating deeply into East Prussia, *around* the lakes. This gave the Germans a chance, albeit a small one, to defeat each Russian army in succession.

Steady and competent generalship was thus essential to the Russian invasion. Rennenkampf and Samsonov both had combat experience: Rennenkampf participated in the suppression of the Boxer Uprising in China and in the Russo-Japanese War; Samsonov fought in the Russo-Turkish War of 1877–1878 and the Russo-Japanese War. Peers recognized Rennenkampf as dashing and brave, Samsonov as efficient and competent. In 1914, though, neither Rennenkampf, Samsonov, nor Zhilinskii was up to his tasks. This was not entirely their fault, for the nature of warfare was changing rapidly, and all armies in 1914 faced serious challenges of adjustment. Samsonov's mission was particularly difficult, for the southern sector of the East Prussian frontier was ill-served by railways and roads. His troops had to march for days after leaving their railheads to reach German territory and confront the Eighth Army, so reconnaissance and communications were accordingly more difficult. A widely circulated myth claimed that Rennenkampf and Samsonov shared a visceral hate for one another dating back to a fight on a train platform in the Russo-Japanese War, but there is little evidence to substantiate the story, and the physical and technical obstacles to a coordinated Russian advance were serious enough. The three

Russian commanders were at best average, but the situation they faced demanded better.

Prittwitz was competent, and time would show the German troops at his disposal were sufficient to defend the frontier, but he suffered from a critical weakness of nerve. His chief of staff, Georg von Waldersee, was not much better. Prittwitz was blessed, though, in a talented staff officer, Lieutenant-Colonel Max Hoffmann, who joined the Eighth Army at the outbreak of war and was destined for bigger and better things. Hoffmann had extensive experience in Russia and in Russian affairs. Prittwitz's basic plan, despite his later cracking under pressure, was essentially sound. He understood that his only hope was an active defense. Passively waiting meant disaster; only offensive action could bring success. He accordingly left his XX Corps to defend East Prussia's southern frontier alone against Samsonov's entire Second Army, concentrating the rest of his troops in the east against Rennenkampf.[11]

THE EASTERN FRONTIER: RENNENKAMPF'S FIRST ARMY

Small-scale skirmishes between cavalry patrols and border guards had begun from the first days of the war. On 12 August, Zhilinskii ordered Rennenkampf to cross the border on 17 August. In keeping with the need for maximum speed, Rennenkampf did not wait for completion of mobilization or full harmonization of his communications and supplies. The whole point of Rennenkampf's invasion was, in operational terms, to engage the Eighth Army on Prussia's eastern frontier and, in strategic terms, to force the German high command to reduce the pressure on France. Both goals depended on speed. Rennenkampf sent his three infantry corps across the border in line from north to the south: the XX, III, and IV. He kept his cavalry on both flanks to screen against possible counterattacks. One cavalry division under Vasilii Gurko protected the left (southern) flank of the Russian advance; a much stronger cavalry corps under the Khan of Nakhichivan had a more ambitious mission: to sweep north around Stallupönen and Gumbinnen, the first two towns on the Russian route into East Prussia, on a deep raid aimed at the more substantial city of Insterburg. Despite Russia's overwhelming advantage in cavalry, the Khan accomplished remarkably little. Zhilinskii had outlined the importance of using cavalry aggres-

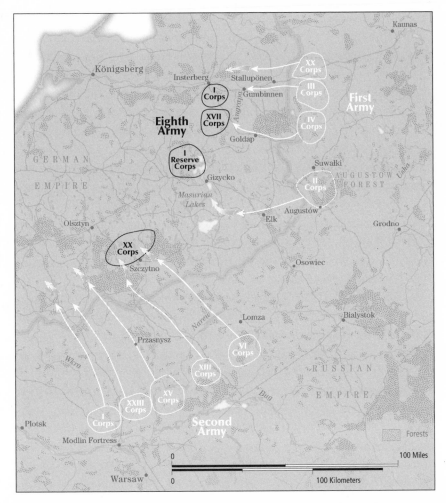

Map 2. Rennenkampf's First Army Invades East Prussia, 18 August 1914

sively "to screen and hide from the enemy the movements of our corps, garrison the most important points, seize river crossings for us, and wreak havoc deep in the rear, in order to disrupt railroad transportation." Thanks to the Khan's desultory pursuit, this simply did not happen.[12]

Prittwitz intended to defend the line of the Angrapa River, 40 kilometers inside the German border. First sending forward his I Corps under the aggressive and ambitious Hermann von François, and following that on 14

August with the balance of his troops, Prittwitz expected to hold his ground and allow the Russians to commit themselves. He was wrong-footed by his own subordinate. On his own initiative, François advanced his I Corps east to meet the Russians head on. At Stallupönen on 17 August, he blundered into the Russian III Corps, commanded by the experienced General Staff officer Nikolai Yepanchin, producing a head-on collision between two fresh formations eager for a fight. Three Russian divisions concentrated on Francois's 1st Division, but Yepanchin never managed to coordinate an attack that might have destroyed it. In fierce fighting, both sides rushed reinforcements to the sound of the guns, and both took heavy losses. Newly arriving German troops caught the flank of the Russian 27th Division and mauled it badly, inflicting 3,000 casualties, but François's single corps was heavily outnumbered and in imminent danger, facing an entire Russian army. François's reckless advance had left both his flanks unprotected, with any German reinforcements well behind him. Faced with advancing Russians threatening to envelop him from both sides, he had no choice but to withdraw back west toward the rest of the Eighth Army. The fight at Stallupönen could have been an even worse disaster had the strong cavalry formation on the Russian right flank properly flanked the German left to cut off retreat. Rennenkampf told the Khan of Nakhichevan that his performance had been "completely unsatisfactory" and ordered him to "in the future be more energetic and mobile."[13]

Yepanchin's III Corps was slow to pursue after the hard fighting at Stallupönen, only following François late on 18 August. The first clash had done equal harm to both sides, but left Russians in possession of the field and the Germans in retreat. Heartened by this initial victory, Rennenkampf's First Army pushed cautiously further into East Prussia, aiming to force the Angrapa River, separate Prittwitz's troops from Königsberg to their north, and hammer the German Eighth Army back onto the anvil of Samsonov's Second Army, now crossing the southern border of East Prussia. At the same time, three of Prittwitz's corps (from north to south, the I, XVII, and I Reserve) had reorganized after the withdrawal from Stallupönen, and now moved east to meet the advancing Russians for a second trial of strength.

The result was another bloody meeting engagement as the two armies collided just inside the East Prussia border, between Stallupönen and Gumbinnen.[14] On 19 August, the Khan of Nakhichevan's cavalry corps on the Russian far right met an advancing *Landwehr* brigade, sending the in-experienced Germans fleeing back in disarray and stripping the German left of its protection. More aggressive action by the Khan could either have pushed west toward the important crossroads at Insterburg or alternatively turned south to fall on the flank of the three German corps in line at Gumbinnen. The Khan did neither, withdrawing his own cavalry to rest and resupply, losing the vital contact with German forces that might have provided Rennenkampf with a sense of what he faced. François had with-drawn to Gumbinnen, east of the Angrapa River and still in front of the main German defensive line. Spoiling for a fight, he convinced Prittwitz to attack again. Accepting that a passive defense would give Samsonov's Sec-ond Army more time to cut off his line of retreat, Prittwitz saw no choice but to attack. The German plan was for François to engage the Russians with a frontal attack directly east, while at the same time a collection of mis-matched garrison troops and reservists formed an improvised strike force to outflank the Russians on the north and August von Mackensen's XVII Corps outflanked them from the south. Overconfident after beating back the Germans in the initial skirmishes, Rennenkampf's divisions moved for-ward without particular attention to maintaining a continuous front and coordinating their advance.

The German I and XVII Corps attacked the advancing Russian XX and III Corps at dawn on 20 August. Taking advantage of the poorly aligned Russian advance, the German I Corps first hammered the leading Russian 28th Infantry Division with artillery, then followed with infantry attacks from multiple directions. Despite the terrible pounding the 28th Division took, German attackers suffered nearly as much from Russian fire as they left their field fortifications. Farmhouses and stands of trees provided ample cover for defending Russians. Just as at Stallupönen, firepower took soldiers and commanders by surprise in its capacity to inflict losses, and the Russians continued to give as good as they got. Francois's men made steady but expensive progress against the XX Corps on the Russian right. Mackensen, commanding the XVII Corps on the German right, thought he spotted an opportunity. To his left, the German I Corps was locked in com-bat with the Russian 28th Division. All reports, including badly mistaken aerial reconnaissance, told him that the Russians in front of him were press-ing north and northwest against the I Corps, presenting him their vulner-able left flank. Supported by the I Reserve Corps to his own right, Mackensen drove forward into what he expected to be empty space, hoping to cut off the Russian XX Corps's escape route back into the Russian heartland. Mackensen, who proved later in the war to be a supremely talented operational commander, was badly mistaken. His aerial observers had missed a full Russian corps, Yepanchin's III Corps, lying directly in his path. Convinced in his ability to break through behind the Russian XX Corps, and unclear on just how many Russian divisions he faced, Mackensen's corps pressed forward against ferocious resistance, took terrible losses, and went reeling into retreat, leaving at least a thousand prisoners in Russian hands. Mackensen had no help from the German I Reserve Corps on his right. As it pushed forward, it was caught by a flank attack from a Russian division and brigade of the IV Corps at Gołdap, halting its forward movement and forcing it to turn south against this new threat.[15]

In this confused sequence of flank attacks that were subsequently themselves outflanked, the German emphasis on operational initiative and aggression had played them false. Misjudging the lethality of Russian artillery and machine gun fire, German troops had blundered forward into devastating fire. Mackensen had lost a third of his corps in the first days of fighting. By the afternoon of 20 August, his troops of the XVII Corps lost their vaunted discipline and cohesion and fled in disorder, though the Russian 28th Division did precisely the same in the opposite direction. But the situations of the two sides were very different; Rennenkampf's troops, outside of the 28th Division, remained in good order and ready to advance; Prittwitz had two broken and exhausted corps, the I and XVII, incapable of renewed offensive action. By the night of the 20th, Prittwitz grasped the seriousness of his situation. His plan to first defeat Rennenkampf and then turn on Samsonov was disintegrating, while his subordinate François, seeing only the 28th Division retreating in disorder in front of him, was convinced victory was at hand despite the terrible losses the German attackers had taken.

Rennenkampf had a rare opportunity, for German troops in panicked flight were a rare occurrence. Pleased in his soldiers' ability to outfight the Germans, but discomfited by the slaughter and chaos of the fighting around Gumbinnen, he gave his troops two days to rest and reorganize before resuming the pursuit west past the Angrapa River. Despite his superiority in cavalry, he did not use them to track German movements or harass the retreating enemy. When he finally began the chase on 23 August, his troops advanced into empty space, with no Germans to be found. He kept his cavalry close at hand, tied to his slow-moving infantry. They met only the most scattered resistance as they advanced, continually monitored by German aircraft. Rennenkampf told Zhilinskii as late as 26 August, when Samsonov's Second Army was already marching into a trap, that "we still do not have any information as to where the defeated formations of the German I and XVII Corps have fled," that "our cavalry have not to this time uncovered the direction of retreat of the main German forces."[16] As a result, Rennenkampf could not answer the most important question: where had the German Eighth Army gone?

Facing defeat, Prittwitz had lost his nerve. Already badly outnumbered, and with the Russian First Army pushing him back steadily west, Prittwitz could not bear the news of Samsonov's Second Army invading East Prussia from the south on 20 August. Good intelligence actually worked against him. Aerial reconnaissance and radio intelligence alike informed Prittwitz of the Russian Second Army approaching his southern flank and threatening to cut off his escape west across the Vistula. He gave up hope of holding East Prussia. In a panic, he prepared full evacuation and told Moltke late on 20 August that he could not defend anywhere east of the Vistula, abandoning East Prussia to Russian occupation. Such a withdrawal would have led inexorably to German military and political disaster. Hoffmann recalled later with the benefit of hindsight that he argued strenuously that Prittwitz should not abandon hope. Though Gumbinnen had been a temporary setback, Hoffmann was confident there was time to pull formations away from the east to deal with Samsonov's invasion from the south. In any event, retreating beyond the Vistula and regrouping to attack Samsonov's invading army both began with the same action: pulling the German corps facing Rennenkampf out of line and moving them west, a step Prittwitz began immediately. Though Prittwitz did rally his courage and work to salvage the situation, the damage to his reputation and Moltke's trust had been done. Moltke decided that Prittwitz had lost his effectiveness as a commander. Prittwitz had to be replaced, but most of Germany's effective generals on active duty were fully engaged on the Western Front.[17]

Moltke's choice for command of the Eighth Army fell on two men whose subsequent wartime careers would grow from their victory in this first campaign. Erich Ludendorff was the brains. Fresh off spectacular successes in the Belgian campaign, he was tapped by Moltke on 22 August to serve as chief of staff for the Eighth Army. Ludendorff had a brilliant tactical and operational mind, a quality that made him perfect for salvaging East Prussia. His flaws were equally marked. Personally abrasive, he lacked strategic and political judgment, which ultimately did terrible harm to Germany's war effort. A son of respectable German gentry, his social stock was sufficiently bourgeois that he lacked the gravitas to command the defense of the Junker heartland of East Prussia. Thus the public face of the Eighth Army would be not Ludendorff, but Paul von Hindenburg. Hindenburg had enjoyed a distinguished but not spectacular career in the Prussian Army. He had done well enough be considered in 1906 for chief of the General Staff, the post that eventually went to Moltke. Though Hindenburg had retired in 1911, he was brought back for his calm and unflappability. When Prittwitz panicked, Hindenburg's solid presence was needed to steady the Eighth Army and prepare a defense.[18]

The German forces were in far better condition to resist the Russian invasion than Hindenburg and Ludendorff could have dreamed. Prittwitz's momentary panic had dissipated quickly. German troops facing Rennenkampf had withdrawn just enough to disengage from their slower Russian pursuers, and thus could be shifted to deal with the threat from the south. A more vigorous Russian pursuit could have entangled the German divisions and held them at the eastern border, but Rennenkampf remained passive. The new German plan, begun under Prittwitz, developed by Hoffmann, and then endorsed by Hindenburg and Ludendorff, was to leave only a token screening force of a single cavalry division facing Rennenkampf. The rest of the Eighth Army would move by road and rail 21–25 August to meet the unsuspecting Samsonov's invasion. Ludendorff had arrived at a similar plan independently before arriving in East Prussia, and let Hoffmann proceed. The German I Corps had the farthest to go, shifting by train and foot from the northern end of the line facing Rennenkampf to the far western flank of German defenses in the south. The XVII and I Reserve Corps did not have as far to go but lacked the luxury of rails, marching southwest behind the Masurian Lakes to put themselves in position to hammer the advancing Samsonov's right flank. The gamble was predicated on Rennenkampf's failing to take advantage of the flimsy defenses the Germans left in front of him; he did not disappoint. The question now was whether Samsonov and his Second Army would fall into the German trap.

THE SOUTHERN FRONTIER: SAMSONOV'S
SECOND ARMY DESTROYED AT TANNENBERG

As the German defenders of East Prussia regrouped to meet the threat from the south, Samsonov's Second Army marched north in ignorance. His forces took longer to reach German territory than the First Army had. Deploying further from the border, and ill-served by poor frontier roads, his army began its advance on 17 August, the same day the First Army crossed into East Prussia. Samsonov only reached the border on 20 August. Though his troops suffered in the summer heat, Samsonov had real mass at his disposal. In line from west to east on a broad front, his main body contained four full army corps: I, XV, XIII, and VI. Two additional corps were poorly deployed and unable to bring their full weight to bear: the XXIII Corps was split, protecting the distant approaches to his left and right wings. The II Corps was even further to Samsonov's right, at the eastern edge of the Masurian Lakes to screen the German garrison at Giżycko. In the event of crisis, this would leave an entire corps too far east to help Samsonov and too far south to help Rennenkampf. His divisions were also undersupplied and undermanned due to the need to invade East Prussia as quickly as possible. Nonetheless, Samsonov still crossed the border with the four corps in his main force opposed by only one, the German XX.[19]

Samsonov was pushed to haste. Zhilinskii had read the results of the fighting at Gumbinnen as a decisive German defeat, and believed Prittwitz was abandoning East Prussia entirely. Throughout the march into East Prussia he urged Samsonov to greater speed, and on 23 August, told Samsonov that "the enemy has left only insignificant forces in front of you" and ordered him to "attack energetically" in order to "meet the enemy retreating before Rennenkampf and cut off the German retreat to the Vistula."[20] Though Samsonov could not get more speed out of his exhausted troops and overstretched supply lines, he concurred with Zhilinskii on the direction of his offensive, shifting his advance west, away from Rennenkampf's First Army, to prevent German escape. His mission then was not to be cautious but to push north as quickly as possible to put his army squarely across the Eighth Army's line of retreat.

Even though Samsonov's advance was slow, the movement of three German corps to Samsonov's flanks took time. The German XX Corps had to delay Samsonov just long enough to prevent the Russians from penetrat-

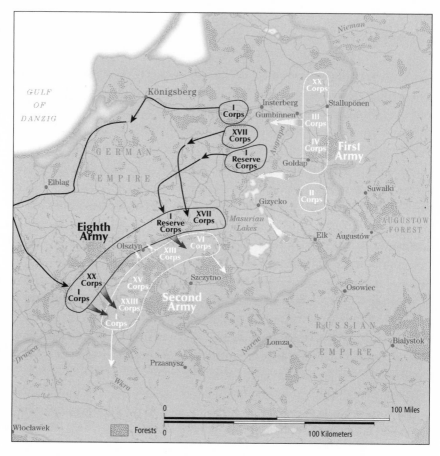

Map 3. Samsonov's Second Army Invades East Prussia, 26 August 1914

ing deep into East Prussia and catching the moving German columns stretched out along railroad and forest tracks. As Samsonov's divisions advanced through marshes and forests, they fought several sharp and bloody engagements with elements of the XX Corps, each of which drew Samsonov still further forward into the German noose he could not see tightening around his army. The XX Corps conducted a fighting withdrawal north, enticing Samsonov into visions of a general German retreat and leading him to press on. In his haste to cut off Prittwitz's path to the Vistula, Samsonov allowed his army to spread itself thin.

Hindenburg and Ludendorff then benefited from a stroke of luck, favoring as always the well-prepared. Late on 24 August, a listening post at Königsberg picked up radio intercepts, then delivered by motorcycle to Hindenburg and Ludendorff, that gave them a rough idea of Russian positions. By the morning of 25 August, additional signals intelligence, supported by aerial reconnaissance, confirmed that Rennenkampf's First Army was continuing its leisurely pursuit, giving the Germans valuable time to deal with Samsonov. German victory against the more numerous Russian enemy depended absolutely on the ability to accumulate information quickly and act on it decisively. Though German aircraft went overwhelmingly to the Western Front (thirty of thirty-three flights), those few aircraft in the east were disproportionately important. In the east, the Germans had four field aviation sections and four fortress aviation sections, for a total of forty aircraft. In addition, the Eighth Army had two old dirigibles, one of which was so antiquated that the addition of a radio set weighed it down to the point of ineffectiveness. Nonetheless, these limited assets proved effective and important in tracking Rennenkampf's pursuit after Gumbinnen, and Samsonov's broad and uncoordinated advance. Throughout August, German aviators provided a steady stream of information. As Hindenburg himself noted, "without the airmen no Tannenberg."[21]

Much was made in retrospect of poor Russian radio security, that the Russians stupidly broadcast *en clair* (i.e., without encoding their messages) and thus handed the details of their operations to the Germans. Certainly it is true that as the First and Second Armies moved away from their railheads into the lakes and woods of East Prussia, messengers became increasingly unhelpful. The Russians could not string telephones laterally, as they were constantly moving forward. Any telephone connection would thus have to run backward from the advancing corps and army headquarters through trackless terrain, but the Second Army possessed only 350 miles of wire. Since division commands lacked radios, corps headquarters used their scarce wire to maintain those connections, forcing the use of radio for communications between corps and with Samsonov at Second Army headquarters. The chaos of mobilization meant that ciphers and keys were poorly distributed. Combined with the pressure of time and the delays imposed by ciphering and deciphering, sending messages *en clair* was a natural expedient. As John Ferris has remarked, "before 1914, no European army came fully to terms with the cryptological consequences of the radio age, because none of them expected wireless to be used routinely in war." Furthermore, armies defending their home soil had the luxury of using existing land networks; it was only armies crossing into foreign territory that had to rely on messengers and radio. The same German Army that benefited from Russian messages *en clair* in East Prussia sent at least fifty messages *en clair* to be intercepted and used by the British and the French on the Western Front in the fall of 1914.[22] The Russians thus were at fault for broadcasting without codes or ciphers, but it was a fault they shared with other armies, and a fault dictated by objective circumstances. Less excusable, though, was Russian failure to employ its available means to get a better picture of what the Eighth Army was doing. Hindenburg and Ludendorff used their small number of aircraft effectively. Zhilinskii, Samsonov, and Rennenkampf, despite having one of the largest air forces in the world at their disposal, failed to spot the Germans' redeployment. Rennenkampf enjoyed an enormous cavalry force that neither disrupted the Germans with deep attacks behind their lines nor provided adequate intelligence of the Eighth Army's withdrawal.[23]

By 26 August, all German forces were in place: the I and XX Corps poised on Samsonov's left flank, the XVII and I Reserve on his right. Samsonov continued to push blindly forward, heading for the town of Olsztyn on the main railroad line running down the spine of East Prussia. His troops skirmished at intervals with German troops as they stumbled into contact. Relying too heavily on Zhilinskii's incorrect information that Rennenkampf had broken the Germans, leaving no chance of their further resistance, Samsonov did not expect anything like the trap he found. The detached Russian VI Corps on Samsonov's right collided with the German XVII and I Reserve Corps. These Germans, worn out from the fighting around Gumbinnen and their days of march, did not press the VI Corps hard. The VI Corps, by contrast, now experienced its first combat and its enthusiastic officers leapt to attack, only to learn the power of machine guns and artillery. Outflanked in the confusing morass of lakes and forests, and finally recognizing that he was outmanned, the commander of the VI Corps had to retreat southward by the night of the 26th. Samsonov's right flank was, as a result, entirely uncovered, and German aviation detected the gap between the retreating VI Corps and Samsonov's main body further to the west. Leaving a small force to screen the VI Corps at Szczytno, the German XVII and I Reserve Corps were now free to continue their forced march southwest to turn Samsonov's right flank. Poor communications meant that Samsonov was ignorant of the VI Corps's retreat and the developing threat on his right.

At the same time, the German I Corps, having completed its redeployment to the western flank of Samsonov's army, launched probing attacks on the Russian I Corps, positioned on Samsonov's left flank. Though the Germans pushed the Russians out of a number of towns and villages, not achieving any substantial breakthrough, the result was nonetheless fateful. Samsonov's left wing was anchored in place by those German fixing attacks, but his center kept advancing. Just as the German XVII and I Reserve Corps were bearing down from the east, Samsonov's XV and XIII Corps in his center and on his right continued to push deeper into East Prussia. To make matters worse, the XIII Corps, the easternmost of those two corps, separated itself from the XV Corps on 26 and 27 August by stretching north to Olsztyn, a pointless feat in the midst of the threatened destruction of an entire Russian army. By 26 August, Samsonov was well aware of the two German corps on his left flank, but nonetheless continued to press his center forward. Russia's commander in chief pushed him to do exactly that: Grand Duke Nikolai Nikolaevich declared to the Northwestern Front that "the foremost task of the First and Second Armies is to finish as soon as possible with East Prussia." Any halt to Samsonov's offensive north was "extremely undesirable."[24] Only an unusually perceptive general with great moral courage could have halted the Second Army's seemingly victorious march north; Samsonov lacked both qualities. Thus the XV and XIII Corps pushed on to Olsztyn, stretching their connections to the corps on Samsonov's left, the I and XXIII, to the breaking point. Samsonov, incredibly, still remained ignorant of the defeat of the VI Corps that he believed was shielding his right.[25]

Samsonov's right flank was already exposed by the retreat of the VI Corps; his left flank was next. Under the continuing pressure from François's German I Corps, the Russian I Corps, protecting Samsonov's left, finally broke and withdrew south away from the rest of the Second Army. This opened a gap through which François's infantry raced toward Nidzica to cut off Russian retreat. The Russian position rapidly disintegrated as Samsonov's troops lost their cohesion and ceased acting as a single unit. Samsonov himself contributed to the muddled communications and general chaos. Zhilinskii had "categorically demanded" that Samsonov maintain constant communication with the Northwestern Front. On 28 August, incredibly, Samsonov instead broke his telegraph connection with Zhilinskii. Seemingly convinced that nothing could replace his physical presence at the key point of the battle, he went to personally lead the fight of the XIII and XV Corps at Olsztyn.[26] Four German corps closed a ring around Samsonov, probing for gaps to further slice his pocketed divisions. The German I Corps from the west and the XVII Corps from the east rushed to shut any route of escape by sending small flying columns to seize towns and crossroads. Samsonov and three Russian corps, the XXIII, XV, and XIII, still did not know the absolute desperation of their position. Zhilinskii had a somewhat better understanding, ordering the Second Army to retreat while simultaneously urging Rennenkampf to press forward quickly to Samsonov's assistance. Both orders came much too late. Only on the morning of 28 August did Samsonov realize the true condition of his army, when he finally received word that his eastern shield, the VI Corps, was in fact miles to the southeast and retreating at top speed. His ability to reverse course and withdraw south himself, however, was disappearing. Decisive action on Samsonov's part to turn all available forces south and southwest, where the German ring was nowhere near complete, might still have extracted the bulk of his men though abandoning any hope of the conquest of East Prussia. Samsonov delayed making that decision, and each hour that passed cost him men, ammunition, and reserves. Only by late on 28 August did he finally give the order to withdraw, through a confusing and difficult tangle of lakes, swamps, and forests quickly being blocked by a German screen.

At this point, the endangered Russian divisions were hardly outnumbered by the Germans encircling them, and the eastern and western spearheads south of Samsonov only linked up on 29 August. Even then, only small detachments blocked escape to the south. Two full Russian corps, the I and the VI, were outside the thin German screen and could easily have broken back through if their leadership had managed to rally. But the Russians were exhausted at this point by nearly two weeks of marching in the summer heat and confused by the sounds of fighting in all directions. Lacking effective wireless communication, the Russians could not either correctly evaluate their position or devise a strategy. Devoid of decisive leadership, the encircled divisions lost any semblance of order and disintegrated into a mob, incapable of serious resistance. Retreat south took them into thick forests that broke their cohesion even further. They lost any capacity to fight the German units that sliced their shrinking pocket into smaller and smaller chunks and compelled Russian soldiers to surrender by the thousands. Over 29 and 30 August, with the surviving I and VI Corps far to the southwest and southeast and in no condition to bring relief, cohesion and chain of command disappeared. Isolated pockets of Russian soldiers continued to fight, either as intact units or as scratch collections of troops, but could not escape destruction. Hindenburg reported victory to the Kaiser on 29 August; on 30 August, Samsonov rode away from his staff officers and shot himself. Nikolai Martos, commander of the Russian XV Corps, was captured the same day and Nikolai Kliuev of the XIII Corps the next. This last day of August marked the end of organized Russian resistance. Zhilinskii had spurred Rennenkampf to greater speed on 27 August, when Samsonov's army was already falling apart. Zhilinskii's calls continued until the afternoon of 29 August, when they suddenly were canceled in the belief that Samsonov was retreating south and thus needed no relief. Rennenkampf told his corps commanders at noon on 29 August to halt their pursuit, for "the Second Army has withdrawn to its initial positions on the border." It had not; it had been annihilated.[27]

The sacrifices that Rennenkampf's and Samsonov's soldiers had made were not pointless. As they did not destroy the Eighth Army or occupy East Prussia, the Russian plan in that sense failed, but all the powers fell short in their initial hopes. As S. L. A. Marshall wrote, "All four of the Continental powers suffered delusions; all tried at the same time to swing for a knockout blow; all four failed."[28] More importantly, the Russian invasion of East Prussia did make the German high command weaken its drive on Paris in order to shore up German defenses in the east. Russian troops on German soil had galvanized public opinion. Wilhelm Düwel, a Social Democrat and not inclined to take the kaiser's word at face value, nonetheless warned of "semi-barbarians, who scorch, murder, loot, who shoot at Samaritans, who vandalize medical stations, and spare neither women not the injured." Rumors of Russian atrocities drove refugees west toward safety and required immediate action. Hans von Plessen, military aide to Kaiser Wilhelm, wrote in his diary "East Prussia . . . occupied by the enemy! The Russians burn and pillage everything!—We must make haste to finish up in the West as quickly as possible in order to come to the rescue of the East."[29] The result was that two corps, the Guard Reserve and XI Corps with a cavalry division, went east on 26 August. Too late to have any effect on the invasion of East Prussia, they did weaken the German drive on Paris, a close-run affair where the presence or absence of two corps might have made a difference.[30]

Tannenberg was unquestionably a major defeat for the Russians, but its significance is easy to overstate. The cost to the Russian war effort was the devastation of the Second Army, the total destruction of two corps (XV and XIII) and partial destruction of another (XXIII) out of thirty-seven corps in the Russian order of battle, and the loss of 50–70,000 casualties and 92,000 prisoners of war. Foreign Minister Sazonov told an American correspondent that Russia had lost 165,000 men in three days.[31] Of Samsonov's original corps, however, the I and VI remained largely intact in defensive positions along the Narew River, along with substantial remnants of the XXIII Corps; the II Corps was now part of Rennenkampf's First Army. Thus half of the Second Army remained to screen the northern approaches to Warsaw against the very real chance that the Eighth Army might press south into Poland to relieve Germany's hard-pressed Austrian allies. Austria-Hungary begged Germany for such a step, hoping for a German attack on Warsaw or Siedlce. The German high command had no such intention, not while Rennenkampf's First Army still remained on German soil. Even while the remnants of Samsonov's shattered divisions were being mopped up, the German high command ordered Hindenburg to clear East Prussia in preparation for a later offensive south into Poland.

RENNENKAMPF'S FIRST ARMY EXPELLED
FROM EAST PRUSSIA

While Rennenkampf's First Army remained on German territory, the initial East Prussian campaign was not complete. Half of Samsonov's army had been destroyed; his surviving corps had withdrawn back across the border to regroup. Rennenkampf, however, was still inching west into East Prussia, and now faced Hindenburg's Eighth Army alone. At Zhilinskii's urging, Rennenkampf had sent his cavalry ranging ahead toward the pocketed Samsonov. At the same time, Zhilinskii had sabotaged this rescue effort by instructing Rennenkampf to divert troops to screen Königsberg, whose garrison was utterly irrelevant to the campaign. In any event, the cavalry sent to Samsonov's relief were withdrawn by the end of August when Samsonov's destruction became clear.[32]

The ongoing mobilization of reserves on both sides was already beginning to change the nature of the war, only weeks into the fighting. The initial battles in East Prussia had been fought by formations that had been forced to fight with open flanks, since the density of manpower and wide spaces of East European terrain meant that there were simply not enough units to maintain continuous fronts. The Russian mobilization system was beginning to tap into the country's colossal human reserves, though, creating an entire new army, the Tenth (made up of the I Turkestan, II Caucasus, III Siberian, and XXII Corps), to cover the gap between the remnants of the Second Army to the west and the First Army to the north. As the names of its corps suggest, the new army drew from far-flung corners of the Russian Empire. In addition, Rennenkampf's forces had been filled out by the earlier addition of the II Corps and the newly arrived XXVI Corps as well. By early September, Rennenkampf's army held a line stretching approximately eighty kilometers from just east of Königsberg south to the northern fringes of the Masurian Lakes. Rennenkampf had seemingly anchored both ends of his position. If the Germans were going to expel him, Rennenkampf reasoned, they would have to do it by a frontal assault, not by outflanking him and forcing a retreat. Zhilinskii badgered Rennenkampf to renew his offensive west into East Prussia. After his own fight and Samsonov's defeat, Rennenkampf had no stomach for more blood, and was content to remain on the defensive. He told Zhilinskii that any offensive would require a paired offensive west of the Masurian Lakes over the ground Samsonov had covered, a requirement that guaranteed substantial delay, until mid or late September at the earliest.

Rennenkampf then waited to see what Hindenburg and his Eighth Army would do. Leaving only a token force to screen the southern border of East Prussia against the reorganizing Second Army, Hindenburg sent the rest of his troops—an impressive five corps—east against the First Army. Hindenburg had (from north to south) the Guards Reserve, I Reserve, XI, XX, and XVII Corps. In purely numerical terms, the situation was fairly even, for Rennenkampf likewise had five corps: XXVI, XX, III, IV, and II. Both sides had just over 200 infantry battalions and roughly a thousand guns. That quantitative equality concealed a deep qualitative difference. Rennenkampf had already shown remarkable passivity, heightened by Samsonov's dire fate. The Russian soldiers, heartened by their early victories over the Germans at Stallupönen and Gumbinnen, had now been disheartened by German triumph. In addition, Rennenkampf's defensive line was not so secure as it seemed. At its far southern end, the Germans had an extensive fortified complex at Giżycko, a natural base for any attempt to turn Rennenkampf's left flank. Still preoccupied with Königsberg, Rennenkampf had shifted troops to the northern end of his line. This left a long stretch of his left flank held by the II Corps, asked to defend a much greater frontage than the rest of Rennenkampf's corps. It was precisely here that Hindenburg and Ludendorff intended to infiltrate their reinforced XVII Corps through the Masurian Lakes, and on emerging from them, to break through the defending II Corps and roll up the Russian line from south to north.

German probing attacks on 7 September revealed that the chief exit from the lakes was held by only a single Russian division, the 43rd Infantry of the II Corps. A full-scale assault on 8 September forced the 43rd to withdraw, and on the next day Hindenburg used fixing attacks all along the line to engage Rennenkampf's First Army and hold it in place while the German XVII and I Corps along with some of the scarce German cavalry emerged from the Masurian Lakes and broke into the Russian rear. Recognizing his danger, Rennenkampf threw the 54th and 72nd divisions from his reserves into the breach on his left. At the same time, he pulled the XX Corps from the northern end of his line opposite Königsberg, dispatching it south to create additional reserves if those proved necessary.

They proved exceedingly necessary. German spearheads raced north behind the Russian line, threatening the First Army with a second Tannenberg. Here, at least, Rennenkampf's timidity proved an asset. Recognizing his danger, he ordered withdrawal on 9 September, declaring to his army that "the enemy has turned the left flank of our army, and the Tenth Army cannot help us."[33] He hoped to pull his troops east, particularly his left flank, before they were cut off and annihilated. All along the line on 10 September, German troops moved into energetic pursuit as the Russian withdrawal became general. Key to the Russian retreat was their escape route—one good road stretching from Königsberg through Insterburg, Gumbinnen, and finally Kaunas. While Russian infantry and cavalry might withdraw overland, vital artillery and supplies would fall into German hands without that road back to Kaunas. German flanking forces from the south fanned out as they pushed north to cut the road. Unable to mount a coherent defense, Rennenkampf threw regiment after regiment piecemeal in front of the flanking Germans to slow their attack and allow the bulk of his army time to escape east. The momentum of the vast German right hook slowed as exhausted troops simply could not maintain the pace of their pursuit.

Rennenkampf continued to retreat on 11 September, withdrawing to a line almost precisely where his troops had won Russia's first victory at Stallupönen, three weeks and an era before. The Russians managed to temporarily outdistance their German pursuers, and so established a new defensive line in relative safety. As the First Army regrouped, Zhilinskii briefly entertained thoughts of ordering them back on the offensive, before the total exhaustion of his human material made him accept reality. The Russian withdrawal halted only briefly to give soldiers a scant few hours rest before continuing east out of East Prussia onto Russian territory. The First Army halted temporarily in mid-September on a line 30–40 kilometers inside the Russian border, before finally withdrawing still further behind the protection of the Nieman River.

The rebuilding and recriminations began as soon as the Russians had been expelled from East Prussia. With Samsonov dead and the Second Army gutted, Sergei Sheideman, previously commander of the II Corps, was appointed the Second Army's new commander and began its reconstruction. Vasilii Flug commanded a new Tenth Army, created at the junction between the First and Second Armies southeast of the Masurian Lakes. More serious repercussions followed for those responsible for the East Prussian debacle. Zhilinskii blamed Rennenkampf for Russian failure, telling *Stavka* that "Rennenkampf pays more attention to the safety of his staff than to commanding the army, which has been completely neglected." He accused Rennenkampf of "losing his head" and abandoning his post. The accusations did not work, and Grand Duke Nikolai Nikolaevich lost confidence in Zhilinskii, not Rennenkampf. He kept Rennenkampf in place but on 16 September dismissed Zhilinskii as head of the Northwestern Front and replaced him with Nikolai Ruzskii, a General Staff officer and previously commander of the Third Army in Galicia. While Zhilinskii's leadership had been ill-conceived and indecisive, it is difficult to argue that Rennenkampf's had been any better. Nonetheless, he remained in place as commander of the First Army, though Yanushkevich and others remained deeply suspicious of his honesty and his nerve.[34]

Rennenkampf's retreat, presaging a much greater retreat in summer 1915, was itself a military feat of a sort, and a triumph in the negative sense that it avoided disaster. The operation was undoubtedly a defeat. His army had retreated nearly 200 kilometers in two weeks, and his army had lost 80,000 killed, wounded, or captured along with 150 guns, making the combined losses of the First and Second Armies close to 250,000 men.[35] The fact remains, though, that Rennenkampf's army withdrew intact despite the difficult circumstances under which it fought. While many of his soldiers were lost, the units they belonged to did survive to fight another day. The fact that few of Rennenkampf's artillery pieces were lost to the enemy indeed suggests that the Russians withdrew in relatively good order. The battle for East Prussia had begun with great hopes but ended in disaster. Though they suffered a demoralizing defeat, the Russians were simultaneously engaged in an ever-larger struggle with Austria-Hungary for the plains of Galicia in the south, a struggle in which the Russians acquitted themselves much better.

4

The Opening Campaigns: Galicia, 1914

In historical literature and popular consciousness, the campaign for East Prussia unjustly overshadowed the simultaneous struggles between Austria-Hungary and Russia in Galicia. By comparison with East Prussia, the battles in Galicia in 1914 involved more Russians: four armies instead of two, and double the number of component corps. They fought against more troops of the Central Powers: at first three and then four Austrian armies, instead of one German. They fought a war that the Russian state actually wanted to fight for a concrete political objective—hegemony in the Balkans—long a Russian priority. The campaign ended in substantial Russian victory. By all standards aside from the attention paid by subsequent historians, the Galician battles loom far larger than those for East Prussia. Despite this, the Galician campaign has received substantially less attention. Tannenberg benefited from the retroactive efforts at self-promotion of three of its key participants on the German side: Hindenburg, Ludendorff, and Hoffmann. The Galician campaign lacked any glorious victory and suffered from a dearth of those willing and able to promote their accomplishments to English-speaking audiences after the war.

Galicia was also horrifically bloody. Rather than the brilliant maneuvers of East Prussia, Galicia degenerated into a grotesque slugging match. The campaign was a perfect storm of elements to create a slaughterhouse. The terrain was flat and open, allowing mass armies to maneuver and clash. Unlike East Prussia, where the Germans absorbed Russian offensives and then counterattacked to restore the status quo, both sides in Galicia

81

planned massive offensives into enemy territory, but had not yet learned how deadly it was for men to move in the open within range of modern artillery, machine guns, and rifles. Conrad was dazzled by his dream of a great drive north by his First and Fourth Armies to link up with the Germans (who had informed him on 3 August that they were not coming) to cut off Russia's Polish salient. Blinded by visions of victory, he discounted the possibility of a Russian attack from the east smashing into the flank of any drive his armies made to the north. Nikolai Ivanov, commander of the Southwestern Front, planned a concentric attack on Austrian Galicia by four armies converging on L'viv. When the armies collided, at least a hundred thousand men died in a month of fighting, leaving the Russians badly bloodied but the Austrian army shattered.

The Russian-Austrian frontier in Galicia formed a great arc from north to east, bowed toward Russia. While there was considerable high ground inside the Austrian frontier, the border itself lay on flat and relatively open terrain, leaving great scope for generals to plan vast maneuvers. Russian communications in the territory behind the frontier were relatively good; a series of major towns lay in a semicircle along a railroad that paralleled the frontier, stretching from Dęblin in the north around clockwise through Lublin, Chełm, Kovel, Lutsk, Rovno, and finally Kamyanets-Podilsky in the east. Austrian communications were not quite so good: the Carpathian mountains ran roughly east–west across the southern boundary of Galicia. As a result, Austrian railroads from Galicia ran west toward Krakow, not south through the mountains. The border itself was not well served by rail; upon debarking, both armies would have substantial marching to reach enemy territory.

Conrad's plans for the upcoming conflict in Galicia were both deceptive and deceived. The Austrians had initiated staff conversations with the Germans in 1909 to nail down the precise intentions of both sides, but the clearly divergent interests of the alliance partners meant that paper assurances were quite different from actual intent. From the German point of view, Austria's Serbian enemy was at best a side show. Complete Austrian victory in Serbia meant nothing if it allowed Russian armies to march to Berlin. The German General Staff thus wanted a full Austrian commitment against Russia to relieve pressure on the German eastern border. Based in part on German assurances, Austria-Hungary by contrast anticipated a German offensive out of East Prussia to occupy the Russians, not merely an active defense. Both sides were duly disappointed; Conrad's visceral hatred of the Serbs made Serbia a priority; Germany's wholehearted commitment to an all-out drive on Paris made an offensive out of East Prussia unthinkable.

In subsequent histories, Conrad has suffered a great deal of highly justified criticism for his inability to think clearly about the Habsburg Empire's strategic problems. In his defense, though, Austria-Hungary's geographical position made strategic decisions extremely complex. Conrad had to plan for mobilization under a host of contingencies, including a localized war against Serbia and a more general European conflict. To cope with this uncertainty, Conrad intended to commit to the Russian frontier a set portion of his mobilized forces: A-Staffel, of twenty-eight infantry and ten cavalry divisions. A smaller force of eight infantry divisions—Minimalgruppe Balkan—was dedicated to dealing with Serbia, where it provided at best rough parity with the eleven divisions of the Serbian army. B-Staffel, a swing force of twelve infantry and one cavalry division, was scheduled for mobilization and deployment in either direction depending on circumstances, allowing overwhelming force against Serbia or substantially reinforcing the armies invading Russia.[1]

This contingency planning was a reasonable approach to a difficult problem, but Conrad's management was so vacillating and incompetent as to defy belief. The Austrian plan required clear thinking and decisive action about where B-Staffel should go: south to Serbia or northeast to Galicia. As the July crisis raced toward war, Conrad had to choose. Once the decision was made, any change would produce chaos, since the railway timetables were not amenable to improvisation or alteration. On 25 July, Conrad mobilized Minimalgruppe Balkan against Serbia, and waited to see the proper course for A-Staffel and B-Staffel. All signs pointed to imminent Russian intervention, and simple strategic calculation told the same story. If Conrad mobilized B-Staffel against Russia without need, Serbia was in no position to threaten Austria and could be crushed at leisure. If B-Staffel went to Serbia, however, Russia threatened the capture of major parts of Austrian territory with the most serious consequences. Despite concrete evidence of Russian preparation for mobilization against Austria from 27 to 30 July, Conrad permitted B-Staffel to begin moving south on 30 July. He did not attempt to reverse B-Staffel's pointless journey to the Serbian front until 6 August, at which point those troops had to finish their deployment to Serbia, then reboard their trains for the slow journey back north to fight the Russians in Galicia. Whether Conrad was motivated by deep denial of Russia's intent to enter the war or by a visceral desire to punish Serbia no matter what the cost, his policies are impossible to regard as rational.

Likewise puzzling is the precise deployment of A-Staffel in Galicia. Contrary to previous Austrian war plans, Conrad's armies mobilized well back from the Russian border. Conrad's grand strategy envisaged a vast pincer closing north out of Galicia in conjunction with Germany, so deploying his divisions well south of the border makes little sense. In addition, Russia's relatively slow mobilization meant that the military balance would steadily turn against the Austrians over time, underlining the importance of acting quickly. Conrad's actions may be explained by the betrayal of his war plans to the Russians by the Austrian counterintelligence officer Colonel Alfred Redl, compelling revisions of previous plans. In any event, Conrad's actions meant his troops were exhausted by their march to the frontier and that the Russians had time to adjust their own plans to the unexpected Austrian mobilization.

Conrad's dithering and the odyssey of the Austrian B-Staffel meant that the Austrian offensive across the Russian border lacked any numerical advantage. In opposition to Russia's four armies it initially had only three, shielded on their flanks by two scratch formations equivalent to understrength armies. Conrad's chief striking force pushing north from Galicia into Russian Poland was made up of two armies, the First Army under Viktor Dankl to the left and the Fourth Army under Moritz von Auffenberg to the right. They deployed in a line stretching from the Vistula River to their west to L'viv to their east. They were protected on their left by the Kummer Group, an understrength army of territorial militia, on the far bank of the Vistula. On their right, another task force under Archduke Joseph Ferdinand, detached from the Austrian Third Army, protected the bend of the Austrian line. Conrad envisaged attacking north toward Lublin and Kovel. Success would cut Russia's lateral railroad line behind the frontier, and if all went well, enable a further push north to sever Warsaw from the rest of Russia. Conrad mistakenly expected that the Germans would join a pincer movement toward Warsaw by attacking south out of East Prussia. To the east, the Austrian Third Army, later reinforced by the Second Army when B-Staffel arrived from its detour to Serbia, defended Galicia against Russian assault.

Ivanov, commanding Russia's Southwestern Front, lacked the aristocratic background and bearing of much of the tsar's high command. A simple and straightforward man, with an enormous square-cut beard enhancing his peasant image, he had a war plan equally devoid of subtlety. His plan was based on Redl's information, which predicted a relatively aggressive Austrian deployment close to the border. As a result, the Russian plan envisaged all four armies converging in a relatively shallow envelopment of L'viv. Conrad's deployment was also substantially further west than the Russians expected, so Russia's plans had its armies converging on empty space. Conrad's odd deployments thus worked to his advantage, at least initially. In addition, the Russians expected, contrary to Conrad's actual plan, that the weight of the Austrian army would be directed east, rather than north. As a result, the two Russian armies in the east, Nikolai Ruzskii's Third and Aleksei Brusilov's Eighth, were substantially stronger than the two armies in the north, Anton Zal'tsa's Fourth and Pavel Pleve's Fifth. In effect, the Russian and Austrian allocation of forces were complementary: the Russian northern wing (sixteen to seventeen infantry divisions) was weaker than its eastern wing (twenty-two divisions); the Austrian eastern wing was weaker than its northern. The ground was prepared for offensives that moved like a revolving door—the larger Austrian armies pushing north out of Galicia with the larger Russian armies advancing west into Galicia.[2]

Under pressure from the French to hasten Russian offensives, even though Russian advances in Galicia could have only the most indirect effect on events in the West, on 14 August Yanushkevich ordered the Southwestern Front to attack before its mobilization was complete. On 19 August, the two Russian armies on the east side of the Galician salient (the Third to the north, the Eighth to the south) moved across the Austrian border. Russian divisions advanced without fully prepared support systems in their rear and with many troops still en route to the front. Moving roughly in parallel, they drove forward against the cavalry screens of Austrian defenders, the Austrian Third Army to the north and the Kövess task force (an understrength army) to the south. The Austrians took advantage of four rivers flowing north to south as defensive lines: three tributaries of the Dniestr (the Seret, the Zolota Lipa, and the Gnila Lipa) and then the Dniestr itself.

THE NORTHERN THEATER

The bloody battles for Galicia began in the north.[3] On the northern side of the Galician salient, the two Russian armies (Fourth to the west, Fifth to the east) began to move on 23 August. The Fifth Army, like the Third Army to its southeast, aimed at L'viv; the Fourth Army marched south parallel to and west of the Fifth, advancing toward the fortress of Przemyśl on the upper San River. The Russian Fourth Army was therefore on a collision course with the Austrian First; one headed south to Przemyśl, the other north to Lublin. Similarly, the Russian Fifth Army was set to brush past the Austrian Fourth. The Austrians were advancing north to Chełm just to the west of where the Russians were moving south toward L'viv. The stage was set for a massive meeting engagement in open terrain. The Russian right flanks were exposed as a result of their converging attack on L'viv, but *Stavka* had noted as early as 22 August that the Russian plan was relying on outdated intelligence. Yanushkevich told Ivanov that "it is possible that the Austrians as a result of caution have deployed the bulk of their forces further west than we had presumed. In that case, the path of our offensive . . . will not correspond to the situation." Ivanov, Yanushkevich suggested, should modify his orders accordingly.[4] The notice came too late, though, for Russian deployment was already essentially complete. The path of advance was, however, redirected slightly to the west to better account for the Austrians' real position.

Dankl's Austrian First Army collided with the Russian Fourth Army, weakest of the Russian armies in Galicia. The Fourth Army was initially commanded by seventy-year-old Anton Zal'tsa, whose physical and mental faculties were long past handling the strain. As the battle began, he was replaced by the younger and more capable Aleksei Evert, a stern disciplinarian and cautious commander. Evert's army, made up (from west to east) of the XIV, XVI, and Grenadier Corps, was deployed on a 60-kilometer front advancing south from Lublin. Evert was shorthanded, as his XX Corps had been transferred to Rennenkampf's First Army prior to the battle. Though Dankl likewise had three corps (the I, V, and X), overall Austrian manpower was much greater: approximately 230,000 men to Evert's 110,000. Both armies moved behind cavalry screens, whose initial clashes fixed the approximate locations of both formations as the mass of the two armies slowly converged. Dankl's divisions stretched in front of an

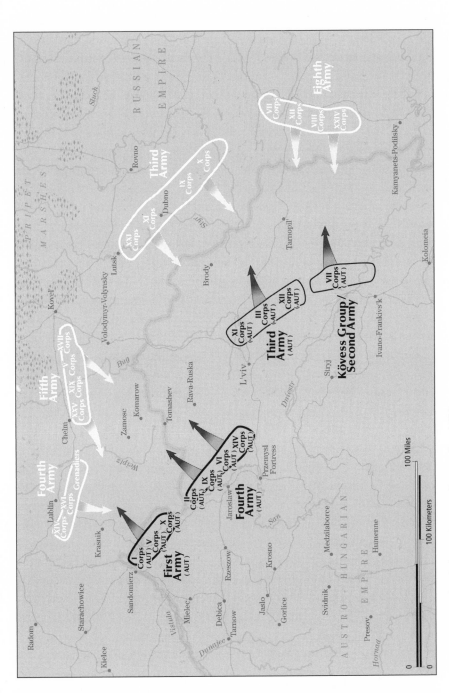

Map 4. Battles for Galicia, August–September 1914

east–west belt of forests north of the Tanew River, centered on the small town of Kraśnik. The two armies' infantry first clashed on 23 August. Dankl concentrated his forces on his left wing, forcing the Russian right, the XIV Corps, to bear the brunt of the first day's fighting. Unable to sustain the punishment and in imminent danger of being encircled on its right, the XIV Corps withdrew north, exposing and endangering the other two Russian corps to its left. Feeling the painful absence of the XX Corps, Evert's two remaining corps could not sustain Austrian pressure, and on 24 August also retreated northeast toward Lublin, only stabilizing the line on 27 and 28 August with local counterattacks that halted the Austrian advance. *Stavka* transferred reinforcements from the Third Army along with the XVIII Corps from Warsaw to shore up the Fourth Army's position and protect its right flank against encirclement by Austrian forces operating on the opposite, western bank of the Vistula River. By 28 and 29 August it was clear the Russian lines were holding, but there was no room to retreat without surrendering vital ground. Key road and rail links ran east–west through Lublin, and Austrian capture of the city would cripple Russian ability to shift troops around the theater.

While the Russian Fourth Army was forced into a steady withdrawal, it maintained its cohesion and was never threatened with defeat in detail. The Russian Fifth Army to its east found itself in much greater danger. Its commander, Pavel Pleve, though he appeared old and sickly, was mentally sharp and maintained calm in the face of extraordinary pressure. Pleve's 150,000 soldiers (from west to east, the XXV, XIX, V, and XVII Corps) were matched against roughly 250,000 in von Auffenberg's Fourth Army (II, IX, VI, and XIV Corps). The clash began only days after the similar collision to the west, but Pleve allowed dangerous gaps to form between the corps under his command. Unlike Evert's Fourth Army, which advanced while keeping its constituent corps in close contact, Pleve's four corps advanced as individual compact masses, leaving wide spaces between them as a result of the broader frontage he had to cover. On 25 August, the Southwestern Front ordered Pleve to relieve the pressure on the embattled Russian Fourth Army by attacking the right (eastern) flank of the Austrian troops engaging them. The Austrian Fourth Army was spread as widely as Pleve's Fifth, but its advantage in manpower gave it a substantial edge in the game of feeling for gaps in the line to find and turn enemy flanks.

Pleve's move south became a wild and confusing melee. Since the battered Russian Fourth Army was already in retreat to his west, Pleve's task was to send his right wing southwest in order to cover the gap left by the Russian Fourth Army's withdrawal. Evert's retreat, combined with poor coordination between Evert and Pleve, left a gap between the two armies, a gap that opened the way to the important railroad line running east from Lublin. As Pleve moved to cover the breach, his divisions collided on 26 August with Auffenberg's main force as well as the far right wing of Dankl's. Pleve's force on his far western wing, the Russian XXV Corps, fought in isolation for two days before finally breaking and retreating on 27 August. As it withdrew, it failed to maintain contact with the XIX Corps to its east, opening another gap. This left the exposed right flank of XIX Corps protected only by Cossack cavalry. The XIX Corps met the Austrian VI Corps head on in frontal attacks, but its position quickly became untenable as divisions of the Austrian II and newly arrived IX Corps began to move around the open western flank created by loss of contact with the XXV Corps. It also had to withdraw north to Komarów on 27 August. By the next day, the XIX Corps's right flank was bending back dangerously under Austrian pressure, and the entire corps was in danger of being enveloped and destroyed.

Pleve's two westernmost corps, the XXV and the XIX, were now either in full retreat or in danger of imminent destruction. He tried to rally the XXV Corps to attack south into the gap between the Austrian First and Fourth Armies, but its half-hearted efforts made no progress. He attempted to wheel his two remaining corps, the V and XVII, to the west to strike the eastern flank of the Austrian advance north, but the XVII Corps was too far east to bring any force to bear. To make matters worse, while strung out on its march west to come to the assistance of the rest of the Fifth Army, the XVII Corps was itself struck on its southern flank by the advancing Austrian XIV Corps and badly mauled, losing several dozen guns and 5,000 prisoners. The V Corps, however, proved much more successful. Close enough to the embattled XIX Corps to bring meaningful aid, the V Corps struck the eastern flank of the Austrian divisions engaging the XIX Corps, smashing the Austrian 15th Division almost as badly as the Russian XVII Corps had suffered. While the V Corps had temporarily salvaged the Russian position, the Fifth Army's overall situation was still grave, broken into two widely separated fragments. The Russian northern wing arcing around Galicia no longer presented any semblance of a coherent formation. The Fourth Army had dug in before Lublin, the isolated XXV Corps to its east had retreated, and the remaining corps of the Fifth Army, the XIX, V, and XVII, were huddled together in a defensive salient centered around Komarów. The numerical superiority of the Austrian First and Fourth Armies now threatened the Russians with encirclement, defeat in detail, and annihilation, especially as an Austrian task force of three infantry divisions under Archduke Joseph Ferdinand began to encircle the Russian enclave from the southeast. Temporarily unified under the authority of the XVII Corps's commander Pyotr Yakovlev, the XIX, V, and XVII Corps held out for two days, 29 and 30 August, against the combined assaults of four Austrian corps. As the Austrian assault worked its way around both flanks of Yakovlev's hard-pressed divisions, a second Tannenberg threatened. The other corps of the Fifth Army, the XXV, was still in retreat north toward Chełm. But just as the Austrians seemed on the verge of a crushing victory, one that could have meant the abandonment of Poland and possibly even Russian exit from the war, circumstances changed with astounding rapidity.

The Austrians had fought hard and well, contrary to the general perception of the Habsburg army's performance in World War I, but there were limits to Austrian reserves of men, supplies, and energy. The long advance and bloody fighting of the advance north into Russian Poland had drained all those. As the Austrians moved north, their lines of supply and communication became increasingly tenuous. Reinforcements flowed more easily to the Russians than to the Austrians, who had now far outdistanced the railheads from which supplies had to be hauled by wagons. A week of desperate fighting meant that both sides were exhausted, but the physical and mental strain was harder on the Austrians, who bore the burden of the offensive and of fighting on foreign soil. The energy of Austrian assaults began to fade.

More importantly, though, the Southwestern Front had begun its advance into Galicia before the completion of Russian mobilization. As the fighting continued, more and more Russian battalions flowed in to bolster the beleaguered Fourth and Fifth Armies, and these fresh and unbloodied troops tilted the balance in Russia's favor. On the right flank of the three isolated corps of the Fifth Army clustered at Komarów, the XIX Corps was close to its breaking point, opening the gate to complete encirclement, when two Cossack cavalry divisions stormed into the rear of the attacking Austrians, routing two divisions. Additional contingents flowed in to

bolster the Fourth Army to the west, eventually giving it numerical superiority even over the combined forces of the Austrian First Army and the
Kummer Group, which now crossed to the east bank of the Vistula to assist in the attack on Lublin. Evert added the newly arrived XVIII Corps,
sent south from Warsaw, to shore up his right flank and the Guard Corps
to protect his left. When the balance between the two sides had shifted
enough, Dankl's right flank began to cave in: his X Corps had to withdraw
on 2 September, followed by the rest of the Austrians. Though the Austrians had advanced 100 kilometers, their offensive had never reached Lublin.
Advance units had managed to briefly cut the railroad east of the city at
Trawniki, but could not sustain themselves once the Austrian withdrawal
began.

Most importantly, the overarching Austrian strategic gamble had failed.
Conrad had counted on his strong northern wing achieving victory before
his weak eastern wing collapsed under the pressure of the Russian Third
and Eighth Armies. By the end of August, that wager had failed, and Austrian attacks, carried out by exhausted troops, no longer brought success.
On 31 August, Austrian aerial reconnaissance spotted Russian troops from
the Third Army closing in behind the Austrian Fourth Army. The victorious Austrian advance deep into Russian territory now threatened to become a trap. Pleve did not realize this: on the night of 30–31 August, he
ordered his Fifth Army into retreat, but the exhausted Austrians were in no
condition to pursue. Indeed, the Austrian command was considering retreat as well. Withdrawing in relatively good order, the Russian Fifth Army
regrouped 50 kilometers behind its previous lines.

THE EASTERN THEATER

As already suggested, Conrad's plan was a gamble: that success in the
north would be faster than failure in the east. That depended on the Austrians holding off the Russian Third and Eighth Armies invading Galicia.[5]
The Austrian forces—the nine to ten infantry divisions of the Third Army
and the Kövess Group to its south—were far outnumbered by the Russians,
who deployed 350,000 men and more than twenty infantry divisions. As
evidence of Conrad's strategic bankruptcy, an entire army was missing
from the Austrian defense of eastern Galicia. It had gone to Serbia as B-

Staffel while Austria-Hungary faced a terrible threat from the Russians. Eventually the Austrian Second Army would take the place of the Kövess Group, and by the end of August six of its divisions arrived, though another six were still entangled in the Balkans.

From north to south, Ruzskii's Third Army had the XXI, XI, IX, and X Corps in a line stretching southeast from Lutsk, a line continued by Brusilov's Eighth Army with the VII, XII, VIII, and XXIV Corps. Since in the eastern theater the Austrians remained on the defensive rather than advancing to contact, it took longer for serious fighting to begin. The Eighth Army moved forward on 18 August, crossing the frontier on 20 August, and the Third Army moved out on 19 August. Both advanced for a week without serious opposition. The Third Army, slightly ahead of the Eighth, made the first contact with the main Austrian forces on the Zolota Lipa River around Złoczów, 60 kilometers east of L'viv. The three corps of the Austrian Third Army—the XI, III, and XII—waited for the Russians to advance across the Galician plains, then attacked on a broad front in hopes of catching the Russians on the march and poorly prepared for battle. The Russians, however, were ready and present in overwhelming force, as those three Austrian corps were engaging in frontal attacks against a full six Russian corps: four from the Third Army and two from the northern wing of the Eighth. Russian weight of numbers repelled Austrian attacks on 26 August and sent all three Austrian corps reeling back toward L'viv. Ruzskii was delighted with his troops' performance, declaring to *Stavka* that "our troops are ready to make any sacrifices, they strain to reach the enemy, not even holding back from frontal assaults."[6] The Russian victory might have been still more complete but for the caution of both Russian army commanders. If the Eighth Army's left wing had pushed forward more aggressively around the southern extreme of the Austrian line, the victory might have been complete. Both Russian armies were advancing cautiously, and Brusilov, the Eighth Army's talented commander, did not wish to extend himself without knowing the precise nature of Austrian resistance. Austrian reinforcements flowed in rapidly, and Conrad directed the Austrian Second Army under Eduard von Böhm-Ermolli, newly arrived from its long detour to Serbia, to shore up the Austrian Third Army's southern flank.

After his initial victories, Ruzskii wanted to halt and regroup his Third Army on the Gnila Lipa River before making a further push onward to

L'viv. Southwestern Front Commander Ivanov and *Stavka* alike were skeptical of this suggestion, knowing the increasingly desperate situation of the Fifth Army to the northwest. Ivanov initially agreed to Ruzskii's request for a pause on condition that active cavalry probes continue, but *Stavka* vetoed a halt altogether and insisted the Third Army continue toward L'viv, shifting to the north to provide more indirect support to the hard-pressed Fifth Army. Ivanov then ordered Ruzskii on 29 August to speed his advance to bring Pleve some assistance. Ruzskii complied, ordering a general offensive for his Third Army on 30 August, but without full consideration of the needs of the Russian northern wing. Fixated on his own advance, Ruzskii responded with an advance directly west by the four corps of his Third Army to steamroller Austrian resistance and take L'viv, ignoring the needs of the Fifth Army to the northwest.

When fighting began again on 29 August along the Gnila Lipa River, the most intense combat took place in the center of the Russian advance just east of L'viv, where the Austrian III and XII Corps, dug in to strong defensive positions with ample artillery, came under the combined assault of four Russian corps. Ivanov harangued Ruzskii and Brusilov to move more quickly, putting the fate of the Fourth and Fifth armies in their hands. By the next day, the Russians had smashed a 15-kilometer gap in the XII Corps, through which a cavalry division raided Austrian supply lines and harassed retreating soldiers. The XXI Corps on the far right of the general Russian advance was north of L'viv by 2 September, thereby creating a dual threat: either to turn south against L'viv or north to attack the rear of the Austrian armies engaged against the Russian Fifth Army. All along the line, Austrian counterattacks failed to stem the steady Russian advance. The Austrian position would have been even more disastrous but for the failure of Russian cavalry to exploit the breach in Austrian lines in full force. On 31 August, the Austrian Third Army ordered general withdrawal from the Gnila Lipa, though not yet abandoning L'viv to Russian occupation. The Austrian Second Army pulled back as well, abandoning Halych and destroying the bridges across the Dniestr River. Though suffering heavy losses, the Austrians had managed to keep their forces intact and in some order. Nonetheless, the Russian advance was relentless, capturing outlying Austrian fortifications around L'viv on 2 September and taking L'viv itself the next day.

As a result, while the north still hung in the balance, the Austrian position in the east was collapsing. The battle for Galicia then turned on whether the Austrians could hold on long enough in the east to enable victory in the north. Ivanov stressed that "even the capture of L'viv cannot compensate us for losing the battle in the north,"[7] and so the highest priority for Ruzskii's Third Army had to be pressing northwest to the relief of the Fifth Army. Conrad belatedly recognized the danger of his situation. Resentful at the lack of a German offensive into Poland but more conscious of their own need, the Austrians appealed to Germany for aid, the first step in a pernicious process that deprived the Habsburg Empire of its autonomy. Germany dispatched a task force of *Landwehr* divisions under Remus von Woyrsch to prop up the faltering Austrian First Army. Shaken by the loss of experienced officers in the first battles, the Habsburgs found that German militia fought more effectively than Austrian first-line troops. Abandoning hope of further advances in the north just as the Russians were planning to renew their pressure there, Conrad rested his hopes on a counterattack against the Russian troops advancing from the east. The retreat of Pleve's Fifth Army gave the Austrian high command some room to maneuver, and on 1 September, Conrad ordered the Fourth Army to turn southeast, away from the beaten Russians, and to attack the Russian Third Army at precisely the moment that army was moving northwest to attack the Austrian Fourth. Conrad split the Austrian Fourth Army, screening the Russian Fifth Army with two weak corps under Archduke Joseph Ferdinand, while sending three corps south to attack the northern flank of the advancing Russian Third Army.[8]

Thus, at the beginning of September, the northern sector had hit a temporary lull. While the Austrian First Army was retreating south, the Austrian Fourth Army had turned in place to move south against the northern flank of the Russian Third Army. In the eastern sector, the Austrian Third and Second Armies had been badly beaten and were temporarily incapable of halting to counterattack the pursuing Russian Third and Eighth Armies. Sensing the possibility to annihilate the northern Austrian armies, Ivanov ordered a general advance all along the Southwestern Front on 3 September. *Stavka* reorganized its troops in the north for greater flexibility, separating out the two westernmost corps from the Fourth Army to create a new Ninth Army under Platon Lechitskii. Lechitskii, a priest's son and former seminarian, was down-to-earth, solid, and effective, uniquely remaining in command of his army, suffering neither promotion nor demotion, through 1917. It, along with the Fourth Army, was assigned to pursue the Austrian First Army as it withdrew south. To make matters even more complex, the Russian Fifth Army had been assigned to halt its own retreat and instead pursue the Austrian Fourth Army as it moved southeast, fighting its way through the screen erected by Joseph Ferdinand's task force.

In essence, then, the renewed Russian offensive on 3-4 September repeated the pattern of the first offensive just over two weeks earlier: a concentric offensive by all the Southwestern Front's armies, converging on the Austrian fortress at Przemyśl. The difference, though, was that two weeks' time had allowed Russian advantages in manpower to accumulate. Austrian forces, smaller to begin with and drained by two weeks of bloody maneuver warfare, were far less capable of resistance. On the northern wing, Russian advantage in numbers (now roughly thirty-six divisions to twenty) began to take its toll. The previous two weeks had also split Austrian forces facing the Russian northern wing. The Austrian First Army occupied a concave arc directed toward Lublin and its Russian defenders; the Austrian Fourth Army to the east had focused on trying to encircle and destroy the Russian Fifth Army before being ordered to the southeast. As a result, a gap of almost 50 kilometers had opened between the right flank of the Austrian First Army and the left flank of the Austrian Fourth. Such gaps had almost destroyed Pleve's Fifth Army just weeks before; now the Austrians were faced with the prospect of destruction. Ivanov threw four corps into that gap to isolate the two Austrian armies and defeat them in detail.

On 4 September the Austrian X Corps, stationed at the gap between the Austrian First and Fourth Armies, began to collapse. Assailed from the front by repeated assaults and outflanked by the XXV Corps moving into the space separating it from the Fourth Army far to its east, beleaguered Austrians surrendered in substantial numbers or withdrew quickly south. Despite the developing crisis on its eastern flank, the Austrian First Army continued to hold elsewhere, repulsing frontal assaults from the Ninth and Fourth Army. If the Russians continued to push into the gap in Austrian defenses, though, that stand could at best be temporary. With the Austrian X Corps broken, the Russian Fourth Army on 7 September hammered the next unit in the Austrian line, the V Corps, which still stubbornly held its ground in the face of overwhelming Russian artillery and weight of numbers. Timely reinforcements by the German *Landwehr* of von Woyrsch's task force stiffened the Austrian line. Even at this early point in the war, the relative worth of the two Central Powers was clearly established: small numbers of German militia commanded by a general nearly seventy years old made an enormous difference in the combat effectiveness of Austrian formations, staving off complete Austrian collapse.

While the Russian Ninth and Fourth Armies had struggled desperately to defend Lublin and then push the Austrians back across the frontier, Pleve's Fifth Army, occupying the hinge of the Russian line, remained remarkably passive after narrowly escaping envelopment and annihilation in the battles around Komarów. As a result, when the Austrian Fourth Army split in two, leaving a task force under Joseph Ferdinand to delay Russian advance while the bulk of the Fourth Army moved south to deal with the crisis at L'viv, the Russian Fifth Army failed to take advantage of the opportunity. Instead, it crept south in slow pursuit of Joseph Ferdinand. By 7 September, though, rest and resupply put it in a position to move decisively either west to smash the right flank of the Austrian First Army or south to avenge its near destruction by attacking the Austrian Fourth. Given this opportunity, Ivanov split the difference, sending the XXV Corps west to assist the Ninth and Fourth Armies, and the rest of Fifth Army and the XIX, V and XVII Corps, along with cavalry, south to the aid of the Russian Third Army.

Through the early days of September, the combined forces of the Russian Ninth and Fourth Armies on the western wing of the enormous arc stretching through Galicia pushed steadily south and southwest in pursuit of the Austrian First Army. The Austrians held their positions in relatively good order, bolstered by a steady flow of reinforcements. Given the slow Russian progress, on 8 September Evert suggested a halt to rest and reorganize, a proposal that Ivanov endorsed on condition that the Ninth and Fourth Armies surrender some divisions to more active fronts. Unwilling to do that, Lechitskii and Evert renewed their attacks, and on 9 September the combined weight of their armies finally broke the Austrian First Army. Independent attacks finally smashed through stubbornly defended Austrian positions south of Lublin, forcing rapid retreat that abandoned artillery and thousands of prisoners. The Ninth and Fourth Armies moved to full pursuit the next day. The Fifth Army's XXV Corps, earlier detached to outflank the Austrian First Army from the east, now forced the disorganized Austrian retreat to move southwest rather than directly south. This withdrawal thus meant the First Army's retreat put increasing distance between itself and the three embattled Austrian armies further east. The other Austrian armies in the theater were now entirely open to Russian attack from the north, a vulnerability that would prove crucial to the outcome of the battles in the eastern sector.

In the east, Ruzskii's Third Army had moved northwest, seeking battle with the Austrian Fourth Army; the Fourth Army had moved southeast to meet it. On 5 September, elements on Ruzskii's right wing began to meet Austrian resistance, and by the next day the two armies were fully engaged all along their front in the wooded terrain north and west of L'viv. The bloody and vicious fighting centered around the village of Rava-Ruska, where the advancing Russians hammered at the Austrian center. The Austrian Fourth Army countered by trying to work its right flank around the Russian left to wedge troops into the junction between the Third Army and the Eighth Army to its south. If successful, this could break through to L'viv and divide the two Russian armies. Two separate developments ended this threat. On 7 September, the Russian XXI Corps on the Third Army's right wing pushed forward toward a link-up with the left wing of the Fifth Army, strengthening the threat to collapse both Joseph Ferdinand's task force and the Austrian Fourth Army: the two Russian armies were close to crushing the Austrians between them. At the same time, the developing crisis on the Third Army's left forced its neighboring armies to rush to its aid. From the Eighth Army to the south, Brusilov sent his VII and VIII Corps north to smash into the southern flank of the developing Austrian breach in Russian lines. To the north, the Fifth Army's two eastern corps, the V and XVII, pressed south hard against the stop-gap defense of Joseph Ferdinand's task force, striving to drive it back into the rear of the Austrian forces hammering away at Ruzskii's Third Army. The developing battle had spread north and south along the front from its center at Rava-Ruska, drawing more and more elements from both armies into the confused fighting.

Despite the net of Russian armies closing around his troops in eastern Galicia, Conrad was not yet prepared to abandon hope of victory. He ordered all three of his armies, the Fourth, Third, and Second, to launch a combined drive on L'viv on 9 and 10 September, regardless of their deteriorating situation. Though the Fourth Army's attacks stalled, this desperate attempt to salvage a lost battle came remarkably close to success in an unexpected sector. While the Austrian Third Army still pressed hard to rip open the junction between the Russian Third and Eighth Armies, the Aus-

trian Second Army, a marginal element at the far southern extreme of the
Austrian line as a result of its late deployment from the Balkans, now finally made its weight felt. As the far southern anchor of the Russian line,
the XXIV Corps of Brusilov's Eighth Army suffered the full force of an attack by the Austrian Second Army on 9 September, forcing it to retreat several miles and thereby bending back the southern fringe of the Russian line.
Brusilov reported that his army was "in an extremely difficult position in
view of the threatened envelopment from the left and a sharp attack into
the gap between itself and Ruzskii's Third Army."[9] The further Brusilov's
left wing retreated, the more the way lay open for the Austrian Second
Army, operating at the southern end of the fighting, to push north to L'viv
and roll up the Eighth. Brusilov's troops fought stubbornly and desperately
to keep the Russian left wing from breaking: could they hold until the Austrian Fourth Army finally gave way?

Ignoring the growing Austrian crisis in the north—the Austrian Fourth
Army was hopelessly entangled in the ferocious fighting around Rava-
Ruska while the First Army on its left was in rapid retreat homeward—the
Austrian high command continued to hope for decisive victory. Only on 11
September did the hopelessness of the Austrian position become clear. The
Russian Fifth Army was slowly but relentlessly pushing south, driving
Joseph Ferdinand's task force in front of it and caving in the northern flank
of the Austrian Fourth Army. Even though Ivanov noted the "difficult po-
sition created by extended and stubborn fighting on the front of General
Ruzskii's army and especially General Brusilov's" and the "exhaustion of
our troops created by uninterrupted marching and extending battles," the
Austrians were in far worse shape. On that afternoon Conrad gave the
order for general retreat.[10] He told his troops to withdraw west to the San
River, anchored on the south by the Przemyśl fortress, followed by further
withdrawal west to Krakow, retreating first across the Wisłoka River before finally halting before the Dunajec River. Russian pursuit across the San
was slowed by rains and the resulting high water, allowing the Austrian
army to gain distance on the Russians and reestablish a defensive position.
They left behind horrific losses. The struggle around Rava-Ruska in the
center of the Russian Third Army line was particularly intense. One American reporter described "stepping from shell hole to shell hole, each surrounded by strips of blue uniform, fingers, bones, and bits of humanity
blown to pieces by high explosive shells."[11]

After almost three weeks of bloody warfare, Russian pursuit was slow and desultory.[12] The exhausted troops of the Russian left—the Third and Eighth Armies and elements of the Fifth Army—were wholly unable to manage an active pursuit of the beaten Austrians. Nonetheless, an important opportunity was missed. The slow Russian pursuit allowed the transfer of German forces from East Prussia to redeploy as a new German Ninth Army in the region north of Krakow, on the west bank of the Vistula. This halted any potential Russian advance along the north bank of the Vistula toward the vital industrial region of Silesia, and laid the groundwork for a subsequent German offensive against Warsaw, discussed in the next chapter. South of the Vistula, the slow Russian pursuit was equally fateful. The four Austrian armies that had fought and lost in Galicia withdrew west into a steadily narrowing space between the Vistula to the north and the Carpathians to the south. Russian cavalry had outdistanced the Austrians on the north side of the Vistula, but proved unable to cross back south behind them and complete the battle of annihilation. The Austrian flight was so rapid that it often outdistanced even Russian cavalry. Russian cavalry pursued the Austrians all the way to the eastern bank of the Dunajec, but they lacked mass and heavy artillery. As a result, Russian horsemen could only harass the Austrian retreat, not force them to battle and destroy the disorganized and demoralized force. In addition, the Russian command, both at the Southwestern Front and at *Stavka*, feared overreaching in pursuit of the Austrians as Russian supply lines lengthened and the Austrian retreat neared substantial fortress complexes. The Austrian retreat swept past the Przemyśl fortress, leaving its garrison to be besieged by the Russians. As late as the end of September, only the Russian Ninth Army, just south of the Vistula, was nearing Austrian positions. The remainder of the Southwestern Front—the Fourth, Fifth, Third, and Eighth Armies—was still advancing slowly, in no hurry to repeat the experience they had just gone through.

The Galician campaign was an undoubted Russian victory, though achieved at great cost. The Russians had seized Galicia and inflicted horrific losses on the Austrians, albeit at enormous expense to themselves. Precise casualty figures are impossible to determine, but the Austrians likely lost in the neighborhood of 400,000 killed, wounded, or captured in the first month of the war, of which 100,000 were prisoners in Russian hands. That casualty total amounted to half the men who began the campaign. By the winter of 1914–1915, Austrian casualties had climbed to nearly one million. As losses were particularly heavy in the vital infantry divisions and among junior officers, the cumulative effect was to destroy the bulk of the prewar fighting force, and leave the Austrian army scrambling to rebuild its experience and professionalism for the rest of the war. It shared this challenge with Russia and the rest of the countries at war, but Austria was hit particularly hard and particularly early.[13] In less than a month of fighting, it was clear to all parties at war that they faced a test on a scale greater than any in living memory.

5

The Struggle for Poland, Autumn 1914

After the battles in the north in East Prussia and in the south in Galicia, the fighting on the Eastern Front shifted to Poland, which was a political as much as a military battlefield. With Poland divided between Prussia, Russia, and the Austrian Empire at the end of the eighteenth century, the Polish people were a potentially useful force if their collective loyalty could be won to one of the warring parties. The ferocious battles of the first weeks of war had raged before the tortuous process of inter-Allied negotiations could begin. Quickly, though, the Entente powers worked out plans for what the world would look like once the war was won. Russia had a series of priorities, including the fate of the Turkish straits. As of the late summer and early fall of 1914, however, the Ottoman Empire had not yet joined the war, so the key question for Russia to negotiate with its allies was the fate of Poland. As early as August 1914, Grand Duke Nikolai Nikolaevich had issued a manifesto promising a unified Poland that upon victory would be "free in faith, speech, and self-government" but "under the scepter of the Russian tsar." While the promise of autonomy and full rights for the Polish language and the Catholic Church was an improvement on prewar Russian practice, it was far from full independence, promising instead something like Finland's status: self-government within the Russian Empire. Russian officials undermined the Grand Duke's proclamation as soon as he made it. While Northwestern Front commander, Zhilinskii prohibited Polish flags and the Polish national anthem, and Governor-General A. O. Essen told Polish elites that the grand duke's manifesto clearly could not mean what it said. Indeed, Tsar Nicholas's inner circle regarded the manifesto as a transparent ploy by the grand duke to raise his own standing. The Allies were also disquieted. By envisaging a Poland including territory from Germany and Austria-Hungary, the Russian declaration complicated any hope of a separate peace that might detach the Habsburgs from Germany. The same was true of Russia's offer to Bucharest later that autumn that Habsburg Transylvania would be a fair price for Romania's joining the allies. But Britain and France had far greater priorities than the fate of Poland, and so deferred to Russia on Eastern European questions. On 5 September 1914, Britain, France, and Russia signed the Pact of London, committing themselves to cooperating in the determination of war aims and peace terms and to rejecting any separate peace. Though often hard-pressed, the Russian Empire would hold to this commitment through its final collapse.[1]

The Central Powers were formulating war aims as well. The German government's September Program, a think-piece discussing potential goals, envisaged Russia stripped of its non-Russian periphery and opened to German economic exploitation. Austria-Hungary had little interest in Russian territory and looked elsewhere for its rewards, including the annexation of Serbia (thus worsening its minorities problem). To match the Russian bid for Polish loyalty, the Austrians proposed in 1915 an autonomous Poland with a Habsburg monarch. As junior partners to the Germans, though, the Austrians had to defer to Berlin's desires for Poland as a political and economic satellite. Over the course of the war, the Austrian bargaining position grew steadily worse, and by 1917 Germany envisaged a Poland fully integrated into a German economic empire, and Austria-Hungary with only slightly more independence.

FOCUS SHIFTS TO CENTRAL POLAND

Despite the seeming threat that the enormous Polish salient seemed to present to Germany, both warring sides left that sector relatively unmanned during the late summer of 1914. The geography of the Polish salient created an odd no-man's land. The border between Russia and Germany marked a vast arc stretching west. The Vistula was a rough mirror image of that: the river flowed east through Krakow, turned north at Sandomierz toward Warsaw, turned west again north of Warsaw where it met the Narew, then flowed northwest into the Baltic. The territory between the western curve of the Russo-German border and the eastern curve of the Vistula was largely devoid of troops. The Russians feared that any strike west out of the Polish salient toward Berlin would be vulnerable to counterattack from north and south, and relied on the array of fortresses stretching northeast from Warsaw for protection against German attacks on Poland. The Vistula south of Warsaw, however, was relatively unguarded. In response, though, the Russians prepared for future operations against Berlin by organizing Lechitskii's Ninth Army at Warsaw. In August and September, Russian troops generally stayed behind the protection of Poland's fortresses and the Vistula River, sending only relatively small formations, mostly cavalry, to cover Poland west of the Vistula. The Germans, clear enough on the general pattern of Russian deployments, concentrated their defenses against Russia in East Prussia, leaving the Polish border in front of Berlin covered by only a third-rate corps of *Landwehr* militia. As a result, the ground between Warsaw and Berlin was oddly empty for the first two months of the war, though over the autumn the Russians built up their garrisons and mobile formations in the region.[2]

The demilitarization of central Poland changed after the initial fighting for East Prussia and Galicia. Both sides then focused on central Poland, west of the Vistula, as the new theater of operations. German calculations changed when the failure of the Schlieffen Plan in the west became apparent. Quick victory against France was no longer possible, so shifting resources east to attempt quick victory against Russia became much more attractive. A rapid capture of Warsaw might bring Polish opinion solidly behind the Central Powers and convince the Russians to come to terms. The exposed position of Russian Poland meant the German high command had several options: an attack from the north, where Hindenburg and Ludendorff's Eighth Army had just crushed Samsonov's Second Army and could descend on Warsaw; from the northwest, where German troops could attack up the Vistula River, using the river itself as protection for their left flank while pushing toward Warsaw; or from the southwest, concentrating around Krakow and pushing northeast, focusing on the Vistula south of Warsaw. Finally, an Austro-German offensive from Krakow that drove east along the south bank of the Vistula rather then northeast on the river's north bank offered the prospect of liberating the besieged Austrian garrison at Przemyśl.[3]

After expelling Rennenkampf from East Prussia, Hindenburg and Ludendorff had no desire for the moment to pursue his retreating First Army east past the Nieman River toward Vilnius and further into Russia's endless depths. Another possibility was more tempting: driving south through the gap where Samsonov's Second Army had once been, crossing the Narew River and thereby cutting off Warsaw and the Polish salient. The two were eager to follow up their triumph over the Second Army with a march on Warsaw. They were then unhappy to find from German headquarters in mid-September that they were to halt all plans for forcing the Narew and moving south. Instead, they had to release two corps to be transported around the vast bulge of the Polish salient for a new concentration at Krakow in order to support the hard-pressed Austrians. Given authority over this newly formed Ninth Army in addition to his Eighth, Hindenburg argued hard for operations to continue in the north, but again found himself forced for political reasons to operate in support of the Austrians. Hindenburg was dealing with a new master. Germany's Chief of the General Staff Helmuth von Moltke had broken under the strain of command and been replaced by Erich von Falkenhayn, more coldly rational than Moltke. From Falkenhayn's point-of-view, failure to stem the Austrian retreat in Galicia would mean a Russian invasion of the vital industrial region of Silesia and possible Austrian collapse. This produced a new plan: rather than provide indirect support to Austria by invading Poland from the north, German troops shifted counterclockwise around the Polish salient to attack toward Warsaw from the southwest.

As a result, while the three Russian armies around the perimeter of East Prussia—the remnants of the Second, the Tenth, and the First—withdrew away from the frontier, a weak German Eighth Army was left in East Prussia. In just under two weeks, Hindenburg and Ludendorff took most of the Eighth Army's formations out of East Prussia for the new Ninth Army between Częstochowa and Krakow. The Ninth Army was given five corps and intended to operate in conjunction with Dankl's Austrian First Army, regrouping after the Galicia battles. The plan was a drive along the northern bank of the Vistula to cross the river south of Warsaw, breaking in between that vital communications center and the bulk of the Southwestern

Front to its south. By the end of September, the new offensive was ready. The Austrians would assist the Germans by pushing back east against their Russian pursuers south of the Vistula.

Russian calculations had changed as well. While the Germans were creating the new Ninth Army in central Poland, the Russians were preparing their own attack in the same theater. A 22 September *Stavka* conference at Chełm between Grand Duke Nikolai and the Front commanders Nikolai Ruzskii and Nikolai Ivanov agreed on the likelihood of an attack on the Polish salient from the west, based on intelligence of German concentrations west of the Vistula. Russian intelligence had detected the German shift from East Prussia to Silesia. While German operational efficiency could transport masses of men and supplies with great speed, it was impossible to conceal movement on such a scale.[4] The Russian high command came to a consensus to cease pursuing the Austrians south of the Vistula and instead to shore up Russian defenses in central Poland. On 23 September Evert's Fourth Army was ordered to halt its crossing of the San River, and instead move north to Dęblin on the Vistula. The rest of the Southwestern Front's armies were instructed to halt their pursuit of the retreating Austrians and instead dig in to defensible positions. On 25 September, Yanushkevich confirmed a massive German buildup west of the Vistula, and urged concentration on the central Vistula to parry any potential attack. The Southwestern Front, having beaten the Austrians in Galicia, had three choices on how to proceed: force its way through the Carpathian mountain passes to its south to move into Hungary, attack west through Krakow into Silesia with its vital coal mines, or halt its advance west out of Galicia and instead redeploy north to counter the German threat. The first two options seemed unattractive. If the Southwestern Front continued to push west along the southern bank of the Vistula, or instead turned south into the Carpathians, it would be vulnerable to an attack from the north by the new German concentration. "Would not it make sense," Yanushkevich argued, "to give the armies of the Southwestern Front new tasks, ones that would put them face-to-face with the main body of the enemy?"[5]

Yanushkevich's question illustrated a growing offensive spirit. The mood of the Russian commanders was an odd mixture of excitement and dread: the possibility of a decisive offensive west out of central Poland toward Berlin, along with the fear of the massive German assault on Warsaw that Russian intelligence had detected. In a second meeting at Chełm between Grand Duke Nikolai and Ivanov on 26 September, the two men agreed on not simply defending the central Vistula but preparing an offensive. Nikolai Nikolaevich ordered on 28 September that "the general task of the armies of both Fronts . . . is to prepare to go on the offensive from the middle Vistula . . . for a deep strike into Germany." That would require as much as three full armies from the Southwestern Front, and a wholesale reorganization, pulling one or more armies from south of the Vistula and transferring them to the middle Vistula south of Warsaw.[6] Lechitskii's Ninth Army, which had advanced far west along the southern bank of the Vistula, was ordered to backtrack. It moved east on 28 September in order to prepare for an offensive from the middle Vistula, and was in place by 3 October. The Fifth Army, preparing to continue along the southern bank of the Vistula toward Krakow, was likewise ordered back toward Dęblin on 29 September. The Third and Eighth Armies were left to hold the southern fringe of the Russian line, with the Third assigned the siege of Przemyśl.[7]

One problem was the continuing weakness of Russia's Northwestern Front in the wake of the East Prussian disaster. Ruzskii, the newly appointed commander of the Northwestern Front, displayed an odd mixture of confidence and anxiety for neither the first nor the last time. He was nervous about just how many Germans were lurking in East Prussia, and wanted the western extreme of his sector, the reconstituted Second Army, pulled back east toward safety deeper inside Russia. While providing for his own security, this would open up Warsaw to attack from the north and make any major offensive out of the Polish salient into Silesia extremely vulnerable. *Stavka* rejected his proposal, and after repeated requests finally ordered Ruzskii on 1 October, over his reservations, to shift the Second Army toward Warsaw in order to support the Southwestern Front. At the same time, though, Ruzskii was confident enough to plan an offensive on the Nieman to restore the East Prussian frontier. On 28 September, Rennenkampf's First Army, supported by Flug's Tenth Army to its south, attacked across the Niemen to recapture lost ground. Though the attack was slow and cautious, Flug was pleased with its initial successes, and wanted to pursue the Germans opposite him more aggressively. When Ruzskii ordered a halt, Flug carried out an ambitious night attack anyway, which compelled German withdrawal and generally restored the prewar frontier.

The heavy losses Russian forces suffered during this advance, however, left Ruzskii but no choice but to withdraw his armies again, meaning that great loss of life (50 percent casualties in some regiments) had achieved almost nothing. Ruzskii dismissed Flug as commander of the Tenth Army, replacing him with Faddei Sivers, a veteran General Staff officer.

In retrospect, Russian thinking in late September 1914, culminating in an ambitious plan for attacks in central Poland and requiring massive reorganization of Russian deployments, is difficult to evaluate as anything other than a substantial misreading of Russian offensive capabilities. In any event, Russian offensive preparations were preempted by something far more substantial: the German attack on Warsaw.

THE GERMAN DRIVE ON WARSAW

The German-Austrian offensive against Warsaw from the southwest unfolded in stages, with the Vistula River forming a natural dividing line.[8] North of the Vistula, Hindenburg's new Ninth Army, assisted by the Austrian I Corps on its right flank, pushed ahead on 28 September against a half-dozen Russian cavalry divisions stationed west of the Vistula to monitor German movements and provide early warning of any action. Ivanov, acting with extraordinary caution, held his armies on the eastern bank of the Vistula. He refused to expand the limited bridgeheads the Russians held on the west bank of the river, particularly at Dęblin, where General Aleksei Evert pushed hard for permission to move the bulk of his Fourth Army to the western bank to meet the oncoming Germans. Hindenburg's divisions curved northeast, following the bend of the Vistula and approaching Warsaw from the south. The three Russian armies defending the Vistula—the Second Army at Warsaw, then the Fifth and Fourth to its south, barely had time to deploy their divisions across to the western bank of the river before being hit by the eight corps that Hindenburg had assembled for his attack, and were forced into quick but orderly retreat back to the Russian side of the Vistula.

Hindenburg's offensive had quick success in pushing the Russians back to the Vistula, but then ran into serious trouble in developing that initial tactical victory into more lasting strategic success. The Russians retained two large and important bridgeheads on the western bank of the Vistula:

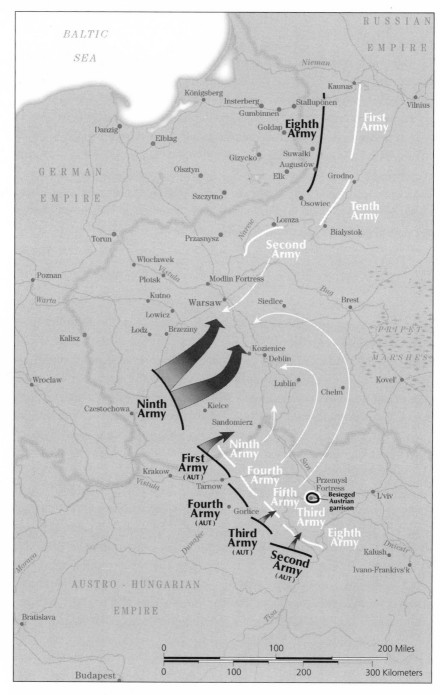

Map 5. The German Attack on Warsaw, 1 October 1914

Warsaw and its environs, and Dęblin and nearby Kozienice 100 kilometers further south. This presented Hindenburg with a conundrum. If he satisfied himself with the advances so far, he had gained territory but had neither destroyed Russian formations nor taken a major city, or indeed done anything to bring himself closer to victory. Crossing the middle Vistula to advance further east would leave him vulnerable to an attack on his lines of communication from the Russian enclaves on the western bank. Reducing those fortified Russian bridgeheads would maximize Russian advantages in manpower and dogged determination and surrender German advantages in rapid maneuver over open terrain. To make matters worse, the Russians enjoyed a decided advantage in numbers. The bulk of the offensive was being carried by a single German army with some Austrian assistance, against the better part of three Russian armies fighting on the defensive.

Faced with unpleasant choices, Hindenburg decided to push north toward Warsaw along the western bank of the Vistula, a decision that took his point of effort further away from his hard-pressed Austrian allies to the south. He created a task force under Mackensen (soon to become his successor as Ninth Army commander) of the troops on his left—an ad hoc corps under Rudolf von Frommel and the XVII and XX Corps—sending it north along the Vistula on 9 October to attack Warsaw before sufficient Russian forces could redeploy north to reinforce the Second Army. On that same day, Ivanov laid out his own plan for countering the Germans—a full-scale offensive by the Second Army out of Warsaw along with a crossing of the Vistula by the Fourth and Fifth Armies. Sheideman, commanding the Second Army, pushed his perimeter well west and south of Warsaw to meet the German attack. Mackensen's troops thus encountered fierce Russian resistance outside Warsaw, and made slow headway on 10–12 October as Sheideman's divisions fell back slowly toward the ring of forts around the city. Ivanov berated Sheideman for his tactical withdrawals and urged him to an offensive, but Sheideman insisted instead on the need to keep his army intact. *Stavka* dispatched a stream of reinforcements, including the vital presence of the excellent I and II Siberian Corps, to maintain Warsaw's southern perimeter. Constrained by the Vistula to their east, the Germans had little choice but to pound ahead directly at substantial cost. Russia's much-maligned fortifications here showed that they did indeed have some worth in modern warfare. On 13 October, bolstered by reinforcements,

Sheideman's soldiers counterattacked and drove Mackensen back from the city. Even as Mackensen's forces were fighting their way north toward Warsaw, Russian troops of the XXIII and II Corps crossed over the Vistula to attack the German right flank, providing welcome relief to Warsaw's defenders, though the bridgehead could not be maintained.

Ivanov likewise saw an opportunity to attack further south when Hindenburg sent Mackensen north to Warsaw. Without manifesting particular subtlety in his planning, on 9 October he ordered a general advance westward across the Vistula by the Second, Fifth, and Fourth Armies. While the Second Army, hard pressed by Mackensen's attack on Warsaw, could manage only limited offensive action on its own, the Fifth and Fourth Armies expended considerable lives and time battering their way to establishing limited additional footholds on the western bank of the Vistula. At Dęblin and particularly at Kozienice, the Russian transfer of substantial forces to the west bank of the Vistula, though costly in lives and producing no substantial advances, kept Hindenburg's Ninth Army off-balance and did not allow it to concentrate its forces for a decisive blow at Warsaw. Evert continued to throw fresh units into Kozienice from 10 to 15 October, and rejected requests from his corps and division commanders to evacuate their bridgeheads back to the east bank.

Even though the Russian army had contained the danger, keeping the Germans on the west bank of the Vistula, barring Mackensen's task force from Warsaw, and maintaining a steady pressure against the Germans from bridgeheads, the ongoing strain of the fighting brought Ivanov to the point of breakdown. He lost confidence in Sheideman, commander of the Second Army at Warsaw, and wanted to replace him with Sivers, commander of the Tenth Army. There was little sense in this move—Sheideman's defense of Warsaw had been conducted well, and disrupting it with a change of command in the middle of the battle made little sense. Nikolai Nikolaevich accepted Ivanov's proposal, only to be stymied by Ruzskii's categorical objection as Northwestern Front commander to removing Sivers from the Tenth Army so soon after he had taken it over.

By mid-October the Germans had shot their bolt, and the strain of two weeks of constant attacks had exhausted both men and supplies. The Russian Second Army at Warsaw and the Fifth Army just to its south were transferred to Ruzskii at the Northwestern Front on 14 October and charged with carrying out a renewed offensive to drive the Germans back from Warsaw.[9] On 16 October, Yanushkevich told Ivanov and Ruzskii that information about possible German reinforcements from the Western Front "compel[s] us to move quickly with the development of a broad offensive" and asked them how quickly their forces could be ready, and on 17 October Grand Duke Nikolai ordered a major Russian counteroffensive, to drive the Germans back from the Vistula, to begin the next day.[10] Ruzskii and Ivanov both protested that their troops were simply not ready, but received only a few days' respite. On 18 October, the Second Army moved to the attack, assisted by renewed Vistula crossings by the XIX and V Corps south of Warsaw. Mackensen and Hindenburg had no choice but to recognize the failure of their offensive, and the need to withdraw to fight another day. On 20 October, the Germans began pulling back from Warsaw at the same time that *Stavka* ordered pursuit.

With the German retreat from Warsaw, the Russians renewed their efforts to break out of their bridgeheads at Dęblin and Kozienice. By 21 October, they had the better part of two corps, the XVII and the III Caucasus, across the Vistula and attacking west into the flank of the withdrawing Germans. The Austrian First Army countered the Russian breakout with an attack of its own north along the Vistula into the southern flank of the expanding Russian salient at Dęblin. Though Conrad hoped this would succeed in crossing the Vistula where the Germans had failed, his troops were hopelessly outnumbered by the Russians, who were further heartened by their recent successes. Conrad's attack temporarily checked the Russian advance across the river, but the Russian Second Army was still moving south from Warsaw. The Austrian counter thus provided only a brief respite, as more and more Russian divisions crossed to the west bank of the Vistula or joined the pursuit south from Warsaw. By 26 October, the Austrian I and V Corps on the southwestern face of the Russian bridgehead had sustained such heavy losses in the fighting that they could no longer hold. With the line broken, Hindenburg had no choice but to withdraw still further. On 27 October, the German Ninth Army was ordered into general retreat. German operational and tactical experience was still evident— though hard-pressed by the Russians, Mackensen's and Hindenburg's soldiers withdrew in a controlled and orderly manner, and quickly outdistanced their Russian pursuers. The Russians were not so lucky; the dividing line between the Russian Northwestern Front and Southwestern Front split the pursuing armies between two commanders and hindered effective coordination. The pursuit was slow and desultory; even Russian cavalry failed to keep pace with the German retreat, just as in the pursuit of the Austrian retreat west from Galicia six weeks before. While the Russians could take heart in seeing the backs of the Germans, the Russian failure to maintain contact allowed the Germans to shift their troops for a surprise offensive elsewhere, with fateful consequences for the Russians. What's more, Russian losses had been heavy. Incomplete figures for three of the four armies involved at Warsaw (Second, Fourth, and Ninth) suggest at least 140,000 casualties.[11]

THE AUSTRIAN OFFENSIVE SOUTH OF THE VISTULA

As Hindenburg attacked northeast toward Warsaw, Conrad had engineered a simultaneous Austrian offensive south of the Vistula toward Przemyśl, an offensive that produced a month of bitter fighting along the San River.[12] In the wake of the initial Galicia battles, the defeated Austrians had retreated west, outdistancing their Russian pursuers, and rallying by mid-September roughly along the Wisłoka River. The pursuing Russians remained 50 kilometers or more behind them, just west of the San River. By late September, as described above, three of the five Russian armies that had fought in Galicia had been pulled north into Poland to defend Warsaw and the central Vistula, leaving only the Russian Third and Eighth Armies behind to hold the Austrians away from besieged Przemyśl (surrounded by a half-dozen infantry divisions of the specially created Blockading Army). This left the two remaining Russian armies, the Third and the Eighth, spread thin with a major Austrian garrison bottled up behind their lines.

Immediately after Hindenburg began his offensive, the Austrian First, Fourth, and Third Armies attacked south of the Vistula, while the Second Army operated to the southeast in the Carpathians. The Third and Eighth Armies had relatively little room to maneuver, bounded by the Carpathians to the south and needing to hold the Austrians away from Przemyśl. They did, however, have ample time to decide on their course, given the space separating them from the main Austrian forces and the extensive Russian cavalry screen harassing the slow Austrian advance. The possibility of retreat led the Russians to attempt a rushed storm of Przemyśl on

5–7 October, culminating in a dawn attack that managed to take a handful of outlying posts but nothing more. This effort in turn hastened the Austrian advance east to Przemyśl's relief. Recognizing further efforts as pointless, Brusilov ended efforts to storm the fortress and ordered his Eighth Army to withdraw east past Przemyśl, abandoning the siege for the moment. Radko Radko-Dmitriev, a Bulgarian in Russian service, now commanded the Third Army after Ruzskii's transfer to the Northwestern Front. He was willing to stand and fight, but Brusilov's withdrawal left him with few options but to follow. Retreat began the night of 7 October back to the San.

Hard pressed in central Poland by the German offensive against Warsaw, Ivanov desperately wanted a Russian counteroffensive in the south to relieve the pressure and preempt an Austrian attack along the right bank of the Vistula that might assist the ongoing German effort on the left bank. Brusilov responded that such an offensive was impossible. In any event, by 9 October the Austrians had finally closed with the Russian Third Army and serious fighting began along the San, preventing any hope of a Russian offensive in the near term. While Conrad was pleased with the relief of Przemyśl, his goals had now expanded to include moving still further east to capture L'viv. Where the Russians could defend along the San River, the Austrians made little progress. At Przemyśl, however, the Russian line continued straight south, breaking away from the course of the San, and there the Austrian Second Army tried to turn the Russian far left flank to break through to L'viv. Desperate fighting 11–13 October around Khyriv over ground sodden with fall rains cost the Austrians thousands of casualties but failed to dislodge the Russian flank. Austrian attacks continued through October, until ammunition shortages, exacerbated by muddy roads, slowed the pace of the fighting.

Over two nights, 17–18 and 18–19 October, Radko-Dmitriev's Third Army finally gave in to Ivanov's pleas for an attack and crossed back west over the San in a new offensive and carved out a series of bridgeheads on the Austrian bank. Both sides became locked in battle, struggling day after day to defend, seize, or expand bridgeheads along the river. By 23 October, failure to advance and heavy losses led the Austrian Fourth Army to suspend further attacks, at the same time that Radko-Dmitriev reached the same conclusion and suspended Russian attacks. Soon, the deteriorating German position north of the Vistula after the failure to take Warsaw convinced the Austrians they could no longer hold along the San. Hindenburg's withdrawal at the end of October created an imminent crisis for the Austrians operating on the south bank of the Vistula. The German retreat exposed the left flank of the Austrians fighting along the San, creating an opportunity for the pursuing Russians to turn south across the Vistula behind the Austrians. On 4 November, the Austrian Fourth Army had to begin its retreat from the San. Further to the south, the Second Army had ceased its own offensive and likewise retreated.

On 5 November, the Russian Third and Eighth Armies pursued the Austrians west, crossing the San for the third time since the start of the war. Delays at the San meant that the active pursuit was again left to Russian cavalry, while Russian infantry divisions advanced more systematically and prepared for a second siege of the Przemyśl fortress, a task entrusted to a newly created Eleventh Army. The renewed Russian encirclement of Przemyśl was complete by 14 November, and the Austrians had been pressed southwest to defend the line of the Carpathian mountains.

The Russian pursuit of the Austrian divisions retreating west inevitably lost momentum. For one, geography worked against the Russians operating south of the Vistula. Krakow, a glittering strategic goal, lay at the apex of a triangle pointed west, bounded on the north by the Vistula and on the south by the Carpathians. As the Russians advanced west toward Krakow, then, the Third Army found it inevitably had less room to maneuver and had to attack on a narrower front; the Eighth Army was constantly on guard against an attack on its southern flank from Austrians firmly ensconced in the Carpathians. In addition, there were limits to what could be asked even of legendarily patient Russian soldiers, and exhaustion from weeks of fighting and marching slowed the chase. The Russian armies south of the Vistula had barely over half their allotted manpower left by mid-November. Russian logistics needed time to reestablish the rail and wagon networks to bring food and ammunition to the front lines. The Russian high command was tantalized by the prospect of reaching Krakow, but the cumulative supply and manpower difficulties created by the previous months of fighting made that impossible. The Germans and the Austrians halted the Russian advance along a line running from just east of Częstochowa to just east of Krakow. By the end of November, the Russian Ninth Army, operating north of the Vistula, and the Third Army, operating south, had clawed to within 25 kilometers of Krakow, but could go no further.

THE ŁÓDŹ CAMPAIGN

While the Russians south of the Vistula pursued the Austrians west toward Krakow during November, a simultaneous struggle centered around Łódź was taking place between the Germans and the Russians, a November sequel to October's failed German drive on Warsaw from the southwest. The failure of Germany's earlier Warsaw-Dęblin offensive, coming on the heels of the apocalyptic struggles for East Prussia and Galicia, did not end the epic clashes in 1914 as both sides struggled for advantage while marching millions of soldiers across the plains of Eastern Europe. What became the Łódź campaign, probably the most complex and dramatic operation of the war in the east, originated in the offensive hopes of both the Russians and the Central Powers. The Russians, heartened by German failure at Warsaw and convinced their victory was more decisive than it had actually been, hoped to finally carry out their invasion west into Germany, perhaps even threatening Berlin; the Germans still hoped that a renewed offensive might slice off Russia's Polish salient, trapping one or more Russian armies and repeating their dramatic victory at Tannenberg. In the November 1914 fighting around Łódź, both the Russians and the Germans enjoyed moments of seeming triumph and endured near disasters, only to end the campaign with thousands of dead strewn across central Poland and the front lines essentially where they had been a month before.

The Russian high command's plan at the beginning of November was to solidify its positions on the shoulders of the Polish salient (East Prussia to the north and Galicia and the Carpathians to the south), enabling a push from the westward bulge of the salient directly into eastern Germany. Eschewing subtlety, the plan imagined a broad advance and frontal assault by four full armies. Chief of Staff Yanushkevich suggested this to his front commanders as early as 2 November, and *Stavka* began planning to bring the war to German soil in a coordinated operation that would involve the full range of Russian formations on the Eastern Front. While limited offensives pinned down Austrian and German forces in the Carpathians and East Prussia to prevent shifting of reserves, a massive Russian offensive would, the plan envisaged, roll west out of the Polish salient and into eastern Germany. While *Stavka*'s conception was breathtaking in its scope, it also entailed a substantial division of effort. Of Russia's thirty-seven corps on the Eastern Front, sixteen would be detailed for the invasion of Ger-

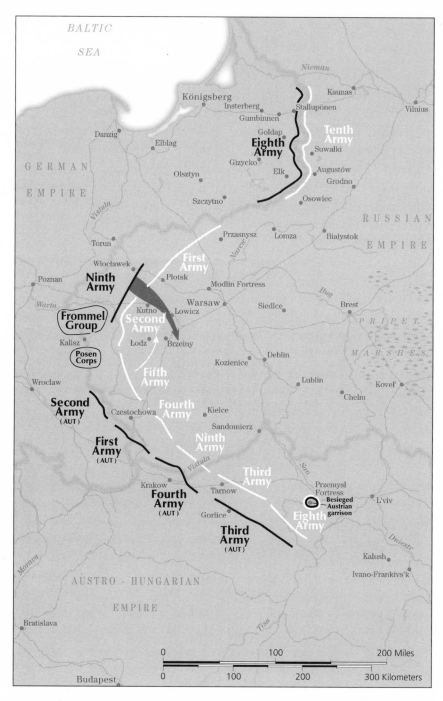

Map 6. The Łódź Offensive, 10 November 1914

many, leaving the rest for operations on the flanks in less important sectors. Even that concentration of force seemed excessive to some. Alekseev, chief of staff of the Southwestern Front, was deeply concerned about the ability of weakened Russian forces in Galicia and the Carpathians to contain a still active Austrian army, and Ivanov, commanding the Southwestern Front, shared Alekseev's sense that Austrian resistance must be dealt with first. *Stavka* ignored these concerns and on 10 November issued orders for a rushed offensive to begin within three days by four armies advancing abreast: from north to south, the Second, Fifth, Fourth, and Ninth. There was little maneuver in the plan—the Second Army would drive for Kalisz on the prewar border. The Fifth and Fourth would cooperate in defeating German formations concentrated at Częstochowa before continuing the march west, and the Ninth Army would take Krakow.[13]

Unfortunately for the Russians, the Germans had plans of their own. The German high command debated the relative merits of focusing on the Eastern Front or the Western, but the danger of a Russian attack raised the stakes and produced general agreement on the need for an offensive in the east to preempt it. At the beginning of November 1914, Hindenburg was named *OberOst*, or commander in chief of all German forces on the Eastern Front. Together with Ludendorff, he planned an ambitious attack from the northwestern corner of the Polish salient. The Ninth Army, under Mackensen's command since 1 November, would counter the forthcoming Russian offensive by attacking down the left (southern) bank of the Vistula. That path would, in the German conception, bring their forces down on Łódź, an industrial center and transportation hub, severing the Russian road, rail, and telegraph connections from the western face of the Polish salient back to Warsaw. With remarkable speed, Hindenburg, Ludendorff, and Hoffmann shifted the bulk of the Ninth Army from southwest of Warsaw to northwest, where now in front of Poznan and Torun a line of five German corps—three (the XI, XVII, and XX) from the Ninth Army and two (I Reserve and XXV Reserve) newly attached from the Eighth—included 150,000 men. By 10 November, Mackensen's Ninth Army had assembled its divisions on the northwestern face of the Polish salient and was ready for its offensive. On Mackensen's far right, to the southwest, he additionally had two scratch formations of roughly corps size—the Frommel Group and Posen Corps—intended to attack directly east toward Łódź.[14]

The Germans chose their point of their attack remarkably well, and

Russian organization and deployments made the German offensive simpler. Mackensen's strike aimed at the vulnerable junction between the hap-
less Rennenkampf's First Army, defending Poland's northern flank, and
the four Russian armies in the invasion force. The First Army, though it had
approximately 125,000 men, was split by the Vistula River, with the V
Siberian Corps on the river's left bank, directly in the path of the German
onslaught; the VI Corps and VI Siberian Corps lay on the northeast bank
of the river and the VI Siberian in particular had to scramble to cross the
Vistula when the attack began. The brunt of the German attack, however,
fell on the 160,000 men of Sheideman's Second Army. Sheideman's divisions primarily faced west to carry out their offensive, not toward the
northwest, where the German attack would come. As a result, Mackensen's
Ninth Army faced only two Russian corps at the weak junction between
the Russian First and Second Armies. On the ground the Germans had chosen, two rivers, the Vistula to the northeast and the Warta to the southwest,
funneled the German attack toward Łódź and provided protection for the
attack's right and left flanks.

Though Russian intelligence had picked up on the transfer of German
units to the northwest sector of the Polish salient, and even the immediate
German preparations for attack, the real scope of the approaching German
offensive had been missed. Yanushkevich, typically dismissed as utterly
incompetent in military affairs, had mused, the day before the German offensive began, about the Russian danger: "Losing contact with the Germans during their retreat toward their own railroad lines was exceedingly
unfortunate for us, since using these railroads our enemy could easily alter
the location of his forces, creating an advantage for himself at some desired
point."[15] Believing that a German redeployment was still in progress rather
than substantially complete, *Stavka* imagined the best course was to disrupt it by speeding the Russian attack west, and set the date for its own
general offensive at 14 November. Once again, the Russians found themselves wrong-footed not so much by German battlefield prowess, but by
the German ability to move troops long distances faster than the Russians
could respond. Mackensen began his attack on 11 November with overwhelming superiority. By starting before the great Russian push west into
Silesia and eastern Germany, Mackensen gained the element of surprise
but gave the Russian high command a certain freedom. Had the Russian
armies begun their offensive and become entangled in German defenses

around Breslau, they would not have been able to turn north to assist the embattled Second Army at Łódź.[16]

Mackensen's march forward moved initially into empty space. The Germans met their first serious resistance at Włocławek from the V Siberian Corps. Though the Siberians held a strong position with their right flank firmly anchored on the Vistula, they were facing the combined forces of three German corps, and their left flank hung in the open, protected only by a Cossack cavalry screen. Over 11 and 12 November, three German divisions launched a frontal attack at the Siberians, while another division supported by cavalry pushed back the Cossacks and turned the Russian flank. The V Siberian Corps had no choice but to fall back southeast toward Łódź and Warsaw, while Ruzskii, commanding the Northwestern Front, was forced to send the VI Siberian Corps across the Vistula to join frantic efforts to stem the German tide. At Ruzskii's direction, the II Corps also wheeled its frontage from west to northwest, taking its place in line beside the Siberians, with the gap in between still covered only by Cossack cavalry. Steadily forced back, the Russian line grew increasingly tenuous at the vulnerable connection between the First and Second Armies. Even though the German advance was rapidly collapsing Russian defenses, Ruzskii still insisted that the First Army had to hold its position in order to enable the Russian offensive west into Silesia by the Second, Fifth, and Fourth Armies to proceed. *Stavka* concurred and continued the same messages, while sending additional divisions to Warsaw as a reserve. On 13 November, Ruzskii continued to hold out hope for an offensive west, declaring that "the Supreme Commander wishes that the armies on the left [west] bank of the Vistula move to a general offensive with the ultimate goal of a deep penetration into Germany," and set the start date for the next day.[17] Even while Mackensen's troops began their knifing attack toward Łódź from the northwest, the Russian offensive planned for 14 November began anyway in the southwest. The Fourth and Ninth Armies attacked west toward Częstochowa but achieved only limited success. The desperate situation around Łódź prevented significant reinforcements to their offensive or the accumulation of reserves to deal with temporary reverses.[18]

Mackensen's advance continued toward the town of Kutno on 14 November. The Russian defenders—the two Siberian corps and the II Corps—could not hold their ground against the pressure of four German corps—the XXV Reserve, I Reserve, XX, and XVII. A cavalry strike smashed through the Cossack screen in the center of the Russian line, and the natural response of local Russian commanders brought a much greater danger. The cavalry breakthrough threatened the Russian corps with being outflanked to their south, so the entire Russian defense began to swing back east away from the German attack, leaving the northern approaches to Łódź wide open. By 16 November, Mackensen could leave the single I Reserve Corps on the Vistula to contain three beaten and exhausted Russian corps, and send the rest of his Ninth Army south to surround Łódź, aiming to trap the Russian Second and Fifth Armies. The question was whether the Russians, always a step behind the Germans, could react in time.

Ruzskii, commanding the Northwestern Front, nearly fell into the German trap. He was slow to realize the scale of Mackensen's attack and believed his offensive could continue. On 13 November Ruzskii ordered the invasion of Germany to proceed, and still maintained this policy on 15 November. By 16 November, though, he finally grasped his danger. The German offensive could not only envelop Łódź from the north, but from there proceed to roll up the length of the Russian line facing eastern Germany. Abandoning hopes of pushing west into Germany, he took a risky but unavoidable step of pulling divisions of Pleve's Fifth Army out of line in the west in order to march them north to shore up the hastily assembled defense at Łódź against the German Ninth Army's breakthrough. If he had miscalculated—if the Germans still had troops waiting in the west to take advantage of Russian weakness—the result would have been disaster. Instead, his decision saved the Second Army. The confused fighting north of Łódź left the Russian commanders scrambling to figure out precisely what the Germans were doing. As Ruzskii complained to Sheideman late on 17 November, "The picture is still not clear to me. What should we have your Second Army do?" The next day, Grand Duke Nikolai Nikolaevich still thought the fight around Łódź was only a sideshow, and prepared for "our transition to a general offensive to be crowned with complete success for . . . God is with us." He too quickly came to realize just how uncertain things were: he informed the tsar on 21 November that "from all the information I've gotten from General Ruzskii, I still cannot assemble even an approximate picture of how things stand on the west bank of the Vistula."[19]

Mackensen was gambling. He had sent four of the five corps in his army against Łódź. The XI and XVII attacked the city from the north, while the XX moved southeast to cut Łódź's communications east to Warsaw. The

XXV Reserve (reinforced by the 3rd Guards Division to form a special task force under Reinhard von Scheffer-Boyadel) swung even wider to the east to engage in a deep envelopment, intended to pass between Łódź and Warsaw, then circle around to the southern outskirts of Łódź. While the Ninth Army attacked Łódź from the north and east, Mackensen was counting on a series of scratch formations and glorified garrison troops—the Frommel Group, the Posen Corps, and the Breslau Corps—to attack from the west and southwest, linking with Scheffer-Boyadel to completely surround Łódź and its defending Russians. The potential gains were enormous—the isolation and destruction of two Russian armies. The risk lay with the potential threat Mackensen had left to his rear. Having left only a single corps, the I Reserve, to hold back three Russian corps, he had to count on being able to envelop and destroy the Russian forces around Łódź before those three corps could reorganize, follow his own troops toward Łódź, and attack the German rear.

The race was a near-run thing. By 18 November, Scheffer-Boyadel's group was already east of Łódź and circling around to the south of the city, while the Russian I Corps, deployed west of Łódź to prepare for the offensive into Germany, now raced east past Łódź to shore up its eastern defenses. It was soon joined by the II Siberian Corps, which made a similar trek from west to east. By 21 November, six Russian corps from the Second and Fifth Armies were clustered in a steadily shrinking arc around Łódź while Scheffer-Boyadel's group to the southeast and the Posen and Breslau Corps to the southwest tried to close the ring around them. The Russian defenders fought desperately to keep the jaws of Mackensen's trap from closing. On 20 November, Ruzskii's telegraph lines from Northwestern Front headquarters to Sheideman and Pleve and their half-encircled armies at Łódź were cut. He had to rely on occasional radio messages relayed out through stations south of the city to get updates and to transfer overall command in the embattled city to Pleve. On the same day, Sheideman got a radio message (not encoded) out via the Russian fortress at Modlin declaring "All reserves expended. Little ammunition. Troops fighting heroically."[20]

By that time, though, the Germans were about to run out of time, and the trappers to find themselves trapped. The three Russian corps that had been shoved east along the Vistula and out of the battle by Mackensen's initial onslaught had now rallied at Łowicz, 50 kilometers northeast of

Łódź. A miscellany of units, including two Cossack cavalry divisions and a main striking force consisting of the II Corps, the 6th Siberian Division, and additional garrison units and infantry brigades, moved south on 20 November. Their target was the rear of the German divisions attacking Łódź from the north and northeast. Their attack threatened to cut off Scheffer-Boyadel's three divisions, trapping them southeast of Łódź and deep behind Russian lines. By the evening of 22 November, help came to Łódź in two forms. *Stavka* reestablished communications with the two armies fighting there, and the Łowicz group hit the Germans attacking Łódź from the north. The Russians captured two key road junctions at Strykow and Bshesiny, which closed Scheffer-Boyadel's avenue of retreat. As was already becoming the pattern, though, Russian maneuvers were parried by quicker and more decisive German responses. Elements of three German divisions north of Łódź—the 35th, 37th, and 41st—did an about-face, turning from south to north to engage the newly arrived Russians in the Łowicz group. At the same time, Scheffer-Boyadel's divisions slackened their pressure on Łódź. They pulled into a defensive perimeter as scattered Russian units closed in on all sides, scenting the possibility of a battle of annihilation with the Germans as the victims. Scheffer-Boyadel and his German reservists never lost their nerve. Just as they had initially circled clockwise in their struggle to surround Łódź, on 23 November they now fought their way counterclockwise to retrace their steps and escape the trap. The Russians, in a position to isolate and destroy three German divisions, only detected the withdrawal after it had already begun, losing vital hours. The Russians observed German columns moving north and empty trenches in front of their own lines only on 24 November. A step too slow to weld shut the ring around Scheffer-Boyadel, the Russians advancing from Łowicz were pushed back, as the Germans north of Łódź switched the focus of their effort from taking Łódź itself to reopening the corridor through which Scheffer-Boyadel could escape. His XXV Reserve Corps fought its way back through Strykow and Bshesiny and the 6th Siberian Division. Scheffer brought out not only 2,000 of his own wounded but several thousand Russian prisoners, and returned to German lines on 25 November. Mackensen's men began to pull back west, recognizing the failure of their gamble at Łódź.

Russian front and army commanders were torn over how to proceed, and Grand Duke Nikolai was, as usual, reluctant to impose a single strategic concept. The Germans were retreating rapidly west, but Russian troops, at least around Warsaw, were exhausted. Those in the south around Krakow were much more optimistic. The deep Russian advances north and south of the Vistula and the presence of Russian armies at the gates of Krakow created some of the same contradictory views—simultaneous pessimism over exhausted troops and exhilaration over potential victory—that had characterized Russian thinking over a potential invasion of Germany early in the fall. The whirlwind campaigns for Poland exhausted Russian reserves and seemed to compel a policy of at least temporary restraint. In order to determine policy for the onset of winter, *Stavka* held a conference at Siedlce on 29–30 November with the two front commanders to get their sense of the proper course of action. What that discussion showed was deep division on the potential for Russian offensive action. In preparation for the meeting, Quartermaster-General Danilov reported that only a relative handful of reserves remained, on the order of a few divisions. Divisions already in line had gone through extraordinarily hard fighting, and badly needed rest, replacement soldiers and officers, and stocks of ammunition. All this did not prevent Danilov, still gripped by a deep commitment to the offensive, from arguing for still more attacks, primarily toward Krakow along the northwestern bank of the Vistula. Ivanov, commanding the Southwestern Front, saw great potential for further offensive action to drive Austria from the war. Third Army commander Radko-Dmitriev, operating southeast of the Vistula, was likewise enthusiastic about continued offensive operations, or at the very least holding in place in their advanced positions. The desperate situation in central Poland trumped all that. The actual conference at Siedlce was dominated by the exceedingly vulnerable position of Russian units west of the Vistula, vulnerable to German attack and worn down by the attrition of the previous months' campaigning and their pursuit of the Germans retreating from Warsaw and Łódź. Even as Mackensen prepared to retreat from his overextended positions, Ruzskii was arguing as early as 23 November for the need for the Russians to pull back eastward once the armies trapped in Łódź were freed. By the end of November, he had convinced *Stavka* of the need for a tactical withdrawal. He had no stomach for further offensives, and hoped for withdrawal back toward the fortified bridgeheads at Warsaw and Dęblin. He could rightly claim that his ranks were too thinned to maintain their positions as far west as they were: one division was reduced to 15 officers and 2,000 men. The *average* strength of Russia's fighting battalions across both the Northwestern and Southwestern Fronts was one-third of their statutory level. Ammunition shortages had already affected Russian operations at the time of the fighting around Warsaw. Half of arriving reinforcements lacked rifles.[21]

Russia's more optimistic generals were finally checked by two things: first, Ruzskii's insistence on withdrawing his own troops in central Poland left Ivanov little alternative to doing the same. Second, the Germans launched a major counteroffensive. After Mackensen withdrew his troops from their attempt to encircle Łódź, he received four additional corps from the Western Front, which he used for a renewed attempt to break through Russian lines west of Łódź. That city, for which the Russians had fought so hard, was still only a dozen kilometers behind the front lines and a vulnerable target. On 30 November, the newly arrived German II Corps advanced rapidly through thinly stretched defenses of the Russian XIX Corps southwest of Łódź, threatening to encircle the city from the south. Łódź itself was well defended by three Russian corps, but that would do little good if the city was enveloped and cut off. Another newly arrived corps, the German III Reserve, pushed up the Vistula toward Warsaw. Since *Stavka* had already ordered a withdrawal to a more defensible position, the Russian armies in central Poland—the Fifth, Second, and First—did not put up a serious fight and instead retreated. Łódź was abandoned in early December and never recovered, and the Russians established a new line on the Bzura and Rawka Rivers, east of Łódź and west of Warsaw.

Both sides now took stock of their positions after months of uninterrupted campaigning. Troops settled into positional warfare and established more elaborate trench systems. Prior to that point, soldiers routinely dug field fortifications, but the front lines had advanced and retreated so rapidly that there was little time to establish the elaborate networks of trenches and bunkers characteristic of warfare on the Western Front. South of the Vistula, local offensives by Ivanov's Southwestern Front failed to make substantial progress, and finally halted by the end of December. As the relentless pace of offensive and counteroffensive finally slowed at the end of the year, following six months of relentless campaigning, the Russian high command cleaned house. Rennenkampf, whose command of the First Army continued to be lackluster, was relieved of duty and replaced by Aleksandr Litvinov; Sheideman at the Second Army was likewise replaced by Vladimir Smirnov.[22]

Though the battles at Łódź cost the Russians territory, their armies escaped encirclement and annihilation. This was particularly important, as Russia's supply of fresh formations was already beginning to dry up (Austria-Hungary was in the same situation). Russia's enormous size and relatively slow mobilization had been a double-edged sword. While Russia began the fighting in 1914 without its full complement of manpower and units, it necessarily enjoyed a steady stream of reinforcements as those units finally made it to the front. The massive battles of 1914 in Galicia, Poland, and the Carpathians took a terrible toll on all the combatants, but particularly on Austria-Hungary. It had the smallest population of the three empires at war, and its chronically underfunded military had the smallest officer corps—30,000 at the outbreak of war. By the end of 1914, its officer casualties (predominantly suffered against Russia, though some against Serbia) amounted to 4,800 dead, 12,000 wounded, 11,200 sick, and 4,700 missing or captured, totaling 32,700, or more than the prewar total. Some of the sick and wounded would return to duty, and many of those casualties were suffered by mobilized reserve officers and new trainees. Nonetheless, the impact of those early campaigns on the experience and cohesion of the Austro-Hungarian officer corps was immense. Its losses among rank-and-file soldiers were a staggering 1.3 million killed, wounded, sick, and captured from an army that in peacetime had only 450,000 men. Russia was hardly better—by the end of 1914, its frontline armies were half a million men short of their full complement of soldiers. Both sides were desperate for some respite from the fighting. A *Stavka* conference at Brest on 13 December resolved to halt offensive action temporarily, withdrawing as necessary to more defensible positions. As badly as the Russians needed time to mobilize manpower and replenish stocks of war materiel, the Austrians and Germans would not allow it.[23]

6

The Masurian Lakes and the Carpathians, Winter 1914–1915

The brief halt at the end of 1914 and the beginning of 1915 was only a short-lived respite from high-intensity campaigning. Despite the terrible losses of the first six months of the war, the Russian high command continued to think in offensive terms. The only question was the proper theater. Russia enjoyed an overall numerical advantage on the Eastern Front: almost one hundred Russian divisions against around eighty-five German and Austrian.[1] While this was not overwhelming, the extended length of the front gave Russia the potential to choose a point at which to mass superior force. This opportunity was, however, squandered. A dispute over the proper point of maximum effort—against Germany in the north or against Austria-Hungary in the Carpathians—led Grand Duke Nikolai Nikolaevich and *Stavka* to make precisely the same mistake as at the beginning of the war: failing to impose clear priorities on Russia's commanders and thereby splitting resources between the two theaters, providing adequate support for neither. *Stavka* made East Prussia the main theater, but failed to ensure that Ivanov, commander of the Southwestern Front, subordinated his own goals and priorities to Russia's overall grand strategy. In January 1915, unlike at the outbreak of war, the Russians even lacked the excuse that the plight of their French ally mandated an offensive against Germany. Russia had a free choice at the beginning of 1915, but its high command failed to choose. Russian indecision allowed the Central Powers to carry out dangerous offensives of their own.

At *Stavka*, Quartermaster-General Danilov believed Russia lacked the resources to launch two major offensives, particularly before newly trained
recruits and stocks of ammunition arrived, and so had to choose its priorities carefully. In mid-January 1915 he proposed two options: to attack directly west out of the Polish salient toward Berlin, or instead to strike at
East Prussia. Since a move directly on Berlin was too vulnerable to counterattacks on its flanks, he advocated clearing East Prussia prior to a subsequent attack on Berlin itself. Chief of Staff Yanushkevich agreed. The next
question was how to attack East Prussia. On its eastern frontier, north of
the Masurian Lakes, the Russian Tenth Army under Faddei Sivers possessed twice as many divisions as the eight facing it in the German Eighth
Army, but German positions were well-fortified and Sivers lacked the
heavy artillery and ammunition to grind through them. Prospects looked
better on the northern face of the Polish salient, where an Russian offensive
might advance either directly north into East Prussia or northwest along
the Vistula. Ruzskii, commander of the Northwestern Front, argued that
available manpower should be employed to create a new Twelfth Army,
based south of East Prussia along the line of Russian fortifications on the
Biebrza and Narew Rivers to attack northwest into the southern face of East
Prussia at Mława. By attacking on a broad front stretching from the Russian fortress at Modlin east to the Masurian Lakes, Ruzskii's plan repeated
the concept of Samsonov's invasion in 1914. Like Samsonov's doomed offensive, Ruzskii's attack offered the tantalizing hope of cutting through to
the Baltic Sea and clearing all territory east of the Vistula from German control. After a *Stavka* conference at Siedlce on 17 January, Ruzskii received
Grand Duke Nikolai's approval to proceed with this plan. The grand duke
transferred Pavel Pleve, a General Staff officer with combat experience in
the Russo-Turkish and Russo-Japanese Wars, to command of the new
Twelfth Army from the Fifth, replacing him as Fifth Army commander with
Aleksei Churin. The start date for the new invasion of East Prussia was set
as 23 February.[2]

Lack of clear strategic direction meant that Russian efforts and resources
were divided, for this emphasis on the Northwestern Front sat poorly with
those who saw Austria-Hungary as the more vulnerable target. Ivanov,
commanding the Southwestern Front, had a quite different view of Russia's proper priorities and prepared his own offensive to knock Austria
from the war. He considered and rejected attacking either west in Poland

along the Vistula or alternatively south into Bukovina, where the Austro-Russian border met Romania. Together with his chief of staff, Alekseev, Ivanov planned for Brusilov's Eighth Army to break through the Carpathians into the Hungarian plain with the assistance of elements of Radko-Dmitriev's Third Army to its northwest, thus attacking through mountains in the dead of winter.[3]

The Central Powers were planning their own initiatives for the early months of 1915. German strategy, for neither the first nor the last time in the war, showed terrible defects. The German-Austrian alliance fell victim to crippling division of effort, just as the Russian. Falkenhayn, chief of the German General Staff, faced a fundamental decision at the end of 1914. The German Army had scraped together a strategic reserve by thinning its divisions, converting from square organization, where each division had four regiments, to triangular organization with three. At the same time, artillery batteries were reduced from six guns to four. While this necessarily reduced manpower and firepower of individual divisions, the Germans counted on greater efficiency and their man-for-man, unit-for-unit advantage in tactical and operational effectiveness to make up any shortfalls. This produced a net gain of four corps as a new strategic reserve. The question was how to use it. German hopes for a quick victory in the west had been disappointed, and now Falkenhayn had to determine what to do: continue to hammer away in the relatively confined space of the Western Front, or instead turn the bulk of German power east against Russia? Wary of the industrial and human resources of the British Empire, Falkenhayn believed the key to victory lay in the west, through attrition, submarine warfare, and careful husbanding of German resources.[4]

For the moment, Falkenhayn enjoyed the support and confidence of Kaiser Wilhelm, but his views on strategy were opposed by a substantial coalition, notably Hindenburg and Ludendorff backed by the Habsburgs. At a series of meetings in December 1914 and January 1915, Conrad argued for the importance of campaigning against Russia, not least to relieve the surrounded Austrian garrison of Przemyśl. He proposed an offensive in the Carpathians, intended to rescue Przemyśl and push the Russians away from Austrian territory. Hindenburg and Ludendorff supported this idea, since it entailed a coordinated German attack on the northern flank of the Polish salient to draw Russian reserves away from the Austrian relief of Przemyśl. Conrad's plan offered a pair of things that always attracted Hindenburg and Ludendorff: grandiose scale and self-glorification. The two men, conscious of the power their victories in 1914 had given them, argued to the point of insubordination for putting the main effort in the east. Victory in the west, Hindenburg later said, "could only be reached over the body of a Russia stricken to the ground." Falkenhayn was more skeptical. Germany could not afford to strip more troops from the west, and he saw no way that four German corps, thrown into the vast spaces of the east, could win a decisive victory against Russia. In addition, the rough terrain of the Carpathians was perfect for chewing up scarce and skilled German soldiers without permitting German operational superiority to come into play. The Russians could (and later did) lose huge swathes of territory without being driven from the war, and Britain and France could (and later did) keep fighting after Russian defeat. Falkenhayn therefore wanted to use Germany's four new army corps in the west. His plans came apart along with the Austrian war effort. Fighting in Galicia and the Carpathians had exhausted Austrian reserves, leaving no reinforcements for Austria's Serbian front, where the Serbs had already inflicted a humiliating defeat on the Austrians. Directed by Kaiser Wilhelm to assist the Austrians, Falkenhayn resigned himself to maintaining a defensive position in the west and using his new formations in the endless spaces of the east, under "the conviction that Austria-Hungary must otherwise collapse in a short time."[5]

As a result, the precious four corps Falkenhayn had scraped together went east to Hindenburg to create a new German Tenth Army for offensive operations out of East Prussia. Hindenburg's concrete plan focused on the destruction of the Russian Tenth Army, screening the eastern border of East Prussia. The Russian Tenth Army was particularly vulnerable, as its right flank hung more or less in air, depending on the remoteness of theater and a thin cavalry screen to prevent German outflanking maneuvers. Its left flank at the Masurian Lakes was poorly connected to the newly forming Russian Twelfth Army, which was itself more focused on preparing its forthcoming offensive than forestalling German attacks. Hindenburg intended a lightning double-envelopment of the Russian Tenth Army, using his left wing in the north (the new German Tenth Army under Hermann von Eichhorn) to sweep around the Russian right wing on the Nieman River, while in the south his right wing (the German Eighth Army under Otto von Below) attacked east from the Masurian Lakes around the Russian left wing. The two German spearheads converged on the Augustów

Forest. If successful, this envelopment created opportunities beyond simply destroying the Russian Tenth Army: the path to Petrograd, though distant, lay open, or German troops could turn south to roll up the four Russian armies in Poland. The Germans massed a substantial predominance
in manpower: perhaps 250,000 men to the 125,000 in the Russian Tenth
Army. Conrad, as usual, had his own ideas about the proper course for the
Eastern Front. Desperate to relieve his besieged troops at Przemyśl and remove the danger of Russia's forcing a passage through the Carpathians
into Hungary, Conrad agreed with Hindenburg that the Eastern Front
should receive priority in allocation of troops and supplies. His forces had
been so weakened by the battles of 1914, however, that his armies received
German divisions to stiffen his own wavering armies, and he planned an
offensive to liberate Przemyśl.

THE AUGUSTÓW OFFENSIVE AGAINST THE TENTH ARMY

Faddei Sivers, commander of the Tenth Army, came from a Danish-
Swedish family with a long and distinguished history of service in the
Russian military. On taking command of the Tenth Army on the East Prussian frontier, he actively probed the German front lines for possible weaknesses. His first attacks in early October tried but failed to break through
German defenses in front of Stallupönen and Gumbinnen, where fighting
had begun in 1914, and had only slight success advancing into German prepared defenses around the Masurian Lakes. Follow-up attacks in November had more success. Initial assaults on 7–8 November by the Russian XX
Corps south of Stallupönen made no progress, but renewed attacks on
12–13 November, combined with a successful cavalry attack around the
northern end of the German line, proved more effective. As Russian cavalry threatened to cut Stallupönen's road west to Gumbinnen and the rest
of East Prussia, the Germans withdrew to more defensible positions. By
late December, the German line lay roughly along the Angrapa River, well
inside the prewar frontier. In late January and early February, Russian
troops on the far northern flank of Sivers's army continued tactical attacks
to improve their positions for the offensive they expected to begin soon. In
preparation for the Twelfth Army's offensive, planned for mid-February,
Russian cavalry also swept regions along the border to hinder German re-

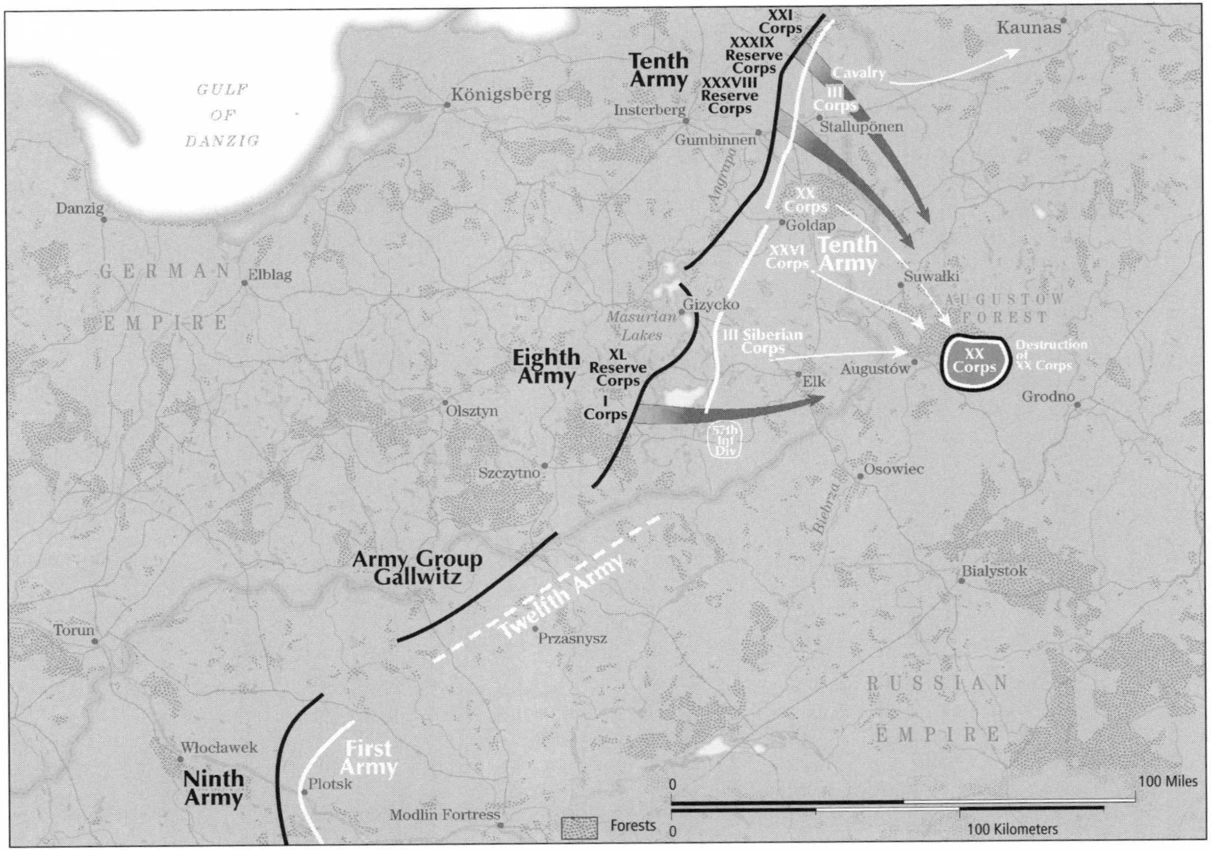

Map 7. The Augustów Forest, February 1915

connaissance. While certainly Russian successes, these small-scale en-
counters prepared the ground for later defeat: the Russians had little time
to prepare positional defenses on their newly seized ground. Finally, an
otherwise insignificant German diversionary attack on 31 January against
the Russian Second Army at Bolimów, between Łódź and Warsaw, used
poison gas for the first time. The agent, xylyl bromide, was not especially
effective since cold weather hindered the gas from forming a cloud of sufficient concentration to be lethal.[6]

Sivers's offensive spirit meant that the Tenth Army was deployed for attack rather than defense, aiming to coordinate with the Twelfth Army's
planned offensive. The bulk of his force consisted of four corps, stretched
in a long, thin, cordon northeast from the Masurian Lakes, from the III
Siberian through the XXVI, XX, and III Corps. He had few forces in reserve,
and his right flank was protected only by a cavalry screen. Given the limited German forces he thought he faced, this forward deployment did not
seem risky. He evidently expected only limited German actions. Unlike
other Austro-German offensives, where deserters, prisoner interrogations,
and Russian aerial reconnaissance provided some warning of German concentrations, winter conditions in forested East Prussia meant that Sivers
was wholly unaware of the mass of German troops in front of him. In ac-
tuality, Sivers was in grave danger: the Germans had carefully assembled
eight corps to his four. They were deployed in massive force opposite both
his wings, including a task force of three corps opposite his lightly defended right wing. The Russians and Germans alike were preparing for attack in February 1915; the Germans moved first.[7]

The Russian Twelfth Army's offensive was planned for 20 February and
the Tenth Army's for 23 February; the preemptive German attack came on
7 February.[8] The first blow against the Russian Tenth Army came from von
Below's Eighth Army. On the far southern end of Sivers's positions, a task
force under Karl Litzmann (the German XL Reserve Corps and elements
of the I Corps) emerged from the tangle of woods and lakes of the Johan-
nisburg Forest to smash through the Russian left flank, defended only by
cavalry and a single infantry division. Following the prewar border as it
moved from west to east, Litzmann's divisions outflanked a series of potential Russian defensive lines, bypassing them on the south. The III Siberian Corps found its own left wing swinging back, forced to retreat or be
encircled. Despite the danger, this southern wing of the Tenth Army

fought effectively and withdrew southeast in good order, fighting the whole way.

The heavier blow came on 10 February, when von Eichhorn's three corps on the German left wing, undetected by Russian reconnaissance, emerged from the forests north of Gumbinnen. This German Tenth Army was an enormously powerful strike force. Leaving a *Landwehr* division to maintain a connection with von Below's Eighth Army, six divisions of the XXXVIII, XXXIX, and XXI Corps moved as a tight, irresistible mass southeast behind the Russian Tenth Army's positions. Winter weather made it difficult for Sivers to judge what he was facing, and he only slowly grasped how grave his situation was. Having missed the buildup of German power against him, he could not conceive that there were significant troops left for an offensive on his right wing, given the scale of the threat on his left. Despite the collapse of both his flanks, he ordered only a slow and partial withdrawal, creating a real possibility that his four corps might be surrounded and annihilated, surpassing Samsonov's disaster six months before. Lacking significant reserves, he had nothing to throw in the path of the oncoming German left wing to slow his encirclement and destruction.

Sivers's partial and orderly withdrawal threatened to become a rout when the III Corps on his far right buckled and broke on 11 February under the weight of the German flanking attack. German advancing troops moved faster than the Russians could turn their defenses from west to north to meet them. German spearheads seized the town of Kudirkos Naumiestis and then cut the railroad east to Kaunas. Much of the III Corps withdrew east toward Kaunas, leaving the right flank of the XX Corps open to German attack as it retreated. The rest of Sivers's Tenth Army was increasingly compressed into a smaller space as it pulled back toward the Augustów Forest. The lines of communication, supply, and retreat for the XX and the XXVI Corps in Sivers's center came under increasing threat. Over the objections of Northwestern Front commander Ruzskii, still fixated on the forthcoming Russian offensive against East Prussia, Sivers ordered a retreat on 11 February, and followed this with a subsequent instruction to his corps on 13 February to withdraw all the way to the Nieman River. He sent his XX Corps east and the XXVI southeast toward the Augustów Forest, while the III Siberian conducted a fighting withdrawal to maintain connections between Sivers and the line of Russian fortifications on the Biebrza and Narew Rivers to the southwest. Sivers hoped his troops' retreat could escape the rapidly closing German net, but his actions were too late. As of 16 February, the Northwestern Front's headquarters thought Sivers's army was doomed.

In sending his XX Corps east, Sivers underestimated the speed and power of the three German corps moving around his right flank. Burdened by poor communications and delayed realization of the extent of the danger, by 14 February the XX Corps was trapped at Suwałki with escape east blocked by German spearheads. It had no choice but instead to turn south into the Augustów Forest, where the XXVI Corps was already in retreat. Two full Russian corps sought refuge on narrow tracks through the dense old-growth wood, slowing their withdrawal further. On 15 February, the German troops that had penetrated furthest east began skirting south around the eastern fringes of the forest to cut off any exit, threatening the complete encirclement of Sivers's embattled army. Moving clockwise, German troops closed road after road. Sivers had to sacrifice some of his troops to save others. He ordered the XX Corps, furthest to the north, to screen Suwałki and the road leading south to the town of Augustów so that the XXVI and III Siberian could escape through the only route still open. By 17 February, those two corps had fled to relative safety on the south bank of the Biebrza River. The XX Corps was not so fortunate. Left with only the dense Augustów forest as its exit, the increasingly scattered units of the XX Corps fought bravely, inflicting severe losses on the German 42nd Division as they battled southeast through the forests in hope of escape. Only with ammunition exhausted and the German ring complete did the last elements of the corps—the better part of four divisions—surrender on 21–22 February. Sivers had given up hope on 21 February, canceling any efforts to break through the German ring. Thirty thousand prisoners (including nearly a dozen generals) went into German captivity.

While the German Tenth and Eighth Armies attacked east out of the East Prussia, an improvised German task force of mismatched infantry and cavalry under the overall command of Max von Gallwitz attacked south out of East Prussia against Russian defenses on the Narew–Biebrza river line. One focus was to the northeast against the Osowiec fortress on the Biebrza, close to Sivers's embattled Tenth Army. Osowiec had been built in the 1880s, and its main citadel lay on ground above the marshy lowlands of the Biebrza, where an important railroad ran northwest from Białystok toward Königsberg. The fortress had already seen action in the first weeks of the war, when it held the hinge of the Russian line between Rennenkampf's

First Army and the shattered remnants of Samsonov's Second Army. German attacks on Osowiec began on 16 February 1915, but geography made their efforts difficult. In the marshes along the Biebrza, solid ground funneled German attacks into a strongly held Russian forward position, which lay in an arc 8–10 kilometers northwest of the central bastion of the fortress, just within range of Russian heavy artillery. The fortress's defenders thus benefited from the prewar Russian strategy of relying on fortresses and heavy guns to protect the Polish salient. Possessing seventy heavy guns, including thirty-nine 152mm cannon, they pounded the relatively restricted avenues of German approach through the marshes. After five days of fierce resistance that cost the Germans 5–6,000 killed and wounded, the Russian defenders staged a night withdrawal, pulling back into a second defensive line closer to the main fortress. The Germans continued to pound this line from 22 to 24 February, but again without breaking through to the fortress or forcing further Russian withdrawal. Taking the outermost Russian defenses put German artillery in range of the main fortress, however, and on 25 February sixty to seventy German heavy guns began smashing Russian positions with the aid of aerial correction, reducing brick and wood installations to rubble. Despite the constant pounding, the Russians maintained their perimeter around the fort and managed to hold it through summer 1915.[9]

Von Gallwitz also struck the northern flank of the Polish salient at Przasnysz with the idea of cutting off Warsaw. His 18 February attack was two-pronged, aiming at encircling Przasnysz from the west and east. To the west, stiff Russian infantry resistance blocked one wing of the envelopment. To the east, however, the troops of the I Reserve Corps swept past Przasnysz, then wheeled in behind the town and stormed it on 24–25 February. Von Gallwitz could not preserve his gains, for he lacked strategic reconnaissance. Poor weather and lack of aircraft meant that he was surprised by a vigorous Russian counteroffensive, ordered on 23 February even before Przasnysz fell. The I and II Siberian Corps followed the German east wing as it circled around Przasnysz, driving the Germans from the town by 27 February. The Russians pushed the remnants of the I Reserve Corps 20–25 kilometers to the northwest and took 10,000 German prisoners. Only a sharp rearguard action kept the Russian pursuit from doing even more damage to the German position.[10]

Despite the loss of the XX Corps in the Augustów Forest, matters could have been far worse in the wake of February's fighting in the north. When presented with an opportunity to collapse and disintegrate, the Russian army showed remarkable ability to recover, parrying Austro-German efforts to shatter its cohesion and drive it from the war altogether. Though badly battered, three of the four corps in Sivers's Tenth Army remained intact—the III at Kaunas and the III Siberian and XXVI at Grodno. They had been reinforced by the hasty dispatch of two additional corps, the II and XV, to shore up Russian defenses. Sivers's men had even managed a counterattack, albeit unsuccessful, to break through to the encircled XX Corps before its surrender. Successful defense of Russian fortresses left no open path south for a renewed German offensive to roll up the Russians in Poland, and the exhausted German troops of the Eighth and Tenth Armies needed time to rest, reorganize, and replenish their supplies before any further action. Nonetheless, Sivers was cashiered for his defeat and died soon after.

The Russian offensive, originally intended for 20 and 23 February but preempted by the German offensive, finally began on 2 March. Though grandiose in the forces involved (three armies: the First, Twelfth, and Tenth), the exhausting struggles of February meant that major gains could no longer be expected. Grand Duke Nikolai had specifically declared on 1 March that "it is impossible given the current state of our troops and their resources to cross our border into East Prussia. . . . The task of the troops of the Northwestern Front is limited to inflicting short, sharp blows with pursuit extending only to the border." No longer an effort to expel the Germans from East Prussia, the offensive sought only to restore the prewar frontier. This goal was aided by the German decision to withdraw some troops from East Prussia, either to serve on the Western Front or to assist the hard-pressed Austrians in Galicia. Russian frontier attacks met small-scale German counterattacks, including renewed fighting north of the Augustów Forest and a second German attack on Przasnysz. After inconclusive results and limited advances, *Stavka* called a halt to any further Russian offensives on 15 March. Exhausted and sick, Ruzskii stepped down as commander of the Northwestern Front. He was replaced by Alekseev, a favorite of Grand Duke Nikolai transferred north from his position as chief of staff for the Southwestern Front. As Alekseev had never supported the invasion of East Prussia, he was well-placed to wind down the Russian offensive. The winter fighting had done substantial damage to

both sides, costing the Germans 80,000 casualties, including 14,000 prisoners. Russian losses were unquestionably greater, though nonetheless exaggerated by German wartime propaganda: the Tenth Army alone lost at
least 56,000, including the almost complete annihilation of the XX Corps.
Total losses were perhaps 200,000 casualties with 90,000 taken prisoner.
Those lost to the Germans as prisoners could never return to the front lines,
unlike a substantial number of wounded soldiers who recovered to fight
another day. Despite those casualties, the fighting in the north over the first
months of 1915 did not provide the Germans with the strategic victory that
Hindenburg and Ludendorff had craved. Russia lost no vital territory, nor
was the captured ground especially useful to the Germans. Russia's larger
population still allowed it to sustain personnel losses that far outstripped
German casualties.[11]

Fighting in the north was still not yet complete. Through March 1915,
combat had centered on the eastern and southern borders of East Prussia.
Little combat had taken place on East Prussia's northeast frontier, facing
the port of Liepāja and beyond it, Riga. This relative quiescence led the
Russians to leave that section of the frontier largely unguarded. In an effort to penalize this short-sightedness and force the Russians to extend their
forces to cover the full length of the frontier, the German high command
assembled a task force under Otto von Lauenstein. Consisting of only three
cavalry and three infantry divisions, it crossed the frontier on 27 April.
Sending his cavalry racing ahead to cut the Liepāja–Vilnius railroad, then
cooperating with the German navy to take Liepāja on 7 May, Lauenstein
rapidly consolidated his control over a large swath of the Baltic shore.
Stavka had to deploy the Fifth Army under Pleve for defense of the Baltic,
from the seashore to the Nieman River.[12]

WINTER BATTLES IN THE CARPATHIANS

The simultaneous fighting in the south, where the Austrians bore the chief
burden, showed that German superiority on the battlefield was counter-
balanced by Austrian strategic and operational deficits. Austrian Chief of
Staff Conrad sent his army into a quixotic three-month campaign in the
frozen heights of the Carpathians, which further devastated divisions already hard hit by the fighting of 1914. In January 1915, the Russian South-

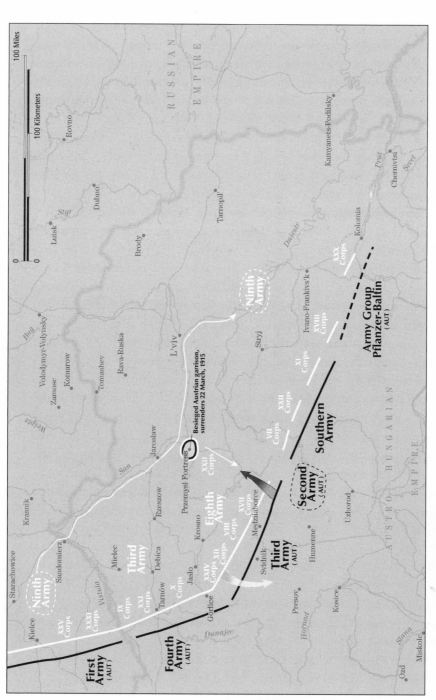

Map 8. The Carpathians, January 1915

western Front lay essentially along the crest of the Carpathians, stretching from the Romanian border in the southeast (thinly manned by both sides) roughly north and west to Gorlice, where the front line turned north. This meant that action by either side would necessarily take place in horrendous conditions: at high elevations in the middle of winter. Nonetheless, both sides prepared ambitious attacks. The Russian plan was for the main strike to come from the armies southeast of the Vistula, in order to break through the Carpathians into the Hungarian plain. An advance down out of the mountains would not only have an enormous political impact in Hungary, but enable a subsequent attack west toward Krakow.

The events in East Prussia—a planned Russian attack interrupted by a Central Powers offensive—were paralleled by similar developments in the Carpathians. While Ivanov and Alekseev were arguing for and preparing an offensive by the Southwestern Front, the Germans and Austrians were preparing to preempt Russian actions by an offensive of their own. Conrad desperately needed a victory to shore up his own battered personal standing and to keep neutral Bulgaria, Italy, and Romania from joining the Allies. Temporarily abandoning efforts to drive Serbia from the war, Austria-Hungary transferred troops to the Russian front. Germany as well moved forces to the Austrian sector to bolster its ally. Conrad's plans for his new offensive lacked all subtlety; these consisted of a general assault along a frontage of over 300 kilometers running to the Romanian border, carried out by the equivalent of four armies. On both flanks, the Austrian effort was largely diversionary: to the far northwest, the Austrian Fourth Army had been stripped of much of its manpower to provide troops for other sectors. To the far southeast, a task force named for its commander, Karl von Pflanzer-Baltin (one of Austria's better field commanders), was hardly larger than a corps, poorly equipped, manned by substandard conscripts, and intended primarily to distract Russian efforts through a mobile offensive over thinly held ground. The main burden of the offensive fell on the two armies in the center: the Austrian Third Army under Svetozar Boroević and the Southern Army, commanded by the German Alexander von Linsingen but including both German and Austrian units. Conrad's hope was that his troops, aided by the better German divisions, could smash through Brusilov's Eighth Army to relieve Przemyśl.[13]

On 22 January 1915, the Central Powers opened their attack, stretching along nearly the whole length of the Southwestern Front, with preliminary attacks in limited sectors and a full-scale assault the next day. Its progress depended greatly on the observer's vantage point. Fighting under horrific conditions and suffering terrible losses from the cold, Austrian troops particularly suffered from poor supplies as a result of limited railroad net from Budapest into the southwestern slopes of the Carpathians. The Austrian Third Army's left wing managed no gains at all. The Third Army's right, however, did manage some limited local successes: Paul Puhallo von Brlog commanded a two-corps task force (the V and XVIII) that pushed back the left wing of Brusilov's Eighth Army and struggled toward Przemyśl. These initial Austrian successes were quite limited. At the junction with the German Southern Army, Puhallo managed to advance only 10–15 kilometers against a front held mostly by Russian cavalry, ill-prepared for static defense, before the Austrian advance lost momentum. Even this success, however, put Puhallo's troops into grave danger as their own advance outdistanced supporting troops to their right and left. All sectors of the Austrian advance produced little besides a few kilometers of territory, frozen horses, and Carpathian passes filled with Austrian dead.[14]

Ivanov wanted to counterattack but believed he needed more manpower. Two days after the start of the Austro-German offensive, shaken by Puhallo's limited advances, Ivanov begged *Stavka* for reinforcements, but without initial result. *Stavka* was concerned about the developing German offensive in the north, and felt Ivanov had ample resources to contain the Austrian offensive without additional troops. Reconsidering this judgment as Brusilov was slowly forced backward, on 26 January *Stavka* did finally send the XXII Corps from Ruzskii's Northwestern Front to halt the Austrian push. Ivanov hoped for the XV Corps as well, but the destruction of the XX Corps at Augustów made it impossible for *Stavka* to transfer additional resources from the north. Though this was not all that Ivanov had hoped for, it was enough for him to respond to the slow Austrian advance with a counterattack. He had already planned on Brusilov's Eighth Army attacking. As the Austrians pushed back Brusilov's left, on 2 February Ivanov ordered an attack by Brusilov's right, toward Prešov and Humenné. In effect, the Russian counterattack would swung around the Austrian advance like a revolving door. The Russian Eighth Army's hammering counterattack, carried out by the XII, XXIV, and VIII Corps against exhausted and frozen Habsburg troops, advanced 15–20 kilometers and took thousands of prisoners, brought the Austrian advances on its left wing to a halt, and seized the key railroad station at Medzilaborce by 5 February. The Austrian offensive had cost it 90,000 casualties from the 165,000 men Conrad had poured into the battle. The German-commanded Southern Army, to the Austrian Third Army's right, did little better in coping with the terrain, the weather, and the dogged Russian defense.[15]

After Brusilov's Eighth Army carried its successful counteroffensive on its right, it then rolled back the limited gains Puhallo had scratched out on its left. Since Ruzskii's hard-pressed Northwestern Front could provide no reinforcement, Ivanov instead weakened his Ninth Army to the southeast in order to strengthen the Eighth. Conrad was forced into a series of desperate countermeasures. The Austrian Fourth Army, holding the front line to the left of the exhausted Austrian Third Army, attacked on 10 February. It had itself been stripped of formations to bolster the initial Austrian offensive, so could do little but provide a distraction. Conrad also deployed an additional army, the Second, between the Third and the German Southern to stop the Russian advance and, if possible, rekindle a breakthrough. As a result, Brusilov failed to make further headway against stubborn Austrian defenses and even more frustrating geographic and climactic conditions.[16]

To the southeast, the Austrian task force under von Pflanzer-Baltin conducted an ambitious mobile campaign, taking advantage of low unit densities and the weakened Russian Ninth Army in the remote region where the Austrian, Russian, and Romanian frontiers came together. In January 1915, the front had stabilized roughly along the prewar border. Moving to the attack in late January and early February in conjunction with the Austrian offensive toward Przemyśl, von Pflanzer-Baltin in rapid succession shifted his operations from east to west along his front. Despite terrible cold and troops consisting largely of *Landsturm* militia, he managed to push back the Russian Dniestr forces and draw in reserves that the Russians badly needed elsewhere. He first trapped Russian forces against the Romanian border, shifted northwest to seize Chernivtsi by mid-February, grabbed Kolomyia shortly after, and finally found his lightning advance frustrated at Kalush, where a hastily assembled force, primarily the Russian II Cavalry and the XI Corps, managed to save the town and contain his advance at the end of February. He then had to give ground throughout March and abandon some of the territory he had taken. Skillfully using cavalry to cover the gaps between his thinly spread infantry divisions, he conducted a mobile withdrawal that kept several Russian corps committed against him rather than fighting elsewhere.

Pflanzer-Baltin's local successes notwithstanding, the Russians had coped quite well with the Austrian offensive. The problem was how to proceed. Ivanov repeatedly insisted that victory in the Carpathians was close and that only a few divisions stripped from East Prussia would allow his troops to break into the Hungarian plain and knock Austria-Hungary out of the war. This would be, of course, a direct rejection of the restrained policy *Stavka* had earlier endorsed. At a conference at Siedlce on 17 February, Ivanov was left in no doubt that his task was to hold his position, not to dream of breaking through the Carpathians. Indeed, his fixation on the Carpathians had left the Dniestr troops so weak, enabling Pflanzer-Baltin's successes, that *Stavka* compelled him to reinforce his far southeastern flank by trasferring the Ninth Army there.[17]

Obsessed with his Carpathian offensive and driven by his concern for his encircled troops at Przemyśl, Conrad was frantic to try a renewed offensive despite the failure of his first. He pushed Eduard von Böhm-Ermolli, commander of the newly deployed Second Army, to attack immediately. Böhm-Ermolli doubted the capacity of his army to achieve anything, given the continuing poor weather and the exhausted state of the armies on his flanks. In addition, he had good reason to doubt the capacity of his own troops—roughly half his divisions were not actual reinforcements, but instead thoroughly wrung-out divisions transferred on paper from the Third Army to the Second. Conrad would not be denied, and as soon as weather cleared the Second Army attacked Russian positions on 27 February 1915. The same circumstances—skilled Russian defense, difficult terrain, and horrific weather—produced the same outcome: failed attacks and massive Austrian casualties before the offensive was called off in early March. Brusilov's Eighth Army engaged in constant limited, local counterattacks that took advantage of the depleted condition of Habsburg units and kept the Austrians off-balance. Brusilov's Eighth Army, particularly its VIII Corps, continued to make slow but steady progress against Austrian units that had exhausted themselves in fruitless attacks.[18]

As Conrad's own offensive ceased, Austrian exhaustion and overcommitment to a narrow sector aimed at Przemyśl seemed to the Russian high command to offer the opportunity for a more decisive counteroffensive, finally offering Ivanov the opportunity he had been begging for. On 10 March, Ivanov ordered preparations for a far more ambitious attack, centered on Svidník and Medzilaborce to break through the Austrian Third Army and then turn southeast down the far slopes of the Carpathians, cutting off the German Southern and the Austrian Fifth Armies. *Stavka* confirmed Ivanov's plan on 19 March, putting the Northwestern Front on a defensive footing in order to allow the Southwestern Front to pursue its grandiose goals. Yanushkevich suggested "actively . . . advancing in the general direction of Budapest and further to envelop the entire line of Krakow, Poznan, and Torun." This might, Yanushkevich speculated, even convince Romania to join the Allies.[19] The major Russian offensive began that same day, carried out primarily by two corps on the left wing of the Third Army—the XXIV and XII—and the Eighth Army's rightmost corps— the VIII. It aimed at the vulnerable junction of the Austrian Third and Second Armies, where the Russians had already fought their way through much of the Carpathians. A secondary but still dangerous attack focused further west on the junction between the Austrian Fourth and Third Armies. Though the advance began slowly as a result of difficult terrain, the Austrians were near collapse after their repeated and disastrous offensives. By the end of March, elements of the Russian Third Army had managed to advance most of the way through the Carpathians, threatening further moves down river valleys through the Carpathian foothills into the Austrian rear. A massive section of the Austrian line—from the right flank of the Fourth Army through the Third and to the left flank of the Second— was in imminent danger of full collapse. Once past the Carpathians, the broad open spaces of the Hungarian plain, tailor-made for Cossack ravaging, lay defenseless.[20]

Precisely as the Russians were crossing the crest of the Carpathians and threatening to break out southward, the Austro-Hungarian garrison of besieged Przemyśl finally fell. The reduction of the fortress had been assigned to Andrei Selivanov's Eleventh Army, but Przemyśl was a formidable defensive position, with an outer ring of bunkers and strongpoints 10 to 15 kilometers in diameter, and an inner ring round the town itself. Though the Russians could not take the fortress by storm, starvation proved effective. As matters deteriorated inside the fortress, cats sold for 10 kroner and dogs for 25, but the thoroughbred horses of the Austrian officers remained sacrosanct. With supplies running out, the fortress garrison launched one final desperate attempt to break the Russian ring on 19 March. Attacking *east*, away from Austrian lines, a force of approximately three divisions in strength moved against the Russian trenches, but failed to make serious headway before a flank attack against the right wing of the breakout ended any hope of success. The fortress surrendered three days later, on 22 March 1915. After the fortress finally fell, a Russian officer described "the most horrible sight I have ever seen in war . . . Hungarian soldiers, crazed for want of food, their hands and faces smeared with blood as they devoured the raw and dripping bits of flesh, gouged with their knives and fingers from the dead bodies of newly-killed horses." Though the Russians expected 70,000 prisoners, they had in fact captured 130,000 Austrians and nearly 1,000 guns. In addition, the Eleventh Army's divisions, previously focused on the siege, were now freed to fight in the Carpathians, though Selivanov himself retired from active service as a result of age and illness.[21]

The capture of Przemyśl only convinced Ivanov and *Stavka* of the opportunity to deal a mortal blow to the Austrians in the Carpathians. The difference was where that breakthrough should take place. *Stavka* hoped to use the Ninth Army against the overextended Pflanzer-Baltin group, while Ivanov by contrast continued to dream of turning southeast to either trap a huge collection of Austrians and Germans against Romania or force them into precipitate withdrawal west away from the Russian border. Ivanov's plan, formulated in the wake of the fall of Przemyśl, held that "our immediate tasks will be crossing the Carpathians and clearing the Dniestr River of enemy forces," breaking south through the mountains then sweeping east.[22] Brusilov's Eighth Army was tasked with the breakthrough, and pounded relentlessly against Austrian positions in the Beskid mountain chain. Both sides relentlessly marched reinforcements into the mountains. At the beginning of April, a hastily assembled Beskiden Corps under the German Georg von der Marwitz, combining Austrian and German divisions, took over the junction between the Third and Second Armies. Deploying behind the shattered Austrian X Corps, Marwitz met the Russian Eighth Army's advance head-on. Ivanov continued to hammer away at the Germans and Austrians, even as his own units were decimated by the constant attrition of mountain fighting. Brusilov, never one to avoid a fight, had to report on 9 April that his troops were making no further progress. "My units," he told Ivanov, "have suffered considerable losses and are completely exhausted by 20 nights of fighting and maneuver under exceptionally difficult conditions."[23] By 10 April Ivanov had to admit that his progress had been halted. His troops were exhausted, his stocks of ammunition were spent, and the dispatch of German reinforcements to the threatened sector had stiffened Austrian resistance. On 10 April, he ordered his Third and Eighth Armies to "fortify yourselves in the positions you occupy, taking action only to seize tactically important points or immediate operational goals."[24]

As would happen again, the Russians took an undoubted tactical success—the horrific losses suffered by the Austrians in their Carpathian offensives—and transformed it into a bloody stalemate by relentless attacks of their own under poor geographical and climatic conditions. By April 1915, Russian reserves of men and ammunition had been exhausted without managing to break through either west to Krakow or south through the Carpathians. While the cost in lives to the Central Powers had been equally great, the Germans in particular now enjoyed an overwhelming advantage in heavy artillery and especially ammunition, an advantage they would soon employ to deadly effect against the depleted Southwestern Front.

7

The Great Retreat, 1915

After the winter battles of early 1915, the nature of combat on the Eastern Front fundamentally shifted. The front now became essentially continuous, with a solid line of troops from the Romanian border in the south to the Baltic Sea in the north. To be sure, the density of those troops varied greatly: the two extremes—the Carpathians at the Romanian border and the flat, marshy ground on the Baltic—were manned by relatively small formations supplemented by cavalry. Nonetheless, the nature of strategic planning had to change. No longer was it possible to find unmanned sectors or open flanks for an offensive. Instead, commanders had to think in terms of forcing a breakthrough against prepared defenses either by finding weak points or through the application of overwhelming force, thereby creating a gap to exploit. The Germans, benefiting from their experience in trench warfare on the Western Front, used their substantial advantage in heavy artillery to inflict terrible losses of territory and manpower on the Russians in the late spring and summer of 1915, threatening the Russian army with total collapse.

The Great Retreat of 1915—the Russian expulsion from Galicia, Poland, and Lithuania—was a military and political disaster of enormous scale. The Russian army abandoned 300,000 square kilometers of territory. While precise figures are impossible to determine, the Russian army may have suffered a million soldiers killed, wounded, or captured. The fragile political and social accord created by the outbreak of war shattered into backbiting, recrimination, and xenophobia. Nonetheless, it is important to keep in mind one overarching fact: in the face of disaster, the Russian military machine never disintegrated. Its units remained capable of organized defense, and despite its losses in soldiers, territory, and equipment, it remained a force that still, in September 1915, held at bay 12 Austro-German armies on the Eastern Front, including 110 infantry and 20 cavalry divisions.

The Great Retreat also illustrates the particular problems of the Russian army in fighting the Central Powers and particularly the Germans. The Russians were perfectly capable of outmatching the Habsburgs, but the German army routinely responded to crises and opportunities more quickly that the Russian army was capable of doing. German expertise also propped up Habsburg performance. In almost all the significant actions of 1915, the leading role was taken by German divisions, supported and assisted by Austrians. Over the course of the war in the east, as Austro-Hungarian casualties mounted and morale fell, the Habsburg army became more and more dependent on such assistance. German officers, senior sergeants, and whole units were with time organically integrated into Austrian formations. Barracks humor regarded these Germans as "corset-stays" for their ability to keep Austrian soldiers ramrod-straight, upright, and in fighting trim. Joking aside, the Habsburgs lost autonomy with each German officer commanding their formations. Habsburg victory seemed an increasingly meaningless concept, as it would inevitably bring with it German political hegemony.

While in retrospect the Great Retreat seems like a steady and inexorable German advance and Russian retreat, a close look at the actual events shows a different pattern. The fighting of 1915 proceeded in fits and starts. Mackensen's Eleventh Army, the formation that did the lion's share of German fighting over the summer, engaged in at least four offensive cycles: preparation, attack, breakthrough, pursuit, exhaustion, and recovery—before beginning again. In almost all cases, the Russian high command detected the buildup of enemy forces, though often not the full scale or intent of German action, and prepared to meet the attack. In each case, though, the Russians came up short: not enough heavy artillery, not enough ammunition, not enough divisions, not enough time to shift reinforcements. Each German victory made the next easier—Russian artillery lost or captured, trained divisions decimated, fortifications abandoned—and the Russian army simply could not break of the cycle of German victory until German supply lines had been stretched to the breaking point and the approach of winter in late 1915 provided some respite. The Russian performance in 1914 was not bad, but it was worse than the German; over 1915, that difference became magnified.

GERMANY'S STRATEGIC CHOICE

In spring 1915, initiative lay with the German high command. Falkenhayn knew he had the luxury of choice. His strategic reserve could be directed to the Western Front, used to finish off Serbia, or sent to the Eastern Front. Austria-Hungary's travails, though, had stripped much of that seeming freedom. Conrad's desperate and failed efforts to relieve Przemyśl had gutted the Habsburg army and wrecked Austrian morale. The Eastern Front required immediate measures to prevent complete collapse of the Habsburg war effort and with that, defeat. At the close of March, Falkenhayn concluded he needed to devote his reserves to the twin tasks of propping up Austria-Hungary and thereby discouraging Italy and Romania from joining the Entente powers to take advantage of Austrian weakness. Decisive victory in the east might even convince the battered Russians to accept a separate peace. He had thus reluctantly come to share to some degree Hindenburg's conviction that victory lay in the east. German troops in the east were perfectly capable of defending against Russia without additional reinforcements, but would need additional manpower to take the offensive. The question, then, was how precisely to use German resources in the east most effectively. Direct German assistance to the Austrians was necessary and ongoing, but the piecemeal reinforcement of individual Austrian armies and corps with German divisions would at best delay defeat, not bring decisive results. Reinforcing Austrian troops in the Carpathians would only grind down German units under circumstances offering little hope for effective action. After considering several options, including an offensive in the far north at the Nieman, or alternatively German participation in the final destruction of Serbia, by the end of March Falkenhayn came to a decision. He sent German strategic reserves east to carry out a third option: an offensive against the southwestern corner of the Russian salient in Poland. Russian lines were thin, since Ivanov's Third and Eighth Armies had spent the last ten days of March pounding against Austrian defenses in the Carpathians to fight through the Dukla Pass. While these attacks gained ground, they cost valuable lives and ammunition when the Russians would soon need all they had. Though Falkenhayn made no effort to inform Conrad of his plans, the ongoing flow of information on Austrian demoralization and gradual disintegration gave increasing urgency to keeping Austria in the war. Only on 13 April, once preparations were well underway, did Falkenhayn finally tell Conrad of his plan, informing him in the process that the Austrian Fourth Army would participate in the operation under German authority. Conrad had little choice but to acquiesce.[1]

The weight of the German offensive was concentrated in the new, secretly created German Eleventh Army, led by August von Mackensen, Germany's ablest field commander of the First World War. Two of Mackensen's subordinates later played vital roles in building and then commanding Hitler's *Wehrmacht*: Mackensen's highly capable chief of staff was Hans von Seeckt, central to reconstructing the German Army under the strictures of the Versailles Treaty, and Fedor von Bock, operations officer, led Hitler's drive on Moscow. Falkenhayn could spare four corps from his strategic reserve for the Eleventh Army's eastern offensive. The eight German divisions of Mackensen's Eleventh Army—the Prussian Guards Corps (still with four regiments to each division and thus more possessing more manpower), the XXXXI Corps, a nonnumbered corps under Paul von Kneussel, and the X Corps in reserve—were bolstered by three additional Austrian divisions: two in the Austrian VI Corps and an additional Hungarian cavalry division. To his immediate north, Mackensen could also draw on the Austrian Fourth Army, subordinated to him and commanded by Archduke Joseph Ferdinand. Troops were deliberately chosen for their experience and effectiveness, and all available artillery, particularly heavy artillery, was massed for the offensive. The Germans emphasized secrecy and distraction, attempting to draw Russian attention away from the Southwestern Front. All this was done with great speed—beginning the concentration in mid-April, the Eleventh Army was ready for action by the start of May.[2]

Russian intelligence noted the presence of new formations opposite the breakthrough sector around Gorlice, but failed to grasp the full scope of German intentions, noting instead Austro-German concentrations in East Prussia and the Carpathians, far away from the actual site of the planned breakthrough. *Stavka*, rather than preparing for the German attack, continued to throw troops into stalled offensives. On 27 April, Yanushkevich emphasized the centrality of continuing operations in the Carpathians, still hoping for a breakthrough into the Hungarian plain. "At the present time," he wrote, "the operations we have begun in the Carpathians, particularly in view of the alliance signed by ourselves and our allies with Italy, continue to have their preeminent significance and demand the utmost effort towards the vigorous completion of what we have begun."[3]

The Russian Southwestern Front, entrusted with an enormous sector of the line, had been exhausted by the fighting in the Carpathians over the winter of 1914–1915, leaving few resources to protect other vulnerable sectors. The sole reserve Ivanov had at his disposal was the III Caucasus Corps, though even that was intended more for further fighting in the Carpathians than defense along other sectors. Mackensen's target sector was held by Radko-Dmitriev's Third Army. Within the Third Army, the weight of the German attack fell on the three divisions of its X Corps, entirely outclassed by the forces thrown against them. The divisions manning Russian defenses were not wholly unready. Defending troops had managed to assemble three belts of trenches: one primary and two reserve, each separated by several kilometers. The trenches were shallow and poorly supplied with reinforced bunkers, however, in part because of the region's high water table. Perfectly adequate against rifle fire or light artillery, the Russian defenders were utterly unready for an onslaught of German heavy artillery honed by the experience of the Western Front. Even worse than the disparity in artillery was the crippling shortage of ammunition on the Russian side, where the Third Army set ten shells as the total daily allotment for a six-gun howitzer battery.[4]

Mackensen and von Seeckt chose a narrow sector just southeast of Krakow between Tarnów to the north and Gorlice to the south. The German advantage in manpower was substantial but not overwhelming: 125,000 to 60,000, or approximately 2:1, in the narrow attack corridor. Measured by divisions, Radko-Dmitriev's Third Army had fourteen infantry and five cavalry against twenty-three German and Austrian. The Russian Third Army as a whole was outnumbered perhaps 3:2, with 219,000 troops facing over 350,000 Germans and Austrians. The key was not in manpower, however, but heavy artillery. Mackensen had amassed over 700 guns and mortars, including some 160 heavy artillery pieces, to support eight divisions attacking on a frontage barely 30 kilometers wide. The German plan was remarkably straightforward: annihilate the Russian frontline defenses with heavy artillery, focusing on the Russian IX and X Corps and particularly the vulnerable junction between them. Once that had been accomplished, German infantry would penetrate the resulting breach, advancing just far enough to cut off the lines of communication and supply to the three Russian corps southeast of the point of breakthrough—the XXIV, XII, and XXI—which were still hanging on to a toehold on the southern face of the Carpathians. Indeed, the Russian advance deep into the mountains had created in the Russian high command a fixation on just how close they were to a breakthrough to Hungary. The reluctance to withdraw them, combined with the difficult mountain terrain that would slow any Russian retreat, created real danger those corps could be cut off and trapped.[5]

MACKENSEN'S INITIAL BREAKTHROUGH

After two days of skirmishing to improve their position for the coming offensive, Mackensen's forces moved to their jumping off points on the night of 1–2 May 1915. Intermittent artillery fire continued through the night, intended to prevent movement of reserves, harass Russian defenders, interrupt their rest, and draw them out of trenches during brief intervals of quiet. A storm of intense bombardment began at 6:00 AM on the morning of 2 May. Russian trenches were neither deep nor well-constructed enough to sustain pounding from the heavy artillery Mackensen brought to bear. Artillery barrages, briefly interrupted to prevent the Russians from judging the precise moment of German attack, continued until 10:00 AM. By this point, Mackensen's 700 guns had erased the foremost Russian trench belt and shredded its barbed wire obstacles. In the sector defended by the 61st Division, "the trenches had been leveled and losses are great."[6] A subsequent Russian report declared that German heavy artillery, which the Russians had nothing to match, "literally destroyed our trenches, inflicting enormous losses on the defenders."[7] The artillery's targets then moved from the front lines to the second belt of Russian defenses. For Russian peasant soldiers, Germany's evident superiority in machine guns, artillery, and all forms of technology was hard to bear, and made the overwhelming barrage that much more difficult to withstand.[8]

When the German Eleventh Army's infantry assault jumped off at 10:00 AM on 2 May, Mackensen's soldiers encountered little organized resistance from the Russian IX Corps and the X Corps immediately to its south. On the IX Corps's right wing, territorial militia conscripted into the regular army (and thus either inexperienced, old, physically unfit, or some combination of the three) shattered under German pressure. The Germans had their greatest success, however, at the junction between the IX and X Corps. In particular, the 70th Infantry Division, the southernmost of the IX Corps, was spread over a wide frontage and ill-prepared for what it faced. Nikolai Protopopov, commander of the X Corps, begged his 31st Division to maintain the continuity of the front line: "Take all measures to sustain the connection between your right flank and the left flank of the 70th Division. A breakthrough cannot be permitted. Hold more stubbornly. Take measures to reinvigorate our artillery fire."[9] His urgings did no good. When the Russian line buckled at the seam between the two corps, the X Corps withdrew its affected divisions to the second belt of trenches. As a result, the initial German advance had no trouble achieving its first day's goal of capturing the first Russian trench belt, bagging 17,000 stunned prisoners. All along the line, the picture was consistent. The Prussian Guard Corps advanced three miles. Even the Austrian VI Corps had shown uncharacteristic initiative, moving several miles alongside its German counterparts. François's XXXXI Reserve Corps had taken the town of Gorlice itself and advanced two miles. Despite moments of hard fighting and occasional spirited Russian counterattacks, von Kneussel's corps had advanced a mile by nightfall, well through the first Russian belt. Only in a few isolated places did unbroken Russian infantry and intact machine guns briefly delay the German advance. Mackensen had emphasized the importance of flexible and responsive artillery, however, and remaining Russian strongpoints were quickly smashed or outflanked.

The struggle was not over. From the first day of the assault, Radko-Dmitriev recognized the seriousness of his position and threw his limited reserves—a few infantry regiments and additional cavalry—in front of the advancing Germans. By the end of the first day, he told Ivanov that "the troops of the X Corps have fought splendidly, as witnessed by their enormous losses, but the inability to counter the destructive hurricane of enemy artillery fire has destroyed their ability to resist."[10] He begged for and received the release of the III Caucasus Corps to help plug the gap. This left no additional reserves should the new line not hold. Though the Russian first line had been taken with little trouble, two further reserve trench belts still barred German progress. As Mackensen's men hammered forward, the soldiers of the Russian X Corps were steadily forced backward. They had not yet either broken or shattered, though, and there was still some hope of containing the German assault.

On the second day of the offensive, 3 May, Mackensen committed one of his two reserve divisions to Corps Kneussl to consolidate and extend the previous day's success. The problems his troops faced became more complex. Unlike the capture of forward Russian positions, the Germans now dealt with Russian systems that had not been surveyed previously. The first Russian lines, within sight of German observers, had been the target of carefully planned and directly observed artillery fire, something not possible with the trench belts further to the rear. German artillery thus improvised its fire support rather than relying on careful preparation. On the other hand, Russian morale was wavering, and the continuing momentum of the Austro-German advance made it difficult for the Russians to establish a new defensive line. Individual counterattacks by Russian formations temporarily checked the Austro-German onslaught in one sector, but the general pace of German advance again outflanked any Russian defensive stand. Should a Russian regiment or division hold its ground, this only provided time for German heavy artillery to advance along traffic-choked roads and annihilate the defender with shell. Once forced out of their inadequate frontline trenches by the initial German attacks, the Russians were forced to fight under even worse circumstances, costing them even more lives.

The key break came on 4 May. On that day, IX Corps commander Abram Dragomirov was already reporting critical shortages of artillery ammunition and his doubts about his ability to hold any longer, and Ivanov, who might have been quick to blame his corps and army commanders, instead emphasized to *Stavka* the crippling effect of ammunition shortages on the Russian ability to resist.[11] Russian counterattacks had been clumsy, frontal assaults into the teeth of the advancing Germans, and succeeded only in exhausting units that might otherwise have been able to defend in place. The III Siberian Corps had staved off complete collapse on the northern sector of the breakthrough, but the southern sector, relatively quiet to this point, now broke. The Corps Kneussl on the far right of the German assault cracked the gap between the Russian 9th division, the southernmost of the X Corps, and the 49th Division, northernmost of the XXIV Corps. This penetration pushed toward the Wisłoka River, lying behind the Russian line, and on to the confusingly named Wisłok River lying 25 kilometers behind it. The XXIV Corps now found its escape route under threat.

The X Corps, now outflanked on both wings and its divisions reduced to 1,500 effectives, was in no position to resist further. Radko-Dmitriev authorized general retreat behind the Wisłoka River on the night of 4–5 May, warning Ivanov that he might not be able to hold this new line or maintain connections with the Russian armies to his left and right. Ivanov and *Stavka* stressed the urgency of maintaining this new position to enable the Russian Fourth Army to the north and the Eighth Army to the southeast to hold their positions. Defeat was rapidly becoming disaster. Confusion and clogged roads made organized withdrawal impossible. Not fully aware of the extent of the German advance through the X Corps's shattered left wing, Radko-Dmitriev directed elements of the XXIV Corps (including the later counterrevolutionary Lavr Kornilov and his 48th Division) to retreat through territory already under German control, where they found their retreat cut off by a German spearhead and had to fight their way through to Russian lines. As a report to the Third Army Staff put it on 6 May, "three [of four] of the 48th Division's regiments have not escaped from their position."[12] Half the division and Kornilov himself were captured.

By 5 May, disaster was clear. Fresh divisions were on their way to the breakthrough, but there was a real question whether they could arrive in time to salvage the situation. The Southwestern Front began a scorched-earth policy of destroying all material of use to the Central Powers as part of Russian withdrawal. Ivanov's headquarters relayed to his constituent armies instructions from Yanushkevich "to take the most energetic measures towards the complete destruction of all remaining railroad, road, and telegraph links. I believe it is necessary to direct your attention to this, since experience has shown that our troops are careless in this regard."[13] Dragomirov reported that Mackensen's army had captured essentially the entire Russian defensive zone—three full belts of trenches. By 7–8 May, Mackensen had reached the Wisłok River, the only significant natural barrier behind the Russian trench system, across the breadth of the Third Army's defensive front. Breakthroughs in single sectors rapidly propagated up and down the Russian line. Each neighboring unit in turn had to withdraw or be outflanked and cut off itself. Radko-Dmitriev saw little alternative to further retreat behind the San River. On the Third Army's left,

Brusilov's Eighth Army was warned on 6 May that it would likely have to withdraw, given the slim chances of the Third Army's holding in place. Though opinion in the Russian high command blamed Radko-Dmitriev for the Third Army's collapse, German superiority in heavy artillery and Russian shortages of shells had far more to do with it.

The Austrian Third and Fourth Armies, on the right and left shoulders of Mackensen's Eleventh, advanced slowly against the Russians without Mackensen's spectacular success. On 6 May, the order to advance was extended further south to the Austrian Second Army. Mackensen's forces, having expelled the Russians from their prepared defenses, continued to make steady progress. But merely pushing the Russians back with local offensives inflicted Russian casualties at a rate little greater than that which the Austrians and Germans would themselves suffer. In isolated instances the Central Powers bagged a significant number of prisoners, as in the Austrian capture of Tarnów or the Austrian encirclement and capture of the 48th Division. Generally, though, the Russian formations retreated in good order and in time to prevent the mass surrenders that had befallen the Second Army at Tannenberg. The question for the Central Powers was how best to exploit the breach in Russian defenses to turn a local and limited success into a strategic victory; for the Russians, it was how to stop a retreat that only seemed to be gaining momentum.

By a week into the German offensive, the Russian position was difficult, and the *Stavka* could not decide how to respond. There were few reserves to plug the major hole blasted in the Russian line. Divisions to the north and east of the breakthrough were now in an untenable position, but withdrawal meant abandoning trench systems to fight in the open during a demoralizing retreat. The Russian generals, lacking any consensus on how to respond, bickered instead. On 5 May, Grand Duke Nikolai indicated he would not permit any retreat from the Wisłok River to the San. He met with his commanders at Chełm on 7 May, and again insisted on the inviolability of the Wisłok River line. There was little the grand duke could offer Radko-Dmitriev's Third Army, though, to make that task possible. A single division was pulled from the Northwestern Front and dispatched to the Third Army, and another was available in the event of emergency. The only other directive was to strip units from the other armies of the Southwestern Front, making them increasingly vulnerable just as the Austro-German offensive seemed to be widening. Radko-Dmitriev wanted to withdraw still further to gain time and reorganize a coherent defense, but had to order his troops on 8 May "to die in their position but not to retreat."[14] Radko-Dmitriev's direct superior, Ivanov at the Southwestern Front, ordered the Third Army to surrender no more ground and to strike back westward immediately. Ivanov's chief of staff, Vladimir Dragomirov, backed Radko-Dmitriev's desire to retreat; *Stavka* backed Ivanov's determination to stand and fight. The grand duke, in effect, accused Dragomirov of cowardice: "In view of the uninterrupted attempts by the Southwestern Front staff entrusted to you to withdraw for some or other reason from various sectors of the front in turn, I categorically command you to carry out no retreat without my express permission under concrete circumstances of combat."[15] In the confusion and recriminations flying between his army headquarters, the Southwestern Front, and *Stavka*, Radko-Dmitriev found it impossible to organize a defense. He had pulled Yakov Shkinskii's XXI Corps out of the front line south of the breakthrough in order to provide himself with a reserve. On 8 May, Radko-Dmitriev ordered Shkinskii to prepare to attack west into the face of the German breakthrough, striking toward Rymanów, where the Germans had forced a breach between the XXIV and XII Corps. At midday on 9 May, Radko-Dmitriev begged Shkinskii to speed his delayed attack, but by early on the morning of 10 May, Radko-Dmitriev was already reporting failure in the face of overwhelming German superiority. The XXI Corps had achieved only limited success, opening a gap in the German line that was quickly closed again.

Upon that failure, Radko-Dmitriev ordered his Third Army on the morning of 10 May into a general retreat to more defensible positions. Given the pounding the Third Army had taken, it withdrew in remarkably good order, leaving few of its guns behind. Begging *Stavka* to consider a general withdrawal of all the armies in Poland, he declared his troops "had fulfilled their duties to the utmost; many divisions have only a few hundred combat troops left. Given the delay in receiving reinforcements, we have no chance of holding in our new positions." He insisted to Ivanov that "we need a more radical decision in order to preserve the remnants of the army."[16] Faced with the inevitable, Ivanov ordered Brusilov's Eighth Army to retreat as well. On 13 May, Radko-Dmitriev withdrew further to the San River as part of Ivanov's directive to use that as the new basis for defense. As reward for extracting his army from destruction, he was removed as commander of the Third Army and replaced with Leonid Lesh on 20 May; Dragomirov was removed as Southwestern Front chief of staff for "nervous exhaustion" and replaced by Sergei Savvich.

The German high command did not suffer from indecision or chaos, but like the Russians felt a crying shortage of manpower. Sensing early in the offensive that the momentum of the German attack might be converted into substantial gains, Falkenhayn began the transfer of reinforcements to Mackensen only days into the offensive, but had available only a single division. Given the power of static defenses, Falkenhayn wrote later, it was imperative to take advantage of an enemy forced into the open: "It seemed of less consequence than usual merely to gain ground. The essential thing was to smash the enemy's fighting machine. This could be done nowhere better and more swiftly than in the breach where the enemy was forced to give battle on unprepared terrain." Since Italian intervention against Austria seemed imminent, it was vital to inflict as much damage as possible to the Russians in as short a time as possible. [17]

RUSSIAN RETREAT TO PRZEMYŚL

By 13 May, the Third and Eighth Armies had withdrawn to the San River, but their divisions had been gutted, down to some 2,000 men each, and their respite would last only a few days. On 12 May, an Austro-German conference had already agreed on the next step. Taking advantage of Russian disorganization, the German Eleventh Army would continue to push past the Wisłok River toward the San River, establishing bridgeheads across the San at Jarosław and Radymno, while the Austrian Third Army, advancing on its right, would recapture Przemyśl.[18] Over the next two to three days, Mackensen's divisions sped east to the San to catch up with the retreating Russians without meeting significant opposition, quite fortunate given their expenditures of men and ammunition to achieve the breakthroughs at the beginning of May. As the Austro-German advance rolled east toward Jarosław and Przemyśl, it forced the Russians to abandon their footholds in the Carpathians or risk being trapped in the mountains with enemies behind them.

By 14 May, the Germans and Austrians reached the San, where the Russians had left outposts on the western bank of the river to slow the enemy

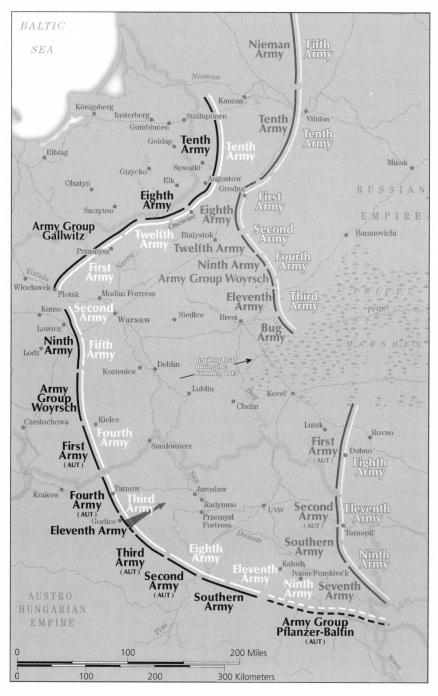

Map 9. The Great Retreat, May–August 1915

advance. Radko-Dmitriev was confident that these fortified bridgeheads would slow any Austro-German crossing, and told his corps commanders that "once again I insist that we will maintain our corps on the left [west] bank of the San."[19] His hopes proved beyond the ability of his exhausted troops to sustain. Repeated Austro-German attacks on the San River line began on 14 May at Jarosław, forcing the Russians to withdraw some bridgeheads to the east bank on the night of 15–16 May. Radko-Dmitriev wanted a general retreat to the east bank: the Russian defenders, crammed into small bridgeheads, were perfect targets for German heavy artillery. Ivanov, nonetheless, still insisted on the absolute necessity of holding the San and keeping some presence on the west bank.

Orders to hold fast were not enough to maintain the Russian footholds west of the San. As Brusilov explained the situation, each corps under his command was reduced to division strength, and he stressed to Ivanov that one of his regiments was short 67 officers (of 80) and 3,390 men (of 4,000). A Lieutenant-Colonel Lazarev presented his evaluation to the quartermaster-general of the Third Army and found "The River San can hardly be held with the support of strong, heavy artillery, in view of the lack of prepared defenses, crippling shortages of manpower in the units, and the extreme moral and physical exhaustion of the troops. The question consists of temporarily holding our position until the Germans concentrate heavy artillery north of Radymno." Shkinskii reported to Radko-Dmitriev on the state of his XXI Corps: six of his regiments were 3,000 men short (that is, reduced to one-quarter strength), other regiments were down to 200 men by the time they reached the San, and his troops had marched for seven days and not slept for eight.[20] On 17 May, Radko-Dmitriev had to report to Ivanov that his men could no longer even remain on the east bank of the San opposite Jarosław. The Germans and Austrians themselves crossed the San in several places on 16 and 17 May to establish bridgeheads for subsequent exploitation. Ivanov, despite the exhaustion of his men's physical resources and ammunition, ordered the full force of Third Army to carry out a counteroffensive to liquidate the Jarosław bridgehead on the night of 18–19 May. By mid-morning on 19 May, it was already clear that the attack had produced no results, shattering against hastily prepared German defenses and draining further strength from the Russian divisions close to breaking. At this point, though, the Russians finally received a temporary reprieve. The Austrian and German soldiers, although heartened by victory, were themselves as exhausted as the Russians. Mackensen's Eleventh Army was now operating 150 kilometers from its railheads and short on supplies and ammunition. The relentless pressure on the Russians eased while German railheads were pushed east and supplies at the front replenished.

Once Mackensen had replenished his supplies, secured his rail connections, and rested his soldiers, he prepared another offensive. Opening with an artillery barrage on 23 May, moving to infantry assault on 24 May, Mackensen applied strategic misdirection. Instead of striking directly east from his Jarosław bridgehead toward L'viv, his troops moved southeast in order to descend behind Przemyśl to either trap its defenders or force them to abandon the fortress without a fight. The dynamic was similar to the initial breakthrough at Gorlice: heavy artillery destroyed Russian field fortifications, forcing a breakthrough that then forced the Russians to retreat and fight in the open. Ivanov and his army commanders pressed early for the abandonment of Przemyśl, but Grand Duke Nikolai Nikolaevich, resistant to surrendering one of Russia's great prizes from the first year of the war, insisted on defending Przemyśl and holding the San as long as possible. That was not long: bombardment of the fortress began on 30 May, Russian posts on the western bank of the San were abandoned the next day, and on 1 June the Austrians captured some of the fortress's outer defensive works. When a Russian counterattack on 2 June failed to secure the last route east out of the fortress, Przemyśl was evacuated. Despite the lengthy Russian resistance, the Austrian haul at Przemyśl was remarkably small: 8,000 prisoners and forty guns.

The Southwestern Front's staff anticipated that the Austrians and Germans would pause temporarily to digest their gains, believing Italy's joining the Allies would force Austria to redirect troops from the east to the west. Through the first year of the war, Italy had carefully weighed its options, seeking the most advantageous moment to join the war. Though a member of the Triple Alliance since 1881, the Italian government felt no obligation to join Germany and Austria-Hungary unless it saw concrete advantage. The problem for the Central Powers was that Italy's key territorial desires were Austrian lands, and the Habsburgs saw little point in giving away territory in hope of victory. After the Austrians' final rejection of Italian demands in spring 1915, the Italians looked for and found a much better offer from Britain, France, and Russia. In the secret Treaty of London, signed 26 April 1915, the Allies promised Italy territory in the Alps, around the Adriatic, and a sphere of influence in Anatolia upon Ottoman defeat. Italy declared war on Austria-Hungary on 23 May 1915. Delayed Italian mobilization, however, meant that the Austro-Hungarian army had substantial time to organize effective defenses in the Alps. Despite commitments on the Russian and Serbian fronts, the Austro-Hungarian army enjoyed a number of advantages, including a year of experience in modern war, fighting on the defensive, and the commanding advantage of defending the high ground of the Alps against the lackluster Italian Army. Italy made little gain at huge cost in repeated but futile attacks. Nonetheless, Austria-Hungary's limited supply of aircraft were redirected to the Italian theater, there was a temporary lull in pressure against the Russians, and Conrad's focus was divided. Previously consumed by hatred of the Serbs, he now became obsessed with Italy to the extent of considering a separate peace with Russia as a path to victory.[21]

The cycle of rest and renewed attack thus repeated itself without serious delay from Italian entry. Mackensen's divisions, after capturing Jarosław and Przemyśl to establish themselves firmly on the east bank of the San, replenished their supplies and incorporated reinforcements and replacements. In early June, the natural next step for the Germans was continued advance east to L'viv.[22] Mackensen's renewed attack, once again spearheaded by the German Eleventh Army, supported by the Austrian Fourth Army to his north and the Austrian Second to his south, pushed east with an artillery bombardment on the night of 12–13 June and infantry assault on 13 June. The German attack fell primarily on Brusilov's Eighth Army, still exhausted from the struggles on the San River and in no position to effectively resist. The dogged Russians nonetheless contained the German advance for three days, collapsing into rapid retreat only on 16 June. On 20 June, *Stavka* ordered the evacuation of L'viv, and by 21 June, the Germans were just outside the city. They occupied it the next day.

Mackensen had achieved a stunning success—in seven weeks, his divisions had advanced some 250 kilometers from Gorlice to L'viv (dwarfing the movement of the Western Front over four years of war), taken perhaps a quarter of a million prisoners, and inflicted at least as many additional casualties on the Russians. *Stavka* reckoned that its frontline armies after the fall of L'viv were down by 500,000 men. As an early Soviet history of the war put it:

Our technical poverty and cultural backwardness created a vicious circle: conscious that we were close to the complete disintegration of our units, we nonetheless made enormous human sacrifices, since our lack of equipment deprived us of the means to create a strong defensive belt; wishing to conserve soldiers and bullets, at the same time we were ordered not to surrender to the enemy without a fight even an inch of ground. We dreamed of maneuver, but did not want to give up a yard of space.[23]

While Russian operational command had certainly not been good, too slow to withdraw embattled divisions from exposed positions and quick to engage in wasteful and undermanned counterattacks, German superiority in heavy artillery had done the important work of smashing Russian defensive positions and forcing Russian divisions into open ground and mobile warfare at which the Germans were far superior. Ivanov, though certainly an interested party, explained the Russian failure this way:

Neither artful maneuver, nor the combat quality of enemy soldiers, but solely his predominance in artillery fire, inflicting enormous losses and shaking the moral strength of our soldiers, allowed him break the steadiness and steadfastness of our glorious troops and force them into successive retreats. . . . Thanks to the strength of this fire the enemy could achieve quick results in his offensive operations along his chosen axes. Unfortunately, we could not answer him because of insufficient ammunition for our rifles and light artillery. Our offensive actions and counterattacks, deprived of the necessary powerful artillery fire, either developed very slowly or did not take place at all, meeting a wall of fire from the enemy and obstacles and fortifications not destroyed by our artillery fire.[24]

RENEWED AUSTRO-GERMAN OFFENSIVE

Anticipating a brief respite with the loss of L'viv and Italian intervention, the Russians reorganized their defenses in the south. Ivanov, left in place as Southwestern Front commander despite his string of uninterrupted defeats, had his armies stretched thin by the Austro-German advance east to

L'viv. Ivanov's armies retreated in divergent directions—the Third Army north toward Lublin and Volodymyr-Volyns'kyi; the Eighth and Eleventh Armies east toward Kiev. In an effort to alleviate Ivanov's burden of command, *Stavka* had narrowed his geographical scope by transferring the Third and Fourth Armies to Alekseev's Northwestern Front. Intended to allow Ivanov to concentrate on the region of greatest danger, this well-intended action would prove instead to divide command when the next German offensive began.

By mid-June 1915, Mackensen's successes in the Gorlice-Tarnów offensive, together with the subsequent recapture of Przemyśl and his approach to L'viv, reduced the danger of invasion of Hungary but raised again the same question that had agitated the German and Austrian high commands earlier in the spring: what to do now? There was some sentiment for directing the main effort elsewhere than against the Russians. British forces continued to arrive on the continent in greater numbers, and Italy had joined the war on the Allied side. The Central Powers enjoyed the luxury of choice, but lacked real consensus: focus on the west, the south, or the east? Russia had sustained a serious defeat, and might be brought to accept a negotiated peace if commitment to that front were sustained. Conrad wanted to focus on Italy. Falkenhayn thought the Italians could be contained by minimal commitment in the Alps, and manpower could better be directed to the Western Front, or to the final defeat of Serbia. While operations in the east had inflicted serious losses on the Russians, they had not managed to achieve the wholesale destruction of entire formations. In effect, Russian troops had been pushed back, at the cost of human and material losses on both sides. Russian losses had been greater than German and Austrian, but not enough to be confident in grinding the Russians to defeat through attrition.

Despite the attraction of other fronts, their very successes against Russia made it difficult for the Germans and Austro-Hungarians to abandon their operations in the east. The campaigns of the first half of 1915 thus laid the groundwork for Russia's final disaster of the year: the complete loss of Poland. Russia's divisions and regiments had been hollowed out by casualties, and lack of rifles slowed the flow of march companies of reinforcements to the front. Instead of the 1.5 million frontline soldiers that tables of organization would suggest for its field army of 49 corps and well over 100 infantry divisions, Russia had only a million men at the front. Less

evident but equally crippling was the lack of heavy artillery and ammunition. Finally, Russia's own ill-advised Carpathian campaigns, extended
long past the point of diminishing returns, had set up the Russian army
perfectly for a knock-out blow. In the north, Hindenburg's campaigns had
expanded German control well outside the bounds of East Prussia, stretching Russian lines and providing a wealth of potential targets. In the south,
Mackensen's Gorlice-Tarnów breakthrough and the six weeks' retreat that
followed gave him control of Galicia. Taken together, those advances in the
north and south made Russian control of the Polish salient even more precarious, and the Russian armies stationed there—from north to south, the
Twelfth, the First, the Second, the Fourth, the Third, and the Thirteenth—
even more vulnerable. With all this, continued pressure on the Russians
came to seem the natural next step.[25]

Even as Mackensen's army group was pushing toward L'viv, German
planners considered what to do when the city fell. Consensus quickly centered on an ambitious plan: turning north from L'viv to attack the Polish
salient from the south, perhaps in conjunction with an attack from East
Prussia in the north, to trap and annihilate the Russian armies around Warsaw. Von Seeckt, chief of staff of the German Eleventh Army, proposed just
such an attack on 15 June. Falkenhayn and Conrad quickly agreed on the
general outlines of the plan; Hindenburg and Ludendorff required more
convincing, as von Seeckt's concept was not nearly ambitious enough for
them. While Falkenhayn wanted them to attack south into the Polish
salient, they dreamed instead of attacking east from East Prussia, hitting
first Kaunas and then Vilnius in a deep penetration toward the Russian
heartland, an ambitious strike that would strain German logistics to the
breaking point and leave their extended troops vulnerable to being cut off
deep inside Russia. At a 2 July 1915 meeting with Falkenhayn and Conrad,
Kaiser Wilhelm uncharacteristically proved the voice of reason, compelling
Hindenburg and Ludendorff to accept the more limited and realistic plan.[26]

The concrete plan prepared in late June involved a strike by two armies:
the Austrian Fourth Army and Mackensen's Eleventh Army. Having
pushed east from Gorlice to L'viv, they would now in effect turn left, driving north to cut off the Polish salient. These two armies were joined on 8
July by a newly created German Army of the Bug, formed from elements
of the German Southern Army and commanded by Alexander von Linsingen. Mackensen had overall control of the three armies. The sector for their

attack was the north–south corridor formed by the Vistula River on their left and the Bug River on their right, providing protection on both flanks and, in addition, barriers that might hinder Russian escape east. Falkenhayn intended a secondary blow from the north. This responsibility fell to Max von Gallwitz's army group on the northwestern corner of the Polish salient at Przasnysz, where a German double-envelopment had gone badly wrong just a few months before.[27]

Before the main blow between the Vistula and the Bug, the Germans and Austrians carried out limited operations at the end of June and beginning of July to distract attention from the coming offensive, disrupt Russian defenses, and generally improve the position of their armies. On 26 June, Mackensen's Eleventh Army began probing attacks around the town of Rava-Ruska against the Russian Eighth Army and a task force under Vladimir Olokhov just to its west. These became hard fought engagements, inflicting heavy casualties on both sides in four days of fighting. Alekseev reinforced Russian defenses in the area, upgrading Olokhov's group to a full army under Vladimir Gorbatovskii. Though in order of creation it was the Thirteenth Army, demands of superstition meant it was generally called the Special Army instead. On 2 July, well before the main offensive began, Mackensen renewed his attacks further west against the Russian Third Army. This time the Austrian Fourth Army attacked toward Lublin, gaining 10–15 kilometers of territory before being halted and partially reversed by the Third Army's vigorous counterattacks, assisted by the XXV Corps from the Fourth Army to its west. Though the Austrians seized Kraśnik, site of much bloody fighting in 1914, none of their gains justified the expense in lives lost. The stiff Russian resistance did convince the Germans and Austrians of the need to reinforce their planned offensive, adding the Army of the Bug to the Austrian Fourth and German Eleventh in the attack plan.[28]

Stavka had not been idle, but crippling shell shortages necessarily restricted any spoiling attacks to disrupt German preparations. Besides the creation of Gorbatovskii's Thirteenth Army, *Stavka* had limited means at its disposal. Alekseev, commanding the Northwestern Front, did transfer three corps from northwest of Warsaw, where he had expected the main German attack, south to where Mackensen had been probing Russian defenses. He also prepared his armies for retreat in anticipation of further German offensives: on 5 July he had been given preliminary permission to withdraw in order to keep his armies intact and preserve manpower. Russia had two armies awaiting the forthcoming German offensive between the Vistula and the Bug: Lesh's Third Army covered most of the territory between the rivers, and Gorbatovskii's new Thirteenth Army lay to its east on both banks of the Bug. The Thirteenth Army was thus quite awkwardly placed astride the Bug, rendering it vulnerable to being pushed to the river's east bank and effectively out of action, and hindering lateral movement of the army's divisions. Russian higher command structures were also poorly organized. Gorbatovskii's Thirteenth Army, though at the far southeastern corner of Poland, was part of the Northwestern Front. Alekseev, the Northwestern Front's commander, as a result had responsibility for a front line that wound 900 kilometers from the Baltic coast to eastern Galicia and included eight armies under his control. While this did at least mean that the defense of the Polish salient was under one command, it put far more responsibility on Alekseev than he was capable of bearing.[29]

Mackensen's new offensive began with diversionary attacks in the northwest and northeast. On the northwest corner of the Polish salient, Gallwitz did not repeat the mistakes of the first battle of Przasnysz. On 13 July, the massed artillery of his Twelfth Army annihilated many defenders of Litvinov's First Army in their first belt of trenches, as Litvinov had imprudently not kept the foremost trenches thinly manned to prevent just such losses. In a single day, the 11th Siberian Division went from 14,500 effectives to 5,000. Once the first belt of two trench systems had been smashed after a day of hard fighting, German advance was rapid. Przasnysz itself was encircled on the second day of the offensive, and Gallwitz's divisions penetrated the second, rudimentary Russian trench belt, 15 kilometers behind the initial line, by the third day. Alekseev pulled troops from neighboring armies and fortress garrisons, which in combination with Russian forts slowed the speed of German advance. Nonetheless, Alekseev was pessimistic about his ability to hold much longer in place, and on 19 July received permission, if necessary, to withdraw east from the Vistula and abandon Warsaw.[30]

Russian defenses in northern Poland relied heavily on river fortresses. Among the most formidable was at Modlin (Novogeorgievsk), guarding the point at which the Narew flowed west into the Vistula, about 30 kilometers northwest of Warsaw. While a formidable position by the standards of the 19th century, it was far less defensible in an age of heavy artillery. To make matters worse, the garrison commander, Nikolai Bobyr', had a reputation for corruption and lacked any field experience, while his competent officers and stock of artillery had been drained since the outbreak of war to supply the field army. As garrison troops, Bobyr''s soldiers were a low priority for small arms as well, having rifles for only a fraction of the total garrison strength of 50,000 men in four divisions. Evacuation was the only reasonable option for the Modlin garrison once von Gallwitz's offensive began, but the region around the fortress had long been poorly served by railroad connections. The bulk of the fortress complex lay on the north bank of the Narew-Vistula, and bridges across the Narew and Vistula were crude. In any case, the existing transport network had been strained to the point of complete collapse by the flood of refugees from Russian Poland, either Jews forcibly relocated out of the combat zone or Russians and Poles striving to escape from the fighting into safety within Russia.

In any event, von Gallwitz simply screened Modlin and prepared to force the Narew. The Germans could not cross the Narew and its string of fortifications without a few days to reorganize after their rapid advance, but once this regrouping was complete the fortifications proved their worthlessness. On 23 July von Gallwitz's divisions simultaneously attacked the fortified towns of Pułtusk and Rozan, 50 kilometers behind the initial front lines. While German artillery smashed the fortresses, German infantry easily forced the Narew at several points above and below the two towns. This broke the Narew River barrier, opening the way to a further advance. The fortifications held out only an additional day. Taking Pułtusk put the Germans halfway to Warsaw. The Russian Second Army, well to the west of Warsaw, resisted tentative German attacks. Its remaining in place only invited encirclement, particularly once the main offensive began in the south. Alekseev decided on withdrawal. On 24 July, he gave preliminary orders to his armies to prepare for retreat east, a retreat that on 4–5 August abandoned Warsaw to occupation and Modlin to encirclement. Once the Germans finally began a siege of the isolated and abandoned Modlin, it fell relatively quickly on 19 August. Tens of thousands of men and 1,600 artillery pieces were lost.

In the far north, the Germans once again took advantage of relative Russian neglect of the quiet front lines of the Baltic. Lauenstein's army group, now upgraded to a full Army of the Nieman under Otto von Below,

again demonstrated remarkable initiative and originality. On 14 July a mobile force of cavalry and infantry crossed the Venta River to outflank Pleve's
Fifth Army, which was thin on infantry and relied instead on cavalry to
hold the empty spaces of the region. The German main attack toward Delgava aimed at circling the northern flank of Pleve's troops in order to trap
and destroy them. Lacking real mass, Pleve was in no position to stop the
German offensive. Like Alekseev at Warsaw, he chose to withdraw and preserve his army intact instead of fighting for territory and risking destruction. After fierce fighting at Delgava lasting several days, German troops
finally took the city on 20 August. German troops had thus reached the
Gulf of Riga and threatened Riga itself before Pleve could establish a defensive position on the Aa River and the Dvina. Though by no means a decisive campaign, this operation further undermined Russian confidence in
their ability to resist the Germans and hold ground, and brought the war
to the outskirts of one of Russia's major industrial centers. *Stavka* shifted
the Twelfth Army to the defense of Riga. The Army of the Nieman's advance also pushed a German salient deep into the space between Riga to
the north and Kaunas to the south, threatening Kaunas with encirclement.
The Kaunas fortress fell on 18 August in a particularly humiliating fashion:
the garrison commander, Vladimir Grigor'ev, fled the fort, allowing the
Germans to capture 20,000 prisoners and 1,300 guns at low cost in casualties.[31]

The real attack, however, came not to the north in the Baltic but from
Mackensen's three armies in the south, supported by Woyrsch's army
group west of the Vistula and the First Army east of the Bug. The offensive
between the rivers began in the east with the Army of the Bug on 15 July,
followed further west the next day by the Eleventh Army, Mackensen's
most effective force, and the Austrian Fourth Army. The restricted terrain
between the rivers, the elaborate Russian trench systems, and the timely
arrival of Russian reinforcements meant that the Austro-German advance
north was slow and costly. The Central Powers found no open Russian
flanks to turn or weak points to penetrate, but instead slogged ahead by
the massive application of artillery in the face of repeated but costly Russian counterattacks. This pushed Russian divisions back, but did not isolate and destroy them, and the Russians extracted a substantial cost in return. In addition, the poor railroad net running north from Galicia meant
that German superiority in ammunition quickly decreased as preassem-

bled stocks were depleted. This was not a path to victory, given Russia's enormous resources in space and manpower. Giving in to remorseless German pressure, the Russians began evacuating the western bank of the Vistula on 22 July, but still maintained stubborn resistance around the edge of the Polish salient.[32]

German success finally came not from Mackensen's armies but from their flank support to the west. After two weeks of bitter fighting, Mackensen's three armies had succeeded in grinding ahead between the Vistula and Bug only 25–40 kilometers. On the German left flank across the Vistula, however, Woyrsch's army group proved much more successful as the Russians conducted a fighting withdrawal. By end of July, it had outstripped Mackensen's troops on its right. Despite a preponderance of *landwehr* militia and Austro-Hungarian troops, Woyrsch managed to make excellent use of his unprepossessing human material. At Falkenhayn's instigation, Woyrsch took two *landwehr* divisions fighting southeast of Dęblin and sent them on a long circling march. Bypassing the well-defended outskirts of Dęblin, these divisions crossed the Vistula northwest of the town on 29 July with the support of Austro-Hungarian cavalry to establish bridgeheads on the river's east bank, at the juncture between the Russian Fourth Army to the south and the Russian Second Army defending Warsaw. This step presented *Stavka* with two serious threats. First, if Woyrsch turned east, that would put Austro-German troops *behind* the Russian Fourth Army holding back Mackensen between the Vistula and Bug, making its position untenable. If Woyrsch turned north, however, he could link up with von Gallwitz's army group east of Warsaw, trapping much of the Russian First and Second Armies.

At the same time Woyrsch crossed the Vistula behind the Russian Fourth Army, Mackensen renewed his offensive between the Vistula and the Bug. This time he enjoyed real success, as *Stavka* grew increasingly pessimistic about holding any territory west of the Bug. Position after position was abandoned. Russian Poland had become untenable, and *Stavka* had no choice but to pull troops east or see them cut off and annihilated. Lublin fell on 31 July. On 2 August, Alekseev ordered full evacuation from the west bank of the Vistula, and on 4 August, the Russians blew up the Dęblin fortress and withdrew all troops there east of the Vistula. Worst of all, on 5 August the Germans took an abandoned Warsaw, though celebrations were muted in hopes of easing the sting for the Russians and thus expediting a possible separate peace. The Russian Third and Fourth Armies withdrew north between the Vistula and the Bug, and Mackensen's troops followed behind. Despite the inherent difficulty of retreat while actively engaged with the enemy, the Russians pulled back in good order and maintained discipline, thus preventing any overwhelming German victory.

With the Russians lacking any viable line of defense west of the Bug, the Austro-German high command could focus on the final liquidation of the Polish salient and the tying up of loose ends. After a brief halt to consolidate his gains while resupplying and resting his exhausted troops, Mackensen renewed his attack on 11 August, chasing the retreating Russians toward the Bug, aiming at the fortress and communications hub of Brest-Litovsk. By 17 August, even while the Russian Third Army still retained a substantial bridgehead on the west bank of the Bug, the Germans and Austrians had established bridgeheads of their own north and south of Brest-Litovsk at Drohiczyn and Włodawa. Once the Central Powers had crossed the Bug, Brest-Litovsk, as the Russians had learned from bitter experience, could not be held and was abandoned. The Germans and Austrians established a new defensive line well east of the Bug.

THE GERMAN NORTHERN OFFENSIVE

Only one obstacle remained to a thorough vindication of Falkenhayn's original vision of a short, successful offensive to save manpower in the east: Hindenburg and Ludendorff's ongoing insistence on still more ambitious goals. The fall of the Russian fortresses on the Narew, and particularly Kaunas's surrender, convinced Hindenburg and Ludendorff that the moment had come to renew their original concept from earlier in the summer: a deep attack directly east through Vilnius toward the Russian heartland. Russian actions played into this, as the threat to Riga had drawn Russian troops north away from the region around Kaunas, Vilnius, and Dvinsk, weakening the Russian Tenth Army. On 17 August, *Stavka* had finally split the unwieldy Northwestern Front in two, making Ruzskii commander of a new Northern Front. Alekseev was briefly left as commander of the new Western Front, but quickly pulled back to *Stavka* to serve as chief of staff. Aleksei Evert then became commander of the Western Front.[33]

After the fall of Kaunas, Hindenburg's Tenth Army had not paused but continued to attack east along the Kaunas–Vilnius road, and the Russians threw the V Corps in its path on 21 August to halt the advance. Temporarily stopped, Hindenburg reorganized his troops and devised a new plan, badgering Falkenhayn for permission and resources to keep pushing deeper into Russia. He intended to use his own reinforced Tenth Army, supported by the Army of the Nieman to the north and the Eighth Army to the south, to seize Vilnius by enveloping the city from the north. In conjunction with the Niemen Army, the Tenth Army's goal was to punch a hole in the Russian front line wide enough to send an enormous cavalry force—six divisions—through the gap to swing south behind Vilnius and descend on Minsk from the north. To give Hindenburg and Ludendorff some credit, this was not merely an unthinking attempt to seize territory, for taking Minsk would cut important lines of supply and communication to the entire Russian Western Front.[34]

Hindenburg's new offensive began on 8 September. The Army of the Niemen drove the Russian III Corps east toward Dvinsk, while the German Tenth Army immediately to its south pushed the Russian Tenth Army southeast, back toward Vilnius. As the two Russian armies retreated on diverging paths, this opened a gap covered only by weak Russian cavalry troops between Vilnius and Dvinsk at the town of Švenčionys. A cavalry corps of four divisions under Otto von Garnier poured through this gap by 10 September, taking Švenčionys late on 12 September. Speeding through Russian rear areas, Garnier's divisions aimed for the major east–west connections running through Minsk. The Russian Tenth Army's right flank stretched further and further east to try to contain the breakthrough, finally bending south again. Tsar Nicholas, newly in place as commander in chief, did not want to preside over the loss of Vilnius so soon after taking command, and so insisted on the active defense of the city rather than its abandonment. This did no good; Vilnius fell to the Germans on 16 September, and only Pleve's desperate but improvised defense kept Dvinsk from capture as well.[35]

The Russian response was hampered by the exhaustion of available reserves from months of fighting as well as the remarkable speed of the German cavalry penetration. Nonetheless, within three days after the beginning of Hindenburg's offensive, Alekseev agreed with Evert, commanding the Western Front, on the deployment of a new Second Army under Vladimir Smirnov in the path of the German advance. Ordering a general withdrawal by most of the Western Front to escape encirclement, Evert detached four corps freed from the retreating armies by the shortening of the front—the XXXVI, IV Siberian, XXVII, and XIV—for dispatch to the site of the breakthrough. Marching northeast from the wreckage of Russian Poland, the four corps of the new Second Army began arriving on the threatened line between Vilnius and Minsk within days, and on 17 September Alekseev approved the withdraw of the Tenth Army toward Minsk, back to greater safety. Just as the Tenth Army was withdrawing, the new Second Army immediately to its east launched its own offensive north on 18 September, halting the German advance and providing a breathing space for the safe withdrawal of the full Western Front. The German attack, faced with increasing Russian resistance from these hastily assembled divisions, now began to retreat back north. On 25 September, *Stavka* approved a suggestion of Evert's and created a new First Army of three corps, temporarily placed under Smirnov's command, at the eastern edge of the threatened zone. The Germans had no choice but to evacuate the breach they had created at Švenčionys. Once again, Russia had suffered defeat but managed to avoid disaster.

Heartened by the summer's victories, Conrad overestimated his army's capabilities and planned a renewed offensive, much more exclusively an Austro-Hungarian affair, in western Ukraine. He intended to take advantage of a gap in the Russian lines created by the retreat from Poland. As Mackensen's offensive had pushed north between the Vistula and Bug, the Russian Third Army, on the far southern wing of the Northwestern Front, had retreated north along with it. This opened a gap east of Kovel, a breach covered only by the wide-ranging IV Cavalry Corps, between the Third Army and the armies of the Russian Southwestern Front, which were slowly withdrawing east. An Austrian attack into that gap could outflank the Southwestern Front's northernmost Eighth Army, centered on the town of Lutsk. On 27 August Conrad thus sent his First Army to outflank Brusilov's Eighth Army, while the other armies of the Central Powers—the Austrian Second, German Southern, and Austrian Seventh—attacked the Southwestern Front further south. Racing around Brusilov's right flank, the Austrians tried to descend on Lutsk from the north and cut off the Eighth Army's retreat. A vigorous counterattack on 29 August halted the Austrian advance long enough to enable Brusilov's Eighth Army to withdraw. Not quite on the scale of the summer battles in Poland, this Austrian autumn offensive managed to gain territory, but at a cost in lives far out of line with its strategic achievements. It failed to turn a Russian flank or achieve a major breakthrough, and as a result degenerated into an exhausting six-week slugging match. The Southwestern Front retreated east, but by 10 and 11 September were able to halt, rally behind the Seret River, and then reverse the Austrian gains with sharp local counterattacks, at first on the southern end of the Russian line and then on the northern. These captured 70,000 Austrian prisoners before the Central Powers stopped the Russian advance at the Strypa River in mid-September. Once his failure had become clear, Conrad pulled his troops back to the Styr River. By mid-October, both sides had accepted a peace of exhaustion, and the front lines temporarily stabilized in western Ukraine.[36]

Grand Duke Nikolai Nikolaevich had been driven close to nervous breakdown by stress of the long retreat. While the Russian Army's ability to withstand a series of blows and carry out an effective retreat over hundreds of kilometers was a real accomplishment, it was nonetheless a negative one. The sequence of disasters in summer 1915 and the political discontent it generated seemed to Tsar Nicholas and his government to require some scapegoat. Tsar Nicholas determined that Nikolai Nikolaevich had to go, dismissing him in September 1915 and assuming the role of commander in chief himself. The grand duke took his dismissal and new assignment as viceroy of the Caucasus calmly, even with good cheer. Alekseev, briefly placed in command of the Western Front, transferred to *Stavka* to replace Yanushkevich as chief of staff. He became Russia's de facto commander in-chief as a result of Nicholas's relative inexperience in military matters. Though like all members of the royal family Nicholas had some exposure to military life, he had nothing like the extensive military career of Nikolai Nikolaevich. Alekseev's calm and steadying presence, combined with thorough professional competence, meant that *Stavka*'s performance improved markedly. The son of a former noncommissioned officer, Alekseev was modest and reticent, which unfortunately only worsened Nicholas's own tendency to indecisiveness. A tireless worker and wary of delegating authority, Alekseev dealt with much of *Stavka*'s responsibilities singlehandedly until his health failed in late 1916.[37]

War Minister Sukhomlinov also fell as a result of the summer's disasters. The evident shortage of supplies that crippled Russia's ability to resist meant that someone had to be held responsible for failures behind the lines. On 24 June, in the midst of the Russian retreat, Sukhomlinov was dismissed for mismanagement, particularly the shell shortage that had crippled the Russian military effort. Sukhomlinov certainly had faults, including a propensity to take bribes and a resolute resistance to cooperating with Russian civil society, and he owed his position to his skill at glad-handing fellow officers and courtiers. In these, though, he was little different than hundreds of other tsarist bureaucrats. He combined these faults with undoubted talents, and had been decorated for bravery during the 1877–1878 Russo-Turkish War. Nonetheless, as war minister, he was well-placed to serve as the focus of criticism for the undeniable and widespread failings of Russian supply. Someone needed to be sacrificed to public opinion. In Sukhomlinov's place, Nicholas appointed Sukhomlinov's chief aide, Aleksei Polivanov, who was cut from a quite different cloth. Initially an engineer, a far more technical and less aristocratic branch than the infantry or particularly the cavalry, he was also a trained General Staff officer. He did not last long in office as minister of war, in part because of his excessive willingness to cooperate with Russian civil society, but he was competent and efficient in his time there.[38]

Sukhomlinov's downfall was not simply the result of battlefield defeat. He had become personally and professionally close to Sergei Miasoyedov, a colonel who had previously served in the gendarmes policing a post on the Russo-German border. Miasoyedov had married the daughter of a German-Jewish businessman. He took advantage of his position to befriend both Russian and German officers stationed along the border, and quite likely to engage in intelligence gathering on behalf of the Russian government as well as the opportunities for personal enrichment that came with control over a border post. Miasoyedov became a valuable aide for Sukhomlinov's various shady dealings as war minister, managing to create many enemies before his discharge over a sordid duel with one of Sukhomlinov's political rivals, the Octobrist political leader Aleksandr Guchkov. Moving back into the army on the outbreak of war, Miasoyedov became an intelligence officer for the Tenth Army in East Prussia. On thin and dubious evidence, he was arrested as a German spy on 4 March 1915, tried by a military court in Warsaw on 31 March, found guilty, and executed that same night.[39] Sukhomlinov's enemies were not satisfied with his dismissal from office, since they either genuinely believed him to be a traitor like his friend Miasoyedov, or cynically believed guilt by association

with Miasoyedov to be a handy political maneuver. The Duma voted overwhelmingly to recommend criminal prosecution against Sukhomlinov. He
was discharged from military service and then arrested in May 1916. Tried
and found guilty in September 1917 of treason and failure to prepare the
army for war, he was sentenced to life at hard labor. Amnestied in 1918 because of his advanced age, he went into exile.[40]

AFTERMATH OF THE GREAT RETREAT

Though World War I began with an Austro-Serbian conflict, the demands
of other fronts meant that Austria was unable to mass sufficient troops
against Serbia to drive it out of the war. Serbia had enjoyed a brief respite
from serious attack while Austrian energies were focused elsewhere, first
on fighting the Russians in Galicia and then in spring 1915 dealing with
Italian entry to the war. By late 1915, Russia's great retreat from Poland and
the Austro-German troops thereby released from the Russian front guaranteed that Serbia's brief survival as a small power between great powers
would end. Austria-Hungary had managed to contain Italy at relatively little cost, and Serbia itself, which had already suffered significant manpower
losses in the Balkan Wars and then in the first year of the World War, suffered as well from epidemic typhus triggered by the war's privations and
so neared the end of its reserves of manpower.

The ongoing strategic stalemate in the war as a whole made both sides
desperate to bring in additional allies in hopes of tipping the delicate balance of forces in their favor. Ongoing Austro-German diplomacy to recruit
Serbia's neighbor Bulgaria finally bore fruit when Russian defeats suggested
Bulgaria had limited time to cash in on joining the war. At the same time,
the Serbian government saw no point in conceding its own territory to keep
Bulgaria out of the war; Germany and Austria-Hungary, by contrast, had
no objection to gifts to the Bulgarians at Serbia's expense. On 6 September
1915, Bulgaria signed a convention with Germany and Austria-Hungary in
return for promises of substantial territorial concessions. All parties agreed
to a renewed offensive against Serbia in a month's time. Bulgaria's preparations for war, particularly the massive mobilization of hundreds of thousands of soldiers, were impossible to conceal. Russia attempted to keep Bulgaria out of the war through threats, but its ultimatum failed.[41]

The new campaign in the Balkans began with nearly simultaneous actions by the Entente and the Central Powers. On 5 October, French and British troops under Maurice Sarrail landed at Thessaloniki in Greece in order to march north and relieve pressure on the Serbs by forcing Bulgaria to defend its southern frontier. This expedition proved to be singularly ineffective. The next day, a joint German-Austrian force began the final invasion of Serbia with a massive bombardment of Serbian fortifications and the city of Belgrade itself. Geography and numbers weighed heavily against the Serbs, and the combined German Eleventh and Austrian Third Armies crossed the Danube and made slow but steady progress against dogged Serbian resistance. The Serbs might have held out until winter, but on 14 October two Bulgarian armies invaded Serbia from the east. Though terribly outnumbered (approximately 200,000 Serbians against 500,000 for the combined Central Powers), Serbia managed to maintain its positions in the north for a week, but the Bulgarian attack rendered Serbia's position hopeless. By late October, the Bulgarian attack had shattered Serbia's southern defenses, and in early November the Austro-Germans and Bulgarians linked up at Niš, Serbia's wartime capital. Facing certain annihilation if the Serbian army remained to fight, the Serbian command instead chose evacuation. The Serbian army and government, together with tens of thousands of civilian refugees, marched in the dead of winter southwest through Montenegro and Albania to the Adriatic coast, where 120,000 survivors were evacuated by British and French ships to the island of Corfu.

The Great Retreat meant that for the first time in the war, Russia lost significant territory, and with it human and material resources. Warsaw and Poland had been a substantial industrial asset, and relatively densely populated. Ivanov had ordered military-aged men to be evacuated and livestock driven east. This evacuation, predictably, turned into a spontaneous scorched earth policy, as soldiers destroyed private property rather than leave it to the enemy.[42] Losses to the Russian army were, of course, equally devastating. Precise figures on casualties are difficult to determine because of the scale of the operations, but were disastrous for both Russia and Austria-Hungary. In terms of Russian prisoners, Falkenhayn claimed 750,000, German archival sources suggest 850,000–950,000, and incomplete Russian sources record at least 500,000 captured or missing. Russian casualties of all kinds reached 2–3 million over the year. The year had been at least as hard on the Austro-Hungarians as it had on the Russians. Losses over 1915, suffered against Russia but also Serbia and Italy, were greater than in the six months of fighting in 1914, but with a greater proportional increase in men out of action due to disease. This was likely the result of a combination of circumstances, including the cumulative effects of hunger, cold, and exposure on weakening soldiers as well as sustained combat in the high altitudes of the Carpathians and the Alps. The already decimated Habsburg officer corps lost 4,400 dead, 14,400 wounded, 24,000 sick, and 8,300 captured or missing, for 51,000 total losses. Rank and file soldiers suffered 178,000 dead, 625,000 wounded, 700,000 sick, and 608,000 captured, for total losses of 2.1 million. Of those, 80–85 percent were suffered on the Russian front. German losses amounted to perhaps 200,000 in the east.[43] Though Russia managed to avoid complete collapse over 1915, its losses were staggering. The scale of its defeats makes the subsequent Russian recovery in the next year even more impressive.

8

The Caucasus Campaign, 1914–1917

If the Eastern Front is the neglected theater of the First World War, the war in the Caucasus is the neglected theater of the Eastern Front.[1] Its significance, both for the Russian war effort and particularly for the subsequent history of the region, was enormous. Russia's most important war aims involved control over the Turkish straits, and the war with the Ottoman Turks in the Caucasus belongs as part of the story of Russia in the First World War. Neither the Russians nor the Ottomans were eager for war with one another in 1914, though over the eighteenth and nineteenth centuries, Russia had fought the Ottoman Empire repeatedly for control of the Black Sea, for territory in the Caucasus, and for suzerainty over the Orthodox Christians of the Balkans. The long series of Ottoman defeats at Russian hands enabled the growth and ambition of the small states of the Balkans. The Ottoman government thus had a long series of accounts to settle with Russia when war exploded in 1914, but also abundant reason for caution. The military disasters of the Balkan Wars (1912–1913) forced the Ottomans to be cautious about whether to enter the First World War, and under what circumstances. It would mean fighting the Russians in the Caucasus, as well as the British in the Middle East. Such a step could only be taken with deep trepidation. For Russia, the most important territorial and political goals—domination of the Balkans and control over the Turkish straits—required a prostrate and defeated Ottoman Empire. Russia additionally saw eastern Anatolia and northwestern Iran as natural spheres of influence. Those ambitions were temporarily set aside, however, once war began in

178

summer 1914. The Russians had all they could handle in dealing with the Austrians and Germans, and no need to see the Ottomans join the war. For the Russians, at least, victory could solve all problems. If Germany and Austria were defeated, Russia's foreign policy goals with regard to the Ottomans could be dealt with easily; the only complication would be making sure Russia's *allies* would accept a major advance in Russian power. It took several months before the Ottomans finally joined the Central Powers. When they did, they found they had substantially overestimated their ability to take advantage of the weakness of a distracted Russian army.[2]

THE OTTOMAN ROAD TO WAR

By 1914, the Ottoman political system was in the midst of profound change. On 23 July 1908, a heterogeneous group of liberal reformers, mostly nationalist students and military officers from the Ottoman Balkans, carried out a coup. These Young Turks (more formally the Committee of Union and Progress) ushered in a brief period of enthusiasm for reform on the part of the Ottoman Empire's multiethnic and multireligious political class, eventually deposing Sultan Abdülhamid II and replacing him with the figurehead Mehmed V. Their power was opposed by conservative forces, including the Muslim *ulema* and the empire's military and political elite. Only when the Committee of Union and Progress consolidated its control over the Ottoman army in early 1913 could it be reasonably confident of maintaining itself in power. At least some in Russia, most notably Foreign Minister Izvol'skii, saw the political chaos in the Ottoman Empire as a chance for Russia to initiate a short, victorious war, but cooler heads in St. Petersburg prevailed and maintained peace.[3]

Other European powers were not so restrained. In September 1911, Italy declared war on the Ottoman Empire to seize the Ottoman provinces of Tripolitania and Cyrenaica in North Africa (modern Libya). An October 1912 peace cost the Ottomans Tripoli. This material evidence of Ottoman military weakness signaled the empire's vulnerability to further military aggression. The result was the Balkan Wars (1912–1913). In the First Balkan War, a coalition of Bulgaria, Serbia, Montenegro, and Greece invaded the remaining Ottoman possessions in Europe in October 1912, just as the Italo-Turkish War was ending. Faced with overwhelming odds, and attacked from all directions, the Ottoman position in Thrace and Macedonia was hopeless. Ottoman territory in the Balkans was swiftly overrun, though a tenacious defensive stand by Ottoman troops just outside Constantinople and at isolated fortresses maintained a foothold for the empire on the western side of the Turkish straits. An armistice in December 1912 brought hostilities to a temporary close. When the Ottoman grand council voted to accept peace terms that would ratify the loss of Ottoman Europe, the Young Turks took advantage of popular revulsion at the humiliating terms to seize complete power on 23 January 1913 and rejected the peace. Fighting began again on 3 February 1913.[4]

This time, the Balkan states' overextension and Ottoman recovery meant that the struggle was more even. The Ottomans had no hopes of regaining their prewar possessions, but had instead the much more practical and indeed desperate goal of defending their capital of Constantinople itself. By April, all sides were ready for an armistice. At this point, the victorious Balkan powers squabbled over the division of the spoils. Overconfident from its smashing victories in the First Balkan War, Bulgaria attacked Serbia and Greece at the end of June 1913, beginning the Second Balkan War. With the Bulgarian military fully committed to the west and south, Romania, which had not been involved in the first war, invaded Bulgaria from the north on 10 July. The Ottomans themselves then intervened to recoup some of their losses at Bulgarian hands. Four Ottoman armies, totaling almost a quarter of a million soldiers, faced only desultory resistance from overmatched Bulgaria. Ottoman troops reoccupied important territory on the western side of the Turkish straits, particularly the city of Adrianople.[5]

Turkish defeat in the First Balkan War drew the Ottoman Empire closer to Germany as a result of the need for German assistance in reconstructing Turkish armed forces. The chief German military advisor, Liman von Sanders, arrived in Constantinople on 14 December 1913, enjoying extraordinary powers to overhaul the Ottoman military from top to bottom. Von Sanders and his officers had inspection powers throughout the empire, control over military schools, membership on the empire's Supreme War Council, approval of promotion to general rank, and (in some cases) command of major Ottoman formations. War Minister Enver Pasha cooperated by cashiering over a thousand senior officers on grounds of incompetence. Russian foreign minister Sazonov objected vigorously, of course, to Germany's role in the Ottoman empire, but the British and French did not wish to push this to war. The British did not want to endanger their position as advisors to the Ottoman navy; von Sanders's delegation was carefully calibrated to be precisely the same size (seventy-two members) as the British naval mission. The Russians were unable to act alone, unwilling to risk military action against Turkey if it meant war against Germany without British and French support. As a sop to Entente opinion, von Sanders was promoted to a rank that removed him from direct command over troops.[6]

The 1914 July crisis found the Ottoman Empire only a year removed from devastating defeat, and raised the stakes of joining the war. The Ottomans ordered general mobilization on 2 August. Though mobilization went much more slowly than planned, the Empire's delay in entering the war meant no catastrophe resulted. The leading figures of the Committee of Union and Progress (CUP), in particular Minister of War Enver Pasha, carefully weighed their options. The bulk of the CUP felt that the better opportunity lay with Germany, because of both their sense of Germany's greater military power and the danger of Russian designs on the Ottomans.[7] Even so, it was not a foregone conclusion that Turkey would fight against Russia. The Turks had proposed an alliance to Russia in 1913–1914, and the Russians had little reason to want war. The Ottoman position astride the Turkish straits, one of Russia's key links to the outside world, gave the Ottomans enormous leverage over Russia and provided real material incentive for the Russians to want Ottoman neutrality. Russian trade was extremely vulnerable to any disruption to transit through the straits. Russia's chief grain-growing regions, along with the rich coal deposits of the Donets basin, lay in Ukraine and southern Russia on rivers that drained into the Black Sea. In 1913, 56.5 percent of Russian exports went through the Black Sea, and from there through the straits. In April 1911, during the Italo-Turkish War, the Ottoman government temporarily closed the straits, provoking Russian protest. When Italy bombarded islands in the Aegean on 18 April 1912, the Turkish government closed the straits until May. As a result, grain piled up on Russian docks, cutting Russian grain exports in half. Just before the outbreak of the First Balkan War on 18 October 1912, Ottoman Turkey again closed the straits to Greek and Bulgarian vessels (which carried much of Russia's exported grain), forcing Foreign Minister Sazonov to pressure the Greeks to refrain from any attacks on the straits in hopes of keeping them open. At the same time the Russian government reflagged Greek ships as Russian to maintain exports. In short, conflict with the Ottomans risked economic catastrophe for Russia.[8]

In addition, all Russia's options for naval war in the Black Sea were bad. In the years before the war, Russian strategy had focused on keeping an enemy navy out of the Black Sea, whether through naval supremacy, an amphibious landing to seize the straits, or mining of the straits to prevent passage. Naval supremacy was difficult to imagine, however, if the Turkish fleet were supplemented by the forces of another Great Power. In addition, the Young Turks had committed to expansion and modernization of the Turkish fleet, in large part to protect against Russian encroachment at the straits. An amphibious landing would be difficult to sustain logistically, and Russia never acquired the necessary specialized equipment. During the Balkan Wars, the Russian Black Sea Fleet could promise to transport only 2,000–3,000 soldiers for an amphibious assault, nowhere near enough. As a result, the Black Sea Fleet focused its efforts on the third option: contingency plans for mining the straits at their northern exit into the Black Sea. This was no mean task; Russian naval authorities were highly skeptical of their ability to manage it without substantial additional resources, and it would in any case destroy Russian commerce. Russia had no clear and coherent plan for naval war in the Black Sea, not without more capital ships.[9]

For the Ottoman educated public and political elite, war had much to offer. Given the popularity of social Darwinism in Ottoman intellectual circles, war might transform and modernize Ottoman society. The refining fire of war could revitalize Ottoman creative forces, while at the same time recovering the honor and standing lost by defeat in the Balkan Wars.[10] This desire for war among Ottoman elites did not necessarily mean war against Russia. In addition to Russian reluctance for war with the Ottomans, the Ottomans themselves enjoyed reasonably good relations with Russia's allies Britain and France, a fact that provided at least some brake on Turkish alignment with Germany and Austria-Hungary. Britain built warships for the Ottomans, and a British admiral reformed the Ottoman navy much as Liman von Sanders overhauled the army. In 1908 and 1911, the Turks had pursued a British alliance, albeit without success. The French did not have an important military role in the Ottoman Empire, but assisted the Ottomans in reforming civil administration, particularly the customs service.

In early 1914, the French had organized a major loan to the Ottoman government, one to which the Russians acquiesced for fear of driving the Ottomans to Germany. Finally, the Turks had just fought and lost a war against Italy, Germany and Austria-Hungary's ostensible ally.[11]

During the July crisis, the Ottoman government carefully surveyed its options, determined that Germany offered it better prospects, and began negotiating terms of intervention. Enver Pasha proposed an alliance to the Russian ambassador, but this seems more misdirection than serious intent to join the Entente. The German government responded warmly to Turkish overtures. Kaiser Wilhelm was captivated with the possibility of using Islam and the Ottoman Empire to undermine the British Empire. German efforts to construct the Berlin-Baghdad railway prior to the war, and then active efforts by German agents to foment jihad and Muslim rebellion against Allied rule both paid remarkably few dividends for the time, effort, and money that the Germans invested in them. Nonetheless, Wilhelm was firmly convinced that Turkish intervention would be decisive. On 1 August, the British government seized two essentially complete Turkish vessels, the *Reşadiye* and the *Sultan Osman*, from their British shipyards rather than risk the two battleships serving Germany, further alienating Ottoman opinion. On 2 August, the same day the Turks began general mobilization, Germany and the Ottoman Empire signed a military alliance, but the Turks were in no hurry to fight before their own defenses were prepared and specific conditions hammered out. On 6 August, the Ottoman government offered safe haven to two hard-pressed German cruisers in the Mediterranean, the *Goeben* and the *Breslau* under Rear Admiral Wilhelm Souchon, in return for German promises of concrete territorial gains upon victory. The two ships arrived in the Turkish straits on 10 August, and Turkey's nominal neutrality was maintained by the Turkish purchase of the two vessels (leaving the ships in possession of their German crews).[12]

But the precise moment of Ottoman intervention remained open and the subject of much dispute with the Germans. In September and October, the Germans were increasingly eager to see Ottoman participation in the war. Interior Minister Talat Bey, and particularly War Minister Enver Pasha, who had been trying to convince the other members of the government to start fighting, were at the same time trying to wheedle the best possible bargain out of Germany. They delayed while the increasingly frustrated Germans threatened and cajoled, a problem worsened by the Austrian failure to make any progress against Serbia. The combination of German carrots and sticks finally drove Enver Pasha to take action. The Turkish straits had been closed to commerce, and Arthur Henry Limpus, the British naval advisor to the Ottoman government, resigned his post, opening the door for the German Souchon to become commander in chief of the Ottoman navy. This provided Enver with a mechanism to start the war. On 24 October, he ordered Souchon to take his ships into the Black Sea and attack the Russians. On 27 October 1914, the German ships, now nominally Turkish, took to sea, and on 29 October, Souchon attacked Russian vessels and bombarded Russian Black Sea ports. In Novorossiisk, the port commander received word of the outbreak of war on the morning of 29 October, just before an enemy warship appeared outside the port and delivered a warning of imminent bombardment of the port and any ships remaining in it after four hours' grace. This provoked immediate panic and the flight of half the town's population (including the local governor) while Turkish shelling destroyed 20,000 tons of fuel and sank or damaged several cargo vessels.[13]

Even now, a sizable minority within the Committee of Union and Progress opposed the war and Enver Pasha's fait accompli. Their misgivings were too late; much as Russia might desire to keep the Black Sea and the Caucasus quiet, it could not ignore attacks on its territory. Russia declared war on the Ottoman Empire on 2 November, accompanied shortly thereafter by Britain and France. The Germans finally had what they wanted: the Ottomans at war with Russia. The Russians moved to assure support from their allies for their own aims in the war. In the Straits Agreement of 12 November 1914, Britain agreed to accept Russian control of Constantinople upon victory. France joined the agreement in spring 1915.[14]

The Ottoman army that went to war in 1914 was, like the Russian, in the midst of lengthy and painful modernization, but had much further to go. A German military mission had been created in 1882, and the Prussian officer Colmar von der Goltz became inspector general for the Ottoman army and then head of mission in 1883. A brief war with Greece in 1897 suggested that these reforms were progressing well, though they were far from complete by the Balkan Wars of 1912–1913. Ottoman defeat in the Balkan Wars did not discredit military reform but only underlined how essential it was. The costs of the two Balkan Wars were enormous. In addition to being expelled from the Balkan Peninsula, the Ottoman army had suffered perhaps 340,000 casualties: 50,000 killed in battle, 100,000 wounded, 75,000 dead from disease, and 115,000 taken prisoner. A staggering thirty-six divisions had been annihilated. There was no way to regard the Balkan Wars as anything other than a terrible defeat requiring radical improvements.[15]

At the war's outbreak, and for the rest of imperial Russia's time in it, the Ottoman armed forces were commanded by Minister of War Enver Pasha. As a result of a long heritage of German influence, and von Sanders's crash efforts at reform over 1914, the Ottoman army was organized largely on German lines. It also bore some comparison with its Russian counterpart, but important differences remained. Both relied on a system of ostensibly universal service with extensive exemptions on ethnic or religious grounds (the Ottomans excused non-Muslims from service). The youngest cohorts, drafted by birth year, made up the peacetime army, with two larger groups of older veterans making up first a reserve and then a territorial militia. Both were manned by peasant soldiers who were capable of remarkable feats of endurance and fought well when capably led. By contrast, though, the revolutionary upheavals carried out by the Young Turks purged the Turkish high command of superannuated relics of the old regime, replacing them with young, eager reformers, convinced of the need for aggressive action on the battlefield and disdainful of material and manpower constraints. The contrast with Russia's sclerotic high command was palpable. At lower levels, though, continuing shortcomings of the Ottoman social and educational system meant that middle ranges of the officer corps were quite poor, at the very time when social mobility meant that real talent from a variety of social groups was percolating up through the lower ranks of the Russian army's officer corps.[16]

The biggest contrast lay in the material infrastructure of war. The Ottoman population was only about 20 million, compared to Russia's 170 million. While the Ottoman army was quite large, amounting to a million men on paper, the long frontiers, underdeveloped infrastructure, and heavy reliance on irregulars meant the actual number of effectives was at best half that. It was short on officers—its 12,000 were less than a third of the Russian total, so the war forced the immediate transfer of military cadets from their schools to posts as junior officers. Its industrial infrastructure was entirely inadequate—the Ottoman Empire had only a tenth the railway mileage of British India. Indeed, the Ottomans lacked a single railroad to the Caucasus frontier. The empire possessed "a single cannon and small arms foundry, a single shell and bullet factory, and a single gunpowder factory." While Russia had a long way to go before full technical modernization, the Ottomans lagged well behind in modern field artillery and were particularly short of machine guns. Stocks of equipment and ammunition had not been replenished after the Balkan wars.[17]

THE OPENING CAMPAIGNS

For both the Russians and the Ottomans, the region to the southwest of the Caucasus mountains—eastern Anatolia and the Armenian highlands—was a difficult place to fight. Geographically, it was a tangle of mountains without good lines of communications either east–west or north–south. The Black Sea coast to the north offered few good harbors and was cut off by coastal mountains from easy access to the interior. Cold and snow in the winters and general lack of water made supply an ongoing nightmare, particularly since railroad access was so poor. The Russian railroad ran only as far west as Sarıkamış. The center of Turkish power in the region, the fortress at Erzerum, had no railroad connections as all. The region was ethnically complex. A quarter or a third of the population was Armenian, with a smaller number of Assyrian Christians in the interior and some Greeks on the Black Sea shore. The rest of the population was Muslim, divided between a Kurdish majority and a substantial number of ethnic Turks. Politics were even more complicated. The Russians suppressed Armenian nationalism on their side of the frontier while supporting Armenians and Kurds on the opposite side of the border to destabilize the Ottoman borderlands. At the same time, the Ottoman authorities turned a blind eye to periodic anti-Armenian pogroms on their own territory but backed Armenian nationalists inside Russia.[18]

Neither the Russians nor the Ottomans could spare enough troops to maintain a strong continuous front in the Caucasus. On mobilization, the Ottoman high command expected a field force of 460,000 men, including forty regular divisions and a host of reserve and irregular formations, but that strength was split between the Caucasus, Constantinople, Mesopotamia, and Palestine. The Ottoman strategic dilemma revolved around its lengthy frontiers and the tasks its army might need to accomplish. The Ottomans could move against British-controlled Egypt in order to cut the Suez Canal, put an expeditionary force into the Balkans, or attack Russia in eastern Anatolia and the Caucasus. At the same time, the Ottomans had to be prepared to defend the Turkish straits against British naval attack, Basra and the mouth of the Tigris and Euphrates rivers against British amphibious assault, and the Caucasus against a potential Russian invasion. Ottoman war planning, which lay almost entirely in German hands, proved as indecisive as the Austrian plans had been in August 1914. The German-devised plan concentrated two-thirds of Ottoman forces at Constantinople and the straits. When the importance of Ottoman commitments elsewhere became clear, many weeks and much energy were wasted shifting units around the wholly inadequate Ottoman transportation network. In 1914, defense of the Russian frontier in the Caucasus lay with Hasan Izzet Pasha's Third Army, made up of three corps (the IX, X, and XI). Though the enormous Ottoman losses in the Balkan Wars temporarily reduced troop strength in the Caucasus, by the outbreak of World War I in August 1914 total strength in the Third Army had reached nine infantry divisions (approximately one hundred battalions) and three cavalry brigades. Guerrilla units and irregular cavalry extended the reach of Ottoman regular forces, but were of little use against Russian formations and proved much more effective at massacring civilians.[19]

Similarly, Russia had limited forces available for use against the Ottomans, but a combination of geography and numerical advantage led the Russian command to go on the offensive. Russia had made the Caucasus a low priority, leaving one regular corps and one reserve corps there while sending the rest of the troops in the theater to Poland in 1914. Russia nonetheless enjoyed an initial advantage of approximately 150 infantry battalions to 100, and a similar superiority in artillery. Terrain also pushed a Russian offensive. The Russo-Turkish frontier ran generally east–southeast from the Black Sea coast to Mount Ararat. For roughly its last third, closest to the border with Iran, the frontier followed the line of the Agry-Dag range, a natural defense. In the central section of the front, though—the mountainous territory lying between Russian Kars to the northeast and Ottoman Erzerum to the southwest—the border ran perpendicular to natural barriers, cutting *across* rivers and ridge lines. Since that left no natural line to defend, reasoned the Russian high command, better to push forward and fight on Ottoman territory, seizing high ground and mountain passes. In addition, Russian advance disrupted Turkish communications with Iranian Azerbaijan, where Ottoman support for Kurdish militias threatened the vital oil production center at Baku. Russian deployment concentrated its regular forces in two groups. The larger, with six divisions, massed around Sarıkamış. This key point was the final station on the rail line from the Russian heartland through the city of Kars into eastern Anatolia, which thus served as a logistical center for any further Russian advance. This Sarıkamış group aimed to push forward on the route from Kars west toward Erzerum. The second and smaller concentration of two divisions was further east at Iğdır, just north of Mt. Ararat. It was ready to push southwest into Ottoman territory toward the regional centers of Alashkert and Doğubeyazıt. Smaller irregular formations covered the gap between Sarıkamış and the Black Sea. While Illarion Vorontsov-Dashkov held nominal command in the Caucasus as the tsar's viceroy, his age and poor health meant that real authority lay instead with Aleksandr Myshlaevskii, who prior to the war had served as both chief of the Main Staff and chief of the Main Directorate of the General Staff. Myshlaevskii was ably assisted by his own chief of staff, Nikolai Yudenich, later a key commander for the anti-communist Whites during the Russian Civil War.[20]

At the moment of Turkish attack on Russian Black Sea ports, Russian troops were already at the border and ready for action. Within days after the Turkish bombardment, indeed before Russia's formal declaration of war, Russian troops under Georgii Berkhman pushed forward rapidly across the border to seize positions on local high ground. Berkhman quickly exceeded the relatively modest goals of Russian planning. The Sarıkamış group moved recklessly toward Erzerum, seizing en route the Kara-Derbent mountain pass on its left flank. That passage allowed a connection back east to the Iğdır group, which had streamed through passes in the Agry-Dag. On 7 November, the whirlwind Russian offensive took Köprüköy, a village crossroads only 35 kilometers from Erzerum, and pushed past it to Pasinler, the last populated point before Erzerum itself. The rapid Russian advance carried with it the potential for disaster. Lead Russian units had outdistanced their supplies, no small matter in a Caucasus winter. In order to win time, the Turkish Third Army launched a counterattack from Pasinler toward Köprüköy against Berkhman's overextended advance units with four regular infantry divisions, two Kurdish divisions, and a cavalry division. A host of meeting engagements ensued as both sides struggled for control of hills and passes ringing Russian-controlled Köprüköy to the north, west, and south. Though the Turks sus-

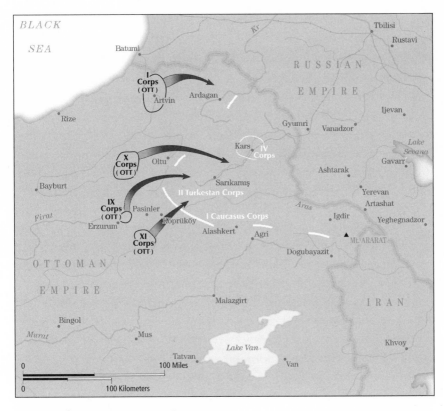

Map 10. The Caucasus, December 1914

tained heavy losses in their improvised counteroffensives, the Russian command was forced to commit the 2nd Turkestan Corps from its reserves at Tbilisi. The Ottomans intensified their counteroffensives on 11 November. By the next day, overstretched Russian forces were giving up ground in fierce fighting all along the leading edge of their push toward Erzerum. By mid-November, however, the Turkish advance lost steam, while worsening weather made rapid road movement impossible. A sharp Russian counterattack on 21 November caught Turkish troops off-guard, and forced a precipitate withdrawal back toward Erzerum. Both sides, now separated by space and exhausted by their back-and-forth pushes through the mountains, settled in to await further reinforcements. With the onset of winter, the Russians moved their troops into defensive positions.[21]

THE TURKISH ATTACK ON SARIKAMIŞ

The Russian halt gave the Turks the opportunity for a riposte. The first weeks of fighting had cost both sides substantial casualties, but the Russians had left themselves vulnerable. Their initial push toward Erzerum had left their troops concentrated well forward, with few reserves and little protection for their flanks. The Russian advance on Erzerum and the similar successes south of Sarıkamış were not matched in the northern sector of the line, between Sarıkamış and the Black Sea. The small and undermanned Oltu detachment, intended to screen and protect the right flank of the Russian drive on Erzerum, had failed to make headway, leaving that northern flank of the advance toward Erzerum dangerously exposed. Russian reliance on small and irregular formations allowed the Ottomans to move forward along the Black Sea coast and created the potential for a Turkish left hook to swing around Russian units and reach deep into Russian rear areas to attack Sarıkamış from the north. If successful, this would cut off Russian troops in dangerously exposed positions in the middle of a bitter Anatolian winter, allowing the wholesale destruction of Russian divisions. Inspired by Tannenberg, Enver Pasha, who had now taken over personal command in eastern Anatolia, prepared an attack on Sarıkamış.[22]

The Turkish plan, which was far beyond the capability of their relatively inexperienced commanders to execute and ignored the harsh climactic conditions, was for the XI Corps to fix the Russian defenders in place by a frontal assault east toward Sarıkamış. The Turkish IX corps on the Turkish left planned a shallow swing north around the Russian right wing, while the X Corps on the far left carried a simultaneous deep envelopment of the Russian right by passing through Oltu. The ultimate goal was to outflank, encircle, and destroy the Russians in a pocket west of Sarıkamış. In the name of speed, the flanking Turkish corps abandoned much of their heavy artillery. At the same time, the Turkish I Corps intended to move inland from the Black Sea coast, aiming toward Ardagan to further dislocate Russian defenses. The Turkish Third Army had about 75,000 troops in the field for this ambitious set of maneuvers, only slightly more manpower than the two Russian corps it faced.

The Turkish offensive opened on 22 December and quickly seized Oltu on its left flank, speeding through it toward the northern approaches to Sarıkamış, the heart of Russian defenses. By 25 December, the Russian situation appeared desperate. The Turkish I Corps from the Black Sea coast had captured Ardagan, and the X Corps on the Turkish far left was racing toward Kars, deep behind Russian lines. The IX Corps had moved through the Bardus pass northwest of Sarıkamış to directly threaten the town, essentially devoid of regular troops for its defense. The situation appeared so dire that the Russian commander Myshlaevskii lost his nerve, ordered retreat, and fled to Tbilisi, leaving Berkhman to organize the defense alone. The reckless stubbornness which had pushed Berkhman to overextend his initial offensive toward Erzerum, however, now led him to ignore Myshlaevskii's flight and take command. Yudenich, Myshlaevskii's chief-of-staff, likewise kept his nerve and continued to direct Russian resistance. In the center, the Turkish XI Corps' fixing attack directly east failed to hold the Russians in place. Berkhman pulled troops out of the line there, withdrawing them back east to Sarıkamış to defend the town until the overextended Turkish offensive collapsed. A scratch force of Russian garrison and service troops held Sarıkamış against the Turkish assault from the north long enough for reinforcements streaming in from the west, east, and south to march directly into battle.

In the conditions of the Anatolian winter, the Turks counted on victory to secure them shelter and supplies. The desperate but ultimately successful Russian defense of Sarıkamış made the consequences of the lost gamble clear. By 30 December, Turkish attacks were noticeably less vigorous and large formations were surrending *en masse*. In bitter cold, the Ottoman divisions were held at bay along the ridges northwest of Sarıkamış, with both flanks open to Russian encirclement. The Russians were quick to grasp their opportunity. Mikhail Przheval'skii, cousin of the more famous Russian explorer, led a detachment that captured the Bardus Pass on 2 January, cutting off Ottoman retreat. The Turkish IX Corps surrendered two days later. The X Corps managed to withdraw from its positions between Sarıkamış and Kars, but lost most of its men and equipment on the way. Of the 75,000 Turkish soldiers who began the offensive, only 10,000 were still under arms and in organized units by 9 January, the day that Enver Pasha abandoned the front to return to Constantinople. Returning stragglers brought the Third Army's manpower back up over subsequent days, but easily half the Third Army had been killed, wounded, or captured in the failed offensive.

Yudenich was rewarded for his performance by promotion to command while Myshlaevskii was put out to pasture for his cowardice. For the moment, though, Yudenich could do little to exploit his victory. Both sides were exhausted, and the remoteness of the theater made replenishing men and supplies extremely difficult. At some points, Turkish positions were 900 kilometers from their railheads. A typhus epidemic among Turkish troops made the situation even worse, but Enver Pasha continued to urge his divisions to bypass Russian positions and invade north-western Iran. Though Turkish troops crossed the border into Iran in December 1914, shortages of manpower and extended supply lines made staying longer than a few months impossible. Reserves of manpower were critically low. The Turkish IX, X, and XI Corps had only 15,000 men by March 1915. At the same time, though, the Russians needed to draw troops from the Caucasus to meet the increasing demands of the Austro-German front. As a result of scarce manpower on both sides in spring 1915, the Caucasus front was relatively quiet.[23]

The military campaigns of 1915 in the Caucasus are thus overshadowed by the beginnings of the Armenian genocide. On most of the fronts of the First World War, civilians largely escaped mass death. In the Ottoman Empire, however, between 500,000 and one million Armenian non-combatants were massacred or deliberately allowed to die from hunger and disease. For the Committee of Union and Progress, the Armenians presented a triple danger: they were an increasingly self-conscious and organized ethnic minority, they were religiously distinct from the Muslim majority, and they were a natural focus for foreign intervention in Ottoman affairs. Local, unsystematic pogroms against Armenians in 1894–1896 and in 1909 had built substantial amounts of ill-will: Armenians organized themselves for self-defense, which only increased official mistrust. By spring 1915, the CUP government moved to the systematic annihilation of the Armenian population, though disarming of Armenian troops in the Ottoman army had already begun earlier that year. The defeat at Sarıkamış had made the Ottoman government increasingly fearful of its ability to hold eastern Anatolia, particularly as irregular Armenian volunteers fought alongside the Russians and harassed the long and tenuous Turkish supply lines. With weaponry in short supply, only enough rifles were issued for one in ten of the ten thousand Ottoman soldiers tasked with keeping supplies flowing to the Third Army. In an atmosphere of growing tension, an Armenian uprising seized control of the city of Van in mid-April 1915. Immediately after the Van uprising, Anglo-French forces landed at Gallipoli, the southern entrance to the Turkish straits. The Ottoman government then arrested *en masse* Armenian political leaders and intellectuals in Constantinople, and began the systematic removal of Armenians from Anatolia. Though the precise nature of the process varied, men of military age were typically killed outright, while women, children, and the aged were marched into the deserts of northern Syria to die of hunger, thirst, and disease. Survivors were seized by local Muslim populations for forcible conversion to Islam and assimilation as wives or adopted children.[24]

In conjunction with the April 1915 Armenian uprising at Van, the Russians launched an offensive in May in the Tortum Valley, north-east of Erzerum, but achieved no great success. Further to the south, another Russian offensive succeeded in reaching and relieving the Armenian rebels at Van by mid-May. Russian advances threatened to outflank the Turkish position at Erzerum from the south. Attacking west from Lake Van toward Muş in July, the Russians were surprised by an unexpected concentration of Turkish forces which forced them to retreat east past Malazgirt. Just as at Sarıkamış, though, an overambitious Turkish attack squandered Ottoman gains and lost still more precious manpower. By September, both sides accepted a temporary peace of exhaustion. The Grand Duke Nikolai Nikolaevich, freshly dismissed from his position as commander-in-chief in the wake of the Great Retreat, was given an honorable sinecure as Viceroy of the Caucasus. He had the good sense to leave operational command of the Caucasus Army in Yudenich's capable hands.[25]

THE ERZERUM CAMPAIGN

In January 1916, the Ottomans appeared to have the luxury of strategic choice. The Allied landing force at Gallipoli had evacuated, freeing the Ottoman Fifth Army for service elsewhere. Enver Pasha's priority was to mass forces in eastern Anatolia to inflict a decisive defeat on the Russians. He expected to have time to reorganize his troops, dismissing the possibility of Russian winter operations. The Ottoman command was so unconcerned about potential Russian offensive action that both the commander and the chief-of-staff of the Third Army in the Caucasus left the front to spend the winter elsewhere. Unexpected Russian initiative denied the Ottomans the ability to use their newly available divisions. Yudenich supplied his troops cold weather gear and established a network of weather stations to prepare a winter campaign. On 10 January 1916, he launched a lightning offensive straight into the heart of Turkish forces defending the approaches to Erzerum, which dominated communication routes through eastern Anatolia. Though the Ottomans had troops to spare after Gallipoli, it was months before the inadequate Ottoman rail network could move them to the Caucasus. The Turkish Third Army fought bravely to defend Erzerum, but it was crippled by the length of front line it was forced to cover, from the Black Sea coast to Lake Van, and the shortage of men in the field. Turkish defenses in mountainous eastern Anatolia were made up of isolated strongpoints rather than a continuous line. Russian attacks infiltrated the gaps between those strongpoints, isolated the Turkish defenders, and destroyed them. In the initial fighting around Köprüköy, the Third Army's defenses were shattered within ten days and Yudenich's soldiers raced southwest toward Erzerum, where the survivors of the Third Army took refuge and rallied. The Russian offensive spread, to the southeast at Lake Van and to the north-west on the Black Sea coast.[26]

At Erzerum, Yudenich continued his pattern of boldness. While he attacked at a time when the Ottomans did not believe he could carry out an offensive, there was nothing subtle about his strategy. Erzerum lay in an east-west valley, protected by a ring of fortifications. As darkness fell on 11 February, after a day-long artillery bombardment, Yudenich's divisions simply struck directly west along the valley, focusing on two forts on a low ridge just to the east of Erzerum. Making slow but steady progress, Yudenich forced the Turks to evacuate Erzerum on 15 February, and took the city the next morning, along with hundreds of artillery pieces and thousands of Turkish prisoners. Though pursuit west from Erzerum was slow, Russian troops elsewhere in the theater achieved similar successes. By mid-April, the Russians captured Trabzon, one of the few good ports on the Anatolian coast of the Black Sea. To contain the Russian advance, the Turks threw seven new divisions into the Caucasus Front along with another army headquarters, the Second Army, to ease the burden of commanding a geographically far-flung theater in difficult terrain. Fatefully, though, the Turks failed to establish an overall theater commander, so the Second and Third Armies failed to work together in confronting the Russians.

After weathering scattered and weak Turkish counterattacks through the late winter and early spring, Yudenich was finally ready for another major offensive, this time aimed at Erzincan, 150 kilometers west of Erzerum. Changing his tactics somewhat, Yudenich did not simply push straight toward Erzincan, instead attacking further north at Bayburt. Beginning his offensive on 2 July 1916, Yudenich captured Bayburt on 17 July and then pushed toward Erzincan from the north-east, capturing it on 25 July. The Turkish Third Army was smashed and in no position to take countermeasures, but the Turkish Second Army to the southeast launched a counterattack on 2 August 1916, attacking north of Lake Van and attempting to cut Erzerum's connections east to the Russian railhead at Sarıkamış. The Russians, taking advantage of the difficult terrain and shifting their reserves south to meet the developing threat, halted the offensive by September, inflicting heavy losses on good Turkish divisions manned with experienced veterans of the Gallipoli campaign. The Turks had no choice but to overhaul their organization once again in hopes of achieving some success against the Russians. The bulk of the Turkish army (24 infantry divisions, many seriously understrength as a result of casualties) was committed to the Caucasus, and thus prevented from fighting against the British in Palestine, Arabia, and Mesopotamia (19 divisions) or on the Eastern Front alongside the Germans and Austrians (seven divisions).

The manpower demands on the Russian army, and as a result the limited means that could be allocated to the Caucasus, left Yudenich no choice but to bide his time for the rest of 1916.[27] After the fall of Tsar Nicholas in early 1917 disrupted the Russian war effort (discussed below), it became even more difficult to imagine further offensive action. Not least, Russian troops in the Caucasus were fighting on foreign soil. Given that Russia's new Provisional Government had to assuage popular opinion by declaring itself to be fighting only for defense of the national territory, not to seize and annex new lands, it could not justify further offensive action in Anatolia. This in turn permitted the Turks to remain on the defensive in the Caucasus, and devote their own scarce manpower to action in Palestine and Mesopotamia. Once the disintegration of Russia's military machine began in earnest in summer and early fall of 1917, Russia's armies in the Caucasus simply melted away. By February 1918, the Turks were ready to reclaim their lost territories, and began an offensive against small and hastily-organized Armenian formations on 12 February 1918. Erzincan, Trabzon, and Erzerum, taken at such pains by the Russians, all fell within a month. The Turks crossed the 1914 frontier into Russia by the end of March 1918, and over the rest of the year swept through the remainder of the Caucasus, reaching Baku on Black Sea on 15 September 1918.

Vladimir Sukhomlinov,
Russian War Minister,
1909–1915. (Imperial War
Museum)

Nikolai Yanushkevich,
Russian Chief of Staff,
1914–1915. (Imperial War
Museum)

Tsar Nicholas II and Grand Duke Nikolai, Russian Commander in Chief, 1914–1915. (Imperial War Museum)

German Emperor Wilhelm II and Franz Conrad von Hötzendorf, Austrian Chief of Staff, 1906–1911, 1912–1918. (Library of Congress)

Tsar Nicholas II with Allied Representatives. (RIA Novosti)

Paul von Hindenburg, Emperor Wilhelm, and Erich Ludendorff. (Library of Congress)

August von Mackensen.
(Library of Congress)

Russian Reservists Mustering for Service. (Imperial War Museum)

Russian Trench. (RIA Novosti)

Russian Troops on the March. (RIA Novosti)

Officers of a Russian Regiment. (Library of Congress)

Russian Artillery. (RIA Novosti)

Russian Antiaircraft Machine Gun. (RIA Novosti)

Russian Soldiers Taken Prisoner. (Library of Congress)

German and Austrian Soldiers Taken Prisoner. (Library of Congress)

Mikhail Alekseev,
Russian Chief of
Staff, 1915–1917.
(RIA Novosti)

Aleksei Brusilov. (Imperial War Museum)

Aleksandr Kerenskii (in vehicle), Russian War Minister and Prime Minister, 1917.
(Imperial War Museum)

Russian Women Soldiers Training. (Imperial War Museum)

9

Russian Society at War

The war brought wrenching transformation to all segments of Russian society, not least the military itself. The Russian army was continually engaged in modernization, transforming into a far more effective and capable organization than it had been at the start of the war. It nonetheless ultimately collapsed in 1917. This failure has two fundamental explanations: first, the army's modernization did not take place in a vacuum, but was measured against similar changes on the other side of the lines. While the Russian army's ability to sustain and transform itself matched and surpassed the Austrian and Ottoman armies, it fell short in comparison to the German. In this, the Russians shared the experience of their British and French allies, who also improved their performance markedly over the war, but nonetheless found the German army outfighting them man-for-man through 1918. Second, while the Russian army was changing, the same was true of Russian society. In comparative terms, Russian civil society—industrialists, local government, charitable and professional organizations—coped with war better than Tsar Nicholas's government. That government made matters worse by its reluctance to cooperate with civil society, preferring to maintain control regardless of potential gains from collaboration. When the final collapse happened in 1917, it began in the heart of the Russian state, in Petrograd, and only subsequently spread to the front lines. The Russian military was not blameless in this. It had many mistakes and blunders on its record, and its management of civil and economic affairs immediately behind the front lines showed its weaknesses. Nonetheless, if there was a weak link in Russia, it was the tsar and his government.

THE RUSSIAN PEOPLE AND THE OUTBREAK OF WAR

Russians, both civilians and soldiers, proved more resilient than many had expected. By 1913, some observers, including Vladimir Lenin in exile, believed Russia on the verge of revolution. Others, particularly in the liberal Cadet Party, hoped for gradual evolution toward responsible government. While the May Day strikes of 1912 included 80 percent of St. Petersburg workers, the geographical extent of participation had been limited. By 1913, Russia had surpassed Germany in its number of strikes and striking workers, obtaining first place in the world, but its strikes were short by Western standards, lowering the intensity of labor unrest. By summer 1914, while the Duma was mired in political crisis, the strike wave escalated substantially. Two hundred fifty thousand Petersburg workers participated in a one-day strike on May Day, followed by a general strike in the oil production center of Baku later that month and a sympathy strike in Petersburg. Labor unrest was still largely confined to the capital; Moscow and other industrial cities remained generally quiet. More reassuring for the regime, worker unrest was not supported by peasants, soldiers, or students, and revolutionary parties were largely uninvolved.[1]

Russia, like the other belligerents, saw crowds of enthusiastic patriots on the streets of major cities at the outbreak of war. Nicholas greeted an enormous crowd outside the Winter Palace on 2 August, and those crowds rallied again for Russian victories through the first few months of the war. Russia's urban, educated society was caught up by a feeling of national unity transcending class and politics. The war was called the "Second Fatherland War," recalling the war to expel Napoleon from Russia. Even before the German declaration of war, massive spontaneous popular demonstrations took place in cities across Russia. The Duma approved the necessary credits to finance the war without a hint of protest. Representatives of Russia's ethnicities whose loyalty might be suspect—Germans and Jews—proclaimed their unceasing loyalty to the Russian Empire and solidarity in time of war. How far this solidarity extended outside urban elites is questionable, though the provincial press claimed extensive peasant interest in news of the war. The Russian popular press hailed the war as a "just cause," though the precise nature of that cause remained obscure to Russia's peasantry. Rural populations and the working class were generally more resigned than ecstatic. Even so, as late as January 1915, when defeats at the front and inflation at home had begun to undermine social solidarity, demonstrations to mark the Bloody Sunday massacre that had sparked the 1905 Revolution still drew only 2,200 workers in Petrograd, by comparison with 56,000 in 1913 and 110,000 in 1914. The morale of Russian soldiers—peasants and workers in uniform—showed remarkable resilience, so far as we can judge. The Russian state monitored their correspondence for indicators on morale. This found that Russia's peasant soldiers did not particularly imagine themselves as Russian, but instead felt connection to their particular home region, their village, and their family. The Russian Empire was far too vast and incomprehensible to engender any emotional bond. Indeed the connection to their homes was so great that one of the greatest incentives to bravery and heroism was the home leave that came with a medal. Nonetheless, little active opposition to the war was evident.[2]

Russians saw the war in religious terms, as a holy struggle, despite all the confessional problems created by the concrete makeup of the warring sides. Orthodox Russia fought alongside Catholic France and Anglican England against Lutheran Germany; turning that into a crusade was not simple. The leading religious philosophers—Nikolai Berdiaev, Sergei Bulgakov, Yevgenii Trubetskoi—regarded the war as one of Christian faith against "Germanism," which was *not* Christian, but overcome by some aggressive and destructive spirit. The war was one of liberation, but liberation of whom and from what was not particularly clear.[3]

This potent blend of patriotism, sacrifice, and duty extended to prohibition: restrictions on alcohol across Europe. In Britain, drinking hours were restricted, and George V banned beer, wine, and liquor at royal residences. The Russian government also instituted prohibition at the outbreak of war, ending the sale of vodka and other strong spirits, and restricting the sale of beer and wine. Government officials and social activists alike had long bemoaned the harmful effects of alcohol as well as the Russian state's unhealthy dependence on alcohol revenue. Early in 1914, Finance Minister Pyotr Bark had prepared to wean Russia off vodka by increased taxes and prices. War Minister Sukhomlinov recalled with horror the drunken riots that had accompanied mobilization for the 1904–1905 Russo-Japanese War. In summer 1914, he removed alcohol from mobilization points and transit routes to the front. The army in order 309 of 22 May 1914 called on officers to set an example of sober behavior and prohibited drunkenness in public, and particularly before enlisted men. Sobriety became part of officer fitness reports, and regimental surgeons were charged with delivering regular educational programs on the harms of alcohol. For enlisted men, hard liquor was entirely prohibited on active duty, and they were urged to join anti-alcohol societies. Their commanders used chaplains and church services to promote morality along with calisthenics and athletic competitions to drain excess energy. In their turn, regimental chaplains were required to verify twice-yearly attendance by officers at lectures on the benefits of sobriety while counseling those in the lower ranks prone to drunkenness.[4]

Wartime prohibition did grave damage to Russian state finances, but may have substantially improved public health. The last prewar budget prepared by Kokovtsov, finance minister and chairman of the Council of Ministers, relied for a quarter of its revenue on alcohol: 936 million of 3,572 million rubles. No one in summer 1914 expected the war to last as long as it did, so the fiscal damage of prohibition was not anticipated. On the other hand, the benefits to Russian society were very real. Women, less prone to heavy drinking but suffering its social consequences, were supportive of prohibition. Grassroots pressure was widespread to maintain the ban on hard liquor and to extend local prohibition to beer and wine. Popular perception was that industrial and agricultural productivity benefited from sobriety and crime fell. To be sure, individuals sought alternatives. Petrograd's consumption of denatured alcohol rose by 30 percent during the war. Some drinkers turned to narcotics, while well-connected urbanites could obtain alcohol from pharmacies. Drugstores in Moscow boosted their consumption of pure grain alcohol by 7.5 times.[5]

As part of Tsar Alexander II's Great Reforms, Russia had established local, elected self-government: councils for towns and cities and equivalent *zemstvos* in rural areas. Over the decades prior to the war, rural Russia had become reliant on the *zemstvos* for basic medical, veterinary, agricultural, and educational services. Though the autocratic tsarist regime regarded them with deep suspicion, these elected bodies responded to war with remarkable voluntary enthusiasm to organize medical services and care for soldiers' families. This expanded over the course of the war to supporting munitions production as well. Not only did the war increase the strain of providing social services, but the trained and educated *zemstvo* personnel, a scarce commodity in rural Russia, were hard hit by conscription. Thirty-five percent of *zemstvo* doctors were conscripted within the first year of the war. Thirty thousand schoolteachers were drafted, largely because their education and administrative experience made them vital as noncommissioned and junior officers. The war also reduced the number of policemen in the already undergoverned countryside. The police who remained behind were resented for their failure to serve at the front alongside other able-bodied men.[6]

The general spirit of communal dedication and sacrifice, particularly when the tsarist state failed to fulfill its expected responsibilities, extended to something as concrete as wounded soldiers. When the Russian government failed to care adequately for its wounded and sick, Russian society organized itself to meet the need. At the outbreak of war, the Russian army was unprepared for the sheer volume of casualties. The wounded piled up at cities and railway junctions behind the lines. The surgeon S. R. Mirotvortsev, veteran of the siege of Port Arthur and no stranger to war, was horrified to visit Lublin and find thousands of wounded lying in the rain without medical assistance. Through heroic mobilization of local resources along with students and medical personnel from Kiev, he managed to evacuate 40,000 wounded men in the space of fourteen days. Over the period from August 1914 to November 1916, 5.8 million sick and wounded soldiers were evacuated from the front to medical institutions in the rear. The Russian state could manage this flood only by relying on the voluntary efforts of non-state or quasi-state organizations. By 14 November 1915, Russia had a network of 783,000 hospital beds, of which 106,000 were provided by the Russian Red Cross and an additional 257,000 by the Union of Zemstvos and Union of Towns. By the time Russia's war effort collapsed in 1917, it had just under one million hospital beds available for an army of 6.5 million. This proved a reasonable match with the 1.2 million soldiers wounded yearly, each with an average hospital stay of seventy days.[7]

That medical network was created by the Russian government's appeal to Russian society for assistance. In Samara, for example, immediately after the outbreak of war a group of local notables created a provincial committee under the All-Russian Union of Zemstvos to care for the wounded, initially by placing them in private homes but more permanently by constructing hospitals. Western provinces were tapped first, but soon the scale of casualties forced streams of sick and wounded soldiers deeper east into Russia. While local authorities set up hospitals and mess facilities, their efforts were constrained by lack of funding and trained medical personnel. As a rule, these early improvised measures to prepare medical facilities depended on the initiative and cooperation of city and provincial authorities and on voluntary contributions by Russian society. While this was workable for the first months of the war, it assumed a short war. The state attempted to provide financial assistance in the form of grants and loans, always insufficient, to the chief private organizations assisting the sick and wounded. The Union of Zemstvos received 2,200 million rubles, the Union of Towns 600 million, and the Russian Red Cross 245 million. As the conflict dragged on and costs grew, Russia's provinces could no longer cope, and the Russian state proved unable to help them.[8]

For wounded Russian soldiers, treatment began with a company medic (fel'dsher). The weakest link in the entire Russian system followed: military transport from the battlefield to a railhead with a well-equipped medical train. While the Russian army's goal was a detachment of twenty ambulances for each corps, it never achieved that. Soldiers typically spent the first stage of their evacuation on stretchers carried by regimental and divisional stretcher bearers to regimental medical posts, potentially still under fire, and from there by horse-drawn cart to divisional medical units, generally out of range of enemy artillery. Lightly wounded soldiers were kept at divisional hospitals. From the front, one set of relatively crude field medical trains moved more seriously wounded soldiers within the combat zone to evacuation points run by individual armies. Those whose recovery would take six weeks or less were kept close to the front; the rest dispatched to the rear. From there, more elaborately equipped medical trains took soldiers by stages to their ultimate destinations deep inside Russia, where the majority of available hospital beds lay. Though mobilization plans had envisaged 100 evacuation trains, Russia went to war with only 46. Capacity grew rapidly, with just over 200 by late 1914, more than 300 by the start of 1915 and 400 by the end of 1916.[9]

Given the standards of the time, Russian medical care was not bad. One experienced observer estimated that of one sample of 1,799 wounded, 958 had their wounds dressed within two hours of injury, and only 51 after twenty-four hours. On the other hand, of those 1,799, only 878 had their wounds treated by trained medical personnel; the rest had their bandages applied by a stretcher bearer, a fellow soldier, or the wounded soldier himself. In another sample of 2,000 wounded, 879 were delivered to a regimental medical facility within six hours, and 243 after a full twenty-four. Once soldiers survived to reach hospitals in rear areas (a measure that excludes the most seriously wounded and the most arduous parts of their journey), their chances were good: 2.4 percent of sick and 2.6 percent of wounded died. Among those hospitalized, 44 percent of wounded and 46.5 percent of sick soldiers ultimately returned to duty.[10]

The patriotism that rallied around the regime and built hospitals had a dark side when turned against internal enemies, a phenomenon evident from the first days of the war. On 22 July 1914, a mob in St. Petersburg left a patriotic rally to destroy German stores and a German-language newspaper before sacking the German embassy. The imperial government clearly saw its interests in the maintenance of public order, and tried to constrain overt hostility. Moscow governor A. A. Adrianov declared flatly that "the legal authorities of HIS IMPERIAL MAJESTY stand in protection of the interests of the motherland, and the chance person on the street is not allowed to resolve the question of who is good or who is harmful for the state." The same was true of much more serious riots in Moscow on 8–11 June 1915: the regime encouraged patriotism, but mob violence was disruptive and counterproductive. Beginning with spontaneous disturbances by a group of women complaining of Germans in the royal family accompanied by striking workers at a print shop, the June disturbances grew far more serious the next day, turning into attacks on German property, German subjects, or suspected Germans. Some were saved from mob attacks by police arrest, but several were killed. The rioting hit its height on 10 June, spreading throughout Moscow and attacking foreign property indiscriminately, whether linked to Germany or to Russia's allies. The Moscow city administration used deadly force to disperse the rioters, but not before at least a dozen people had been killed and hundreds of businesses destroyed.[11]

Given Russia's late economic development in relation to Central and Western Europe, foreign entrepreneurs and industrialists had long played a central role in its economy. This, combined with 3 million ethnic Germans on Russian soil, made them a natural target for discriminatory legislation. The army began the process, using its extensive powers in frontline zones to expropriate German property. In January 1915, the Russian government barred enemy subjects from commercial enterprises and mandated the liquidation of their businesses, and in December it expanded these measures to industry. In February 1915, the Russian government attacked landholding by German or Austro-Hungarian citizens. This served parallel purposes: providing a stock of land to reward Russian soldiers while weakening the economic role of enemy aliens. While much German land was concentrated on the Volga River or in southern Ukraine and relatively far from the front lines, Germans did own substantial land in Volhynia in western Ukraine. Wartime laws barred new acquisition of land and gave enemy aliens owning land in border regions a deadline to divest themselves of their property. Occupation of Poland and Galicia by the Central Powers in summer 1915 made the law a dead letter, but in the meantime it had managed to cause considerable economic chaos and reduce the amount of land sowed in southern regions by 10 percent as German owners prepared to sell. The loss of highly productive German farmers did noticeable damage to agricultural yield.[12]

IMPACT OF THE GREAT RETREAT

Social cohesion and resignation to the war's burdens lasted about a year. Weariness over death and suffering combined with the military catastrophes of 1915 to discourage soldiers, embitter social and political relations, and destroy the fragile concord that had sustained Russia through the first year of war. The process was not rapid or irreversible. Despite the losses at the front, active antiwar sentiment remained limited. Most elements of Russian society were quiescent for most of the war. Conscription was generally met with acceptance rather than evasion or active resistance, at least through 1916. In Saratov, for example, no expressions of resentment or opposition to conscription or the war effort were evident until summer 1915, a year into the war, with peasants unhappy but resigned to their fate rather than hostile. Moods then improved until another period of public discontent in summer 1916. True mass discontent appeared only *after* the February Revolution began destroying central authority. Discontent, at least for the first period of the war, took the form of opposition not to the war or to the tsarist regime, but instead to concrete, local problems centering on support for soldiers' families.[13]

Huge losses of territory in summer 1915, combined with other population displacements, meant that Russia had 6 million refugees by 1917. In addition to burdening Russia's already overworked social services, this refugee population worsened latent national tensions. Though overwhelmingly legal subjects of the Russian Empire, these refugees were typically not ethnically Russian but instead Polish, Latvian, Lithuanian, or Ukrainian, and so ethnically, religiously, and linguistically distinct from the ethnic Russians among whom they were forced to settle. The Russian military and particularly Chief of Staff Yanushkevich had mandated forcible evacuation for whole populations in Russia's western borderlands, not just Germans and Jews who were particularly suspected of disloyalty. Millions of these national minorities found themselves forced to organize to defend their collective interests, and increasingly at odds with a Russian state and society that they had previously had less reason to resent.[14]

The general flood of refugees was joined by Jews who were forcibly removed from areas behind the front lines under suspicion of collaboration with the enemy. Individual violence against Jews was widespread and probably unavoidable: millions of peasant soldiers inevitably generated random violence against women or suspected enemies. In summer 1917, commissar Victor Shklovsky matter-of-factly noted that soldiers had killed two Jews, ostensibly for signaling the enemy. Systematic policies had a different origin. The Jews came in for particular suspicion because of the belief that they were naturally sympathetic to the Central Powers. This is, of course, a quite different pattern than during World War II: no one could imagine the Jews of Eastern Europe supporting *Hitler*'s Germany. Deportation of the Jews grew out of policies of removal of enemy subjects—that is, German and Austrian citizens—from the front lines in fall 1914. That category grew to include Russian subjects of German ancestry, resulting in hundreds of thousands of people forcibly deported to internal areas of Russia by 1916. Russian policies of the forcible deportation of Russian Jews (as opposed to German or Austrian Jews resident in Russia) began in January 1915, when Yanushkevich authorized the removal of Jewish communities in cases where individuals were suspected of spying. Mass and systematic deportations of Jews from large sections of Poland followed in March and

April. Deportation accelerated with the military disasters of the summer, driven by growing panic and hysteria among common soldiers and their commanders. Grand Duke Nikolai Nikolaevich attempted to calm matters by warning against unfounded paranoia about spies, but to little effect. Evacuation from Galicia and Poland thus included the forcible removal of hundreds of thousands of Jews. Protests by Russian civil society, and even the Russian government, against Yanushkevich's blanket measures against an entire ethnic-religious community on grounds of humanity as well as practicality went nowhere. Measures against Jews extended far beyond forcible evacuation from war zones, and included closing Jewish newspapers. Perhaps most traumatic was the taking of Jewish hostages to ensure the good behavior of other Jews. At Modlin fortress, for example, the garrison commander N. P. Bobyr' ordered his troops to take Jewish hostages to serve as guarantors against treason. Measures improved somewhat after the leadership shakeup of early autumn 1915. When Alekseev replaced Yanushkevich as chief of staff, military policies toward the Jews softened noticeably, though Alekseev had certainly participated in expulsions before his promotion.[15]

The Great Retreat necessarily damaged military morale, but soldier morale like civilian proved remarkably resilient, and improved after 1915 in line with Russia's military performance. Censors noted an increase in soldier complaints about Germans and traitors at home, with soldiers resentful of speculators who drove up prices and workers who struck for a shorter work day. Thousands of letters sent to Saratov *oblast'* from the front from autumn 1915 through the end of 1916 show that complaints, criticisms of leadership, or wishes for a quick end to the war peaked in September 1915 at 2.9 percent of the total volume, and dropped in 1916 to a mere handful: 11 letters of more than 18,000 sent in the final week of 1916.[16]

The stabilization of the fronts after 1915 gave the Russian army much needed breathing space, but also saw increased fraternization across no-man's-land. The story of the Christmas truce on the Western Front in December 1914 is relatively well known; on the Eastern Front, fraternization took longer to appear. Isolated instances occurred earlier: V. S. Littauer, writing later in emigration, told of German officers offering cigars and cognac to their Russian counterparts in a gentlemanly greeting in no-man's-land until the Russian division's commanding general forbade the practice. An order of the Russian First Army from 29 December 1914 described German troops on Christmas Day emerging from their trenches, separated from two Russian regiments by a river. Waving white flags and carrying bottles and cigars, they crossed the river in a boat, where they met Russian soldiers and at least one officer. Some of the Russians crossed back over the river with the Germans, where they were promptly taken prisoner. The order directed that the officer be court-martialed and that on any repetition Germans offering a truce were to be met with fire. As a large-scale phenomenon, however, fraternization appeared not at Christmas 1914 but instead at Easter in April 1915. The same thing happened again on a larger scale in April 1916. Though timing varied, the nature of the phenomenon was much the same as in the west. Soldiers carefully emerged from their trenches to meet, exchange handshakes, cigarettes, and alcohol, and show photographs of families. Russian soldiers in particular wondered at the creature comforts they saw in their glimpses of Austro-German trenches. For Brusilov, commanding the Southwestern Front, this was a deliberate effort by the Austrians and Germans to take advantage of "Slavic kindheartedness"; Anton Denikin, reprimanded for his lax approach to fraternization, dismissed it as harmless—indeed, a touching reflection of common humanity.[17]

The Great Retreat of 1915 made desertion into a substantially worse problem. Prior to the war, Russia suffered from desertion like all armies, but at rates that were not particularly alarming considering that Russian soldiers were conscripts: in 1912, 13,000 soldiers deserted from the entire Russian army, or roughly one in one hundred. On the outbreak of war, the disincentives to soldierly life grew far greater, and desertion rates increased. In the space of a single month in the winter of 1914–1915, the Southwestern Front alone apprehended on its rail networks 13,000 deserters. In Russia's vast spaces, desertion was hard to combat. Chief of Staff Yanushkevich argued in spring 1915 that only harsh penalties for villages that failed to report homecoming deserters could deal with the problem. Many deserters left the front from fear for their lives, so the thought of five years in prison (the penalty for a first offense) was not necessarily a deterrent, particularly since sentences were to be deferred to the end of the war when popular opinion held that a general amnesty was inevitable. Likewise, imprisonment or execution (the penalty for a third offense) did nothing to alleviate the army's need for manpower. The Russian army had to do its own policing, establishing checkpoints on railroads and in major cities to catch and return deserters to the front lines. The Northern Front was particularly thorough, registering all inhabitants of villages near its units and preventing contact between soldiers and sympathetic locals.[18]

The Great Retreat not only cost the Russian army killed, wounded, and prisoners, but made desertion significantly easier. The chaos of withdrawal multiplied opportunities for stragglers to separate from their units. Individual soldiers could hide in the flood of refugees streaming eastward, while the guards monitoring railways behind the front lines were overcome by the scale of evacuation. As the number of deserters grew, their ability to do mischief increased. Theft, robbery, and rape by larger groups of deserters made life increasingly perilous behind the front, stretching all the way back to the outskirts of Moscow. While desertion rates climbed steadily over the war; they displayed significant cycles. In particular, Russian soldiers seemed content in the summers, when desertions was generally low, but far more likely to set out for home on the approach of winter. On the Southwestern Front, desertion hit 5,000 per month in spring 1916. A special authority in Petrograd created to deal with deserters apprehended a thousand a week. Precise and comprehensive figures are difficult to come by, since during combat it could be difficult to distinguish missing and the prisoners from the deserted, and the same soldier could also desert several times over. Nonetheless, Russian fronts managed to apprehend approximately 200,000 deserters from 1915 to the February Revolution, while Russian police caught another 225,000 behind the lines in 1915 and 1916. This compares to approximately 35,000 deserters from the British and German armies during the war.[19]

The Great Retreat also had serious political implications. In the summer of 1915, Nicholas dismissed several of his ministers, notably Minister of Internal Affairs Nikolai Maklakov, particularly opposed to cooperation with civil society. This gesture toward compromise did not satisfy Russia's moderates, who in late summer organized the Progressive Bloc, a group at the center of the Russian political spectrum. Including both the moderately conservative Octobrists and the moderately liberal Cadets, the Bloc commanded a majority of the Duma and called on Nicholas to create a government enjoying the confidence of the Duma and more generally to invite public participation in managing the war. Their efforts at political cooperation and calls for the dismissal of particularly reactionary ministers achieved almost nothing, pushing them into increasingly radical opposition. Though some within Nicholas's government (notably Minister of War Polivanov) sympathized with the Bloc's goals, Nicholas himself saw them as anathema. Any sign of weakness at a moment of defeat could lead only to political crisis.[20]

Matters were worsened by Nicholas's dismissal of Grand Duke Nikolai Nikolaevich and assumption of the role of commander in chief. His ongoing presence at *Stavka* removed him from Petrograd, resulting in governmental drift. Nicholas's wife, Alexandra, came to exert increasing influence over politics and ministerial appointments, which in turn increased the power of the charismatic and depraved Siberian holy man Grigorii Rasputin. Rasputin had worked his way into the trust of the royal family by his seeming ability to help Nicholas's son and heir Aleksei in health crises resulting from his hemophilia. Russia's anti-German sentiment, much of it directed at the German-born Alexandra, drove her into increasing isolation and increased Rasputin's power over her. While his influence is often exaggerated, he unquestionably had an important voice in a flood of ministerial appointments, notably the manifestly incompetent and unpopular Boris Shtiurmer, chairman of the Council of Ministers from the beginning of 1916, and Aleksandr Protopopov, minister of internal affairs from September 1916. The ongoing mismanagement provoked Pavel Miliukov, leader of the Cadet Party and important figure in the Progressive Bloc, to ask the Duma in November 1916 if the Russian government's policies were "stupidity or treason." On the night of 29–30 December 1916, Rasputin was murdered by a group of disgusted aristocrats, an action that only served to further discredit Nicholas's regime.

SUPPLYING THE FRONT WITH MEN AND ARMS

The most direct impact of the Great Retreat was on the Russian army itself: millions of men had been removed from the ranks of Russia's soldiers and officers, and needed to be replaced. The defeats had come in large part from shortages of rifles and ammunition, and those shortfalls had to be addressed. Other powers were in a similar bind. As early as November 1914, 80 percent of Austrian officers and 40 percent of soldiers arriving at the front as reinforcements were not new recruits but those recovered from earlier wounds.[21] Russia was in similar straits even before the 1915 catastrophe. On the outbreak of war, the Russian army had grown from 1.4 million to approximately 4.5 million with the addition of 3 million men from Russia's reserves. By the end of 1914, the Russian state had mobilized all its reserves, but in addition had dipped into its essentially untrained *opolchenie*, bringing in those born from 1879 through 1893 who were physically capable of active service but had not been selected to actually complete their active duty. This measure generated an additional 2.3 million men. By the start of 1915, that totaled roughly 6.5 million men called to serve, many of whom had been lost in the first six months of the war. In 1915, as a result of massive casualties, Russia was compelled to return to its large but not unlimited pool of manpower. In January 1915 the regime called up the 1894 cohort (that is, men born in 1894) eight months ahead of schedule. In late spring, it added a portion of the 1895 cohort sixteen months ahead of schedule, and by late summer had added the 1896 cohort, over two years ahead. There was a limit to how far this expedient could go: Russia was losing soldiers faster than boys grew to the age of military service, and speeding the process any further would mean drawing soldiers even earlier in their teens. Under its new War Minister Polivanov, Russia dipped further into the untrained *opolchenie* over 1915, calling up 2 million men from among those less physically suited for military service or previously excused on grounds of age or family circumstance (only sons or sole breadwinners). In total, Russia mobilized 4.65 million men in 1915, and relayed 3.3 to 3.5 million of them to the front.[22]

The process repeated itself in 1916, with the 1897 cohort mobilized early in the year, more than two years ahead of schedule when most of them were 18 years old. The government continued to pull in older and less fit members of the *opolchenie*. There was an inherent limit to this as well—given the poor nutrition and hard life of Russian peasants, men in their late thirties not yet drafted were less capable of withstanding the rigors of campaigning. The army managed to send 2.5 million replacements to the front. In summer 1916, Nicholas issued a directive extending conscription to the nomadic Muslims of Central Asia for noncombat service in rear areas. This policy was a disaster: there were no reliable birth records, and the implementation of conscription provoked uprisings and ethnic riots that killed thousands of people. In early 1917, the 1898 cohort of 700,000 men was drafted as well before revolution finally ended imperial Russian conscription. The decline in quality of recruits was palpable, as older, sicker, and less experienced men took the place of younger, healthier trainees in combat units. The War Ministry made a concerted effort to cull the population for deserters and comb rear-area units for able-bodied men. By the end of 1916, Gurko was experimenting with expanding the number of divisions by the simple expedient of reducing them from sixteen battalions to twelve. By the end of the war, some 15 million soldiers had been called up, over one-sixth of the country's male population.[23]

Russia also ran short of talented officers. Observers have decried Russia's abundance of superannuated officers, political appointees, and blinkered traditionalists in command. These were, of course, all flaws shared by every other European army. There were certainly examples of egregious incompetence or inexperience. General V. F. Dzhunkovskii had never commanded a company, but in 1915 on his retirement from the Ministry of Internal Affairs was placed in the command of the 15th Siberian Rifle Division. In August 1914, Sukhomlinov wrote Yanushkevich (neither characterized by military genius) that "our troops are fighting heroically, but some of our generals? Better if they'd been fighting on the other side."[24] On the other hand, as a result of the Russo-Japanese War, many Russian officers had at least some experience with modern warfare, and the Russian Army routinely cashiered those who failed and promoted those who succeeded. At the beginning of the war, eleven men held the most important positions of command: Grand Duke Nikolai Nikolaevich as commander in chief, Yanushkevich as his chief of staff, Danilov as quartermaster-general, Northwestern Front commander Zhilinskii, Southwestern Front commander Ivanov, and six army commanders directly confronting the Germans and Austrians: Rennenkampf and Samsonov on the Northwestern Front; Ruzskii, Zal'tsa, Pleve, and Brusilov on the Southwestern Front. Of those eleven, only three remained in the same positions a year into the war. Nikolai Nikolaevich had been dismissed, Danilov demoted to corps commander, Yanushkevich shunted off to an administrative post in the Caucasus, Rennenkampf cashiered for incompetence, Zal'tsa retired to an administrative post for age and ill health. Zal'tsa's replacement Evert had himself been promoted to commander of the newly created Western Front. Samsonov was dead by his own hand after humiliating defeat. Ivanov remained as front commander, while Pleve and Brusilov were still army commanders. Brusilov, likely the best Imperial Russian commander of the war, ended his career as commander in chief. Ruzskii had been promoted to command the Northwestern Front before ill health and caution led to his own eclipse. The point is not that Russia flawlessly purged all (and only) its incompetents, but that there was a real effort to find commanders who could fight and win. While Russian generals were, as an overall pattern, risk-averse to a fault, bitter experience at the hands of the more operationally flexible Germans had taught them the virtues of caution. When measured against the Austro-Hungarians or the Ottoman Turks, the performance of Russian generals was much better.

The real crisis for Russian commanders came at lower levels, where a crippling shortage of officers hampered Russia's ability to lead its tough and resilient soldiers. The combat of 1914, when armies had not yet fully internalized the lethality of modern firepower, took a particularly heavy toll on junior officers. While all armies were struggling with the time and effort it took to train new officers and the speed with which they were killed or wounded, Russia in particular suffered from its relatively small population of literate, educated young men to take on those roles. In part because of high rates of loss, officers discarded their distinctive epaulettes and sabers and were directed to take better care of their own personal safety.

The Russian army went to war with a little over 40,000 officers, and mobilized 21,000 reserve officers in 1914. Russia's military schools also rushed the graduation as sublieutenants (*podporuchik*) of all students who had entered in 1913. Put together, this pushed Russia's initial stock of officers to 80,000. An average regiment had 80 officers to command 4,000 men, a 50:1 ratio that approximately matched the total number of officers and men in Russia's mobilized army: 80,000 and 4.5 million. Casualties quickly decimated that population, and showed the necessity of finding new officers. The Life Guards Grenadier Regiment, fighting as part of the 2nd Guards Infantry Division, went into action against the Austrians at Visoke-Tarnovka on 25–27 August 1914. Of the 76 officers who went into battle, 18 were killed and 34 wounded. This casualty rate, about 75 percent, was the same for rank-and-file soldiers, of whom some 2,900 were lost from a regimental strength of 4,000. The Great Retreat wiped out many of Russia's remaining officers. In a 1915 four-day fight at Krupe in southeastern Poland, the Grenadiers lost almost as many officers and men as they had at Visoke-Tarnovka. Approximately 50 of the 76 officers who started the war with the Grenadiers were dead by the February Revolution. Military theorist Aleksandr Svechin saw his regiment in early 1915 drop from 37 officers to 10.

The Life Guards Kexholm Regiment by summer 1916 had only 4 officers (one a junior ensign) in addition to its commander. Each commanded a battalion (nominally 1,000 men). While even the prerevolutionary officers had included a substantial number, even a majority, from outside the Russian nobility, the atmosphere and ethos of the officer corps had been intensely monarchical and aristocratic. In spring 1916, by contrast, 90 percent of the Russian army's 130,000 officers were products of wartime commissioning. By 1917, 96 percent of officers had gone through only abbreviated wartime training, 80 percent were peasants, and only 4–5 percent nobility. By another account, regiments with a statutory strength of 4,000 men might have only 1 or 2 officers with prewar service, and the rest the product of wartime commissions.[25]

As officers were killed, seriously wounded, or captured, they were replaced by reserve officers or graduates of military schools. The Russian pool of reserve officers for new formations and casualty replacement was small, despite requirements that were not especially onerous: four years of secondary education and two years on active duty, or six years of secondary education and one year of active duty. These requirements were made slightly more stringent in 1914 (six years education and two years active duty), but this had only a negligible effect on numbers. Over the course of the war, 220,000 men entered the officer corps; those killed, wounded, or captured totaled 71,298. While some of that number recovered from wounds and returned to the army, an additional number died of disease. The result was that net permanent losses from the officer corps were substantially more than the entire prewar cohort. Losses were particularly heavy among the junior officers, who bore the most responsibility for leading Russia's soldiers in combat. Infantry officers, as in all armies, bore the heaviest burden, with casualty rates of 300–500 percent. According to War Minister Polivanov, Russia's peasant soldiers, lacking the education and initiative of their German counterparts, needed to be led from the front, and officer losses were correspondingly high.[26]

The greatest flow into the officer corps was at its lowest rank, the *praporshchik* or ensign, regarded as a temporary wartime expedient. *Praporshchiki* were distinctly second-class citizens, trained and treated as disposable. The rank lacks a close Western equivalent, ranking socially far below a second lieutenant, the lowest-ranking officer in most armies, and, unlike a second lieutenant, not regarded as a path to a real career. While technically officers, they were barred from promotion to some positions and re-garded as strictly temporary. In keeping with this conception and the des-perate needs of wartime, the Russian army waived its usual examinations in order to verify ability, and standards remained low. Men followed a va-riety of paths into the rank of *praporshchik*. Many came from Russia's sen-ior noncommissioned officers. An *unterofitser*, generally equivalent to a Western sergeant, could receive a battlefield promotion to *praporshchik* for demonstrated ability or for desperate need. There were some 50,000 such promotions over the course of the war. These new officers almost by defi-nition possessed military merit, but they inevitably suffered from a lack of formal military education. Moreover, while the war democratized the officer corps by introducing a broader range of social backgrounds, bat-tlefield commissions still bore social stigma: the standard practice of mov-ing those officers to new units was an effort to deal with that fact. Other *praporshchiki* came from the cadet corps, path to an officer's career for young nobility. The greatest share, however, came from a network of schools set up to train *praporshchiki* from Russia's lower-middle classes. Given the desperate need, education standards for admission to military schools dropped to only six total years of education. As circumstances be-came more desperate, standards fell even lower: four total years of educa-tion with four months on active duty. Over the course of the war, forty-one ensign schools trained officers through three-to-four-month courses. Al-together, those mechanisms produced 170,000 ensigns, well over half the total officer corps and more than three-quarters of those who became offi-cers during wartime. These ensigns, rushed through a short course of train-ing, had barely mastered the personal skills of a soldier, and had little time to develop the leadership and technical knowledge that their new duties would require. A study of a Russian army on the Romanian front in 1917, after three years of war, found that 35 percent of its ensigns had less than two months of frontline experience, and 97 percent had less than a year. To be sure, some more experienced ensigns had been promoted to higher ranks, but many had simply fallen victim to the vicissitudes of the battle-field before they could accumulate experience.[27]

In social terms, the new flood of *praporshchiki* fit poorly with the aristo-cratic ethos of the prewar officer corps, which never fully trusted the liter-ate peasants and urban petty bourgeoisie who made up the majority of the new officers and held dangerous sympathies for Russia's working classes.

One graduate described his classmates as "country teachers, low-level bureaucrats, poor traders, well-off peasants," alongside a much smaller number from the higher ranks of Russian society. Svechin, a perceptive observer, noted that the ideal *praporshchik* was a country schoolteacher, possessing some acquaintance with outdoor life and, more importantly, experience in dealing with peasants from a position of authority. In 1915, General A. A. Adlerberg bemoaned the declining quality of those selected for ensign school, as the desperate need for men swept up tradesmen and the lower levels of urban society. Despite the second-class nature of the ensign schools, Jews, descendants of recent immigrants, and ethnic Germans were barred from participation.[28]

While the Russian army needed soldiers and officers, it also required weapons and ammunition. The Russian economy displayed state mismanagement at its most clear, and failures of economic policy had the most pernicious consequences. Russia was as usual not alone in facing economic crisis. No European economy was prepared for the demands of war, which consumed men and material on an unprecedented scale. Prewar stockpiles of weapons and ammunition were wholly inadequate, and industrial capacity was incapable of accelerating production to cover the need. Britain had stocks of 1,000 rounds for each of its standard 18-pounder (84mm) field guns, and needed six months to produce an additional 500 rounds per gun. Individual batteries had 176 rounds per gun, sufficient for forty-four minutes of firing at the gun's top rate. Rifle manufacturing capability was 47,000 rifles annually, but Britain would need 1.1 million in 1915. France had 1,400 rounds for each of its 3,500 75mm guns, but at the outbreak of war could produce only 10–12,000 new rounds each day, compared to a need of 80–100,000. Austria, desperately short of manpower after the bloodbath of the 1914 Galician campaign, was more constrained by lack of rifles than of men: 200,000 soldiers could not be shipped to the front for want of rifles.[29]

Russia's situation differed in some respects from other European states. First, Russia suffered from its government's deep hostility toward private enterprise. Preparations for war relied far more on state arsenals and state-owned factories than on Russia's small but rapidly growing industrial sector. Indeed, the Russian government was more eager to place contracts abroad with foreign manufacturers than with domestic producers. The result was that Russian industry was poorly prepared to take on the burden of a radical increase in wartime demand for ammunition, while Russian orders with foreign producers were crowded out by British and French contracts. Since Russia's industrial economy was relatively underdeveloped, it had depended heavily on imports of technologically sophisticated goods. Explosives were state-produced, but required precursor chemicals from Germany. Even the relatively mundane production of surgical instruments and medications was dependent on imports, particularly from Germany. Russian chloroform, needed for surgery, was not sufficiently pure for narcotic use. The Union of Zemstvos, more and more involved in supporting the Russian war effort, began building factories for medical production.[30]

By far the biggest industrial problem Russia faced during the course of the war was its 1915 shortage of rifles and shell, when prewar stocks of ammunition ran short and industrial production had not yet increased to meet demand. By the beginning of 1915, Russia suffered from a crippling rifle shortage, forcing a series of desperate improvisations to collect rifles wherever possible and put them into the hands of soldiers at the front. This included stripping rear-area units and civilians of weapons, and carefully collecting them from wounded soldiers and the battlefield. Reinforcements were kept behind the lines rather than sent to their units for lack of rifles to equip them. Wounded soldiers who held on to their rifles received monetary rewards, as did soldiers who retrieved extra rifles from the battlefield (expedients also used by the Habsburg army). Prior to the outbreak of war, the Russian army thought it had the necessary stockpiles of shell to meet its needs: 1,000 rounds per gun. Within weeks of the start of war, commanders in the field were already warning of critical shortages of ammunition. The shortages reached catastrophic levels in 1915, when troops fighting the German spring and summer offensives simply lacked the supplies to compete. Shortage of ammunition does not excuse poor performance by Russian commanders, but the German method in 1915 is instructive: annihilate Russian front lines with tons of shell, and then use the resulting breach to force the Russians into retreat and fighting in the open. Lack of sufficient artillery and ammunition meant the Russians simply had no such option.[31]

The shell shortage made it clear that there was a desperate need for better management of Russia's industrial efforts. In late spring 1915, the leadership of the Duma cooperated with leading Russian industrialists to establish a special conference to coordinate policy with Nicholas's government. Over the summer, this body took formal legal shape as "Special Conference for the Discussion and Coordination of Measures for the Defense of the State" in August 1915. Under the leadership of War Minister Polivanov, the group brought together key representatives of the Russian state and society, including elements from the Duma, the Union of Zemstvos, and the Union of Towns, but particularly the owners of major industrial concerns, to improve the functioning of the Russian economy. Its responsibilities were split into four subsections: defense, fuel, transport, and food. The Special Conference had extensive powers to distribute war orders, take over management of underperforming enterprises, and set wage and price controls. The owners and managers of Russia's smaller enterprises, however, found themselves shut out of this cozy relationship between Nicholas's government and Russia's business elites. At the same time the Special Conference began its own work in late spring 1915, they created a parallel network of War-Industries Committees to distribute war orders among smaller, provincial factories. These War-Industries Committees found themselves outgunned by the combined power of the Russian state and big business, and were still locked out of much of the Russian army's lucrative production contracts. Nonetheless, the combination of these groups functioned reasonably well at reorienting Russian industry toward high-priority war orders through the creation of a whole series of subsidiary boards and commissions to oversee particular aspects of the Russian war effort. Together, they alleviated Russia's munitions crisis, but created a large and extensive bureaucracy without a clearly defined relationship to the rest of the tsarist government, and enriched private industrialists when Russian workers were increasingly going hungry.[32]

By 1917, a crisis in living standards was widespread throughout Europe. Austria-Hungary suffered from economic warfare between its two halves. In Vienna, real wages were a third of what they had been prior to the war. Even in the midst of world war, Hungarian negotiators drove a very hard bargain with their Austrian counterparts. An internal agreement of 24 February 1917 *raised* tariffs on imported food in the midst of a subsistence crisis, and the Austrian government could not risk publishing the terms of an agreement it had negotiated within the bounds of its own empire. Over spring 1917, daily shell production in Austria dropped from 50,000 to 18,000. In Germany, the early imposition of price controls on grain had driven farmers to other crops, forcing still more state intervention. The 1916–1917 "turnip winter" produced unprecedented hardship, as the potato crop failed and extreme cold locked up the German road and rail systems. Two hundred thousand German workers struck in April 1917 over food. In Freiburg, to take one example, official food prices doubled while wages in war industries went up by only 50 percent. Even in the United States, which enjoyed the most robust and advanced industrial infrastructure in the world, stripping railways of equipment and personnel for war use produced a fuel crisis in the winter of 1917–1918.[33]

Russia was no different. At first glance, there was no reason Russia should have suffered from food shortages during the war. Before 1914, grain exports from Russia averaged 11 million tons yearly. With Russian grain no longer flowing to consumers in Germany and Austria-Hungary, and Russia's export route from the grain regions of Ukraine through the Black Sea and the Turkish straits closed, Russia should not have lacked bread. Certainly, production suffered to some degree from the conscription of able-bodied men and horses for the war effort, but the effect of this was less than might have been expected. Russia's countryside had suffered from endemic overpopulation. Though Russia possessed enormous territories, its arable land was much more limited, so the result was a cushion of spare men in the countryside who could be drafted without appreciable harm. Wartime grain production dropped by 10 percent from prewar levels, but the end to exports more than made up for that.[34]

The problem was not in raw production, but instead in distribution. There was enough grain to go around, though the 1916 harvest was certainly weaker than in previous years. Transport difficulties and financial distortions meant that grain was not moving from its producers to urban consumers in anything like the necessary amounts. By the spring of 1917, grain cost 231 percent more in rural regions than it had before the war. In cities, by contrast, the price had gone up 808 percent. The key problem lay with insufficient or actually counterproductive administrative measures. Price caps on food (and the lack of such caps on industrial goods) and restrictions on internal trade between Russia's provinces removed incentives for peasants to put their grain on the market. City governments clumsily interfered in the grain markets to try to establish their own distribution mechanisms. Russian peasants were largely self-sufficient, but those goods they might have purchased from urban producers—cloth, household items, tools, agricultural implements, chemical fertilizer—had been taken over by wartime production for the needs of the army. Shoes and bolts of cloth were now boots and uniforms. The lack of goods to purchase, combined with inflation that both made peasants perceive manufactured goods as poor value and ate away at the value of cash in their hands, had a decided effect on peasant behavior. They had far less reason to put their grain on the market when the cash they received in return was of little use to them. Not least, the restriction on the sale and production of vodka removed an important incentive for peasants to raise cash by selling grain. By the end of 1916, the Russian government had been forced to begin though not fully implement a program of requisitioning to pull food out of the countryside.[35]

The inflationary problem was worsened by the growing crisis of Russia's railroad network. The administrative split established at the start of the war, giving the military extensive powers in large regions behind the front lines while leaving the rest of Russia in civilian hands, had divided a rail network that was clearly best managed as a unified whole. As a result of jurisdictional disputes and petty wars over equipment, coal piled up at mines in the Donets basin for lack of cars to move it. Intensive wear on rails and cars was not matched by investment in upkeep, maintenance, and replacement, given the tyranny of seemingly more urgent needs. By the winter of 1916–1917, the number of Russia's locomotives and cars in service dropped despite extensive purchases abroad. The Ministry of Transportation asked *Stavka* to temporarily reduce or halt troop movements to the front in February 1917 in order to free locomotives, rolling stock, and railway lines to move available food to urban centers. *Stavka* refused.[36]

The result was increasing privation in Russian cities including, fatefully, the capital, Petrograd. Worker wages had grown during the war, but those increases had been eaten up by inflation, particularly in the cost of food and fuel. By February 1917, the real purchasing power of workers had dropped to perhaps three-quarters of what it had been prior to the war. Certain products disappeared altogether from the Petrograd market, and total supplies of flour to the city dropped precipitously. Strikes, which had almost disappeared in the patriotic fervor of the first months of the war, reappeared and intensified, with a serious strike wave in the early months of 1916 and another in late 1916 to early 1917. Finally, food prices spiked at a much higher rate than previously in the first months of 1917. When Russia's armies were finally equipped with what they needed to fight, the Russian home front was on the brink of collapse.[37]

10

The Brusilov Offensive, 1916

After the disasters of 1915, it seemed impossible that Russia could recover from its losses, overcome its shortages of equipment and ammunition, and fight against the Austrians and Germans on anything like an equal footing. In fact, Russian military power was steadily growing. Even though skilled officers and experienced soldiers were in short supply after eighteen months of savage fighting, by 1916 Russian industry was finally providing the troops with what they needed to fight effectively. Russia still had too many timid or unskilled generals, but a harsh process of elimination had finally put Russia's best field commander of the First World War, Aleksei Brusilov, in command of the Southwestern Front. After Russia's other fronts failed to use their improved material position to attack successfully, Brusilov's Southwestern Front unleashed a massive attack in the summer of 1916 that demonstrated what well-led and well-equipped Russian soldiers were capable of doing. In the process, Brusilov smashed the Austrian army beyond repair, turning it into a force wholly dependent on its German ally.

The end of 1915 and the beginning of 1916 were short breathing spaces in the almost constant fighting on the Eastern Front since the outbreak of war, marking the first lengthy respite from combat after eighteen months of almost continuous campaigning. The Russians were exhausted by their lengthy retreats, and the Germans and Austro-Hungarians were almost as exhausted by their pursuit. Both sides used the time to construct much more elaborate trench systems than had been possible for the previous eighteen months. When fully elaborated, defensive systems could consist of two or three trenches in a belt; two or three such defensive belts were separated by several kilometers, all mirrored by enemy systems across the front lines. Whichever side had the burden of attack now faced a much more formidable task. The Austrians in particular benefited from the lull in fighting. While Italy continued to attack in the Alps, Austria's geographic advantages reduced its combat losses dramatically in late 1915 and early 1916. There were some isolated local actions on the Eastern Front in late 1915. *Stavka* had been holding Dmitrii Shcherbachev's Seventh Army in Odessa for a potential amphibious invasion of Bulgaria's Black Sea coast. When Serbian defeat made that pointless, *Stavka* redeployed the Seventh Army north to the Strypa River to join an attack by the Southwestern Front at the end of December. The offensive achieved no notable results, but did identify several basic problems of Russian tactics, including breakthroughs that were too narrow (allowing them to be covered completely by enemy fire), poor coordination between infantry and artillery, and slipshod reconnaissance. Those lessons would pay dividends in summer 1916.[1]

After the massive losses of territory and manpower that Russia had suffered during 1915, the initiative in 1916 clearly lay with the Germans. Following failed efforts to knock France from the war in 1914 and Russia in 1915, the question for the German high command was "what next?" Ludendorff, obsessed with his own potential successes and blind to strategic considerations, urged renewed offensives against Russia. Falkenhayn, as usual, was the voice of reason: with German supply lines already stretched to breaking, and no clear geographic goal in Russia that would assure German victory, renewed offensives offered only unending marches into trackless space. Passivity was likewise not an option. Austria-Hungary was increasingly dependent on Germany in military terms, and both powers were beginning to feel real economic pain from the Allied blockade. Time worked against the Germans. Bereft of other choices, Falkenhayn resolved on the only option left to him: a renewed effort to drive France from the war. He decided to attack the French at the fortress of Verdun, a point that they could not abandon: by using superiority in firepower, he would bleed the French to defeat.

On the Allied side, the priority in early 1916 was achieving a coordinated policy to replace the ad hoc, uncoordinated war Britain, France, and Russia had been fighting. After the outbreak of war, nearly a year had passed before the first major inter-Allied conference, a 6 July 1915 meeting at Calais. A more serious effort at cooperation finally came at Chantilly in December 1915 to organize coordinated offensives. Yakov Zhilinskii, whose command of the Northwestern Front in 1914 had been so disastrous, now served as Russian representative to the Western allies. Zhilinskii brought to Chantilly a proposal for a coordinated Allied offensive in the Balkans, but gained no support. The Western allies saw little point in transferring additional forces to what remained for them a sideshow. Russia's efforts to win binding commitments to come to the immediate aid of any victim of a German offensive likewise went nowhere, stymied by French concern over its low reserves of manpower. Indeed, Russia transferred its own forces to the support of the Western allies in late 1915 and the first half of 1916, shifting four infantry brigades to the west. Two fought on the Western Front and two in Salonika against the Bulgarians, but their small numbers were insufficient to make a difference in either theater. What was reached at Chantilly was an agreement in principle for coordinated offensives in 1916; setting a precise time, place, and direction for those offensives proved more difficult. Preparations for a future conference to answer that question were preempted by the German offensive against Verdun on 21 February 1916. The French immediately urged the Russians to begin an offensive as soon as possible to relieve the pressure.[2]

In keeping with the general Allied commitment to coordinated offensives, and the French calls for assistance, a *Stavka* conference on 24 February 1916 discussed a spring offensive. Russia was in far better condition to contemplate such a step than it had been the previous year. Aleksei Polivanov, who had replaced Sukhomlinov as war minister in the wake of the Great Retreat, was more liberal in his political sympathies and far more competent and professional. He had put the Russian army's logistics, conscription, and training on a much stronger basis, though Nicholas would dismiss him as a result of political intrigues, replacing him as war minister in March 1916 with Dmitrii Shuvaev, who lacked significant experience at the front lines and was quickly overwhelmed by the demands of his position. In any event, at the beginning of 1916, the Russian army had approximately 4.7 million men in the fighting fronts, 4.4 million on the Eastern Front, and the remainder in the Caucasus. Of those, approximately 1.7 mil-

lion were combat troops.[3] Prior to the February meeting, Chief of Staff
Alekseev circulated a memorandum that stressed Russia's advantages in
manpower if only those soldiers could be supplied with the necessary rifles.

The *Stavka* conference resolved on a near-term combined offensive by
the Northern and Western Fronts in the region around Dvinsk and Lake
Naroch. In that theater, north of the Pripet marshes, the Russians enjoyed
a substantial numerical advantage over the Germans of approximately 1.2
million to 600,000. Should all go well, a break in the German line between
Lake Naroch and Dvinsk would allow further exploitation to Kaunas, isolating German troops north of the breach on the Baltic coast and forcing a
withdrawal. The Allies agreed at the same time on coordinated offensives
for later in the spring, the Russians beginning in late April and the other
allies in early May. Zhilinskii, the Russian representative, was unsure of the
depth of the Allied commitment to attack, particularly when it was the Russians who would act first. "The English," he wrote Alekseev, "did not re-
ject a May offensive, but spoke of it guardedly, the Italians still more re-
servedly and conditioned it on the delivery of heavy artillery and other
supplies."[4]

The attack endorsed by *Stavka*'s 24 February conference was allocated
to three armies. For the Northern Front, the Fifth Army under Gurko carried out the main attack; for the Western Front, the armies were Aleksandr
Litvinov's First Army and its immediate neighbor to the south, Vladimir
Smirnov's Second Army. Since the Germans had stripped the Eastern Front
for troops to send west to Verdun, the Russians enjoyed a substantial advantage in manpower. In a sector stretching 400 kilometers, the Russians
massed 550 infantry battalions to approximately 200 German. While numbers worked to Russian advantage, all else was in the German favor. The
Russian generals commanding the attack were doctrinaire and uninspir-
ing, the forested and marshy ground was unsuitable for an offensive, and
German intelligence had detected Russian preparations.[5]

The attack at Lake Naroch opened on 18 March 1916 with artillery bombardment by the First and Second Armies, and in some sectors infantry
began working through German wire obstacles that same day. Full-scale
attacks followed the next day, but units were committed intermittently and
indecisively, nowhere achieving real mass or coordination. Russian troops
slogged forward through snowy marshes and were annihilated by German

artillery and machine gun fire. Fighting dragged on for ten days, but produced no appreciable results. Gurko's Fifth Army, holding the northern edge of the attack sector, delayed its offensive for a short time, given delays in assembling the necessary heavy artillery. On 21 March, it joined in but produced only negligible results. What little gains were made were quickly wrested back by local German counterattacks, a pattern that recurred over the next several days as Russian commanders repeated hopeless attacks. By 26 March, the Fifth Army ceased further efforts as pointless. On 29–30 March, *Stavka* recognized reality and called off the entire offensive. The Lake Naroch campaign was a fiasco from beginning to end. Russian artillery, though beginning to overcome the shell shortage of 1915, was still inferior to the Germans in heavy guns. In the midst of the Russian offensive, thawing winter snows and spring rains turned roads and paths into seas of mud (the fearsome Russian *rasputitsa*), which slowed maneuver to a crawl and was especially crippling to the movement of artillery. In no sector did the offensive achieve any noteworthy successes, with the deepest Russian penetration no more than 2–3 kilometers. Even these advances cost the Russians 78,000 men, with some units suffering 50 percent casualties, while the Germans lost perhaps 20,000.

PREPARATIONS FOR THE BRUSILOV OFFENSIVE

Having committed to a major spring offensive in coordination with Russia's allies, *Stavka* now had to work out the details. The front commanders gathered at Nicholas's headquarters at Mogilev on 14 April 1916: Kuropatkin for the Northern Front, Evert for the Western, and Brusilov, newly appointed to replace Ivanov, for the Southwestern. Chief-of-Staff Alekseev saw signs for real hope despite the failure at Lake Naroch. As he had reported to Tsar Nicholas on 4 April, the combined forces of the Russian Northern and Western Fronts outnumbered the Germans opposite them by almost two-to-one: 1.2 million men to 620,000. The Southwestern Front enjoyed a preponderance over the Austrians of approximately 500,000 men to 440,000. Ammunition for heavy artillery was still in short supply, but the situation for field artillery was much improved. In addition, there were concrete technical reasons to prefer offensive to defensive action. As Alekseev had argued before and would argue again, Russia's underdeveloped railway network meant that allowing the Germans to attack was far too risky—Russian troops were too slow to contain breakthroughs when they occurred, and the length of the Eastern Front meant the Germans could always choose a spot and force a breakthrough if they wished. Thus, it was better for the Russians to attack first. Under Alekseev's guidance, the group decided that the main attack would be carried out by Evert's Western Front in mid-May, moving northwest on the axis from Minsk to Vilnius. The other two fronts were tasked with diversionary attacks, first Brusilov's Southwestern Front at the beginning of May and then Kuropatkin's Northern Front, to pin down the Austro-German forces in front of them and, if possible, draw enemy reserves away from the main attack. Left unsaid, unfortunately, was what greater strategic purpose Evert's attack was intended to serve.[6]

Through May, preparations for the forthcoming offensive fundamentally changed its nature. Shortages of ammunition led to a reduction in the scale of the Northern Front's attack, and two corps were shifted to support the Western Front's main offensive. Evert, in what became a particularly pathological pattern over the spring and summer, bemoaned the shortages of men and ammunition that made it impossible for him to carry out a successful attack. More importantly, Brusilov, commander of the Southwestern Front, grew increasingly ambitious about what his preliminary diversionary attack might achieve. He was eager to fight, and believed Ivanov had lost his confidence in what Russian soldiers were capable of doing. Using careful preparation and drawing lessons from two years of war, Brusilov turned his limited offensive into an attack with the potential to achieve something much greater. He still saw his task as fundamentally diversionary: granted no additional resources by *Stavka*, "my intent," he wrote, "was to strike the enemy forces opposite me sufficiently strongly that they would not be able to transfer any forces to other sectors, and instead would be forced to send reinforcements from elsewhere."[7] The barest outlines of his offensive were stipulated by Alekseev: the main effort of Brusilov's attack should be carried out by the Cossack general Aleksei Kaledin's Eighth Army and directed toward the town of Lutsk in order to draw off Austrian and German reserves.

Brusilov's previous service had demonstrated that he was a highly competent army commander. He had achieved both victories and defeats in an honorable record of service as commander of the Eighth Army from 1914 through March 1916, but had not clearly differentiated himself from the rest of Russia's high command. A cavalry officer from a military family, he had served with distinction in the Russo-Turkish War, but lacked the General Staff training given to the tsarist army's intellectual elite. Thin and unprepossessing in his physical appearance, he was marked by his commitment to discipline, preparation, and the potential of Russian soldiers if competently led. In five good weeks in 1916, he cemented his reputation as Russia's foremost commander of the First World War, and brought the Austro-Hungarian Empire to the brink of collapse. Sadly for the Russian soldiers who fell in the Southwestern Front's offensive, Brusilov was never able to recreate the magic of June 1916. Hundreds of thousands of Russian soldiers were lost in the further pursuit of elusive gains.

The genius of Brusilov's offensive lay in the concrete details of its implementation. Brusilov lacked overwhelming superiority in numbers, and so was compelled to think about how best to use his limited resources. By one Soviet account, he had 1,950 artillery pieces against 1,850 guns for the Austrians opposite him, had a slight advantage in overall manpower, and was substantially outgunned in terms of heavy artillery.[8] Brusilov's plan, laid out in directives to his army commanders on 18 and 20 April, was that each of the four armies in his Southwestern Front (from north to south, the Eighth, Eleventh, Seventh, and Ninth) was to prepare by 23 May to carry out its own breakthrough of the Austrian front lines. At Brusilov's direction, even the individual component corps of those armies were obliged to plan offensives. The most important attack and the bulk of Brusilov's spare men and guns went to the northernmost Eighth Army, since it was closest to the ostensible main focus of the Russian summer offensive by the Western Front. Its mission was to attack west and northwest, toward Lutsk and then Kovel. The Ninth Army at the far southern extreme of Brusilov's line was important for potentially swaying Romania into joining the war on the Russian side. His Eleventh and Seventh Armies, though less important, were still to plan and carry out their own attacks. This division of effort was a clear violation of long-standing military principles about concentration of forces, and Chief of Staff Alekseev unsuccessfully tried to talk Brusilov out of it. Despite Alekseev's misgivings, Brusilov's plan had a number of advantages. It presented him with the potential, at least, of a choice of further options. Rather than committing fully in advance to one particular sector, he could exploit the breakthrough that appeared most promising. This also forced some degree of ingenuity and improvisation on his army commanders, and they responded remarkably well. By Brusilov's account, all four—Aleksei Kaledin, Vladimir Sakharov, Dmitrii Shcherbachev, and Platon Lechitskii—were skeptical at best about the prospects for success, and Brusilov was actively involved in overseeing the plans of each of his constituent armies as they made their preparations. He may be exaggerating their disquiet—they certainly fought well when the offensive began. Though Brusilov's memoirs and postwar comments were uncomplimentary toward his subordinates, and certainly none of them were military geniuses, they did effectively carry out his plan for the initial breakthroughs.[9]

In addition, since large masses of men and material were impossible to conceal from Austro-German aerial reconnaissance, preparing four separate breakthroughs of roughly equal weight prevented enemy intelligence from determining the key sector: there simply wasn't one. In an effort to distract attention from the true goals of the summer offensive, radio stations were set up around Baranovichi in order to generate false message traffic and draw Austro-German attention away from the true concentration of forces. At the same time, Brusilov made extensive use of aerial reconnaissance to develop a complete picture of Austrian defenses opposite his lines. His front had approximately 100 aircraft at its disposal, roughly equivalent to the Austro-German aircraft strength in the same sector, and those concentrated on reconnaissance missions. Bombing, ground attack, and the hunting of enemy aircraft were decidedly secondary. Brusilov employed his reconnaissance aviation to repeatedly photograph enemy positions in their full depth, tracing changes over time and employing oblique angles in order to better detect camouflaged positions.[10]

Brusilov's operational approach required certain sacrifices. As he himself noted, "this means of action [multiple breakthroughs] had, obviously, its downside, in that I could not concentrate at the main point of attack the men and artillery that I could have if I had established just one strike force."[11] In addition, its dispersion of effort made a truly strategic breakthrough at any point less likely, and this Brusilov seems not to have grasped. His focus was overwhelmingly on inflicting casualties on the Austrians opposite his divisions and seizing their trenches, and he devoted little effort to thinking about how his tactical efforts might fit into a strategic plan. Killing and capturing enemy soldiers became an end in itself, regardless of what it might cost the Russian army in turn.

Brusilov insisted on extensive tactical preparations. This included not only careful reconnaissance, but detailed preparation for his attacking waves of infantry. Troops drilled not just on the capture of the first enemy trenches, but on carrying the battle through the depths of the enemy defense. Above all, Brusilov emphasized speed. His plan stressed moving as quickly as possible from one trench line to the next, shoring up the flanks of an advance with machine guns as soon as ground was taken in order to prevent the enemy from reestablishing a coherent defense or organizing counterattacks. In order to make this possible, the Russian army for perhaps the first time in the war developed really close collaboration between infantry and artillery, with careful designation of enemy strong points to be suppressed by artillery fire, detailed maps, extensive telephone links between infantry and artillery, and closely timed infantry attacks designed to reach and seize enemy bunkers and strongpoints just at the moment artillery barrages lifted. All this, in retrospect, seems obvious, but the experience of World War I proved that time and bitter experience were necessary for armies to master these lessons. Brusilov banned altogether unaimed fire behind enemy trenches in hopes of accidentally hitting a target.

Brusilov gave quite specific engineering directives to his subordinates, requiring painstaking preparation of the battlefield. In particular, he insisted that trenches be advanced as close as possible to enemy lines. Dugouts were to be readied to allow Russian infantry to assemble close enough to enemy positions to reach them in one dash. Vast concealed bunkers were dug in rear areas to prevent Austrian reconnaissance from spotting troops massed for the offensive. Brusilov's subordinates carried out his directives with enthusiasm. Kaledin, commanding the Eighth Army, required detailed maps from all the corps under him, indicating precisely enemy positions and Russian trenches and gun emplacements, distinguishing those long existing, those prepared since April when the orders to dig had come, and those set to be completed by the offensive's deadline. In front of Andrei Zaionchkovskii's XXX Corps, for example, the Austrian-held settlement of Chernyzh sat on high ground overlooking a river bend; while this made approaching Chernyzh itself quite difficult, Russian sappers had moved their trenches closer to both flanks of the Austrian salient.[12]

This preparation, while certainly important, is not in itself enough to explain Brusilov's successes. The terrain over which the Southwestern Front was attacking was in many places ill-suited to extensive engineering. The terrain was largely flat, cut by wide, slow-moving rivers, which were in turn surrounded by bogs and marshes. When the front had stabilized at the end of 1915, it often followed rivers, with Russians on one side and Austrians on the other. In many cases, therefore, it was impossible to move closer to the Austrians simply by digging. The 101st Infantry Division, for example, held a frontage that ran along a river for 10 kilometers. Its own program of sapping trenches closer to the Austrians had brought the Russians closer to their targets, but at their closest, as around the village of Boiarka, the Russian trenches were still some 200 paces from the Austrians, and in most of the sector the distance averaged 600 paces or more.[13] What's more important, however, is that the aggressive spirit that Brusilov cultivated—meticulous preparation for attack with the expectation of success—had clearly taken hold. As the XXXIX Corps reported to Eighth Army commander Kaledin, it had pushed trenches forward where practicable. Elsewhere, particularly in a swampy stretch between the villages of Dubishche and Didichi, closer approach was not possible. Along the course of the Putilovka River, the corps's plan for attack was to cross the river at night, occupying trenches close by the river's shore that the Austrians had astonishingly left unoccupied and intact. Russian reconnaissance teams were actually crossing the river at night to improve the Austrian trenches under cover of darkness.[14]

As the start date for Brusilov's offensive approached, Alekseev contacted him on 24 May with a request to advance it even further. On 15 May, the Austrians had attacked the Italians in a major offensive in Trentino. The hard-pressed Italians had appealed to Russia, just as the French had in February, to draw off Austrian forces through offensive action. Brusilov agreed on condition of receiving an additional corps to bolster his attack. He was initially denied before Alekseev relented and transferred a corps from the Northern Front. On 31 May, Alekseev gave the Russian summer offensive plans, weeks in preparation, their final form. "The continuing transfer of Austrian troops to the Italian Front and the difficult position of the Italian army," he told his army commanders, "demands that we inflict a strong blow with the armies of the Southwestern Front against the numerically-weakened Austrians facing them." Brusilov's Southwestern Front would make the initial attack on 4 June, followed six to seven days later by Evert's Western Front.[15]

THE BRUSILOV OFFENSIVE BEGINS

Brusilov's main artillery bombardment began on 4 June 1916. He did not want to tip his hand about the main sector of his breakthrough, so the start times of the main attacks were staggered over 4–5 June. Brusilov's focus was on Kaledin's Eighth Army. Kaledin's main attacking force of four corps (from north to south, the XXXIX, XL, VIII, and XXXII) began artillery bombardment early on 3 June, wrecking the foremost trenches of the badly led Austrian Fourth Army. Despite ample warnings of a possible offensive, Fourth Army commander Archduke Joseph Ferdinand had made no preparations to parry a potential attack. On 5 June, the Eighth Army's offensive began. In the key central sector southeast of Lutsk, the XL and VIII Corps massed eighty battalions into a 16-kilometer frontage, for a density of 5,000 men per kilometer. On that first day, the XL Corps managed to take all the trench lines in the first belt of Austrian defenses. While the initial assault was not as successful elsewhere, that hardly mattered. The gap before Lutsk widened as more Russian troops poured through it. Once the Austrian retreat began, it became almost impossible to stop. Austrian defenses were not well developed, and once out of their frontline trenches, the Austrians lacked any obvious place to make a further defensive stand. The pattern was a mirror image of what the May 1915 German offensive had done to the Russians: any battalion or regiment that stood and fought on its own would be inevitably encircled and annihilated, and the general chaos made it impossible for the Austrians to reestablish a coordinated defense. Once the Eighth Army's penetration was made in force, the Austrians on either side of the breach had to withdraw or be rolled up and destroyed. The Russians reached Lutsk, 30 kilometers behind the front line, on 7 June. Forcing the Styr River running through Lutsk, the Eighth Army reinforced its breakthrough with the V Siberian Corps and drove northwest toward Kovel, a major transportation hub serving the Austrian lines north of the breach. By mid-June, the Eighth Army had managed to carve out a salient 60 kilometers deep in the Austrian lines around Lutsk.[16]

Brusilov had been reinforced with additional cavalry, in hopes that his Eighth Army might achieve a sufficient breakthrough to allow Yakov Gillenshmidt's IV Cavalry Corps, reinforced by additional manpower, to penetrate behind Austrian lines. A deep cavalry strike toward Kovel could destroy supply and communication links while also cutting off the retreat

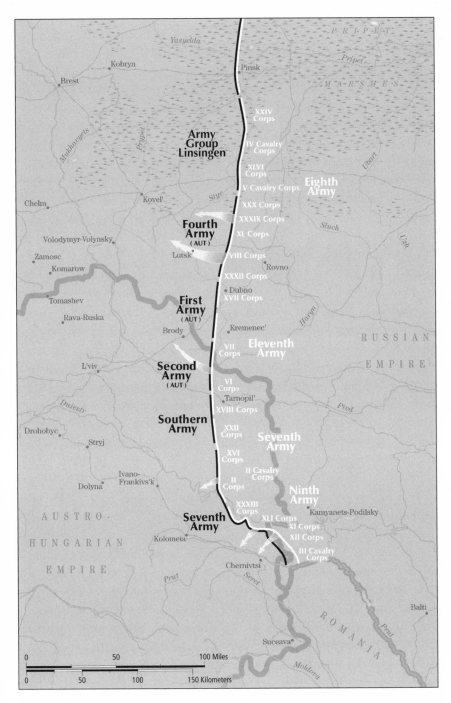

Map 11. The Brusilov Offensive, 4 June 1916

of Austrian units pushed out of their trenches at the front. This never happened, despite Brusilov's repeated entreaties. Both Gillenshmidt's IV Cavalry and Nikolai Istomin's XLVI Corps failed to make significant headway on the northern flank of the Eighth Army's breakthrough sector. The results of the other armies were initially mixed. Sakharov's Eleventh Army, with relatively limited manpower, had only local successes. Its main effort was on the left, where the VI Corps made hardly any headway. On its right flank, where the XVII Corps operated alongside the Eighth Army, the Russians unexpectedly captured most of the initial Austrian defensive belt. The Ninth Army had almost as much success as the Eighth but took a somewhat different approach. In attacking the Austrian Seventh Army under Pflanzer-Baltin, it focused on a very narrow sector of 3.5 kilometers, assaulted by four regiments of the XI Corps. Another sector along the Dniestr was attacked by elements of the XLI Corps. Opening with a relatively short barrage of six hours before attacking at noon on 4 June, the Ninth Army achieved impressive results, smashing through the Austrian 42nd Division on the south bank of the Dniestr and capturing 11,600 prisoners. Its short-term efforts to expand its breach failed, but a much bigger attack on 10 June on a 20-kilometer frontage had even more decisive results, capturing 18,000 prisoners and penetrating 6–12 kilometers into Austrian lines. The Seventh Army was the last to begin its attack, on 6 June. The Austrians, disorganized by their defeats elsewhere along the front, were not capable of sustained and effective resistance. The Russians concentrated 48,000 men, primarily the II Corps, on a 7-kilometer front. At Yazlovets, the Russian infantry quickly captured the entire Austrian first trench belt and forced a panicked withdrawal to the second defensive line. Pflanzer-Baltin's Seventh Army, facing Russian breakthroughs in at least two sectors and split in two, had no choice but to retreat. The Russian Ninth Army's pursuit itself had to spread out as it advanced deeper behind Austrian lines; by 13 June, its penetration was 50 kilometers deep. At some points, this left the Ninth Army 100 kilometers away from its railheads, forcing Lechitskii to slow his pursuit of the shattered Austrians, who left supplies, artillery pieces, and stragglers in their wake as they streamed west.

All along the line, Brusilov's armies captured enormous numbers of Austrian prisoners, many taken by Russian soldiers who arrived at their bunkers just as artillery barrages ceased. Austrian deployments had left them particularly susceptible to Brusilov's specific methods. The Austrians, like the Russians and Germans in the east, set up their defenses as multiple trench belts separated by several kilometers, each belt in turn containing two or three trench lines separated by a few hundred meters. The Austrians, though, had deployed their manpower disproportionately forward, with men and guns concentrated in the first line or two of trenches. This left them vulnerable to the precision artillery barrages and carefully timed infantry rushes that Brusilov mandated. The Austrians had suffered such heavy casualties in killed, wounded, and especially prisoners that they were not in any condition to contain Brusilov's multiple breakthroughs. An incomplete count of prisoners on 6 June, one or two days after the start of the advance by individual armies, registered 40,000 Austrians captured. Three-quarters of the Austrian Fourth Army was lost, and Pflanzer-Baltin, commanding the Austrian Seventh Army, estimated he had lost 100,000 men in two weeks. The German high command quickly recognized the potentially devastating effects on its own war effort if Austria were to collapse. The German high command had no choice, given the desperate situation, but to throw German regiments into the path of the advancing Russians piecemeal rather than assembling a proper striking force. As early as 7 June, Falkenhayn promised Conrad at least four German divisions to plug the hole in the Austrian line at Kovel. In return, Conrad also had to accept von Seeckt as chief of staff for the hard-pressed Austrian Seventh Army.[17]

BRUSILOV CONSOLIDATES HIS GAINS

Despite these initial successes, ominous signs for Brusilov's offensive were already evident. The Eighth Army had begun to encounter German soldiers dispatched to the breakthrough as reinforcements from the defenses facing the Russian Western Front. Brusilov urged Evert to pressure the Germans to prevent transfer of reserves, but to no avail, and appealed directly to Lesh, commanding the Third Army on Brusilov's right, to attack and draw German reserves. Though Brusilov received the dispatch of an additional army corps, this was hardly enough to sustain his offensive. Having achieved an unprecedented success in shattering the Austrian front line, Brusilov then failed to take advantage of the brief but enormous opportunity he had created. Both he and his army commanders focused on consolidating the gains they had achieved instead of advancing more deeply behind enemy lines before the Austrians and Germans could solidify their defenses. The sole exception was Lechitskii, whose Ninth Army's victories took place in the most remote section of the front line. At the same time, *Stavka* proved vacillating and unhelpful, resulting in confusing and frustrating changes in emphasis and direction. As a result, Brusilov's undoubted tactical successes, inflicting terrible losses on the Austrians opposite his troops, never became a truly strategic triumph.[18]

In the middle of the night of 7–8 June, Kaledin reported that the Austrian troops facing his center were in full flight and thrown back over the Styr River. He ordered his troops to maintain energetic pursuit of the fleeing Austrians while directing the XXXIX Corps on his center-right to maintain the defense of the Styr and the XXX Corps on his far-right flank to expand the shoulder of the Russian advance. The main weight of Kaledin's continued offensive came from the XL and VIII Corps in his center, both instructed to push straight west beyond Lutsk toward Volodymyr-Volyns'kyi, not northwest toward Kovel or southwest toward Rava-Ruska. The XXXII Corps on Kaledin's left was to dig in on the Styr River to protect the Eighth Army's left flank. The bulk of Kaledin's divisions were thus tasked with consolidation of gains already achieved, not further expansion of the Russian breakthrough. While there was still some continued effort at an offensive, particularly in the center, much of Kaledin's concern was with protecting ground his army had already seized. Kaledin's priorities were entirely in line with Alekseev and Brusilov's. On the same day, Brusilov directed the Eighth Army to push on the shoulders of the breach they had made in Austrian lines rather than driving west through the breach toward Volodymyr-Volyns'kyi or northwest toward Kovel. He ordered the center of the Eighth Army to halt on the Styr rather than advancing farther west. The task of taking Kovel and achieving real strategic success was left to Yakov Gillenshmidt's IV Cavalry Corps, which was wholly incapable of achieving that task. Brusilov then followed that with instructions to his army commanders at midday on 8 June, declaring that the time had come to "convert the tactical successes achieved by the front's armies into a strategically-completed operation." That did not mean, however, going beyond Lutsk to take really significant transportation hubs such as Kovel or L'viv. Instead he instructed the center of his Eighth Army to hold a north–south line along the Styr River, running roughly 50 kilometers from Sokil in the north through Lutsk and ending at Torgovitsa. This would consolidate advances of 15–25 kilometers from the Russian start lines of four days earlier, but not advance further. Kaledin's center was to maintain an active defense, while attacks were left instead to the Eighth Army's right and left flanks to even out the advance. This was hardly a recipe for strategic victory; Brusilov still believed breakthrough and exploitation would come from the Eighth Army's cavalry, which was stuck attempting to claw through intact Austrian defenses. The cavalry, Brusilov ordered, were "to break through into the enemy rear, regardless of any losses." Instead of using infantry to push against shattered Austrian units, Brusilov planned to send cavalry against unbroken sectors of the Austrian lines, devoid of any surprise, in hopes of strategic success. Predictably, Gillenshmidt's IV Cavalry Corps achieved nothing.[19]

At this point, one week into the offensive, a number of key developments coincided. The day for the beginning of the Western Front's offensive, ostensibly Russia's main effort for 1916, was set as 11 June. On that same day, the Seventh Army's breakthrough was halted by the counterattack of the German 48th Division on its right flank. Shortly thereafter, the Eighth Army's XXXIX and V Siberian Corps, advancing slowly northwest toward Kovel, met a number of German divisions shifted south to plug the gap in the Austrian line. On 14 June, the Russians captured Germans transferred from France, and on 15 June Austrians transferred from Italy. Brusilov's offensive had seized territory and bagged a surprisingly large number of Austrian prisoners, but no key cities had been captured. Whether these territorial advances could be held in the face of German reinforcements and counterattacks was open to question. Short of critical reserves of fresh units to throw into the fight, how would Brusilov's offensive develop?

What began to take shape was a pattern of repeated Russian offensives, unfortunately for the Russian soldiers who bore the brunt of the sacrifice. Each inflicted significant losses on the Austro-Germans but required similar expenditure of life from the Russians, but with diminishing returns over the course of the summer. The victories that Brusilov had won were squandered in increasingly costly offensives that never succeeded in capturing important strategic targets. On 13 June, Brusilov ordered renewed attacks the next day, despite a desperate shortage of reserves and the universal appeals of his army commanders for a slower pace. His goal for the Eighth Army, his most important attacking force, was to reach Volodymyr-

Volyns'kyi to the west and Kovel to the northwest of his salient at Lutsk to prepare for a later push toward Rava-Ruska to the southwest. On 15 June, however, Brusilov ordered the Eighth Army to halt its advance, fearing that his extended troops would be vulnerable to an attack on their right (northern) flank until the Western Front's Third Army began its own offensive, due to begin on 17 June. This order too was changed: on 16 June, Brusilov told Kaledin to prepare to take Kovel, setting aside for the moment any advance toward Volodymyr-Volyns'kyi. Even while this wavering and indecision was taking place on Brusilov's right flank, the Ninth Army on his left continued to advance forward rapidly through the shattered remnants of Karl von Pflanzer-Baltin's Austrian Seventh Army, taking Chernivtsi on 18 June and continuing on to the Seret River.

The offensive by Evert's Western Front, for which Brusilov's offensive was intended as a mere prelude, was repeatedly delayed. Evert flooded *Stavka* with incessant requests for additional men and supplies before he could carry out an attack, and gave every impression of being deeply fearful of actually attacking. His repeated delays suggest some sort of psychological process at work: Brusilov reported speculation that Evert feared his inability to match Brusilov's success, and lamented that a more decisive commander in chief did not simply sack Evert and replace him with someone willing to fight.[20] Evert's half-hearted attack finally took place only on 15 June at Baranovichi with only a single formation, the Grenadier Corps. The Grenadiers suffered 8,000 casualties and found their small gains erased by local counterattacks within a day. Evert's repeated delays and excuses finally led *Stavka* to demand an attack no later than 29–30 June. Evert promised a renewed offensive in greater strength in early July, six weeks later than his initial promises in the spring. Brusilov readied his troops for renewed attack to accompany Evert's offensive. As a result of Evert's chronic inaction, Brusilov was reinforced by the transfer of the Third Army to his authority on 24 June. Instead of the southern extreme of the Western Front, the Third Army became the northern extreme of the Southwestern Front.[21]

Despite Evert's ongoing delays at the Western Front, the Brusilov offensive had an electrifying effect on Russian morale, and judging by Russian intelligence, a devastating effect on Austrian. To be sure, Russian sources were problematic: it was impossible to verify reports from Russian agents on the Austrian side of the line, and Austrian prisoners in Russian hands had every incentive to please their captors by reporting Austrian desperation. Nonetheless, what the Russians heard from their prisoners matches evidence available from other sources, and confirms the deep and permanent damage the Brusilov offensive inflicted on Austrian morale. In late July, the chief intelligence officer of the Southwestern Front's Eighth Army reported a conversation a Russian agent had with the unwitting colonel commanding a regiment of the Austrian 13th Infantry Division, and on the simultaneous interrogation of officers captured near Volodymyr-Volyns'kyi. As a result of Brusilov's offensive, all Austro-German units had suffered "massive losses," and the Austrian colonel doubted whether it would be possible to return the disrupted units to fighting trim. Moreover, the Russian intelligence report concluded, "all officers without exception express their complete certainly in their own defeat and confirm complete confusion in their high command. They also do not believe in the success of the German defense and are certain that the Allies are however slowly, but methodically and carefully, winning." The Brusilov offensive did not do nearly as much damage to German morale, but the Germans hardly escaped unscathed. Though the Russian initial successes had been achieved predominantly against Austrian troops, German units suffered heavy losses in stemming the Russian onslaught and preventing the complete collapse of the Austro-Hungarian army. While German soldiers might remain confident in their own abilities, their evaluation of the worth of their Austrian allies was steadily falling. One Austrian prisoner reported a conversation with the Prussians of the 114th heavy howitzer regiment, who told him five German divisions had already been worn down in the fighting around Volodymyr-Volyns'kyi, requiring the dispatch of an additional three divisions. "The regiment's mood," he said, "was depressed, and no one believed in the possibility of an offensive by the Austrian army."[22]

The improvement in Russian morale was just as noticeable. After the disastrous Great Retreat in 1915, and the failed Naroch offensive in early 1916, the Brusilov offensive demonstrated to the world, and more importantly to the Russians themselves, that they were indeed capable of victory. Brusilov was flooded with telegrams of congratulation. Russian intelligence officers claimed to see the effects of their victory everywhere. In an account that says far more about Russian ethnic politics and the Russian army's growing confidence than it does about the loyalties of Polish Jewry, Colonel Makhrov, acting quartermaster-general of the Eighth Army staff, claimed that a "characteristic and exact sign of the pressure and uncertainty" the Central Powers now felt was "the sharp change in the attitude of Jews in Poland to our soldiers escaping from prisoner-of-war camps. Previously, Polish Jews reacted hostilely to our soldiers, hunting them down and handing them over to German authorities, but now this attitude has changed—the Jews have started to help them by supplying our escapees with food and so on. Attitudes toward the Jews have changed in Austria-Hungary as well—they are not trusted, and are oppressed."[23]

BRUSILOV'S RENEWED OFFENSIVES

As a result of Evert's timidity at the Western Front, combined with general indecision about how best to exploit Brusilov's original breakthrough, the Germans were free to muster their reserves into a powerful striking force. They realized the scope of the breakthrough and the threat to key railroad connections through Kovel. Initially four divisions were pulled in—two from France and two from Italy. The Germans unleashed a counteroffensive at Kovel and elsewhere along the front on 16–17 June. Austrian morale, shattered by two weeks of defeats, placed the burden of counterattacks almost exclusively on German divisions. While this attack failed to break through Brusilov's lines, it did halt any further advance toward Kovel, and forced a halt of several days for Brusilov's armies to rest and replenish their supplies. After a month of fighting, in return for the capture of 200,000 prisoners (overwhelmingly Austrian) and the infliction of 17,000 killed and 125,000 wounded (roughly three-quarters Austrian), Brusilov's own formations had paid a heavy price, with almost 300,000 casualties by the end of June. By mid-July, the bag of prisoners had reached 265,000, but Russian casualties had climbed to 500,000,[24] and Brusilov's stocks of ammunition were almost completely exhausted. The Austro-Germans carried out a second counteroffensive on 30 June with a dozen new divisions transferred from other fighting fronts, again halting Brusilov's progress but not substantially reversing his advances. Disquiet in the German high command continued to grow, since German counterattacks had previously been a reliable means of rolling back and punishing Russian advances. The Russian Ninth Army continued to advance successfully, and Alekseev dispatched additional reinforcements to maintain Lechitskii's momentum.[25]

On 2 July, after enormous delays, the Western Front's Fourth Army, commanded by Aleksandr Ragoza, finally began its own offensive toward Baranovichi, the transportation nexus that had been *Stavka*'s home until its evacuation in late summer of 1915. To all appearances, neither the negative lessons of the Lake Naroch offensive nor the positive lessons of Brusilov's were incorporated into the attack. After artillery preparation lasting most of the day on 2 July, the IX and XXV Corps attacked on a narrow 8-kilometer frontage. Well-placed enemy defenses left largely undamaged by the Russian artillery halted any advance almost immediately. Repeated efforts to break through Austro-German lines were fruitless, expending material and lives against prepared defenses without any element of surprise or misdirection. The Fourth Army suffered 80,000 casualties for negligible gain and the capture of a few thousand enemy prisoners, and Evert cancelled the offensive on 14 July. The Germans counterattacked on the same day, recapturing the trench lines previously lost. A renewed Russian attack by five divisions on 25 July produced no different result. Russia's Northern Front, previously inactive, attacked with its Twelfth Army south of Riga on 16 July, and likewise achieved no meaningful success in return for 15,000 casualties.

Brusilov, despite worsening conditions for his attack as a result of the steady flow of Austrian and German reinforcements, continued to push his offensive beyond the point of diminishing returns. On 28 June, he told his army commanders to prepare for still another offensive, which began on 4–5 July. The Austro-German line formed a salient east of Kovel, and Brusilov planned a pincer attack to eliminate it and then take advantage of the break in the line to push west. From the north, the Third Army attacked south with a special corps under Nikolai Bulatov, and from the south, the XXX and I Turkestan Corps pushed north. The Austro-Germans abandoned the salient and retreated west. Here the German policy of using their own units interspersed with Austrian in order to bolster their ally's ability to fight showed its hazards: Austrian units broke and retreated, leaving German units in danger of encirclement and destruction. Within 4–5 days the Russians had moved 30–40 kilometers west to the Stokhod River, but their pursuit was too slow to prevent the Central Powers from establishing a new defensive line on the western bank of the river. The Third and Eighth Armies together reached the east bank of the Stokhod north of Lutsk, but Kovel still remained far out of Brusilov's grasp. Though German reserves had been exhausted, Brusilov likewise had nothing left to throw into the battle. Much of what he had done to prepare his early June successes was no longer applicable. Not only did the more mobile front lines prevent systematic preparation of offensive action, but additional German aviation prevented the aerial reconnaissance so essential to his troops' effectiveness in the initial offensive. German aircraft seized control of the air over the front lines and barred any systematic study of Austro-German positions. Russian aerial reinforcements went toward protecting Russian rear areas.[26]

Relentless but increasingly fruitless Russian attacks continued. On 9 July, *Stavka* ordered the attack to continue on to take Kovel. The ground along the Stokhod River, though, being low and swampy, literally bogged down the Russian advance, giving the Austro-Germans a substantial advantage and preventing any dramatic success to match Brusilov's earlier accomplishments. On 19 July, after waiting on additional reinforcements from Russia's guards units, Brusilov again sketched out a plan of attack for the Third Army to attack toward Kovel from the northeast, the Special Army from the southeast, the Eighth Army toward Volodymyr-Volyns'kyi, and the Eleventh Army toward L'viv. Those armies would, as a result, be in effect marching abreast to the west, not coordinating on a single strategic goal. This renewed attack, again pounding away at great cost, began with a diversionary attack by the Eleventh Army on 25 July. The rest of the Southwestern Front went on the offensive on 28 July, but the energy of Brusilov's troops had finally run out, and Austro-German defenses held. The one success, as had been consistently the case since the start of Brusilov's offensives, was at the far southern end of the line, where Lechitskii's Ninth Army seemed incapable of failure and even the presence of German infantry divisions could not keep Habsburg troops from continued flight under Russian pressure. Further north, though, early attacks managed to cross the Stokhod or capture the first lines of enemy trenches, but real breakthroughs did not follow. Only east and southeast of Kovel, where the Austro-German front line left the protection of the Stokhod, did Russian attacks make shallow inroads, capturing prisoners and artillery but not making truly strategic gains. Directly east of Kovel, Vladimir Bezobrazov's Special (Thirteenth) Army collapsed a salient held by the Austrian II Corps, but the Austrians were able to hold along a new defensive line 30 kilometers east of Kovel. This transportation center, which might have been taken at the beginning of June off the march when Austrian defenses were in complete disarray, never fell.

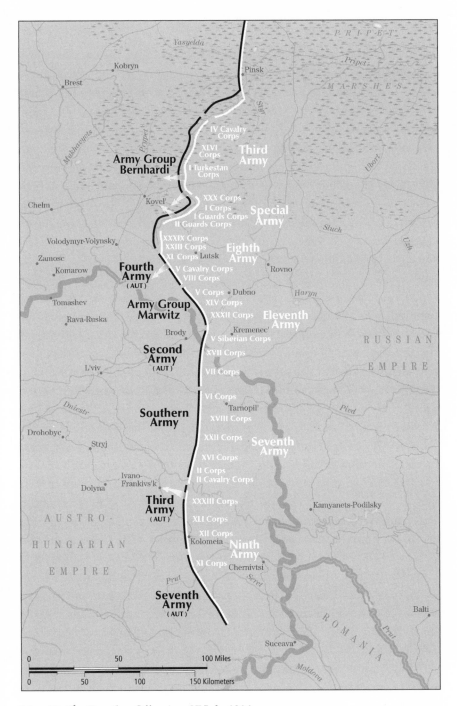

Map 12. The Brusilov Offensive, 27 July 1916

Russian offensives continued through early August. The ongoing fighting took its toll not only in human lives, but in the fighting effectiveness of Brusilov's divisions. Attrition cost the Russian army experienced soldiers and officers, and those who remained were exhausted to the point of losing the attention to detail that had made Brusilov's initial attacks so successful. On 3 August, he warned his army commanders against the complacency that led to poor reconnaissance, lack of coordination between infantry and artillery, and wasted artillery bombardments. He also condemned reluctance to press home attacks in the face of heavy losses: "If an attack is being conducted properly, in a disciplined way, then it must be carried through to the end. Keep in mind that repeating an attack after some interval of time will cost still more lives, since the enemy will be better prepared."[27]

On 9 August, the Third Army again made a serious attempt to force the Stokhod, but with no greater result than previously. The Germans and Austrians were now well-entrenched, and the unsuccessful Russian offensives had done much to repair the morale of Austrian officers and men. Repeated and unsuccessful Russian attacks continued through mid-August. Seeking to make some change, in mid-August *Stavka* and Alekseev removed the Third Army and jurisdiction over the Kovel sector from Brusilov, handing it to the Western Front. After a short period of quiet, Brusilov began yet another costly and futile offensive on 31 August, but only the Seventh Army made appreciable progress. Still another general offensive came on 16 September, and Brusilov drove his armies to repeated attacks despite continually dwindling results. Only further south, away from the most important Russian goals, did the new offensive meet with success: Lechitskii's Ninth Army continued its remarkable run of successes on the far southern extreme of the Russian line, where the Austrian Seventh Army was little more than shattered remnants of fighting formations. By this point, both sides were stumbling toward exhaustion. Ammunition reserves on the Russian side were critically short, and neither the Germans, the Austrians, nor the Russians had fresh divisions to spare to either break the enemy line or repair a breach.

Finally, Brusilov's armies attempted one final offensive, an effort disrupted by a spoiling attack on the Special Army and the Eighth Army on 27 September. The Seventh and Eleventh Armies nonetheless began their own offensives on 30 September, cutting them short on 2 October. On the same day, the Eighth and Special Armies (now under Gurko) began their own offensives after artillery preparation the day before. None of these were pressed with particular enthusiasm or in great strength. This finally marked the end of the terrible cycle of offensives that Brusilov had begun almost four months earlier. Exhaustion, and the desperate need to reinforce Russia's Romanian frontier, compelled a halt to these fruitless and draining attacks. Tsar Nicholas scrawled a note to Alekseev on 5 October that "I am decisively against further development of the operations of the Eighth and Special Armies, operations promising us minimal success and huge losses." Notoriously indecisive, Nicholas *later that day* indicated that he granted permission to carry out an attack if the local commanders wished to. It was too late—amidst the back and forth, the front and army commanders seemed to have lost their will to continue the slaughter. Gurko's Special Army continued desultory offensives, and Lechitskii's Ninth Army in the south was drawn into the Romanian campaign, but the Russian front north of Romania remained largely quiet for the rest of 1916.[28]

BRUSILOV'S AFTERMATH

The Brusilov offensive had a number of important consequences for all sides on the Eastern Front. Intended to relieve the pressure on Russia's allies, it achieved just that. Austria-Hungary and Germany transferred some thirty divisions to contain Brusilov's breakthrough, reducing the pressure on the French at Verdun and the Italians in Trentino at precisely the time that such assistance was desperately needed. At Verdun, Nivelle was able to take advantage of the respite Brusilov provided to build up additional reserves and repair shattered defenses. The Austrians were less fortunate, revealed as almost wholly bankrupt in military terms and in desperate need of German help. The Germans could and did drive a hard bargain, finally attaining unified command of the war in the east to compel Conrad to see the war in German terms. On 27 July 1916, Hindenburg became supreme commander in the east, an important step on his ultimate path to supreme power in Germany itself.[29]

Brusilov's offensive was, however, a decidedly mixed blessing for Russia. Despite Brusilov's success in inflicting enormous casualties on the Austrians, he was as successful at inflicting casualties on his own troops. Beginning immediately after the war, his offensive has been the subject of ongoing debate as to whether its benefits justified the enormous cost in lives that Russian soldiers had to pay. Soon after the war, Nikolai Golovin called Brusilov "absolutely regardless of the loss of human lives." The benefits to Russia were clear: over 400,000 prisoners, nearly 600 artillery pieces, and 1,700 machine guns, as compared to a total Habsburg fighting force of 900,000 on all fronts. The losses hit especially hard, since Austria was approaching famine conditions. Its weakened and demoralized soldiers suffered badly from disease on all fronts, with some 800,000 soldiers lost to sickness in 1916. Brusilov had thus undoubtedly unleashed a crippling blow on Austria. But in order to inflict at least 850,000 casualties on the Central Powers (Brusilov himself claimed 2 million enemy soldiers killed, wounded, or captured), Russia lost 1.5 million men. Brusilov's Southwestern Front alone lost 500,000 men by the middle of June. Offensive action even consumed the lives of the horses that maintained Russian logistics and moved Russian artillery. Requisitioning of horses continued throughout 1916, with peasants losing substantial work time in the spring and summer months of the Brusilov offensive simply traveling to and from military requisition points and draining horsepower from the Russian countryside even as Russia approached a crisis in its urban food supply.[30]

Much of the responsibility for the massive loss of Russian lives lay with Brusilov, since the brilliance of his tactical preparation was not matched by similar strategic vision. To be sure, Evert's criminal passivity while commanding the Western Front was evident even in 1916, and limited potential Russian gains. Nonetheless, Brusilov's strategy of annihilating the enemy in multiple narrow sectors of the front then using those breakthroughs to force the enemy out of prepared fortifications worked stunningly well at the beginning of his offensive, but lost effectiveness as it lost novelty. Devoid of a vision of what his breakthroughs were intended to achieve, by either seizing important transportation and supply hubs or encircling and annihilating large enemy formations, he killed enemy soldiers roughly as quickly as he killed his own.

This was evident even at the time. Tsar Nicholas himself, never the most acute observer, grew appalled by the cost of Brusilov's repeated attacks. Golovin, with the advantage of hindsight, suggested Brusilov's goal should have been converging attacks to encircle and destroy the Austrian armies facing the Southwestern Front, not the diverging attacks he in fact carried out. Zaionchkovskii, who certainly had his own faults as a general, was nonetheless perceptive in diagnosing Brusilov's failings:

> The command of the Southwestern Front gave its particular attention to the irresistible completion of the first part of its task—completing a breakthrough—but did not sufficiently value the second part—the best use of that breakthrough to put our army in a better strategic position. . . . The Brusilov offensive indeed succeeded remarkably, but when we got into the open, when we broke out from the trenches of the enemy's fortified belt, when we needed to maneuver, and when we were confronted with the enemy's evil will in more varied forms than in the breakthrough itself, then our strategy suffered from its neglect and led us to a dead-end at Kovel.

The campaigns of 1916 he characterized as having "1) the choice of main strike points for local tactical significance, ignoring those strategically important 2) the desire to be equally strong at all points along the front, and thus concentrating less force at the desired points than might have been possible 3) repeating attacks at intervals that allowed the defenders to take measures to defeat them."[31] Golovin saw things in much the same way: Brusilov "had prepared the rupture of the enemy's lines where it could be most easily effected," but this was a result of "the inferior strategical importance of the points selected, as for this reason they could be expected to have been less carefully prepared for defense."[32] As the Brusilov offensive finally ended, the question was whether Russia could withstand another such victory, or instead follow success after success down the road to defeat.

11

The Romanian Distraction, 1916

The Brusilov offensive, in addition to the terrible toll of casualties it inflicted on the victorious Russian army, had another pernicious effect by bringing a dubious ally to the side of the Entente. Brusilov's success convinced the Romanian government, which had carefully calculated its own best advantage since 1914, to join the Entente in what it believed to be the imminent partition of Austria-Hungary. While both the Allies and the Central Powers had worked to bring Romania to their side, mesmerized by its 600,000 soldiers, Romania proved to be a disastrous addition to the Russian war effort. Far from adding mass and badly needed manpower, the new Romanian front drew in three dozen Russian infantry divisions and extended Russian lines by hundreds of miles.

Prior to 1914, Romanian foreign policy had been split by cultural affinities with France and concrete political interests in common with Germany. While Romanian elites were Francophile and thus sympathized with the Entente, King Carol was German and thus inclined toward cooperation with the Central Powers. Romania had good reason for hostility to both Russia and Austria. Russia had absorbed Bessarabia, largely populated by Romanian speakers, at the end of the 1877–1878 Russo-Turkish War, but the Hungarian half of Austria-Hungary had pushed an aggressive policy of assimilation on the Romanian peasantry in Transylvania. The Romanian government and monarchy had ignored popular antipathy to Austria-Hungary and secretly aligned Romania with the Triple Alliance. On the eve of war, though, both France and Russia worked to shift Romanian sympathies with the active cooperation of Prime Minister Ion Brătianu. When war broke out, their efforts were successful enough to keep Romania from joining Germany and Austria-Hungary, as the Romanian government remained neutral. From 1914, Romania carried out a careful balancing act that threatened at times to produce a terrible fall. Fundamentally, though, Romania's most important goal was acquiring the Romanian-populated region of Transylvania, ruled by Austria-Hungary, and this tilted Romania increasingly toward the Allies. On King Carol's death in October 1914, the throne passed to his nephew Ferdinand, a weaker personality dominated by his British wife. This combined with Russian victories in Galicia and the seemingly imminent defeat of Austria-Hungary to provide additional political space for Romanian politicians to push for intervention on the side of the Entente. Austria-Hungary's defeats in Galicia and inept showing in Serbia made it seem like an especially tempting target. The intensely pragmatic and cautious Prime Minister Brătianu, however, had no intent of joining a war without clear, concrete benefits. By 1915, Brătianu had convinced the Entente to accept massive territorial gains for Romania at Austrian expense should Romania join the war, though no formal agreement had been signed.[1]

By summer 1916, the success of Brusilov's offensive made the opportunity for Romania's government all the more compelling. Germany's manpower resources were stretched thin, leaving Austria to fight alone in Italy and Ukraine. If Austria disintegrated, as it seemed on the verge of doing, Romania's place at the peace table depended on joining the war while the outcome was still in question. Transylvania, the natural target of any Romanian offensive, was stripped bare of troops by Austria's commitments elsewhere, leaving only a few divisions of territorial militia. After months of hard bargaining over Romanian territorial gains and the degree and nature of Allied assistance, the Romanian government finally resolved to join the Entente. With assurances of a diversionary offensive by the Allies out of Thessaloniki to prevent any Bulgarian strike from the south, Brătianu finally signed a military convention on 17 August, stipulating a Russian commitment to an expeditionary force of 50,000 men in Dobruja and an Anglo-French offensive from Thessaloniki.[2]

On 27 August 1916, Romania declared war on Austria-Hungary and sent its troops into Transylvania, precipitating a crisis for Germany and Austria-Hungary and providing grounds for a halt to the already-failed German offensive against Verdun on the Western Front. Romania's intervention seemed a portent of disaster for the Central Powers: 600,000 additional men on the side of the Entente, and Austria's southern flank extended by hundreds of miles. Thirty percent of Austria-Hungary's grain in 1915 had come from Romania. The Austrian ambassador to Romania, presumably in a position to know the state of Romanian military preparations, anticipated "with mathematical certainly the complete defeat of the Central Powers and their allies," and Emperor Franz Joseph expected to seek peace terms soon. Kaiser Wilhelm himself thought Romanian intervention would bring defeat. The internal crisis that Romanian intervention produced in Germany, particularly after the Russian success in the Brusilov offensive, fundamentally overhauled the management of Germany's war. It toppled Falkenhayn from his position as warlord, handing it to the two men who had made their reputations on the Eastern front: Hindenburg and Ludendorff. Kaiser Wilhelm had been intensely jealous of Hindenburg's popularity. While much of this was mere vanity, Wilhelm also feared that Hindenburg's mass appeal raised the specter of democratization and the consequent undermining of Wilhelm's own authority. Falkenhayn's failure at Verdun, the pressure of the Brusilov offensive, and then Romanian entry compelled a shake-up at the top, particularly given Falkenhayn's prior emphatic dismissal of the possibility of Romanian intervention. Falkenhayn's cold and abrasive personal style left him with few remaining defenders in the army. On 28 August, Wilhelm felt he no longer had any choice and summoned Hindenburg and Ludendorff to a personal consultation on the war at which Falkenhayn was not welcome. Taking the hint, Falkenhayn submitted his resignation. On 29 August 1916, the second anniversary of the victory at Tannenberg, Hindenburg took over as chief of the General Staff, while Ludendorff became quartermaster-general and the real commander of the German war effort. This proved disastrous: Ludendorff's undeniable gift for operations was irrelevant when he turned to grand strategy; his lack of real strategic sense and his emotional instability were magnified.[3]

Had Kaiser Wilhelm better understood the nature of the Romanian military, he would have not have been so disturbed by its intervention. Prior to the Brusilov offensive, the Russians had been quite skeptical of Romanian intervention, Alekseev himself concluding that Russia was better off without Romania as an ally. The Romanian army suffered greatly from its idleness during two years of war. While the other powers of Europe had learned painful lessons about the nature of modern war, Romania lacked such experience. While it had also avoided the mass casualties of two years of fighting, it had neglected to acquire the artillery, machine guns, and reserves of ammunition required if it did intervene. In addition, its leadership seemed to be lacking: the Romanian officer corps had only 220 majors (compared to 145 generals) for command in the field. Royal favor and court politics played a far greater role in promotion than professional competence. Soldiers were largely illiterate, producing in turn a limited pool of noncommissioned officers. At mobilization, the Romanian Army consisted of approximately 800,000 men, but actual combat forces were much more limited: approximately 400,000 men in twenty-three divisions. Given Romania's extraordinarily narrow industrial base, none of its formations were equipped with machine guns and artillery to the standards of contemporary powers, and only the ten first-line divisions had even a modicum of modern equipment.[4]

Entente visions for Romania's proper strategy were deeply divided. Britain and France wanted a Romanian assault on Transylvania to bring about Austrian collapse; Russia argued on the other hand for a joint attack south from Romanian Dobruja and north from the Anglo-French foothold at Thessaloniki to drive Bulgaria out of the war, followed by the Ottoman Turks. Indeed, the Russians committed themselves to an expeditionary force of 50,000 men in Dobruja for just such a purpose. Romanian territorial ambitions, however, could be satisfied only by the dismemberment of Austria-Hungary. To make matters worse, Romanian war plans prior to 1914 had been based on its affiliation with the Triple Alliance, hence envisaging war alongside Austria against Russia. The possibility of war in Transylvania required a fundamental reorientation of Romanian thinking, for little preparation had taken place for mountain warfare in Transylvania. Mountain artillery was in short supply, and the border with Russia was far more heavily fortified than that with Austria-Hungary. Accordingly, geography dictated Romanian strategy. The giant curve of the Carpathians presented the Romanians with the opportunity for converging attacks, while the limited number of passes through the mountains necessarily channeled their advance. Two-thirds of the Romanian army was dedicated to the invasion of Transylvania, with the remainder guarding Bucharest and the land frontier with Bulgaria in the south.[5]

THE ROMANIAN INVASION OF TRANSYLVANIA

On 26 August 1916, three of Romania's four armies, comprising fifteen infantry divisions and supporting cavalry, received orders to cross the border into Austrian Transylvania the next day. Geography presented the Romanians with a real opportunity. Transylvania jutted into Romanian territory, enabling the Romanians to conduct a concentric attack and overwhelm Austria's overstretched troops by crossing the Carpathians at several points simultaneously. Invading Transylvania, however, necessarily left Romania's southern frontier dangerously weak. Though the Austrians and Germans had extensive intelligence suggesting Romanian preparations for war, the notoriously convoluted politics of Bucharest convinced many, including both the German and Austrian ambassadors, that war was unlikely. Nonetheless, the Central Powers had prepared for war, planning the defense of Transylvania while sending Austrian bridging equipment and Turkish troops to Bulgaria to prepare for a crossing of the Danube. Well before Romanian entry, the dynamic August von Mackensen was designated as overall commander of the mostly Bulgarian troops, supplemented by Germans and Turks, which would penalize any Romanian move into Transylvania by an attack from Bulgaria in the south. A sharp and successful spoiling attack against the Allied forces at Thessaloniki on 17 August freed up troops for the Romanian campaign and reduced the chances that the British, French, and Serbian forces could take advantage of Bulgaria's turn north.[6]

Romania's offensive was inherently risky. Its penetration into Transylvania was channeled by the mountains into a few narrow passes. If the Romanians could expand their advance deep into Transylvania and establish lateral connections on the Hungarian side of the passes, their position would become far stronger. If not, they were vulnerable to being contained or, still worse, cut off from the passes to Romania and annihilated. The initial stages of the Romanian invasion of Transylvania proceeded remarkably well, despite the rushed planning and relatively inexperienced officer corps. Brătianu had chosen Dumitru Iliescu as the de facto commander in chief, despite his low standing among the Romanian high command, but Romania's advantages in numbers and geography over the Habsburg defenders of Transylvania allowed for success regardless. Soldiers had mobilized surreptitiously over the weeks prior to the formal declaration of

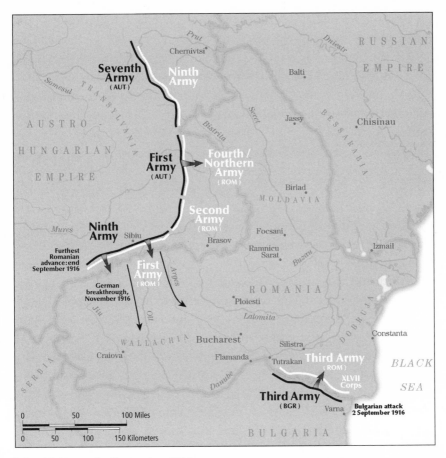

Map 13. Romania, September 1916

war, enabling an immediate crossing of the Austro-Hungarian frontier all around the eastern and southern rim of Transylvania. There had been no prior consultation with the Russian Ninth Army, stationed just north of the Romanian border, so any opportunity for joint action to envelop Austrian defenses from the north was lost. As the Romanian army advanced, hundreds of thousands of German and Magyar refugees fled ahead of them, while ethnic Romanian subjects of the Habsburgs celebrated their liberation.[7]

The first two weeks of easy successes against desultory resistance from outnumbered and superannuated Austrian reservists seemed to endorse the Romanian gamble. The Romanian high command had presumed decisive success could be achieved in the difficult terrain of the Carpathians against thin and poorly prepared Austrian defenses before two inevitable developments followed: the arrival of battled-hardened German and Austrian troops to force the Romanians back out of Transylvania, and Bulgarian intervention into Dobruja and possibly across the Danube into the Romanian heartland.

THE CENTRAL POWERS COUNTERATTACK

The glow of initial Romanian success could not last long. The Russian Ninth Army, exhausted by a summer of almost constant fighting in the aftermath of the Brusilov offensive, could not exert serious pressure on Austrian lines and thus provided the Austrians with vital room to maneuver in assembling divisions for a counteroffensive in Transylvania. The advantage in speed and responsiveness that the Germans enjoyed throughout the war in the east was even more apparent when the experienced troops and officers of the Central Powers were unleashed on Romania. The German high command took the lead in organizing the Central Powers' response with a two-part strategy. Mackensen's polyglot army group of Germans, Bulgarians, and Turks on the south side of the Danube River attacked northeast into Dobruja and then across the Danube toward Bucharest. In Transylvania, the former chief of the General Staff, Falkenhayn, was given an opportunity to redeem himself through command of an army group consisting of the German Ninth and Austrian First Armies to expel the Romanian invasion. The combined forces available outnumbered the Romanians by almost two to one in divisions, but by far more than that when experience, equipment, and leadership were taken into account.

Stavka provided Romania what aid it could. From October 1916, the Romanians pressed the Russians for direct assistance in addition to stretching the Russian front line to cover more of the Carpathian frontier against the Austrians. Lechitskii's Ninth Army, previously the southernmost of the Russian armies facing the Austrians, extended itself south so that its left flank made contact with the right flank of the Romanian Northern Army. Later in the year, as the Romanian military situation degenerated, the Russian Fourth Army moved from the Western Front and the Sixth Army from the Baltic coast to the south to bolster Romanian defenses. In the short term, however, Russian assistance was limited to the new XLVII Corps *Stavka* sent to Dobruja on the Romanian Black Sea coast. The XLVII Corps was a weak and mixed expeditionary force of three divisions: Russian infantry, Cossack cavalry, and Serbian infantry recruited from Russian prisoner-of-war camps. Given the enormous later cost to the Russians of Romanian failure, a more decisive investment of troops at this early stage would likely have paid substantial returns. At the moment, though, Russia committed only this single corps under the resentful and unwilling Andrei Zaion-chkovskii, who viewed Romania as a doomed assignment, repeatedly protested against his appointment, and went on to settle scores after the war in a series of works of military history. Alekseev, by contrast, accused Zaionchkovskii of being so against the Romanian assignment that he deliberately understaffed his own expeditionary force. Zaionchkovskii found in the Romanian Third Army that "the military situation produces a stomach-turning impression. There is complete lack of understanding of contemporary warfare, frightful tendency to panic, the most horrible rumors of a threatening character in official reports but always contradicted by my aerial reconnaissance."[8]

Mackensen's force was the first to move. He employed primarily Bulgarian troops, in particular the Bulgarian Third Army under Stefan Toshev. Politically, Mackensen relied heavily on Bulgaria's Crown Prince Boris, whose German ancestry and extensive military experience made him an excellent go-between to translate Mackensen's campaign plans into Bulgarian action. Only days after Romania entered the war, Mackensen struck back in Dobruja. This flat territory, bounded to the west and north by the Danube and to the east by the Black Sea, had a long southern border with Bulgaria lacking any natural protection. Romania had seized it from Bulgaria in 1913 as a result of the Second Balkan War, and so it was an inviting target for a Bulgarian offensive. Given the Romanian focus on attacking north into Transylvania, the Romanian forces in Dobruja remained defensive and passive, handing initiative to the Germans and Bulgarians. With two and a half infantry and one cavalry division, supplemented by small German detachments, the Bulgarians did not have a substantial numerical advantage over the three Romanian divisions and single Russian corps in southern Dobruja, but enjoyed the advantage of choosing their point of attack as well as an influx of German heavy equipment that far outclassed that available to the Romanians. The Romanian Third Army, responsible for the defense of Romania's southern frontier while the three other Romanian armies attacked Transylvania, consisted only of second-line, poorly equipped divisions.[9]

As early as 30 August, Bulgarian irregular forces crossed the border into Dobruja to spread terror and raise the local Bulgarian population against Romanian rule. The attack began in earnest on 2 September 1916 with a Bulgarian push against Tutrakan. This fortress complex on the east bank of the Danube anchored the western end of the land border with Bulgaria across southern Dobruja. Tutrakan was poorly prepared for a fight. Its defenses were short on heavy artillery and lacked depth, concentrated in a single main defensive ring. Though it was intended as a foothold for Romania on the south bank of the Danube, it lacked a permanent connection to the north bank of the river and thence to Bucharest. When the attack began, Romanian troops manifested little fighting spirit and remained passive, allowing the Germans and Bulgarians to prepare carefully for a final assault. Most of the defensive ring was captured by the Bulgarians on 5 September, and the rest of the complex fell on 6 September, with the bulk of the Romanian defenders unable to escape across the bridgeless Danube: 25,000 were captured. On 9 September, the city of Silistra, just north of Tutrakan, fell without a fight. The significance of the victory at Tutrakan was much broader than a single battle. The poor Romanian performance crushed morale: Prime Minister Brătianu wept openly at a cabinet meeting. As the Russians, the Allies, and the Romanian Third Army's new commander, General Alexandru Averescu, all urged, divisions were immediately transferred from the Romanian invasion of Transylvania south to defend the Danube River line. Romania's inability to fight Bulgarian troops gave the German high command immense confidence in the possibilities of a rapid offensive, one that ran greater risks and extended their lines of supply and communication farther and more quickly than would otherwise be prudent.

Remaining Romanian forces south of the Danube had little stomach to stand and fight, and instead withdrew northeast through Dobruja in concert with Zaionchkovskii's Russian forces. Zaionchkovskii conducted a fighting withdrawal, with his experienced Russian and Serbian divisions far outperforming their Romanian allies. He finally stabilized the front in mid-September 1916 on a line running 70 kilometers east–west between the Danube and the Black Sea, just south of the port of Constanța. Toshev, now reinforced by two Ottoman divisions, failed to push to clear Dobruja entirely, giving Zaionchkovskii time to bring in still more reinforcements.

As Romania's prewar plans came crashing down, Averescu looked for a new alternative. To Russian horror, he devised a plan to retake the initiative and recapture the lost territory in Dobruja, though it was risky to the point of foolhardiness. Alekseev sent him a telegram "long and sad, like an autumn day," begging him to reconsider.[10] With the Bulgarian Third Army bottling up Zaionchkovskii in the northern Dobruja, Averescu intended to cross the Danube far to the west, upstream of the Bulgarian concentration, with his Romanian Third Army. This would cut Bulgarian communications and enable him to crush the Bulgarians between his own forces and Zaionchkovskii's Russians. Receiving royal approval for his plan on 17 September, Averescu chose the village of Flămânda for his attack. While that point on the river was closest to Bucharest and suitable for a pontoon bridge, it lacked any facilities capable of serving the needs of a substantial military formation, let alone the five divisions of his Third Army. In a remarkable logistical feat, considering the primitive infrastructure and utter lack of previous planning at Averescu's disposal, he still managed to have the river crossing ready for the night of 30 September.

Averescu achieved total surprise. Using small boats, he had two infantry divisions across the river by the next day. At the same time, his engineers completed a pontoon bridge that permitted the crossing of artillery. The Germans and Bulgarians had almost no forces in the area, so the Romanian advance was at least initially limited only by the transit capacity of their bridge and boats. At this point, however, the Romanian effort collapsed under a combination of ill-fortune and active Austro-German countermeasures. On 1 October, even before the pontoon bridge was complete, German aerial bombardment harassed Romanian engineers and the troops waiting to cross, though without inflicting serious damage. That night, bad weather and the rising Danube damaged the bridge. The next day, Austrian gunboats raked troops on the bridge with machine gun fire and inflicted some damage on the bridge itself. While the crossing remained intact, the cumulative effect damaged Romanian morale and led Averescu to lose his nerve, and by the night of 2 October the Romanians withdrew back north across the Danube, abandoning the crossing they had taken such pains to achieve. In the wake of the Dobruja fiasco, the damp squib of the Flămânda operation damaged Romanian morale still further. Zaionchkovskii's disgust with his Romanian allies surpassed even its earlier extraordinary levels.

Mackensen's offensive employing the Bulgarian army in the south had compelled the Romanians to halt their advances in Transylvania. A new German Ninth Army under Falkenhayn joined Arz von Straussenburg's Austrian First Army to reverse previous Romanian gains and carry the war back to the far side of the Carpathians. By mid-September Romanian offensives had been stopped and the Austro-German divisions were ready for an offensive of their own. Falkenhayn proved himself a remarkably skilled and flexible operational commander, outmaneuvering the Romanians and rapidly sending them fleeing back over the crest of the Carpathians, pursued by German and Austrian divisions. By 8 October, the Romanians had been forced to abandon all the towns they had taken in Transylvania.[11]

ROMANIAN COLLAPSE

Having sown the wind, Romania was now to reap the whirlwind. Russia had little help to offer, and the Romanians faced attack on two fronts: from Austro-Hungarian troops pursuing the retreating Romanians through the Carpathian passes, and from Mackensen's multinational force in the south.[12] Mackensen now prepared to clear Dobruja of Romanian and Russian forces, prior to crossing the Danube in force. He deployed two Turkish divisions, five Bulgarian divisions, and the equivalent of a division and a half of German troops. The equally polyglot Allied force of Romanians, Russians, and Serbs had few prepared defenses and nothing to match the German heavy artillery. Mackensen's offensive on 19 October quickly became a rout. The Black Sea port of Constanţa was in the hands of the Central Powers by 22–23 October, forcing the Russian fleet there to evacuate. On 25 October, Mackensen captured the damaged railway bridge across the Danube at Cernavoda. With southern Dobruja in Mackensen's hands, he now diverted some of his force from the advance further north into Dobruja to prepare instead for crossing the Danube. Just as Mackensen was weakening his assault troops, the demoralized, underequipped, and inexperienced Romanian divisions were pulled out of the line, leaving the narrow waist of Dobruja held by three Russian corps: Zaionchkovskii's XLVII and two new arrivals, now under the overall command of Vladimir Sakharov. While Mackensen was campaigning in Dobruja, Falkenhayn was engineering the breach of the Carpathian mountains. After a series of probes, he broke through Romanian defenses at the Jiu River pass, at Romania's western extreme. By mid-November, Falkenhayn's divisions had descended from the Carpathians into the plains of Wallachia. The Romanians could not hope to match the Germans, or even the Austrians, at warfare in open ground. Falkenhayn moved east toward Bucharest, rolling up the Romanian defenses on the south slope of the Carpathians as he went. On 22 November German cavalry seized a bridge across the Olt River, the last natural barrier before Bucharest. The next day, Mackensen's troops carried out a meticulously prepared crossing of the Danube well behind Romania's Olt River defenses. On 27 November, cavalry scouts from the two wings of the invasion met. The Romanian high command, underestimating the number of troops they faced, launched a poorly coordinated counterattack with four hastily assembled divisions from 29 November through 1 December. Against all odds, this effort achieved some early successes before Falkenhayn and Mackensen organized effective countermeasures. By 3 December, the exhausted Romanian divisions retreated to Bucharest. Organized resistance in Wallachia collapsed, and Bucharest itself was evacuated. Mackensen entered the city on 6 December, and the oil center of Ploieşti fell the same day.

The German pursuit never slackened, rounding up Romanian prisoners by the tens of thousands. By mid-December, the Romanian First and Second Armies had almost completely disintegrated. The Northern Army, in the more protective terrain of the Carpathians in Romania's northern wing and bolstered by the Russian Ninth Army on its northern flank, was the sole formation in reasonably good order. Only about 70,000 Romanian combat troops remained in organized formations. So many Romanian formations had been destroyed or gutted that those remaining were combined into a single Second Army. Only German exhaustion halted the pursuit and allowed the remnants of the Romanian army, supported by Russian assistance, to establish a new defensive line running west and south of Râmnicu Sărat by mid-December. In effect, the Romanian army went into receivership. The Russians, initially reluctant to commit major resources to Romania, now had no choice but to invest scarce resources in the Romanian front. Romanian entry into the war had now extended the line Russia had to defend by hundreds of kilometers. As Zaionchkovskii later expressed it, "the entire Russian Ninth Army went to the service of our Romanian ally, and behind it others followed." Three full Russian armies—the Ninth Army in the Carpathians and the Fourth and the Sixth further south toward the Black Sea—now propped up the Romanian Second Army and the rump of territory in Moldavia still under control of the Romanian government. Only Tsar Nicholas's sympathies allowed King Ferdinand to remain in nominal control, with the Russian Vladimir Sakharov serving as chief of staff and de facto theater commander.[13]

In late December, the German attack on the Râmnicu Sărat line began. Though Russian troops fought stubbornly in the Carpathians, a direct assault against Râmnicu Sărat itself broke through to the city on 27 December. With the loss of that transportation hub, particularly in winter conditions, the Russians had no choice but to fall back once again behind the Seret River. At the same time, the Russian Sixth Army evacuated its foothold in Dobruja, leaving the marshes of the Danube River delta as a natural barrier against further advance by the Central Powers. Early in the new year, one last major German offensive took the fortified strongpoint of Focşani, the last hope of a Russo-Romanian foothold south of the Seret. By early January 1917, the front lines had settled roughly along the line of the Danube and Seret Rivers and thence into the foothills of the Carpathians, where they would remain essentially unchanged for the next seven months. Two-thirds of Romania was under enemy occupation. At the close of 1916, the Russian alliance with Romania had brought only disaster. The front line for which the Russians were responsible now stretched to the Black Sea, and only about 40 kilometers of that were held by Romanian troops. A full three-fifths of the mobilized Romanian army was now lost. Three Russian armies—the Ninth, Fourth, and Sixth—now held sectors that had not existed prior to Romanian entry, requiring thirty-six infantry and a dozen cavalry divisions.[14]

By stretching Russian manpower resources even further, the Romanian debacle made it almost impossible for the Russians to concentrate a large mass of troops. Even before the February Revolution of 1917 undermined the Russian war effort, offensives were far more difficult to imagine. Even beyond this, though, Romania's collapse had important political consequences on both sides of the Eastern Front. For Russia, it destroyed the faint hopes of forcing victory that had been created by the successes of the Brusilov offensive. For Russia's educated elite, thrilled and heartened by the successes of the summer, the autumn and winter of 1916 were exceedingly bitter. Russia's fragile political peace looked increasingly shaky. For the Central Powers, though, triumph in Romania did not provide a clear way forward. To some, it seemed to open the door to a negotiated settlement with recognition of German and Austrian gains. At Austrian urging, German chancellor Bethmann Hollweg issued a peace proposal through the United States and the Vatican on 12 December 1916, calling on the warring parties to negotiate based on the principle that Germany and the Central Powers had shown their unshakable military might and willingness to persevere to victory. To others it opened the door to unrestrained warfare. Hindenburg and Ludendorff, newly entrusted with supreme power in Germany, transformed victory in Romania into overweening confidence. On 1 February 1917, the German government implemented unrestricted submarine warfare. In this, Hindenburg and Ludendorff discounted the possibility that their actions would provoke American entry into the war against Germany, or that if the United States did intervene, American economic might and manpower would crush Germany as the war dragged on.

12

The Collapse, 1917

As 1917 opened, despite all Russia had lost over two and a half years of war, there were grounds for hope. Russia's economy had shifted to a modern war footing, and the terrible shortage of rifles and ammunition that had crippled Russian armies in 1915 was a distant memory. An ambitious production program for 1917 promised to bolster Russia's inadequate stocks of heavy artillery. Though manpower was running short, all countries at war encountered similar difficulties. Quite quickly, though, the strains of war shattered Russia's tenuous domestic peace. Even while Russian units at the front still fought effectively, the tsar's regime collapsed from within in March 1917. Though the provisional government that replaced Nicholas continued to fight, political and social turmoil destroyed the Russian army. In a series of failed offensives and ineffective defensive operations, Russia's war machine rotted away until the entire structure crumbled. In November 1917, Vladimir Lenin and his Bolshevik party seized power. Though Russia would not know peace until four more years of bloody civil war had passed, imperial Russia's war ended with the end of imperial Russia itself.

In the relative calm that ended 1916, Tsar Nicholas and *Stavka* had reason to be cautiously optimistic. Russia enjoyed a substantial advantage in manpower. In spite of the losses the Russians had suffered and ongoing difficulties in finding able-bodied men, the Russians deployed some 158 divisions on the Eastern Front consisting of approximately 2,350 battalions, compared to 1,900 battalions for the Central Powers. While outclassed in heavy artillery, Russia did outgun its enemies in field artillery.[1] There were tantalizing possibilities for a separate peace with the exhausted Habsburg Empire, allowing Russian strength to focus on the Germans. A separate peace might even create the conditions for a more general settlement that would leave the Russian Empire and the Romanov dynasty intact.

While Russian society was certainly suffering, it was hardly alone; Austria-Hungary in particular was showing signs of wavering. The Allied blockade of the Central Powers was particularly hard on Austria, for that regime's internal divisions made rational management difficult. The dual monarchy's Hungarian half produced food surpluses, while its Austrian half went hungry. The Austrian Emperor Franz Joseph, old and exhausted, died on 21 November 1916, passing the throne to his grand-nephew Karl. This brought a whole host of alterations in Habsburg leadership: Karl took over as commander in chief and secretly explored with France conditions for a separate peace, fearing that German victory would transform Austria into a satellite and destroy it as a great power as surely as Allied victory. The new foreign minister, Ottokar Czernin, shared Karl's sense of the need for peace, but was less willing to act unilaterally. He hoped instead for a general peace involving the Germans and the Entente. Karl commissioned his brother-in-law Prince Sixtus of Bourbon-Parma, an officer in the Belgian army, to approach the Entente secretly. The effort dissolved in misunderstanding, and ultimately became a deep embarrassment for the Habsburgs when revealed by the French in spring 1918. Finally, Chief of Staff Conrad lost his long death grip on the Habsburg military, replaced by Arthur Arz von Straussenburg at the beginning of March 1917.

Russia could be heartened by improved inter-Allied cooperation. In mid-November 1916, Allied conferences at Chantilly and Paris discussed coordinated strategy for spring 1917, driven by French commander in chief Joffre's insistence that the Allies had to take the offensive in order to maintain initiative. The question for 1917 became whether to focus on a single theater, the Balkans, or instead a general offensive against the Central Powers. A Russian-backed proposal suggested an offensive to crush Bulgaria in a pincer movement by Russian and Romanian forces from the north and British and French forces attacking out of Thessaloniki from the south. Alekseev felt this coordinated Balkan attack would sever the connection between the Ottoman Empire and the Central Powers. The British and French, controlling vital flows of war materiel to Russia, won the day for their preference: an offensive by all allies against Germany and Austria-Hungary as early as February 1917, coordinated to prevent superior German staff work and railroad networks from shifting troops between threatened sectors. The Allies agreed their respective offensives would begin within three weeks of one another. Russia thus committed to a spring offensive against the better judgment of its military planners. These plans for a spring offensive, agreed without the presence of the most senior Russian officials, were subject to discussion and ratification at a follow-up conference in February 1917 at *Stavka*.[2]

Stavka accordingly engaged in extensive discussion with its front commanders over plans for 1917. Alekseev, central to *Stavka*'s functioning under Nicholas as the tsar's chief of staff, was now seriously ill. A workaholic, though, he maintained contact with *Stavka* while his post was temporarily held by Gurko. In retrospect, *Stavka*'s preliminary discussions with front commanders over strategy for 1917 are striking in their optimism, with no hint of the disaster soon to strike. While Ruzskii and Evert could be dismissed as engaging in empty rhetoric, given their failure to support Brusilov's offensive in summer 1916, Brusilov himself had grandiose visions for what 1917 spring offensives might achieve. In preparation for the *Stavka* conference, Ruzskii and Evert suggested the Northern and Western Fronts could attack the Germans south of the Gulf of Riga once spring arrived. Brusilov, the most aggressive of the front commanders, pushed instead for a general attack by all fronts in all sectors, employing the tactics for breaking through fortified positions he had developed the previous summer. He even suggested a Balkan offensive against Constantinople. The newly appointed quartermaster-general, Aleksandr Lukomskii, continued to advocate a pincer attack on Bulgaria. On 30–31 December 1916, the Russian high command gathered at *Stavka*. General sentiment was unanimous on the need for delay, regardless of agreements with the Western allies. In addition to the inherent difficulty of a winter offensive, the Russians needed time to assemble men and supplies. This preference for delay was not timidity: each front commander (Ruzskii, Evert, and Brusilov) volunteered his own sector for the decisive offensive. Nicholas was distracted by Rasputin's spectacular murder on the night of 29–30 December, so the *Stavka* conference broke up without resolution. By early February, though, the tsar had endorsed an offensive by the Southwestern Front against the Austrians. Grander in scope than the Brusilov offensive, it envisaged the Eleventh and Seventh Armies attacking L'viv, the Eighth Army in a diversionary attack, the Russian Fourth and Sixth Armies co-operating with the Romanian First and Second Armies in an attack at Focşani, and the Ninth Army pinning down German and Austrian forces in the Carpathians to prevent transfer of reserves.[3]

Inter-Allied relations were always fraught with misunderstanding, and recriminations were especially bitter in early 1917. The British and French begged the Russians for a firm commitment to an early and ambitious offensive, rather than the delayed attack now in the works. The Russian postponement of a major offensive until late spring 1917 at the earliest created understandable alarm in Paris and London, which feared war weariness in Russia: an offensive delayed might become an offensive cancelled. Allied representatives attempted to cajole the Russians into an early offensive. The Russians, by contrast, expected clear and specific agreement to major deliveries of funding and armaments to supply the Russian offensive when it finally came, requesting 16,000 artillery pieces, 100,000 machine guns, ammunition, and machine tools. The British in turn demanded Russian gold as a down payment on eventual settlement, and pointed to enormous stocks of supplies already languishing at Russian ports for lack of railroad capacity to deliver it to the front lines. There was little common ground on which the two sides could meet. Gurko was unbending on his insistence that Russian forces were simply unprepared for a February offensive and any Russian attack was contingent on a substantial materiel commitment from the Allies. Even in the best case, the time needed to deliver those new supplies would make a February offensive impossible. The British and French had little leverage to make the Russians launch an offensive before they deemed themselves ready, and a general Allied offensive was set for April 1917.[4]

Even while the Russian high command was debating the proper course for spring 1917, limited local actions continued. Ruzskii's Northern Front carried out the Jelgava offensive on the Baltic coast at the very beginning of 1917. While this demonstrated that Russian troops were still capable of successful action against the Germans when capably led and provided with necessary supplies, it also indicated Russian limitations. The 1916 Brusilov offensive had drawn all available resources south in hopes of finally breaking the Habsburg army. The Northern Front had accordingly been put on a defensive footing in late summer 1916 and had remained quiet ever since. At the end of 1916, the Northern Front held a substantial bridgehead on the western bank of the Dvina River across from Riga on the Baltic coast. This consisted of a rough triangle with its two short sides stretching approximately 30 kilometers along the coast and 30 kilometers up the Dvina. Though the ground was a morass of rivers, lakes, swamps, and forest poorly suited for offensive operations, the Northern Front prepared a quick strike intended to expand the bridgehead. Russian defenses were poorly placed, with the inland face of the triangle split by the Aa River, Lake Babit, and their surrounding swamps. Should all go well, not only would Russian defenses be put on a much sounder basis in an improved tactical position, but the Russian offensive might cut through to capture the road and rail junction of Jelgava, 20 kilometers behind German lines. This would make German positions on the Dvina harder to sustain and thereby enable further Russian advances.

Accordingly, the Northern Front's Twelfth Army under Radko-Dmitriev prepared an attack on the German Eighth Army. Radko-Dmitriev enjoyed substantial advantages. Not only had German troops lost their sharpness through months of inaction, but the defenders around Jelgava were mostly *landwehr*, not first-line troops. The Twelfth Army had at least a two-to-one advantage in infantry battalions, along with superiority in artillery. The marshy conditions, difficult as they made life for the Russians, presented problems for the Germans as well. They could not maintain a trench line, and so instead occupied strong points on isolated patches of high ground. The Aa River, which cut the Russian position in half, did the same to the Germans, and since the river flowed *behind* much of the German line, a Russian breakthrough might pin the German defenders against the river.[5]

Learning the lessons of the Brusilov offensive, Radko-Dmitriev implemented the Southwestern Front's innovative methods in preparing his more limited attack, and distributed detailed directives for precisely what his units were to do. He decided in the interests of surprise to forgo extensive preliminary bombardment; in any event, German defensive positions were necessarily shallow in the wet and sandy soil of the Baltic coast, so there were no deep bunkers requiring extended pounding by heavy artillery. Radko-Dmitriev mandated extensive training in storming German positions. Deception even managed to convince German intelligence that the Twelfth Army's most effective formations had been transferred to other fronts. Radko-Dmitriev split his attacking forces into three groups, dictated by geography. To the far northwest, split from the rest of his command by the Aa River and Lake Babit, Radko-Dmitriev deployed his Oding group (a reinforced brigade), mirrored to the far southeast by the Olai group (a Siberian rifle division) along the Riga–Jelgava railroad. In the center, his Babit group served as the main striking force: the VI Siberian Corps, supplemented by a Latvian division.

The Russian attack began early on 5 January 1917 without any preparatory bombardment. On the Russian right flank, repeated attacks by the Oding group into marshy forests, channeled into a narrow corridor between a swamp and the Aa River, failed to make any dent in German defenses. In the center, though, southeast of the Aa, the main Babit group of twenty-four battalions achieved impressive success, seizing German positions along the front line and finding no reserves blocking their path to Jelgava. The Latvian battalions had the greatest success, pushing 5 kilometers past the front lines to trap a German regiment against the Aa. On the night of 6–7 January, an attack by the Latvians overran the German position. The German defenders, as was their usual practice, countered the Russian offensive with sharp local counterattacks, but these were contained.

Events on the Russian left wing took an entirely different course. A Siberian rifle regiment refused to attack and instead demanded the installation of a constitutional government. Mutiny spread to other units of the Twelfth Army, while soldiers denounced the tsar and the high command as German traitors. While leaders of the mutiny were executed and soldier-participants sent into hard labor, the left flank's attack toward Jelgava never took place. As news of the mutiny diffused, units in the victorious Russian center refused to continue their advance. Harsh discipline restored order—Soviet sources suggest nearly a hundred executions of mutinous soldiers in January 1917 in the Twelfth Army—but shaky morale and failure to reinforce the offensive doomed further advance. Realizing that momentum had been lost, on 10 January Radko-Dmitriev ordered his troops to clear the eastern bank of the Aa River, then halted his offensive the next day. This provided the Germans welcome time to scrape together reserves for a counterattack on 24 January. This targeted the VI Siberian Corps, which buckled under the combined weight of political discontent and the losses it had suffered in the previous days, giving back much ground.

Nonetheless, the Northern Front commander, Ruzskii, believed the initial success of the Jelgava attack showed the fragility of German lines, and hoped to repeat the effort to break through to Jelgava and reverse the long string of German gains. *Stavka* rejected his proposals, and revolution in Petrograd soon made offensives far more difficult as soldiers became unwilling to sacrifice their lives. This was the last offensive action the Northern Front would undertake. Ruzskii, never dynamic under the best of conditions, was unmanned by the forthcoming revolution and resulting slippage in discipline.

1917'S FIRST REVOLUTION

As miseries mounted in the winter of 1916–1917, increasing numbers of soldiers refused to participate in the war any further. Soldiers' strikes manifested themselves as refusal to attack or occupy frontline positions. While technically mutiny—refusing to obey orders—these strikes expressed discontent without falling prey to the accusation of abandoning the nation's defense. Similar strikes crippled the French Army in 1917. In Russia, the pace of these mutinies mounted with time. In Russia's Southwestern Front, organized demonstrations by soldiers protesting either the war or their living conditions grew from seven in 1914 and eight in 1915 to thirty-five in 1916 and seven in the first two months of 1917.[6] Nonetheless, Russia's collapse in 1917 began not with the hard-pressed soldiers at the front, where discipline remained generally good, but instead with the urban working class, whose living standards had been steadily eroded by inflation and food shortages over the course of the war.

The gathering tension on Russia's home front finally broke on 8 March. On that day, International Women's Day, marches by large crowds of women (who bore the brunt of bread lines and food shortages) triggered spontaneous protest strikes by men as well. Strikes and demonstrations grew dramatically the next day and again the next. Scattered violence had not yet reached crisis proportions, though almost all factories in the city had shut down. On 11 March, troops sent into the streets were ordered to shoot into the crowds, and killed several dozen people. That step destroyed Tsar Nicholas's regime. The soldiers in the capital were not long-service professional troops but recent civilians, unenthused about shooting fellow

Russians or the prospect of transfer to the front. On the night of 11–12 March, unit after unit met and voted to disobey orders to fire on civilians. By 13 March, Petrograd was entirely out of government control.[7]

Key groups responded in very different ways. The revolutionary political parties, surprised by spiraling unrest and the rapid collapse of government authority, scrambled to stay abreast of events. On 12 March the workers of Petrograd, remembering their revolutionary history, recreated the St. Petersburg Soviet, the institution that had coordinated their actions in the 1905 Revolution. Now the Petrograd Soviet, this body was a chaotic gathering of thousands of elected or self-appointed representatives from the factories and workshops of the capital. The revolutionary parties used their unified leadership and organizational experience to take over the Soviet, directing its activities through the Soviet's much smaller Executive Committee. Though enjoying no formal legal standing, the Soviet had far more legitimacy than any other institution among the workers and soldiers of the capital, and indeed of most of Russia. Fearing this revolutionary wave, on 13 March the leadership of the Duma attempted to prevent complete anarchy by declaring themselves the Provisional Government, intended to manage Russia's affairs and provide legal continuity until the establishment of a more permanent system. As soon as the tsar's government collapsed, then, power in Petrograd and soon in all of Russia was split between two contending bodies: the Soviet and its allies, which had popular support but not formal legitimacy, and the Provisional Government, which carried some legal authority from the tsarist days but had at best tepid backing from most Russians.[8]

Neither the Petrograd Soviet nor the Provisional Government had millions of men under arms. The Russian army's high command did, and its response to the collapse of authority in Petrograd was central to what happened next. Tsar Nicholas, at *Stavka* in Mogilev and thus out of touch when the disturbances began, attempted to return by train to his Tsarskoe Selo palace outside Petrograd on the night of 12–13 March. Shunted around the Russian countryside by hostile railroad workers, he finally arrived at Pskov, headquarters of the Northern Front, on 14 March. Messages streamed in to Nicholas from Alekseev and his generals, urging him to abdicate for the sake of the war. Only a new popular government, they argued, could rally support and carry on to victory. High-ranking army officers, a reliably conservative class throughout Europe, now urged the tsar to abdicate, seeing no chance of his retaining even a symbolic role. Bereft of political or emotional support, on 15 March Nicholas abdicated, initially in favor of his young son Aleksei with his brother Mikhail as regent. Mikhail wanted no part of such a role, and the bitter years of the war had almost entirely extinguished monarchist sentiment. The Romanov dynasty ended, and Nicholas was put under house arrest.[9]

Russia's generals had persuaded Nicholas to abdicate in hopes it would improve chances of victory, but Russia's internal collapse and divided authority soon made it clear that victory would be elusive. Even before Nicholas's abdication, the Petrograd Soviet had issued its Order #1, empowering soldiers to check their counterrevolutionary officers, to ensure that the army could not be used against the nascent revolution. Though technically only applicable to the Petrograd garrison, Order #1 was widely taken as generally valid. In addition to easing formal military protocol, the order empowered units to elect soldiers' committees and send representatives to the Petrograd Soviet. Most significantly, the Petrograd Soviet granted itself the ability to countermand the Provisional Government's military orders. The army did not yet have political commissars imposed on it as a means of political control, but the road ahead was clear. Aleksandr Guchkov, new minister of war for the Provisional Government, laid out for Alekseev in no uncertain terms the desperate position the revolution had created. "The Provisional Government," he wrote on 22 March, "does not wield any real power and its orders are carried only to the extent allowed by the [Petrograd] Soviet . . . the troops, railroads, postal service, and telegraph are in its hands. I can say directly that the Provisional Government only exists so long as the Soviet allows it to." This had direct consequences for the army. "The disintegration of reserve formations in internal districts that we have already seen," Guchkov said, "is progressing and those replacements who have been in them three or four months cannot be used for reinforcing the army," meaning no new soldiers for the front. On the same day, Alekseev himself reported to the Provisional Government, in a monument of understatement, that "it is possible that we are close to that frightful hour when individual units of the army will become completely unsuitable for combat."[10]

The revolution brought an immediate overhaul of Russia's high command. Guchkov cashiered three grand dukes (members of the extended royal family) serving in the Russian army. He also dismissed six front and army commanders and dozens of divisional commanders. While there was some resentment at the manner of the purge, even Guchkov's enemies conceded he removed a number of superannuated or incompetent generals. By the time Guchkov's successor, Aleksandr Kerenskii, had completed his own purges in the summer, the dismissals included two commanders in chief, five front commanders, seven army commanders, twenty-six corps commanders, and sixty-nine division commanders. While the Provisional Government may have thereby reduced the odds of a counterrevolutionary military coup, changing commanders wholesale only increased the growing chaos within the Russian army. Even among generals who remained, the majority were at best ambivalent about the revolution. Nicholas's abdication also created a vacuum at the top: who would be the new commander in chief? Grand Duke Nikolai Nikolaevich was briefly named to his old position, but removed by the Provisional Government before taking command. Alekseev, chief of staff and de facto commander in chief, was a natural candidate for the permanent post, but he remained seriously ill. More importantly, Mikhail Rodzianko, chairman of the Duma, moderate conservative, and leading figure in the new Provisional Government, did not trust Alekseev's politics and wanted Brusilov in the job, or alternatively former minister of war Aleksei Polivanov. The result was a long and awkward interregnum where Alekseev, enjoying at least qualified support from most of the generals, coexisted uneasily with the Provisional Government. On 20 May, Alekseev spoke to the All-Russian Congress of Officers and condemned disorders in the army and idealistic slogans of a "peace without annexations." He was finally dismissed and replaced by Brusilov two days later.[11]

After hard years of war, Allied confidence in Russia's prospects was fragile at best, whatever lip service was paid to the glory of Russia's new democracy. The British in particular delayed shipments of war materiel for fear that those weapons would not be used effectively. The Americans did not find the situation much better. Rear Admiral James H. Glennon arrived in Sevastopol on 20 June 1917 to assess the Black Sea Fleet's combat readiness, and found total chaos. The fleet's commander, Aleksandr Kolchak, later to emerge as leader of the anticommunist movement in Siberia, had resigned his position in disgust and thrown his ceremonial sword into the sea just before Glennon's arrival.[12] The German high command was elated that revolution might end Germany's two-front war. Hindenburg described a "sense of military relief" on news of the revolution. Ludendorff felt the same. "How often had I hoped," he wrote after the war, "for a revolution to lighten our military burden . . . I felt as though a weight had been removed from my chest. . . . Our general position had considerably improved, and I could look forward with confidence to the battles in the West." Russia did not leave the war immediately, though, and so any opportunity for the Germans to transfer divisions to the Western Front was slow in coming.[13]

In Russia itself, at least initially, there was more optimism. Like the army's high command, the Provisional Government saw the fall of the tsar as a chance not to leave the war but instead to win it. The Provisional Government had to strike a precarious balance. On the one hand, Russia's high command shed few tears for Tsar Nicholas, but it had no interest in seeing their army disintegrate or the wholesale destruction of social order. In its relations with Russia's allies Britain and France (joined in April 1917 by the United States), the Provisional Government committed itself both to the general war effort against the Central Powers and to the specific agreements and understandings Russia had previously reached with its allies to redraw the map of Europe upon victory. That required encouraging rank-and-file soldiers to fight on. Most left-wing parties and Russia's workers and peasants, however, accepted that the war still needed to be fought but only for national defense, not territorial expansion.

At least initially, rank-and-file soldiers were as thrilled as elite liberals by the fall of the tsar and the creation of a new democratic regime. As best as can be determined, most soldiers still believed in fighting to defend Russian territory. The Provisional Government was unsure how long such loyalty might last and accordingly required, beginning in mid-March, oaths of support from its soldiers and officers. At the same time, it permitted soldier committees as a sop to revolutionary opinion. A massive propaganda effort attempted to convince the soldiers that the Provisional Government worked in their best interests, particularly after Kerenskii took over as minister of war. In addition to standard soldiers' newspapers, this included agitation trains carrying trained orators to rally support. The designation of "Battalions of Death" was awarded units that collectively vowed to fight to the last drop of blood.[14] Even chaplains were politicized in service of the war. Despite Orthodoxy's later identification with counterrevolution, in the heady days of March and April 1917, military clergy were enthused about the new, democratic Russia. Once revolution seemed to threaten that war effort, their attitude quickly shifted to alarm over left-wing sentiments. From 14–22 July, *Stavka* hosted a conference for military chaplains in an effort to channel Orthodoxy as a mechanism for maintaining soldier loyalty. That conference declared that "Russia needs a strong government. Recognize that the Provisional Government is in full the vessel for this power. It is made up of friends of the nation, inspired only by their striving to save Russia." The chaplains called on soldiers to fight and obey their officers, and finally commanded, "Do not fear death!" The message fell on deaf ears; those chaplains were already rapidly losing authority in the increasingly radical atmosphere of 1917.[15]

Army officers were deeply divided by the revolution, with a small minority enthused, a small minority irreconcilable, and most ambivalent, hoping for a revitalized war effort but fearful that anarchy would make their jobs impossible. They formed multiple organizations: the leftist Union of Republican Officers or Soviets of Officers' Deputies, the rightist Military League or Union of Officers arguing for restoration of officer powers, and the broad-based All-Russian Military Union, including both soldiers and officers in an effort to rebuild discipline and solidarity on a collective basis. The very multiplicity of these organizations highlights the deep divisions within the officer corps and the impossibility of speaking with a unified voice. Kerenskii had little interest in an independent voice for the military that might compete with his own authority as minister of war. The All-Russian Military Union never moved much beyond preliminary organizing before disintegrating by the end of 1917.[16]

The Provisional Government in spring 1917 faced a dangerous gulf between the defensive orientation of Russia's workers, peasants, and soldiers, and the annexationist policies of Russia's new foreign minister, Pavel Miliukov. Miliukov, like many Russian liberals, welcomed the political reforms of the revolution but saw them as enabling victory and territorial expansion, not a chance for a negotiated peace. On 9 April, Miliukov had been forced by popular pressure to declare that Russia did not aim at the acquisition of foreign territory. Additional pressure from Russia's left-wing parties compelled him to repeat that declaration to Russia's allies on 1 May, but he included a note stressing Russia's full adherence to its alliance commitments. This enraged left-wing opinion, which did not endorse fighting to further the aims of the alliance. In the resulting political furor, Miliukov resigned as foreign minister, to be replaced by Mikhail Tereshchenko. Guchkov was forced out as war minister as well, replaced by Kerenskii.

Kerenskii, a man of enormously high self-regard, had been the first person to serve in both the Provisional Government and the Petrograd Soviet. Though not yet the formal head of the Provisional Government, Kerenskii quickly became its dominant figure through his ability to bridge the gap between the Provisional Government and the Petrograd Soviet. The reorganized Provisional Government on 5 May unequivocally declared itself in favor of a peace "without annexations or indemnities." This kept the left-wing parties, aside from Lenin's irreconcilable Bolsheviks, behind the war. Their rank-and-file supporters, however, were beginning to waver. Kerenskii self-consciously saw himself as destined to lead the revolution by balancing liberals and socialists and creating a new Russia that would emerge victorious. This required taking a far more deliberate approach to managing military politics. Both the Provisional Government and the Petrograd Soviet had employed political commissars to monitor military units; Kerenskii expanded their use to boost morale and keep watch on potentially counterrevolutionary generals. On 20 May, the War Ministry created a new office to handle political affairs and monitor politics, an office that rapidly expanded its personnel and scope and on 16 August was renamed the Political Directorate.[17]

Kerenskii restructured the high command again, adding to the shake-up that Guchkov had implemented immediately after the revolution. Alekseev's manifest gloom and pessimism made him utterly unsuited to lead the army of a new democratic Russia. If there was any hope that Russian troops would fight enthusiastically, it could come only from someone temperamentally suited to raise morale. Kerenskii dismissed Alekseev, and in the process overhauled the command of most of Russia's fighting fronts. The new commander in chief, Brusilov, though a Russian aristocrat to his bones, possessed a deep conviction that victory was near, was not viscerally opposed to revolution, and had a well-deserved reputation as a successful commander. By moving Brusilov to *Stavka*, however, Kerenskii took him away from the operational command where he excelled, handing him instead overall strategic direction. After the shake-up, Aleksei Gutor (more amenable to the revolution than many generals) replaced Brusilov at the Southwestern Front. Vladislav Klembovskii, Brusilov's chief of staff during the 1916 summer offensive, replaced Dragomirov at the Northern

Front. Denikin replaced Gurko at the Western, and Przheval'skii replaced Yudenich at the Caucasus.[18]

Russian liberals remained enthusiastic about the war in the spring and early summer of 1917, particularly since the American entry on the Allied side in April 1917 promised eventual victory. Indeed, liberal concern focused on the sad fact that too many Russian soldiers had lost enthusiasm. The result was one of Russia's most striking military experiments: combat units made up entirely of women and designed to shame Russia's men into fighting more valiantly for victory. Russia's nascent feminist organizations, dominated by professional, liberal women instead of working-class socialist women, pushed for these new military detachments, and began organizing their own units, even prior to official sanction. Kerenskii approved the creation of the initial women's unit, the 1st Russian Women's Battalion of Death, in early June 1917. Its commander was the tough and experienced Maria Bochkareva, who had already managed to make her way into the Russian army and fight as a noncommissioned officer for two years. The Russian military subsequently created a total of sixteen such units, and almost as many were organized by private individuals.[19]

Russian military morale was indeed collapsing, and the new women's units had no appreciable effect on the process. Desertion increased rapidly after the February Revolution, and grew even worse as the summer offensive approached and soldiers seized any opportunity to escape the front lines and save their lives. Two million men deserted between March and October 1917. Paradoxically, even as the Russian army grew in absolute numbers (6.9 million men as of November 1916), its stock of trained and reliable soldiers continued to fall. It was left with middle-aged men and youths, often politically unreliable. The hundreds of thousands of soldiers in Petrograd, for example, could be transferred to the front only at great risk of political explosion. The stock of able-bodied men left to conscript was almost exhausted. Large numbers of its soldiers were consumed by rear-area work: at the beginning of 1917, for example, the Southwestern Front had 1.7 million men in four armies (many of them in noncombatant positions) but another 1.5 million in rear areas and garrisons.[20]

THE KERENSKII OFFENSIVE

Kerenskii wanted another offensive. Well before Kerenskii took over the War Ministry, France's General Nivelle had informed *Stavka* in March that the offensive in the west would begin on 8 April. A *Stavka* conference, meeting on 31 March, was adamant in its conclusion that there was no hope for an offensive on the previous timetable. Responses from the front commanders were more nuanced, showing how the Russian collapse came from the center outward rather than from the front to the rear. Brusilov was convinced that offensive action, far from being impossible, was in fact the only way to maintain discipline. Gurko, the newly appointed Western Front commander, agreed. Only Ruzskii, who had just dealt with a mutiny of his own in the course of the Jelgava operation, wished to hold back. Alekseev tried to split the difference, ordering on 12 April preparations for an offensive in early May "under good conditions, if possible." He told Nivelle the Russian army was in no condition to attack, at least until the political situation stabilized and the end of the spring thaw allowed troops to move. The Russians might be able to begin an offensive on 1 May. This was still far too optimistic; in fact, the Russians could not manage an offensive before late June.[21]

Kerenskii's motives for intervening decisively in favor of an offensive were complex. Styling himself a dashing revolutionary leader, he desperately wanted a success to shore up his credentials. The excitement of an offensive might restore discipline and spirit to the army. Lack of an offensive was certainly doing it no good. Even Russia's other socialist leaders backed him, hoping that an attack might somehow produce a quicker peace. While, to be sure, many officers believed that the poor state of discipline and morale meant that any offensive would be a disaster, enough high-placed commanders argued for an offensive that Kerenskii had the political cover he needed to proceed. The argument for an offensive posture was not inherently ridiculous. Alekseev, for example, argued that demoralized troops and disorganized transport had consequences equally bad for offensive or defensive operations, so the Russians would lose little and might gain by an attack. On 12 April, Alekseev declared that "our allies began decisive action against the Germans on the Western Front on 9 April [the Battle of Arras]. Taking into account the current situation and our obligations to our allies, bearing in mind the general state of the army and its supplies,

I have decided to preserve the basic idea of the plan and under the right conditions, if possible, to carry out a series of offensive operations in mid-May." Summarizing the front commanders' reasoning to Guchkov, he suggested that "even if we are short on supplies at the present time, it is all the better to attack, even without full assurance of success, than to shift to a dangerous defense and burden ourselves with the need to subordinate ourselves to the enemy's initiatives. The disorganization of the army and its supply system will exert its baleful influence no less on defense than on active operations."[22]

In addition, passivity lost some of its appeal when the Central Powers broke the winter lull in late March and early April with a series of local attacks. Designed as economy-of-force operations to keep the Russians off-balance with minimal expenditure of resources, these met with mixed success. The Germans and Austrians carried out at least five such attacks, beginning on 26 March and continuing through 3 April. One example that particularly alarmed the Russian high command took place at the village of Toboli. Grigorii Ianushevskii's Russian III Corps, an element of the Western Front's southernmost Third Army under Lesh, held a small bridgehead on the western bank of the Stokhod River. Manned by elements of the 5th Rifle and 27th and 73rd Infantry Divisions, the tiny bridgehead was only 8 kilometers long and 3 kilometers deep. Rising spring waters flooded most of the bridges to the small foothold, making the Russian position vulnerable. It was so precarious, in fact, that the Southwestern Front was considering its evacuation, only to be dissuaded by Lesh. At four in the morning of 3 April 1917, the Austrian general Leopold von Hauer's cavalry corps of mixed Austrian and German troops opened an artillery bombardment, concentrating on the foremost Russian trenches and employing chemical rounds. At one in the afternoon, the infantry assault began and quickly broke through the outermost Russian trench line (given the shallow depth of the bridgehead, this was the main line of resistance). Reinforcements from the east bank of the Stokhod were slow to arrive and found it difficult to cross the flooded bridges under German shelling. Cohesive command of the Russian defenses broke down, and the entire bridgehead was taken by that evening, costing the Russians 12,000 prisoners. This was a painful reminder to the Russian high command that quiet sectors might not remain quiet.[23]

Kerenskii, firmly convinced of his own revolutionary greatness and popular acclaim, toured the length of the front in May to stir up support for an offensive and restore discipline. Kerenskii's undoubted charisma produced cheering crowds of soldiers wherever he went, but enthusiasm for a renewed fight was short-lived and shallow. As soon as Kerenskii left the front, the euphoria he created dissipated. And, of course, Kerenskii's motivational speeches boosted morale but abandoned any hope of surprise. Brusilov, now commander in chief, set the start date for the Southwestern Front's offensive at 23 June, but the ongoing disintegration of Russian society and Kerenskii's desire to extend his tours of the frontline units forced a series of delays—first to 25 June, then finally to 29 June. The other fronts were delayed still further, deep into July, in hopes that the soldiers' mood would improve.[24]

Kerenskii's offensive began on 29 June with a two-day artillery barrage, followed on 1 July with attacks by three Russian armies, over the same ground and in greater strength than the Brusilov offensive of the year before. The Southwestern Front, now commanded by Gutor, targeted an Austro-German hybrid army group under Eduard von Böhm-Ermolli. The initial Russian attacks came from Ivan Erdeli's Eleventh Army, pushing toward the town of Pomorzany against the Austrian Second Army, and just to its south Leonid Bel'kovich's Seventh Army, advancing on Berezhany against the Austrian Southern Army. The Special (Thirteenth) Army and the Eighth Army, on the flanks of the main attack, were assigned diversionary duties. In reserve, held out of initial attacks in hopes of exploiting a breakthrough, were three army corps and an additional cavalry corps. The offensive clearly intended to take the lessons of the Brusilov offensive to heart, emphasizing careful reconnaissance and centralized coordination of artillery bombardment. As a sign of just how fragile the Russian army had become, though, divisions drawn from the Russian heartland were conspicuous by their absence from the main offensive sectors. Initial Russian attacks by both armies relied heavily on Finnish, Siberian, and Transamur divisions, and a Czechoslovak brigade.[25]

While the Seventh Army made little headway, the Eleventh to its north managed to use its substantial advantage in manpower and heavy guns to capture the first belt of Austrian trenches and even seize the second defensive belt over two days of offensive action. Gurko committed one of his reserve corps, the I Guards, to the breach in order to expand it further. Russian shock units, modeled on German storm troops and well-equipped with heavy weapons and hand grenades, proved their effectiveness at taking enemy trenches. The initial attacks managed to capture 18,000 Austrian prisoners. At this point, though, further advance proved impossible. Rather than becoming heartened by initial success, Russian soldiers now believed that they had done their part, and had no further wish to risk their lives in a war that had grown quiet over the first half of 1917. They halted in the trenches they had seized and refused to go farther. The small elite formations of shock troops and death battalions that Kerenskii had so carefully assembled were useless unless followed and supported by Russian infantry. A renewed attack by Erdeli's Eleventh Army on 6 July made only insignificant gains, and he reported that "despite the victories of 1 and 2 July, which should have strengthened the offensive spirit of our units, we have not seen this in the majority of the regiments. Some units are dominated by the conviction that they have done their duty and are not obligated to carry on further uninterrupted offensives."[26]

The Russian high command had planned a further attack by the Eighth Army, holding the front line to the south of the Seventh Army. As the attacks rolled south in succession, the plan envisaged, Austro-German reserves would commit to the sectors in front of the Eleventh and Seventh Armies, leaving the Austrian Third Army devoid of support when the Eighth Army joined the offensive. The Eighth Army enjoyed the benefit of a new and charismatic commander, Lavr Kornilov, whose successes (albeit limited) in summer 1917 and outspoken advocacy of harsh measures against revolutionaries would soon make him the darling of Russia's right wing.[27] Despite the limited success of the Eleventh and Seventh Armies to Kornilov's north, he hoped for much better. Kornilov began his attack on 6 July with his left wing, the XVI Corps, to further distract Austro-German attention and reserves from the approaching main blow to be delivered on his right wing by the XII Corps. This initial diversionary attack actually seized a number of Austrian positions, preparing the ground for the main attack the next day. The XII Corps began its own assault on 7 July, just west of the Russian-held town of Ivano-Frankivs'k. Kornilov's infantry and artillery smashed Austrian defenses, taking 7,000 prisoners and forty-eight guns. More importantly, Kornilov's initial successes opened the door for one of the few successful cavalry breakthroughs of the war. Two Caucasian cavalry divisions headed for the important town of Kalush, 25 kilometers behind the front. By 11 July, the Russians had managed to take Kalush off the march and even push beyond it.

This was the high-water mark of Russian success. Though the Seventh and Eleventh Armies had been ordered to renew their attacks after Kornilov's victories, these efforts were no more productive than they had been before. This meant that Kornilov's advance to Kalush left his right flank, well ahead of the immobile Russian armies to his north, unprotected from Austro-German units concentrating around Rohatyn for a counterblow. In addition, after the unsuccessful Nivelle offensives of April 1917 devastated the French army and produced widespread mutiny, the French were utterly incapable of offensive action for the rest of the year. Without significant pressure on the Western Front, the German high command pulled units out of line in the west and transferred them east to contain the limited Russian breakthroughs. The Russians themselves lacked enough battle-ready reserves to support the faltering offensive. There were plenty of soldiers in uniform, but not enough who wished to fight. The specialized shock troops, which had proven immensely valuable in capturing Austro-German trenches, had been ground up in the advance, and there were no others to replace them.

In keeping with typical and tested German practice, the counteroffensive did not strike the newly established Russian salient head-on, but instead broke the Russian advance by attacking its flank.[28] A task force under the Prussian Arnold von Winckler assembled east of Zolochiv to hit the Russian Eleventh Army on its northern flank. While Kerenskii had assembled some fifty divisions for the Russian summer offensive, the key component of the German counterattack was only one Austrian and five German divisions, making up the XXIII Reserve and LI Corps. Attacking east from Zolochiv toward the Seret River on 19 July after a brief but intense artillery bombardment, the improvised Austro-German force quickly shattered hastily constructed Russian defenses. The next day, Brusilov ordered no retreat for the Eleventh and Seventh Armies, along with immediate and vigorous counterattacks. Both directives were equally meaningless. Rolling southeast along the Seret, Winckler's divisions reached the outskirts of Ternopil, 45 kilometers behind the front lines, in two days, and forced the Eleventh Army into headlong retreat.

Further south, Kornilov's Eighth Army had lost momentum. Böhm-Ermolli, in overall command of the Central Powers' response, counterattacked on 19 July, pushed the Russians back, and recaptured Kalush, reestablishing a defensible position on the Limnycja River running through the town. The limited Russian success now made their position even more dangerous: weary troops, convinced that they need run no further risks for the Russian war effort, were vulnerable to the concerted counteroffensive that inevitably followed. When attacked, Russian units simply withdrew. On 21 July, the Eleventh Army's soldiers, ordered to counter Böhm-Ermolli's advance, refused and retreated instead. Brusilov shook up the command of the Southwestern Front; Kornilov now took over the Southwestern Front from Gutor, who had held the command for less than two months. Erdeli was removed from the Eleventh Army and replaced with Pyotr Baluev. It made no difference. Despite Kornilov's undoubted charisma, he could do no better. Each day brought a new attack from the Central Powers and yet another Russian retreat. Once the Eleventh Army's line had been broken in the north, the demoralized Russians could not hold their positions further south. The German breakthrough thus rolled south down the Russian line. Individual Russian battalions or regiments might rally at some town or river line, but the tide of Austro-German troops easily outflanked these isolated positions and forced them to retreat or surrender. Within two weeks, the Russians had wholly abandoned Galicia, the Central Powers had swallowed up 15,000 square kilometers in Bukovina, and only their extended supply lines—and the lack of objectives worth seizing—halted their advance.

The limited initial successes of the Southwestern Front's offensive and the quick German response ought to have discouraged similar attacks by the Northern or Western Front, but invigorating morale at home and convincing the allies that Russia was still a valuable partner trumped the poor odds of success. A joint attack on Vilnius by the Northern Front's Fifth Army and the Western Front's Tenth Army began with artillery preparation on 19 July and infantry attack on 22 July. Despite ample artillery and ammunition, the Russian offensive went no further than the first enemy trenches: Russian soldiers halted, then returned to their own lines.[29] Indeed, the only reason to pay particular attention to these particularly uninspired operations was that they marked the first combat for Russia's first women's unit, Bochkareva's Women's Battalion of Death. Fighting as part of Baluev's Tenth Army, the battalion went into action on 22 July near the Belarusian town of Smorgon', leaving their trenches to attack German positions even when the battalions of men to either side of them refused. Their action shamed their fellow soldiers into eventually joining them, and the Russian attack captured the foremost enemy trenches. In keeping with the general pattern of 1917, the male soldiers then felt they had done their part, and returned to their starting points. A German counterattack then forced the First Women's Battalion of Death out of their captured positions, erasing the day's gains.[30]

As a result of the half-hearted Russian offensives, the Germans had no difficulty pulling troops from quiet sectors to deal with the Southwestern Front's limited breakthroughs. The best summary of Russia's plight at this point probably comes from Anton Denikin, commanding the Western Front, in his remarks to a gathering of commanders at *Stavka* on 29 July:

> Our artillery preparation began. Over three years of war, I never saw such astounding work from the artillery. The spirit of the troops began to lift. The infantry, increasingly demanding of the artillery, were finally satisfied. In the XXXVIII Corps, the infantry even declined further artillery barrages, considering the job completely done. The units moved to the attack, carried out a ceremonial march through two or three lines of enemy trenches and . . . returned to their own lines.

Boris Savinkov, the Provisional Government's commissar attached to the Southwestern Front, rejected Denikin's pessimism and endorsed the possibilities of a new revolutionary army serving a new revolutionary government.[31] It is difficult to regard Savinkov's response as anything but a willful denial of reality. Russian withdrawals in the wake of the Kerenskii offensive continued apace. Once retreat had begun in the poisonous atmosphere of 1917, it was impossible to halt. Only in early August did the German pursuit stop, and with it a new front line stabilized. Kerenskii, having publicly attached his prestige to the summer offensive, desperately needed to find a scapegoat. He thus dismissed Brusilov as commander in chief, replacing him on 31 July with Kornilov.

THE FALL OF RIGA

By autumn 1917, while the Provisional Government and the Russian army were alike incapable of taking productive action, the German high command had to balance a number of competing priorities. The German gamble on unrestricted submarine warfare in early 1917 had not starved Britain into surrender, but had instead brought the United States into the war. While American human and industrial power would take months or years to bring to bear, Germany's long-term prospects looked bleak. The British blockade was causing real suffering on the German home front. Though the German high command did not fully grasp how the spring 1917 Nivelle offensives had brought the French army to the brink of disintegration, there was a real opportunity if Germany could manage to free troops from the Eastern Front in order to devote them to an offensive on the Western Front. Victory in the short term, before the Americans arrived in force, might just be a possibility.

But against all reason, the Russian army continued to maintain a bare minimum of cohesion and combat capability despite ongoing political collapse at home, and the Russian government refused to come to terms. Though not capable of serious offensive action, the Russian army was not yet so helpless that the Austro-German front lines in the east could be denuded of troops. The fall of the tsar had temporarily reinvigorated Russia's will to fight, and the German dispatch of Vladimir Lenin and other Russian revolutionaries back to Russia had discomfited the Provisional Government but not toppled it. Kerenskii's offensive had ended in defeat and retreat, but the Provisional Government had not fallen and the Russian army remained intact, though its officers maintained only as much control as they could negotiate or browbeat out of restive soldiers' committees. The confused street fighting of the July Days, a chaotic and improvised grab at power by Lenin's Bolsheviks, had only succeeded in steeling the Provisional Government's resolve, forcing Lenin to go underground.[32]

With time running out on German victory, the German high command looked for a way to expend minimal lives for maximal effect to drive Russia out of the war and enable a grab for victory in the west. The southern sector of the Eastern Front seemed to offer few prospects. Troops had been drained by the summer's fighting in absorbing and then countering the Kerenskii offensive. Supply lines and stocks of war materiel had to be rebuilt, and soldiers needed rest. The Austro-Hungarian pursuit of the Russians after the failed Kerenskii offensive had lost its momentum, so chances for a successful offensive in the near term looked bleak. The north, though, seemed more promising. That sector had been relatively quiet, but its proximity to the capital at Petrograd suggested that German victories might have a disproportionate impact, compelling the Provisional Government to agree to peace terms. From the German point of view, shifting reinforcements north for a short campaign directed against Riga, a major industrial center on the Baltic, would allow a respite in the south to reorganize, resupply, and expand the railroad network. Once operations around Riga were complete, the Germans could launch a renewed offensive in the south to occupy the last sliver of Romanian territory and drive the Romanian army from the war for good. The outcome of this thinking was a two-part plan for limited offensives in the north. The first, involving solely the army, was an attack to capture Riga. The second, should the fall of Riga not bring down the Russian political system, was an amphibious operation, unprecedented in German military experience, to seize the islands at the mouth of the Gulf of Riga. This would permit the use of Riga as a naval supply base and jumping-off point for still more offensive operations should Russia persevere into 1918.[33]

Riga lay on the east bank of the Dvina River, just above the point at which the river flowed into the southern shore of the Gulf of Riga. The Russian Twelfth Army held the line in that sector, where Russian defenses generally followed the line of the Dvina. There was one prominent exception. The Russians held a substantial salient of flat marshy ground on the western bank of the Dvina at its mouth, the site of the January Jelgava operation. It was well-defended by two corps: the VI Siberian and II Siberian. The German high command saw this Russian bridgehead across the Dvina as both a threat—a potential staging area for another offensive to outflank and roll up their positions further south—and at the same time a vulnerable target to be cut off and destroyed as Russian troop morale deteriorated.

Eighth Army commander Oscar von Hutier, a seasoned veteran of the Eastern Front, recognized the relatively limited manpower and resources at his disposal. Rather than directly reducing the well-manned and fortified Russian bridgehead on the west bank of the Dvina, or attacking Riga directly, he decided on a more innovative approach. His plan was to attack further up the Dvina—approximately 30 kilometers upstream from where the Dvina flowed into the Baltic. By crossing the river south of Riga, he intended to push east then north *behind* Riga, isolating the city, trapping its defenders, and forcing its surrender without a costly attack on the city it-self. By threatening to cut off the city, he could either force a withdrawal or bag a large contingent of Russian prisoners from the west bank bridgehead and the encircled city. Beginning in early August, he massed troops and ar-tillery on the west bank of the Dvina opposite the town of Ikšķile, where the Russian XLIII Corps held the river bank. German artillery expert Georg Bruchmüller devised an elaborate and sophisticated plan to use field guns to suppress the first belt of Russian trenches defending the riverbank, ad-ditional artillery to create a curtain of fire immediately behind the river-bank defenses to prevent the arrival of Russian reinforcements, still more batteries to cut off lateral reinforcement on both sides of the attack sector, and a massive chemical barrage on the second Russian defensive belt, 2–3 kilometers back from the Dvina. He assembled a enormous concentration of artillery, nearly 200 batteries, to allow carefully applied material supe-riority to conserve soldiers' lives. The Russian Twelfth Army was not nearly so well prepared, despite ample advance warning. The German con-centration had been detected, with information coming from both French intelligence and German deserters. The Twelfth Army's commander, Dmitrii Parskii, in place only a few weeks, warned his troops of the precise sector of German attack in a dispatch of 26 August. Russian troops on the west bank of the Dvina pulled back east toward Riga in preparation. Nonetheless, the February Revolution had already had a serious effect on morale and discipline. Russian soldiers were not eager to sacrifice them-selves in defense of a disintegrating state.[34]

The German attack opened on 31 August 1917 with diversionary ar-tillery bombardment west of Riga to draw Russian attention away from the primary attack sector south of the city. The real preparatory bombardment began early on the morning of 1 September with Bruchmüller's coordi-nated artillery barrages disrupting the Russian defense. The precise sec-tor for the crossing at Ikšķile had been the site of a Russian bridgehead on the west bank, abandoned only a month earlier by order of the then-commander of the Northern Front, Vladislav Klembovskii. The Russian de-fenses on the east bank were held by a relatively inexperienced infantry di-vision that broke and fled under German fire, while those defenders who maintained discipline were pinned down in their entrenchments and in-capable of effective resistance. Shortly after 9:00 AM, three German divisions raced across the Dvina in wooden boats and over three hastily emplaced pontoon bridges to seize the eastern bank, unhindered by sporadic Russian defensive fire. Unprepared for the effective German artillery tactics honed on the Western Front, the Russian defenders failed to offer serious opposition to the river crossing. Initial Russian counterattacks were uncoordinated and ineffective, allowing the Germans time to consolidate their positions on the east bank of the river.[35]

Russian resistance improved only once the Germans had begun to exploit their crossing. The leftmost of the three German divisions, the 2nd Guards, raced northwest along the eastern bank of the Dvina toward Riga. The other two pushed northeast across the Dvina, heading toward the rail line connecting Riga to the rest of Russia. Despite the German success in crossing the Dvina, full exploitation of that initial victory proved elusive. The 2nd Latvian Brigade (at this point in the war, Latvian units were among the only ones still willing to fight) stubbornly held up the German advance toward the vital rail line for twenty-four hours. Once the river crossing had been secured on 1 September, the German attack expanded the next day to include the Russian bridgehead on the western bank of the Dvina at its mouth. Though only a single division attacked, the two Russian defending divisions of the VI Siberian Corps quickly broke and ran before reforming at a second line of defense only a few miles outside of Riga. The II Siberian Corps, also defending the bridgehead, remained remarkably passive. Parskii attempted a counterattack with the divisions at his disposal, led by the XLIII Corps, but this failed to make an appreciable dent in German bridgeheads.

The results of the first two days of fighting, in which the Germans had easily accomplished their most difficult task (crossing a river to take prepared defenses) but then found their rapid advance stalling, suggested to Parskii that his Twelfth Army might indeed hold Riga. Out of touch with the concrete situation on the ground as communications broke down, on 3 September he ordered continued counterattacks to contain and then eliminate the German beachhead at Ikšķile. He simply did not grasp that his defenses were barely holding due to the heroic resistance of isolated units. Other formations were in full retreat, and certainly in no condition for counterattack. At the same time, the Germans reorganized their substantial stock of artillery to blast the new Russian defensive positions southeast of Riga. The few remaining Russian units holding their positions, notably the 2nd Latvian Brigade, were too worn down by continuous fighting to maintain their stand, and Parskii had lost all control over the divisions under his command. Refugees and retreating soldiers streamed eastward out of Riga in a disorganized mass, and the Germans managed to capture some 15,000 prisoners and sizable supplies of abandoned weapons and ammunition. The Twelfth Army established a new defensive position some 40 kilometers behind the Dvina, but the Germans had no interest in pressing the Russians any further. Upon the capture of Riga, the German high command halted further pursuit and the German army fortified itself in place, freeing additional troops for more urgent needs in Italy and the West. The Russian collapse was total. Klembovskii, commanding the Northern Front, declared that "the Twelfth Army's retreat has so disorganized it that it is positively in no state at all to stop an enemy attack without a well-fortified position."[36]

THE KORNILOV MUTINY

As a result of the fall of Riga, Russian politics became still more poisonous. Even before the attack, the Moscow State Conference, opening on 27 August, had given Kornilov a rapturous welcome while being cool toward Kerenskii, only fueling Kerenskii's suspicions of a right-wing plot. The conference engaged in wholesale condemnation of soldiers' committees and workers' soviets. Speaking to the State Conference, Mikhail Alekseev and Aleksei Kaledin put full responsibility for failures at the front on revolutionary agitation. The fall of Riga only made matters worse. Kornilov demanded Petrograd be included under his operational authority and the capital be prepared for military defense. To the revolutionary left, this was a sign of betrayal by the officer corps, which intended to put counterrevolution above the war; to the right, it demonstrated the pernicious effect of leftist agitation. In this atmosphere, when the Russian right was recovering its self-confidence after the fall of the tsar, Kerenskii and Kornilov's relationship moved toward an open break.[37]

The final crisis took place in circumstances comically murky and tangled, which makes determining what precisely happened and what the chief actors intended quite difficult. In an atmosphere of mutual recrimination and bitterness between Kerenskii and Kornilov, it seems the eccentric political dilettante Vladimir L'vov took it upon himself to serve as a go-between, meeting Kornilov at his headquarters at Mogilev on 6–7 September to ask him his opinion of the usefulness of establishing a dictatorship in Russia. Kornilov replied it might indeed bring political stability, fully understanding that he himself might be the man for the job. L'vov then met with Kerenskii on 8 September, and presented Kornilov's responses as demands. That evening, Kerenskii contacted Kornilov by telegraph, and the two men talked past one another. Each man succeeded only in convincing the other of his insincerity and unreliability. Following the conversation, Kerenskii dismissed Kornilov as commander in chief on 9 September, and Kornilov in turn dispatched his III Cavalry Corps to Petrograd, likely intending to depose Kerenskii and establish himself as dictator, an intention he declared openly the next day. The coup, at best half-hearted and at worst the result of a misunderstanding, collapsed within days as Kornilov's troops showed no enthusiasm for marching on the Provisional Government. Alekseev arrived at headquarters in Mogilev on 14 September and relieved Kornilov of command, placing him under arrest.[38]

Kornilov's mutiny delivered the final blow to military discipline. Soldiers were far more mistrustful of their officers than before. Some commanders were killed by their own troops; many others were arrested and replaced, sometimes through popular election, by junior officers or even enlisted men based on their revolutionary sympathies. Kornilov's actions seemed to demonstrate the ongoing danger of counterrevolution, and thus produced a radicalization of Russian popular opinion exacerbated by ongoing economic free fall. At the same time, Kerenskii was revealed as ineffective and duplicitous. His popular support, and that of other moderate socialists, dropped precipitously. Worker and soldier support, though not yet that of Russia's peasantry, shifted to the most radical option available to them, untainted by participation in or cooperation with the now-discredited Provisional Government: Vladimir Lenin's Bolshevik party.

The Kornilov mutiny also produced substantial turnover in the high command of the Russian army. Nikolai Dukhonin, a relative unknown with extensive experience as a staff officer at the front level, became chief of staff. Vladimir Cheremisov, whom Kornilov had rejected as commander of the Southwestern Front, now took command of the Northern Front. Baluev took the Western Front; Nikolai Volodchenko the Southwestern, while Dmitrii Shcherbachev remained at the Romanian. Given how little fighting remained to be done, the fact that these generals' revolutionary sympathies outweighed their operational skill mattered little. Only a year away from his own death, Alekseev now saw the situation as essentially hopeless:

All the government's efforts ought to be directed at one thing: the restoration of discipline, the troops' return to normality, to strengthening training, since in fact no serious exercises have been carried for the last five months and the troops don't want any. We need laws which will allow us to begin the rebirth and development of the army, but we don't have those laws yet and the army's illness continues to drag on without hope, threatening fatal and already irreversible consequences. Only when the government takes decisive measures will it be possible in any way to rebuild the army's capabilities and talk about offensive action.[39]

GERMANY CAPTURES THE BALTIC ISLANDS

The fall of Riga was an undoubted German tactical success, but it did not drive Russia from the war. In addition, Riga's potential as a base for further operations closer to Petrograd was limited by geography. The mouth of the Gulf of Riga was blocked by an archipelago of numerous small islands and three large ones (Hiiumaa, Saaremaa, and Muhu) still in Russian hands. Hiiumaa, midway in size between the other two and furthest to the north, was less tactically significant. Saaremaa, largest of the three, stretched across almost the entire mouth of the Gulf of Riga, and the Sworbe peninsula on its southwestern tip commanded the western entrance to the gulf. Muhu, smallest of the three, lay off the eastern end of Saaremaa, connected to it by a causeway. Muhu also housed a Russian naval base at Kuivastu on its south shore. Muhu Sound, separating Muhu from the mainland, formed the northern exit of the Gulf of Riga.

The archipelago's strategic value had been clear well before the war, offering as it did a protected base just off the Russian coast. Naval defenses in the archipelago had been relatively underdeveloped prior to the war, though, for Russian naval preparations had focused on the Gulf of Finland and the near approaches to St. Petersburg, not the Gulf of Riga. The German navy had drawn up contingency plans for seizing the islands in the event of war, but in 1914 the German navy's priorities lay in the west, not the Baltic. Early in the war, the possibility of seizing the islands was raised and dismissed repeatedly. In 1915, attempts to take the islands by naval force through a sweep around their southern coasts failed: Russian mines in the Gulf of Riga presented too great a threat to German capital ships. Taking the islands would require infantry, but troops were at too high a premium for the Germans to make them a priority. This delay allowed the Russians to improve the islands' defenses. Unsure of the Russian fleet's ability to contest the Germans in open water, the Russian command instead emphasized static defenses, installing gun batteries at key points, particularly the Sworbe peninsula, in 1915 and 1916. The combination of these gun emplacements, extensive mines, and the shallow and treacherous waters around the archipelago made any German effort prior to 1917 too costly for the potential gains. Once the February Revolution showed Russian vulnerability, though, and Riga was in German hands, calculations changed. *Stavka* was preoccupied in summer 1917 with the possibility of a German amphibious landing in the Gulf of Finland, particularly because of a strong and growing movement for Finnish independence. For the German high command, however, attacking Hiiumaa, Saaremaa, and Muhu presented the opportunity to maintain pressure on the Russians and drive the unstable politics in Petrograd closer to collapse, while at the same time avoiding the inherent risks in driving still deeper into endless Russian territory. Ludendorff in particular hoped for a "profound impression" on politics in the Russian capital. There was an additional factor at work: discipline in the German navy had slipped as a result of forced idleness for much of the war. Small-scale mutinies and demonstrations multiplied, and the German high command saw action as the most effective medicine to restore fighting spirit. In September 1917, the navy and the General Staff planned an operation that would divert a substantial part of the High Seas Fleet to the Gulf of Riga.[40]

The result was an enormous commitment of German naval power to Operation Albion, intend to seize the archipelago in a further blow at a tottering Russia. The German navy committed ten battleships (only sixteen had fought at Jutland) with a cruiser and nine light cruisers, together with a host of smaller craft. Those were intended to convey an invasion force of 25,000: the 42nd Infantry Division, reinforced with a number of smaller units. Overall command of the operation lay with Vice Admiral Erhard

Schmidt. The German plan was assembled with remarkable speed and efficiency, particularly considering the necessary army-navy cooperation, which the Germans had not previously needed to undertake. There was no tradition of interservice interaction, and no purpose-built landing craft or equipment. Joint army-navy planning began only in mid-September, less than a month before the landings. In addition, the rocks and shoals of the Baltic meant that the key strategic point—Saaremaa's Sworbe peninsula and its naval guns covering the western entrance to the Gulf of Riga— could not be attacked directly. Instead, German troops had to land on the northern coast of Saaremaa, then race south to capture the guns from the landward side. While the Russian defenders did not know the precise details of the German plan, the scale of naval preparations required for the amphibious attack made its general outlines impossible to conceal. There were few suitable targets for amphibious landings in the Baltic, and only a few conceivable landing sites in the archipelago. The Russian fleet in the Gulf of Riga consisted of 118 ships, and was substantially outgunned by the Germans. In terms of capital ships the Russians had only two aged, pre-dreadnought battleships along with a cruiser, later supplemented by two cruisers as reinforcement. Based at Muhu at the northern entrance to Gulf of Riga, the fleet had quite limited mobility. The waters were so shallow that only a narrow dredged channel allowed larger ships passage north and south between Muhu and the mainland. The islands' land defenses, the reinforced 107th Infantry Division under Fyodor Matveevich Ivanov, was far less than a division in actual combat effectiveness. The three Russian regiments on Saaremaa and one on the smaller northern island of Hiiumaa were all understrength, and deeply infected with revolutionary sentiment and war-weariness.[41]

The German invasion fleet left port early on 11 October, and Operation Albion began on the night of 11–12 October. Following minesweepers, the capital ships and troop transports aimed for Tagga Bay on the northwestern coast of Saaremaa, one of the few places suitable for landing. Despite confusion in managing the night maneuvers of such a large fleet to the archipelago, which cost the Germans valuable hours of darkness, the Russian defenders failed to detect the approach. German landings, beginning at dawn, thus enjoyed a vital grace period to get troops ashore without serious Russian opposing fire. Lacking specialized landing craft, the troops were shuttled in on shallow-draft torpedo boats and towed barges. In the waters off Tagga Bay, however, the battleships *Bayern* and *Grosser Kurfürst* and the transport *Corsica* struck mines. Abandoning any hope at surprise, the German ships then opened an artillery duel with Russian batteries overlooking the bay. After a swift and accurate bombardment, the Russian guns were silenced, and German troops once ashore quickly captured the remaining artillery emplacements. A secondary landing force went ashore further east at Pamerort. This contingent included vital bicycle troops, brought in from the Belgian trenches, where their unique mobility had gone unused.[42]

The German troops that landed at Tagga Bay and Pamerort on 12 October pushed inland across Saaremaa as quickly as possible, not pausing to consolidate their hold on the landing beaches or wait for artillery and heavy equipment. Though meeting little resistance on the beaches or in central Saaremaa, these soldiers faced a particularly arduous task. Their three objectives required three diverging advances, contrary to the fundamental military maxim of concentration. Conventional infantry moved south toward the neck of the Sworbe peninsula to capture the Russian gun emplacements, and southeast toward Kuressaare, the island's administrative center and the Russian headquarters. Specialized bicycle units sped east along the island's northern shore, racing to the causeway to Muhu at the village of Orissaare to cut off any Russian retreat. On the first day of action, one detachment of German bicycle troops traveled 50 kilometers to reach Orissaare and seize the causeway. The rapid German advance on all three axes cut Russian lines of communication, both physical and electrical, leaving the overall Russian commander Admiral Dmitrii Sveshnikov in Kuressaare out of touch with his subordinates and the Russian defense uncoordinated and ineffective. Russian will to resist on Saaremaa could not be sustained indefinitely, particularly after Sveshnikov, early in the evening of 12 October, ordered all forces outside of the Sworbe peninsula to flee over the causeway at Orissaare. That night, Sveshnikov himself left by boat to relative safety on Muhu, leaving behind plans of the shore defenses and the minefields in the waters around the archipelago. By the night of 13 October, the Germans had occupied the base of the Sworbe peninsula, trapping the garrison of the powerful Russian shore batteries. The narrow neck of the peninsula, however, was barred by well-constructed fortifications, making a direct German storm an unpleasant prospect. The shore batteries on the Sworbe peninsula, though pounded by German naval guns, manned by inexperienced crews, and with their own guns ineffective from ammunition shortages and mechanical failure, still held out, preventing at least for the moment a German naval sweep around the southern side of the archipelago. After two days of fighting, though, resistance on the peninsula was buckling under combined naval and ground pressure. By the evening of 15 October, Russian defenders at the neck of peninsula lost heart and allowed Germans through. The Sworbe defenders did manage to spike their guns before evacuating by ship or joining the 5,000 prisoners the Germans captured on the peninsula.[43]

The troops that Sveshnikov ordered to evacuate the island collided on 13 October with the defensive perimeter the German bicycle troops had hastily thrown up around the causeway to Muhu. The Russians were desperate to reopen this lone route of escape, and the cyclists were too few to hold them back. Russian units infiltrated gaps in the German line, and by that night the German defenders had to retreat northwest, temporarily reopening the causeway. Two days of desperate seesaw fighting for the bridgehead, with German gunboats providing ammunition resupply and fire support, kept the causeway open for Russian escape to Muhu. By 15 October, though, the remnants of the Russian 45th Division and its commander, Ivanov, had surrendered.[44]

The Germans then turned their attention to the smaller islands of Hiiumaa and Muhu. Though Muhu was the smallest of the three, its position commanding the strait between the islands and the mainland made it more strategically important. While the vital causeway between Saaremaa and Muhu was defended by a thrown-together force of whatever soldiers could be found, the Russian Northern Front attempted to reinforce Muhu. It managed to get some units from the mainland to the island, but found its efforts hampered by soldier mutinies and refusals to board trains for transfer. Those reinforcements that did arrive found a mob of panicked soldiers fleeing the defeat on Saaremaa, infecting fresh troops with their panic. Russian morale had declined so precipitously that the Germans carried out an amphibious crossing to Muhu in broad daylight on 17 October without provoking any defensive fire. By early on 18 October, the Germans had secured both ends of the causeway, and the path to Muhu was open. Russian resistance collapsed, and the Germans managed to capture the island and 5,000 Russian prisoners. On 17 October, the Germans had also landed a regiment on Hiiumaa, and they completed its capture by 21 October.[45]

While the German army was making quick work of Russian defenders on the islands, the German navy was clearing the waters around the islands of Russian ships. Initially, the German fleet pushed east through Soela Sound into the waters in the center of the archipelago, and made quick work of the Russian battery guarding the entrance. Though the waters past the sound were too shallow for German capital ships, torpedo boats harassed Russian ships between the islands and the mainland. Repeated clashes by smaller ships—destroyers, minelayers, minesweepers, and gunboats—from 14 to 16 October in these narrow waters between Saaremaa, Hiiumaa, and Muhu did heavy damage to both sides. By 16 October, when Germans had cleared all resistance on Saaremaa, they could attempt a new approach. With no more Russian shore batteries on the southern coast of Saaremaa, the German fleet tried attacking Muhu by skirting the archipelago through the Gulf of Riga. On the first day, two German battleships and three cruisers, accompanied by destroyers, minesweepers, and other small craft, exchanged fire with Russian ships and shore batteries. Harassed by Russian submarines, the Germans withdrew west. In a second attempt the next day, 17 October, superior German gunnery scored multiple hits on the battleship *Slava*. As one Russian officer described the naval battles around the islands, "our obsolete ships were helpless against the newest German battleships with long-range guns. They showered us with shells when our own couldn't reach them." The Russian ships withdrew north through the strait between the archipelago and the mainland. Since the *Slava* had taken on too much water to escape north through Muhu Sound, the Russians scuttled it at the southern entrance to the sound to block German passage. On 19 October, the Russian capital ships ceased their resistance around the islands and steamed north to the Gulf of Finland. Russian artillerymen guarding the southern approaches to Muhu lost heart with the flight of the capital ships and ceased resistance. They were not the only ones; though they did not yet know it, Operation Albion was the last campaign of Imperial Russia's First World War. A new Soviet Russia was about to take its place.[46]

Conclusion

This book has often talked about contingency; how small changes can have big effects. The end of Russia's war is one such example. Even as Russia was falling apart, the Germans had to keep a huge proportion of their military machine on the Eastern Front. In July 1917, after the Russian Revolution had already begun and the disintegration of the Russian army was proceeding apace, the German Army had 146 infantry divisions on the Western Front. Eighty-nine divisions remained in the east—the peak of German commitment to the Eastern Front. Once the Russian war effort collapsed completely at the end of 1917, Germany was slowly able to draw down its presence in the east, but ongoing danger and chaos meant that it still maintained substantial forces there. The number of German divisions dropped from eighty-nine to seventy-four in December and by 1 January 1918 to sixty-five, still a substantial number. By the time of Germany's last-ditch spring 1918 offensives in the west, there were still forty-seven German divisions in the east. Those spring offensives, empowered by troops transferred from Russia, very nearly won the war for Germany before the full weight of American power could be brought to bear alongside the British and the French.[1] Had Russia exited the war in March 1917 instead of November 1917, the final German offensive in the west would have been far more powerful; had the Provisional Government survived until March 1918, the German spring offensives would likely never have happened at all.

Thus it mattered a great deal how and when Russia left the war. As the autumn of 1917 wore on, the authority of both Kerenskii and the Provisional Government continued to slip away. For Russians in 1917, the most positive interpretation of Kerenskii's role in the Kornilov affair was that he was feckless and ineffective; the most negative was that he schemed toward the dictatorship that he attributed to Kornilov. Left and right alike were increasingly disgusted with him. Popular opinion grew increasingly radicalized, and worker, soldier, and (to a lesser degree) peasant support shifted toward Lenin's Bolsheviks. They were the most radical party in the Russian political spectrum, and their adamant refusal to participate in the Provisional Government meant that they were untainted by its failures. Clear evidence of this was the increasing election of Bolshevik representatives to worker and soldier soviets. On 8 October, Lev Trotskii, close ally of Lenin and hero of the 1905 revolution, was elected chairman of the Petrograd Soviet. He then began to use its authority to make preparations for a seizure of power, a plan that the leadership of the Bolshevik party approved on 23 October. On 6 November, Kerenskii made one last effort to squelch the communist threat by cracking down on Bolshevik organizations. In response, the Bolsheviks quickly and efficiently used their loosely organized worker and soldier militias, the Red Guards, to seize bridges, railroad stations, and telegraph offices throughout the capital. In this last test of strength, Kerenskii failed, fleeing Petrograd to try to find support from frontline soldiers. On the night of 7–8 November, Red Guards arrested the remnants of the Provisional Government, and on 8 November an all-Russian Congress of Soviets retroactively approved Lenin's seizure of power and the creation of a new, Bolshevik-dominated government. Imperial Russia was gone; a new Soviet Russia was beginning to emerge.

After the Bolshevik takeover in Petrograd, *Stavka*, now located in Mogilev, was the clear center of potential resistance. Dual power had plagued the Provisional Government, but a new kind of dual power now threatened the Bolsheviks. While they now held power in Petrograd and enjoyed the loyalty of substantial numbers of workers and soldiers, the military high command was firmly opposed to them and still commanded real (albeit dwindling) military resources. Kerenskii had fled to Pskov and the headquarters of the Northern Front, where he called on *Stavka* to use loyal troops to suppress the Bolshevik uprising in Petrograd. On 12 November, a few hundred Cossack cavalry under the command of General Pyotr Krasnov made a half-hearted attempt to occupy Petrograd, but gave up when confronted with a much larger improvised force of Red Guards. Nikolai Dukhonin, who had been chief of staff at *Stavka* for only two weeks prior to the Bolshevik takeover, proclaimed his support for the Provisional Government. On 17 November, Nikolai Krylenko, People's Commissar of War in Lenin's government, officially informed Dukhonin in a telegram that *Stavka* was now subject to Lenin's newly established Council of People's Commissars in Petrograd. Dukhonin, open and straightforward by nature and well-informed of the army's disintegrating morale, attempted to claim a position outside of politics, but this stance was impossible in the fevered atmosphere of Russia at the end of 1917. *Stavka* hosted a major gathering of non-Bolshevik and anti-Bolshevik activists from the Socialist Revolutionaries, the railroad union Vikzhel', and the Ukrainian Central Rada. The program was not excluding the Bolsheviks from power, but instead forcing the Bolsheviks to accept a broad government of all left-leaning parties. The tensions within this broad left-wing coalition, and between the leftist parties and the far more conservative army high command, meant the *Stavka* talks broke down almost as soon as they began.[2]

On 22 November, Lenin informed Dukhonin he was dismissed as head of the army, to be replaced by Krylenko. Dukhonin refused to cooperate, and won declarations of support from the commanders of Russia's far-flung fronts. This did Dukhonin little good in the short run, as those commanders were too distant to provide any tangible support, and the loyalty of Dukhonin's soldiers close at hand was ebbing rapidly. Dukhonin released Kornilov and other counterrevolutionary officers from prison, freeing them to flee south to begin rallying anti-Bolshevik resistance for the approaching civil war. Dukhonin stayed behind in Mogilev despite entreaties to flee along with the last loyal troops. He was under few illusions about his likely fate. In freeing Kornilov, he declared, "I have signed my death warrant." On 3 December, Krylenko and a body of Red Guards arrived at Mogilev to take over *Stavka*. Taken under arrest to the Mogilev train station, Dukhonin was dragged from his automobile by an angry mob and bayoneted on the spot.[3]

On 22 November, Lenin's government issued a "Decree on Peace," calling for an immediate armistice by all the warring states. It was ignored. On 28 November, they then declared their willingness to open peace talks with the Germans and Austrians, who were eager to do just that. Lenin needed to get Russia out of the war in order to rebuild Russia on Marxist lines, just as Germany wished to free its divisions from the Eastern Front. Since Lenin anticipated that revolution would soon sweep all of Europe, he was not particularly concerned with what terms the Germans might offer. The Bolshevik delegation began peace talks with the Germans at the fortress-town of Brest-Litovsk on 3 December. The Provisional Government and the old army was gone, and with it the Russian Empire. Lenin's new Soviet Russia moved to the reordering of Russian society under fundamentally new principles. Imperial Russia's First World War was over; Russia's civil war was about to begin.

The revolutionary break of 1917 meant that the Bolshevik Party in control of the new Soviet Russia saw itself as fundamentally different from the tsarist regime that had waged the First World War. Lenin and his comrades believed they ruled in the name of Russia's proletarian masses, not as capitalist exploiters, and so the experiences of imperial Russia at war were at best of limited usefulness. Mikhail Frunze, who led the Soviet Army in the mid-1920s, claimed that "our homeland presents itself as a state formation of a wholly new type . . . differing from all other states existing now on the globe."[4] Observers not otherwise inclined to support the Bolsheviks could agree that much had changed: landlords had disappeared from the Russian countryside, while private ownership of most industry had disappeared. One-party dictatorship had replaced a traditional authoritarian monarchy. In strictly human terms, the roughly 2 million Russians, almost all soldiers, who lost their lives during the First World War were dwarfed by the 10 million Russians who perished from combat or political violence or (more importantly) famine and disease during the Russian Civil War from 1918 to 1921. Even from the narrow standpoint of military questions, there was great discontinuity. Only a handful of military units passed intact from the imperial army to the new Soviet Red Army, and much of the tsarist officer corps moved quickly into the anti-Bolshevik White Armies, with many old officers who served the Red Army doing so at gunpoint, with their families held hostage to their loyal service. The 1920s saw the rapid development of tanks and aircraft from the crude beginnings of the First World War, making the lessons of that war seem even more irrelevant.[5]

And yet the undeniable discontinuities across 1917 masked some significant threads that connected the old tsarist empire to the new Soviet Russia. Many, though certainly not all, of the policy innovations of Bolshevik Russia came not simply from communist ideology but from emerging ideas about the nature of modern society that were common across the entire developed world, and so represented evolutionary rather than revolutionary change. The experience of the First World War itself, by requiring governments to intervene in economies and the daily lives of their people in ways unimaginable prior to the war, made many of Soviet Russia's policies look not so different from those of wartime imperial Russia. Food requisitioning to feed hungry cities, massive and routine surveillance and censorship, mass conscription and the resulting militarization of the population, military commissars to monitor the loyalty of officers—all these began before the Bolshevik seizure of power.[6]

For the new Soviet Army, the continuities were equally striking. While few units passed intact across 1917, the central bureaucracy of the imperial army, handling training, conscription, and procurement, transferred to Soviet control largely complete. Unlike in western Europe, where the locked fronts made mobility seem impossible, Soviet veterans of the Eastern Front knew that artillery and machine guns were no obstacle to mobile warfare. The malaise that characterized British and French elites, leading to a profound reluctance to risk another war or even seriously prepare for it, was entirely absent from the Soviet Union. World War I had not been pointless slaughter: quite the reverse. World War I had produced the world's first socialist state, and the next war might bring world revolution. Western Europe's cultural pessimism had no place in a Soviet state whose ideological lodestar was the deep conviction that the future belonged to socialism. As a result, key elements of the developing theory of operational art and maneuver warfare made the jump to the new regime relatively intact.[7]

Even though many imperial Russian officers who survived World War I ended up on the losing side of the civil war, others served the Bolsheviks with varying degrees of enthusiasm. The leading authority on the issue estimates that 75,000 imperial officers served in the Soviet army during the Russian Civil War and afterward. Even after the Red Army's crash demobilization at the end of the Civil War, a third of the officer corps, and a far greater proportion at higher ranks, consisted of imperial officers. This domination by imperial officers continued well into the interwar period. Of the 100 authors of the Red Army's 1929 Field Regulations, for example, 79 came from the imperial officer corps. The Soviet officers in the 1920s who had not been imperial officers came overwhelmingly from the tsarist non-commissioned officers. Often former peasants, industrial workers, or clerks, their formative experience of war was as junior leaders in the imperial Russian army in World War I.[8]

As a result, Soviet military thinkers drew explicit lessons from the experience of World War I. For the Soviets, the vital strategic lesson of World War I was the centrality of politics and economics to the outcome of the war. Napoleon famously remarked that in war, the moral outweighs the material by three to one; the Soviet assumption was that the political outweighed the material by three to one. This was in part wishful thinking, especially in the lean years of the early 1920s when the Soviet military saw itself as hopelessly outclassed by Poland and Romania, let alone the Great Powers of the West. The Soviet state found itself forced to depend on political sympathy abroad for protection from a new interventionist coalition. Nonetheless, the centrality of politics to warfare went deeper than fantasies of foreign revolution. It was the cornerstone of the Bolshevik philosophy of war, and it grew directly out of World War I. When imperial Russia collapsed in March 1917, the Soviets saw its failure as political, economic, and social, not military. It was equally clear that the ultimate collapse of Germany and Austria-Hungary in 1918 was not simply a battlefield defeat. Domestic economic and political failure was as important as allied military success to the sudden end of the Central Powers. As a result, Bolshevik theory stressed the importance of politics, both foreign and domestic, to the outcome of wars. As early as 1918, Joseph Stalin headed his list of five "permanently operating factors" in warfare with "stability of the rear," immediately followed by the morale of soldiers—a direct response to imperial Russia's collapse in 1917. To be sure, those "permanently operating factors" remained permanently operating not because of their profound insight, but because their author was Stalin. Nonetheless, they provide an excellent example of the way the Bolsheviks approached war.[9] Stalin's emphasis on the centrality of political stability to the outcome of wars was not a debated point. Mikhail Frunze opened his essay "Front and Rear in Future War" with: "The basic and most important conclusion from the experience of the past imperialist war of 1914–1918 is the reevaluation of the question of the role and significance of the rear in the general course of military operations." It was the organization and preparedness of society as a whole that decided wars.[10]

This led the Bolsheviks to think of the deliberate use of revolution abroad as a tool of warfare, but also to see the need to prepare the Soviet home front. To an astounding extent, the Soviet military's high command was preoccupied with maintaining social and economic stability at home, a clear lesson from imperial Russia's collapse in World War I. In 1926, N. A. Danilov's *The Economy and Preparation for War* put as the Soviet state's first priority in wartime the maintenance of an adequate supply of food to the urban population. Soviet economic planning for war in the 1920s was remarkably conservative, minimizing disruption to the civilian economy, even at the expense of limiting military production. In addition, the military thinkers of Soviet Russia had in the back of their minds the catastrophic shell shortage of 1915, a disastrous shortfall in supplies of ammunition and firearms. Though Norman Stone in his *Eastern Front* has argued that the shell shortage was overblown, this seems incorrect. Soviet military planners certainly *acted* throughout the 1920s and 1930s as if they had experienced a shell shortage and would take any measures necessary to guarantee that they never would again. In part as a result of their experiences during World War I, they pushed for and won from their civilian leadership approval for the overwhelming militarization of Soviet society, organizing industry and government for war.[11]

Because World War I was so important to the Bolsheviks, the new regime moved quickly to study the war's history and lessons. As early as 18 August 1918, well before the war ended on the Western Front, the Red Army's high command established a Commission for the Investigation and Use of the Experience of the War to analyze Russia's wartime experience. Under the leadership of Vladislav Klembovskii, who had served as chief of staff for the imperial army's Southwestern Front, this commission was responsible for "assembling a description of the war, in order to use that experience in the future to create a combat-ready army." Noted tsarist and Soviet military theorist Aleksandr Svechin served as well. In short order, this group produced a substantial body of work, most importantly the *Strategic Outline of the War, 1914–1918.*[12] Serious historical research and publication on World War I continued throughout the interwar period, culminating in a number of extraordinary documentary collections at the end of the 1930s. By that time, as war with Germany loomed, the Soviet military was desperate to find a usable past, to show how Russians could fight and win against Germans. Brusilov's summer 1916 offensive proved re-

markably useful; it generated a series of monographs studying and cele-
brating his victories, while systematically downplaying the terrible waste
of lives.[13]

There were, of course, enormous differences between the Russo-German
war that the interwar Soviet Union studied and the Nazi–Soviet War it actually fought. Both regimes in 1914 belonged to a common and shared European civilization, however much wartime propaganda exaggerated their
differences. In part as a result of this, the First World War's human toll in
the east was much less than the Second's, and it was by any measure a
cleaner war. Prisoners of war were generally treated humanely. Atrocities
and violence against civilians are unavoidable in war, but the Eastern Front
from 1914 to 1917 lacked anything approaching the mass violence against
civilians that characterized 1941–1945, with the sole exception the mass
slaughter of Armenians by the Ottoman government. World War II in the
east was far different technologically than its predecessor, with the mass
application of the principles of mechanization and motorization and the
key technologies of tanks and aircraft.

In other ways, though, the two wars were remarkably similar. The enormous scale of the Eastern Front was difficult to grasp for military men who
knew only Western Europe. German officers who spent time in the east
were struck by just how different it was.[14] It is a basic but important ob-
servation that Adolf Hitler spent World War I on the Western Front. Had
he fought in the east, he might not have been so cavalier in 1941 about his
army's ability to overcome the difficulties of space and climate created by
fighting in Russia. On the Eastern Front, space created room to maneuver,
which in turn produced operations in both 1914 and 1941 marked by encirclements and the wholesale destruction of entire enemy formations on
a grand scale. During World War I in the east, when the speed of breakthrough and exploitation was that of an infantryman marching with 50
pounds of supplies on his back, battles of encirclement were nonetheless
almost routine: Samsonov's army destroyed at Tannenberg in August 1914;
three Russian corps almost cut off at Kraśnik in August 1914; two Russian
armies isolated at Łódź in November 1914 and a German corps itself cut
off in the attempt; a Russian corps surrounded and annihilated in the Augustów Forest in February 1915. The Second World War added mechanized
exploitation to the mix, and its encirclements were larger in terms of troops
involved and space covered, but the essential elements were the same. In-

deed, under some circumstances the First World War saw *greater* mobility than the Second. Hitler's vaunted panzer divisions were brought to a halt in fall 1941 by the autumn rains bringing the *rasputitsa*, the time when roads disappear into seas of mud. In fall 1914, by contrast, the pace of combat barely slackened, as men and horses were better able to cope with mud than Hitler's partially mechanized *Wehrmacht*. Many of the generals who built the Red Army into a formidable military machine only to be killed in Stalin's purges—Mikhail Tukhachevskii, Ieronym Uborevich, Aleksandr Yegorov, Yakov Alksnis—learned their trade as soldiers fighting for the tsar. Still others who led the Soviet Army to victory over Nazi Germany—Georgii Zhukov, Aleksandr Vasilevskii, Konstantin Rokossovskii, Ivan Konev, Rodion Malinovskii, Aleksei Antonov, Ivan Bagramyan—began their road to the Eastern Front against Adolf Hitler on the earlier Eastern Front in Russia's First World War.

Notes

INTRODUCTION

1. For a similar point, see David R. Jones, "Imperial Russia's Forces at War," in *Military Effectiveness*, ed. Allan Millett and Williamson Murray (Boston: Allen & Unwin, 1988), 1, 250.

2. John Schindler, "Steamrollered in Galicia: The Austro-Hungarian Army and the Brusilov Offensive, 1916," *War in History* 23, no. 1 (2003): 32.

3. Charles Townshend, *Easter 1916: The Irish Rebellion* (London: Allen Lane, 2005), 337–343; Adrian Gregory, "'You Might as Well Recruit Germans': British Public Opinion and the Decision to Conscript the Irish in 1918," in *Ireland and the Great War*, ed. Adrian Gregory and Senia Paseta (Manchester: Manchester University Press, 2002), 113–132.

4. Leonard V. Smith, *Between Mutiny and Obedience: The Case of the French Fifth Infantry Division during World War I* (Princeton, N.J.: Princeton University Press, 1994); Leonard V. Smith, "War and 'Politics': The French Army Mutinies of 1917," *War in History* 2, no. 2 (1995): 180–201; John Williams, *Mutiny 1917* (London: Heinemann, 1962).

5. Ian F. W. Beckett, *The Great War*, 2nd ed. (Harlow, UK: Pearson Longman, 2007), 7.

6. John Keegan, *The Mask of Command* (New York: Viking, 1987).

7. Peter Gatrell, *Russia's First World War: A Social and Economic History* (Harlow, UK: Pearson, 2005).

8. Winston Churchill, *The Unknown War* (New York: Scribner's, 1931).

9. Nik Cornish, *The Russian Army and the First World War* (Stroud, UK: Spellmount, 2006); Michael P. Kihntopf, *Victory in the East: The Rise and Fall of the Imperial German Army* (Shippensburg, Pa.: White Mane, 2000); Michael Neiberg and David Jordan, *The Eastern Front, 1914–1920* (London: Amber, 2011).

10. Norman Stone, *The Eastern Front, 1914–1917* (New York: Scribner's, 1975); W. Bruce Lincoln, *Passage through Armageddon: The Russians in War and Revolution* (New York: Simon & Schuster, 1986).

11. Dennis E. Showalter, *Tannenberg: Clash of Empires* (Hamden, Conn.: Archon, 1991); Richard L. DiNardo, *Breakthrough: the Gorlice-Tarnow Campaign, 1915* (Santa Barbara: Praeger, 2010); Graydon A. Tunstall, *Blood on the Snow: The Carpathian Winter War of 1915* (Lawrence: University Press of Kansas, 2010).

12. For a detailed discussion of the problem of casualties, see Nicholas N. Golovine, *The Russian Army in the World War* (New Haven, Conn.: Yale University Press, 1931), 45–74.

13. Stéphane Audoin-Rouzeau and Annette Becker, *14–18: Understanding the Great War* (New York: Hill and Wang, 2002), 217.

14. On the general complexity of the problem for the better-documented Western Front, see James McRandle and James Quirk, "The Blood Test Revisited: A New Look at German Casualty Counts in World War I," *Journal of Military History* 70, no. 3 (2006): 667–701. For Eighth Army casualties, compare reports for 1 May to 15 May 1916 (old style) and 15 May to 1 June 1916 (old style): RGVIA f. 2314, op. 2, d. 308, l. 21, and d. 303, l. 43.

CHAPTER 1. THE ORIGINS OF RUSSIA'S FIRST WORLD WAR

1. The literature on the origins of the war is enormous. For good introductions to the issues, see James Joll and Gordon Martel, *The Origins of the First World War*, 3rd ed. (Harlow, UK: Pearson Longman, 2007), Richard F. Hamilton and Holger H. Herwig, *The Origins of World War I* (Cambridge: Cambridge University Press, 2003), and Keith Wilson, ed., *Decisions for War 1914* (London: University College London Press, 1995). For an important early work arguing for German responsibility, see Luigi Albertini, *The Origins of the War of 1914*, 3 vols. (London: Oxford University Press, 1953). Fischer's two books are *Germany's Aims in the First World War* (New York: Norton, 1967), and *War of Illusions: German Policies from 1911 to 1914* (London: Chatto and Windus, 1975). Paul Schroeder, "World War I as Galloping Gertie," *Journal of Modern History* 44, no. 3 (1972): 319–345, demonstrates increasing Austrian desperation. For more accessible works arguing viewpoints essentially congruent to Fischer, see V. R. Berghahn, *Germany and the Approach of War in 1914* (New York: St. Martin's, 1973) and Samuel R. Williamson Jr., *Austria-Hungary and the Origins of the First World War* (London: Macmillan, 1991). A. J. P. Taylor's *The Struggle for Mastery in Europe, 1848–1918* (Oxford: Oxford University Press, 1954) is a useful reference for the prewar crises.

2. On Russia specifically, see D. C. B. Lieven, *Russia and the Origins of the First World War* (New York: St. Martin's, 1983); David Alan Rich, "Russia," in Hamilton and Herwig, *Origins*, 188–226; Keith Neilson, "Russia," in Wilson, *Decisions for War*, 97–120. Sean McMeekin, *The Russian Origins of the First World War* (Cambridge:

Belknap, 2011), 6–75, is relevant here, but the book in general focuses much more on Ottoman issues than general European ones.

3. On Bismarck's role, compare S. L. A. Marshall, *World War I* (New York: Random House, 1965), 16, with Taylor, *Struggle for Mastery*, 211.

4. John C. G. Röhl, *Young Wilhelm: The Kaiser's Early Life, 1859–1888* (Cambridge: Cambridge University Press, 1998), 810–813.

5. Randall E. Newnham, *Deutsche Mark Diplomacy: Positive Economic Sanctions in German-Russian Relations* (University Park: Penn State University Press, 2002), 65–68; Niall Ferguson, *The Pity of War* (New York: Basic Books, 1998), 43; Dennis E. Showalter, *Tannenberg: Clash of Empires* (Hamden, Conn.: Archon, 1991), 23–24.

6. Jennifer Siegel, *Endgame: Britain, Russia, and the Final Struggle for Central Asia* (London: Tauris, 2002), xv–xviii, 14–19; Taylor, *Struggle for Mastery*, 441–446; Ye. Iu. Sergeev, "Anglo-russkaia antanta 1907 goda: Novye aspekty," *Novaia i noveishchaia istoriia*, no. 5 (2007): 50–65.

7. R. Raspopovich, "Voennaia konventsiia mezhdu Chernogoriui i Rossiei 1910 goda," *Rossiiskaia istoriia*, no. 2 (2009): 54–67.

8. Newnham, *Deutsche Mark*, 67–68; Showalter, *Tannenberg*, 18–19; Ferguson, *Pity*, 43. V. S. Kotov, "Russko-germanskie torgovye otnosheniia nakanune Pervoi mirovoi voiny v otsenke russkoi pressy," *Voprosy istorii*, no. 2 (2012): 104–118.

9. Dominic Lieven, "Pro-Germans and Russian Foreign Policy 1890–1914," *International History Review* 2, no. 1 (1980): 34–54; Troy R. E. Paddock, *Creating the Russian Peril: Education, the Public Sphere, and National Identity in Imperial Germany, 1890–1914* (Rochester, N.Y.: Camden House, 2010).

10. E. G. Kostrikova, "Bosniiskii krizis 1908 goda i obshchestvennoe mnenie Rossii," *Rossiiskaia istoriia* 2 (2009): 42–43; Iu. V. Luneva, "Bosniiskii krizis 1908–1909 godov: Proval tainoi sdelki Izvol'skogo i Erentalia," *Novaia i noveishchaia istoriia*, no. 2 (2009): 52–55.

11. Kostrikova, "Bosniiskii krizis," 47–49; Luneva, "Bosniiskii krizis," 55–59, 65; David G. Herrmann, *The Arming of Europe and the Making of the First World War* (Princeton, N.J.: Princeton University Press, 1996), 115–130.

12. L. C. F. Turner, "The Russian Mobilization in 1914," in *The War Plans of the Great Powers, 1880–1914*, ed. Paul M. Kennedy (Boston: Allen and Unwin, 1979), 252–253.

13. Ibid., 254–255; David Stevenson, *Armaments and the Coming of War, 1904–1914* (Oxford: Oxford University Press, 1996), 231–278.

14. Holger Afflerbach, "Wilhelm II as Supreme Warlord in the First World War," *War in History* 5, no. 4 (1998): 428–430; Ian F. W. Beckett, *The Great War*, 2nd ed. (Harlow, UK: Pearson Longman, 2007), 30; Stevenson, *Armaments*, 251–253.

15. Turner, "Russian Mobilization," 257–258; Stevenson, *Armaments*, 278–328.

16. Richard L. DiNardo, *Breakthrough: The Gorlice-Tarnow Campaign, 1915* (Santa Barbara, Calif.: Praeger, 2010), 5; R. L. DiNardo and Daniel J. Hughes, "Germany and Coalition Warfare in the World Wars: A Comparative Study," *War in History* 8,

no. 2 (2001): 167–168; Annika Mombauer, "German War Plans," in *War Planning 1914*, ed, Richard F. Hamilton and Holger H. Herwig (Cambridge: Cambridge University Press, 2010), 51–52; Showalter, *Tannenberg*, 20–21; Graydon A. Tunstall, *Planning for War against Russia and Serbia* (Boulder, Colo.: Social Science Monographs, 1993), 10–32.

17. Beckett, *Great War*, 61–64; Mombauer, "German War Plans," 52–62; Showalter, *Tannenberg*, 31–35; Tunstall, *Planning for War*, 33–54.

18. Mombauer, "German War Plans," 63–65.

19. DiNardo, *Breakthrough*, 6; DiNardo and Hughes, "Coalition Warfare," 164–165; N. Stone, "Moltke-Conrad: Relations between the Austro-Hungarian and German General Staffs, 1909–1914," *Historical Journal* 9 (1966): 222–223; Showalter, *Tannenberg*, 44–46; Günther Kronenbitter, "Austria-Hungary," in Hamilton and Herwig, *War Planning*, 37–38.

20. The historical literature on the July Crisis is enormous. Good introductions are Fritz Fellner, "Austria-Hungary," in Wilson, *Decisions for War*, 9–25; Joll and Martel, *Origins of the First World War*, 12–48; Sean McMeekin, *July 1914: Countdown to War* (New York: Basic Books, 2013); Williamson, *Austria-Hungary*, 190–216. For specific information on Russia and its actions during the crisis, see Lieven, *Russia and the Origins of the First World War*, 141–151; David Alan Rich, "Russia," in Hamilton and Herwig, *The Origins of World War I*, 188–226. Christopher Clark, *The Sleepwalkers: How Europe Went to War in 1914* (New York: Harper, 2013), 3–64, 367–376, 387–391 is excellent on the specific Serbian context of the assassination.

21. Konrad H. Jarausch, "The Illusion of Limited War: Chancellor Bethmann Hollweg's Calculated Risk, July 1914," *Central European History* 2, no. 1 (March 1969): 54–59.

22. Afflerbach, "Wilhelm II," 432–433; Beckett, *Great War*, 31.

CHAPTER 2. THE RUSSIAN ARMY

1. For various figures, see Ian F. W. Beckett, *The Great War*, 2nd ed. (Harlow, UK: Pearson Longman, 2007); *Istoriia voennoi strategii Rossii* (Moscow: Kuchkovo Pole, 2000), 93; S. L. A. Marshall, *World War I* (New York: Random House, 1965), 46; S. Kliatskin, "O sistemy komplektovaniia staroi armii," *Voenno-istoricheskii zhurnal*, no. 1 (1966): 108.

2. A. B. Astashov, "Russkii krest'ianin na frontakh Pervoi mirovoi voiny," *Otechestvennaia istoriia*, no. 4 (2003): 73–76; V. V. Izonov, "Podgotovka russkoi armii nakanune Pervoi mirovoi voiny," *Voenno-istoricheskii zhurnal*, no. 10 (2004): 36; I. V. Narskii, "Frontovoi opyt russkikh soldat, 1914–1916 gody," *Novaia i noveishchaia istoriia*, no. 2 (2005): 194–195.

3. David Moon, "Peasants into Russian Citizens? A Comparative Perspective," *Revolutionary Russia* 9, no. 1 (1995), 43–81.

4. I. I. Rostunov, *Russkii front pervoi mirovoi voiny* (Moscow: Nauka, 1976), 49–50; Kliatskin, "O sisteme komplektovaniia," 108.

5. Nicholas N. Golovine, *The Russian Army in the World War* (New Haven, Conn.: Yale University Press, 1931), 17–21; David G. Herrmann, *The Arming of Europe and the Making of the First World War* (Princeton N.J.: Princeton University Press, 1996), 175; Mark Von Hagen, "The Limits of Reform: The Multiethnic Imperial Army Confronts Nationalism, 1874–1917," in *Reforming the Tsar's Army: Military Innovation in Imperial Russia from Peter the Great to the Revolution*, ed. David Schimmelpenninck van der Oye and Bruce Menning (Washington, D.C.: Woodrow Wilson Center Press, 2004), 41.

6. Robert F. Baumann, "Universal Service Reform and Russia's Imperial Dilemma," *War and Society* 4, no. 2 (1986): 31–49; D. Iu. Arapov, "Rossiiskie musul'-mane geroichestki srazhalis' v gody Pervoi mirovoi voiny," *Voenno-istoricheskii zhurnal*, no. 11 (2004): 43; Joshua Sanborn, *Drafting the Russian Nation: Military Conscription, Total War, and Mass Politics, 1905–1925* (Dekalb: Northern Illinois University Press, 2003), 68–74.

7. Baumann, "Imperial Dilemma," 34; A. N. Kurtsev, "Poluterritorial'naia sistema komplektovaniia russkoi armii v nachale XX veka," *Voenno-istoricheskii zhurnal*, no. 4 (2002): 42–44; Rostunov, *Russkii front*, 46–48; Ye. G. Vapilin, "Politicheskie i natsional'nye aspekty armii v XVIII–nachale XX vv.," *Voenno-istoricheskii zhurnal*, no. 10 (2001): 24.

8. Baumann, "Universal Service Reform," 16, 25–26; Vapilin, "Politicheskie i natsional'nye aspekty," 26; Kliatskin, "O sisteme komplektovaniia," 107; Beckett, *Great War*, 55; Rostunov, *Russkii front*, 51–52.

9. Narskii, "Frontovoi opyt," 199; M. V. Os'kin, "Russkaia armiia i prodovol'stvennyi krizis v 1914–1917 gg.," *Voprosy istorii*, no. 3 (2010): 144–147.

10. For extensive information on Russian arms in World War I, see Ye. Z. Barsukov, *Artilleriia russkoi armii (1900–1917gg.)*, 4 vols. (Moscow: Voenizdat, 1948–1949); for balance of artillery, see specifically vol. 1, 168. See also Bruce W. Menning, *Bayonets before Bullets: The Imperial Russian Army, 1861–1914* (Bloomington: Indiana University Press, 2000), 104–107; *Oruzhie pobedy*, 2nd ed. (Moscow: Mashinostroenie, 1987), 242–243; K. Shatsillo, "Podgotovka tsarizmom vooruzhennykh sil k pervoi mirovoi voine," *Voenno-istoricheskii zhurnal*, no. 9 (1974): 94.

11. Izonov, "Podgotovka russkoi armii," 35; Menning, *Bayonets before Bullets*, 257–259; V. V. Murai, "Ustavy sukhoputnykh voisk russkoi armii XVII–nachalo XX veka," *Voenno-istoricheskii zhurnal*, no. 3 (2012): 13.

12. A. A. Budko et al., "V izvestnye momenty na voine, ne meditsina, ne nauka, ne operatsiia igraiut samuiu vazhnuiu rol', a organizatsiia raboty," *Voenno-istoricheskii zhurnal*, no. 8 (2004), 62; B. Frolov, "Razvitie taktiki nastupatel'nogo boia russkoi armii v pervuiu mirovuiu voinu," *Voenno-istoricheskii zhurnal*, no. 6 (1981): 65–66; Murai, "Ustavy," 14.

13. Bruce I. Gudmundsson, *Stormtroop Tactics: Innovation in the German Army, 1914–1918* (Westport, Conn.: Greenwood, 1995), 20–23.

14. Izonov, "Podgotovka russkoi armii," 34–36.

15. Murai, "Ustavy," 14; Shatsillo, "Podgotovka tsarizmom," 93.

16. Baumann, "Universal Service Reform," 23; V. D. Kuznetsov, "Religioznye osnovy podgotovki ofitserov Rossiiskoi Imperii v 1890–1917gg.," *Voenno-istoricheskii zhurnal*, no. 12 (2005): 62.

17. V. A. Avdeev, "Posle Mukdena i Tsysimy," *Voenno-istoricheskii zhurnal*, no. 8 (1992): 4; Bruce W. Menning, "War Planning and Initial Operations in the Russian Context," in *War Planning 1914*, ed. Richard F. Hamilton and Holger H. Herwig (Cambridge: Cambridge University Press, 2010), 99; Rostunov, *Russkii front*, 39–40; Gregory Vitarbo, "Nationality Policy and the Russian Imperial Officer Corps, 1905–1914," *Slavic Review* 66, no. 4 (2007): 684–685.

18. V. D. Kuznetsov, "Religioznye osnovy podgotovki ofitserov Rossiiskoi Imperii v 1890–1917gg.," *Voenno-istoricheskii zhurnal*, no. 12 (2005): 62; Vitarbo, "Nationality Policy," 682–701; K. V. Zhil'tsov, "Generaly musul'manskogo veroispovedaniia v rossiiskoi armii v 1905–1914 godakh," *Voprosy istorii*, no. 12 (2007): 130, 132, 134.

19. I. Grebenkin, "Ofitsery rossiiskoi armii v gody pervoi mirovoi voiny," *Voprosy istorii*, no. 2 (2010): 55; Izonov, "Podgotovka russkoi armii," 36, 38; Peter Kenez, "Russian Officer Corps before the Revolution: The Military Mind," *Russian Review* 31, no. 3 (1972), 226–236; Menning, *Bayonets*, 6–50, 87–151; John Steinberg, *All the Tsar's Men: Russia's General Staff and the Fate of the Empire, 1898–1914* (Washington, D.C.: Woodrow Wilson Center Press, 2010).

20. On the convoluted history of Russian military administration in this period, see Avdeev, "Posle Mukdena," 4–5; A. Kavtaradze, "Iz istorii russkogo general'nogo shtaba," *Voenno-istoricheskii zhurnal*, no. 12 (1971): 77–79; A. Kavtaradze, "Iz istorii russkogo general'nogo shtaba," *Voenno-istoricheskii zhurnal*, no. 7 (1972): 87–92; Dominic Lieven, *Nicholas II: Emperor of All the Russias* (London: Pimlico, 1993), 175; Menning, "War Planning and Initial Operations," 94, 104–105; Rostunov, *Russkii front*, 34–40; A. S. Skvortsov, "General'nyi shtab v sisteme organov tsentral'nogo voennogo upravleniia strany," *Voenno-istoricheskii zhurnal*, no. 1 (2003): 3–4.

21. See Menning, *Bayonets before Bullets*, chap. 7; Menning, "War Planning and Initial Operations," 80–142. See also Rostunov, *Russkii front*, 60–95; L. C. F. Turner, "The Russian Mobilization in 1914," in *The War Plans of the Great Powers, 1880–1914*, ed. Paul M. Kennedy (Boston: Allen and Unwin, 1979), 252–268.

22. *Istoriia voennoi strategii Rossii*, 96; Menning, "War Planning and Initial Operations," 87–91; Rostunov, *Russkii front*, 63–73.

23. Rostunov, *Russkii front*, 73–83.

24. Avdeev, "Posle Mukdena," 2; Menning, *Bayonets*, 239; Menning, "War Planning and Initial Operations," 101–103; Rostunov, 84–91.

25. Avdeev, "Posle Mukdena," 6; Rostunov, *Russkii front*, 42–4. Palitsyn and Alekseev report: RGVIA f. 2000, d. 154, 114. I am grateful to Bruce Menning for this reference.

26. William Gleason, *Alexander Guchkov and the End of the Russian Empire* (Philadelphia: Transactions of the American Philosophical Society, 1983), 31–35.

27. Peter Gatrell, *Government, Industry and Rearmament in Russia, 1900–1914: The*

Last Argument of Tsarism (Cambridge: Cambridge University Press, 1994); David Stevenson, *Armaments and the Coming of War: Europe, 1904–1914* (Oxford: Clarendon, 1996), 6, 53; Keith Neilson, "Russia," in *Decisions for War 1914*, ed. Keith Wilson (London: University College London Press, 1995) has slightly different figures but the same overall pattern.

28. William C. Fuller, *The Foe Within: Fantasies of Treason and the End of Imperial Russia* (Ithaca, N.Y.: Cornell University Press, 2006), 73; Menning, *Bayonets*, 240; Menning, "War Planning and Initial Operations," 109–112; Rostunov, *Russkii front*, 54–55; Hew Strachan, "From Cabinet War to Total War: The Perspective of Military Doctrine, 1861–1917," in *Great War, Total War: Combat and Mobilization on the Western Front, 1914–1918*, ed. Roger Chickering and Stig Förster (Cambridge: Cambridge University Press, 2000), 20; A. Zhilin, "Bol'shaia programma po usileniiu russkoi armii," *Voenno-istoricheskii zhurnal*, no. 7 (1974): 92–96.

29. Beckett, *Great War*, 68; Herrmann, *Arming of Europe*, 147–160.

30. Menning, "War Planning and Initial Operations," 115–120.

31. Menning, "War Planning and Initial Operations," 120–125; Rostunov, *Russkii front*, 92; *Strategicheskii ocherk voiny 1914–1918 gg*, vol. 1 (Moscow: VVRS, 1922), 10–11.

32. Herrmann, *Arming of Europe*, 194–197, 205; Zhilin, "Bol'shaia programma," 92–96; Rostunov, *Russkii front*, 57–59; *Strategicheskii ocherk*, 1:23-30.

33. Gudmundsson, *Stormtroop Tactics*, 18–19; Dennis E. Showalter, *Tannenberg: Clash of Empires* (Hamden, Conn.: Archon, 1991), 117–121; on the German army generally, see Eric Dorn Brose, *The Kaiser's Army: The Politics of Military Technology in Germany during the Machine Age, 1870–1918* (Oxford: Oxford University Press, 2001).

34. Showalter, *Tannenberg*, 123–124.

35. On the prewar Habsburg military, see Günther Kronenbitter, "Austria-Hungary," in Hamilton and Herwig, *War Planning*, 41–43; Gunther E. Rothenberg, "The Habsburg Army and the Nationality Problem in the Nineteenth Century, 1815–1914," *Austrian History Yearbook* 3, no. 1 (1967): 70–87; Rothenberg, "The Austro-Hungarian Campaign against Serbia in 1914," *Journal of Military History* 53, no. 2 (April 1989): 127–146; Rothenberg, *The Army of Francis Joseph* (West Lafayette, Ind.: Purdue University Press, 1976). On the general problem of funding, see John Dredger, "Offensive Spending: Tactics and Procurement in the Habsburg Military, 1866–1918," Ph.D. diss., Kansas State University, 2013.

36. Marshall, *World War I*, 44. On the tendency to overplay ethnic tensions to the neglect of other structural problems, see John Schindler, "Steamrollered in Galicia: The Austro-Hungarian Army and the Brusilov Offensive, 1916," *War in History* 10, no. 1 (2003): 27–59, and more generally Alan Sked, *The Decline and Fall of the Habsburg Empire, 1815–1918* (London: Longman, 1989), chap. 6.

CHAPTER 3. THE OPENING CAMPAIGNS: EAST PRUSSIA, 1914

1. I. I. Rostunov, *Russkii front pervoi mirovoi voiny* (Moscow: Nauka, 1976), 108–109.

2. Razgonov, "Kharakternye cherty sovremennogo boia," *Vostochno-Prusskaia operatsiia: Sbornik dokumentov* (Moscow: Voenizdat, 1939), doc. 763: 487–488.

3. A. Kavtaradze, "Iz istorii russkogo general'nogo shtaba," *Voenno-istoricheskii zhurnal*, no. 3 (1976): 103; Iu. I. Kir'ianov, "Byli li antivoennye stachki v Rossii v 1914 gody?" *Voprosy istorii*, no. 2 (1994): 43–52; Eric Lohr, *Nationalizing the Russian Empire* (Cambridge, Mass.: Harvard University Press, 2003), 14; Joshua Sanborn, "The Mobilization of 1914 and the Question of the Russian Nation: A Reexamination," *Slavic Review* 59, no. 2 (2000): 267–289; J. N. Westwood, *A History of Russian Railways* (London: Allen & Unwin, 1964), 167–170.

4. Boris Kolonitskii, *"Tragicheskaia erotica": Obrazy imperatorskoi sem'i v gody Pervoi mirovoi voiny* (Moscow: Novoe literaturnoe obozrenie, 2010); Anton V. Posadskii, "World War I: A Russian National Perspective, July 1914 to February 1917 (Materials from Saratov Province)," *Journal of Slavic Military Studies* 15, no. 1 (2002): 68; Rostunov, *Russkii front*, 112–113; Paul Robinson, "A Study of Grand Duke Nikolai Nikolaevich as Supreme Commander of the Russian Army, 1914–1915," unpublished paper; Paul Robinson, *Grand Duke Nikolai Nikolaevich: Supreme Commander of the Russian Army* (Dekalb: Northern Illinois University Press, 2014); David Jones, "Imperial Russia's Forces at War," in *Military Effectiveness: The First World War*, ed. Allan Millett and Williamson Murray (Boston: Allen & Unwin, 1988), 291–294; P. M. Portugal'skii, P. D. Alekseev, and V. A Runov, *Pervaia mirovaia v zhizneopisaniiakh russkikh voenachal'nikov* (Moscow: Elakos, 1994), 9–55. I am grateful to Robinson for permission to cite his work.

5. A. Iu. Bezugol'nyi, "Voenno-okruzhnaia sistema v Rossii v period Pervoi mirovoi voiny i revoliutsionnykh sobytii 1917 goda," *Voenno-istoricheskii zhurnal*, no. 10 (2008): 23–24; Rostunov, *Russkii front*, 113–115; Kavtaradze, "Iz istorii," 103; A. S. Skvortsov, "General'nyi shtab v sisteme organov tsentral'nogo voennogo upravleniia strany," *Voenno-istoricheskii zhurnal*, no. 1 (2003): 4; T. Iminov, "Evoliutsiia voennogo iskusstva v gody Pervoi mirovoi voiny," *Voenno-istoricheskii zhurnal*, no. 8 (2004): 5.

6. Dominic Lieven, *Nicholas II: Emperor of All the Russias* (London: Pimlico, 1993), 207–208; Edvard Radzinsky, *The Last Tsar: The Life and Death of Nicholas II* (New York: Doubleday, 1992), 134–166.

7. Bezugol'nyi, "Voenno-okruzhnaia sistema," 22–23; Richard Harrison, *The Russian War of War, 1904–1940* (Lawrence: University Press of Kansas, 2001), 26, 38, 44–45; Iminov, "Evoliutsiia voennogo iskusstva," 5.

8. K. A. Pakhaliuk, "Vostochno-prusskaia katastrofa 1914 goda," *Voenno-istoricheskii zhurnal*, no. 2 (2011): 10; Ianushkevich to Zhilinskii, 10 August 1914: *Vostochno-Prusskaia operatsiia*, doc. 33, 85–86.

9. Dennis E. Showalter, *Tannenberg: Clash of Empires* (Hamden, Conn.: Archon, 1991), 139–142; *Strategicheskii ocherk voiny 1914–1918 gg*, vol. 1 (Moscow: VVRS, 1922), 68–72.

10. Pakhaliuk, "Vostochno-prusskaia katastrofa," 9; A. M. Zaionchkovskii, *Pervaia mirovaia voina* (St. Petersburg: Poligon, 2002), 137.

11. Showalter, *Tannenberg*, 142–144.

12. On the initial border battles, see Pakhaliuk, "Vostochno-prusskaia katastrofa," 11; Showalter, *Tannenberg*, 157–169; Norman Stone, *The Eastern Front, 1914–1917* (New York: Scribner's, 1975), 59–60; *Strategicheksii ocherk*, 1:72–73; Zaionchkovskii, *Pervaia mirovaia voina*, 139–140; Zhilinskii to Rennenkampf, 13 August 1914, *Vostochno-Prusskaia operatsiia*, doc. 100, 146–147.

13. Rennenkampf to Khan of Nakhichevan, 19 August 1914, *Vostochno-Prusskaia operatsiia*, doc. 157, 188.

14. On Gumbinnen, see Rostunov, *Russkii front*, 119–121; Showalter, *Tannenberg*, 169–190; N. Stone, *Eastern Front*, 60–61; *Strategicheskii ocherk*, 1:73–77; *Vostochno-Prusskaia operatsiia*, 186–227; Zaionchkovskii, *Pervaia mirovaia voina*, 140–146.

15. John R. Cuneo, *The Air Weapon, 1914–1916* (Harrisburg, Pa.: Military Service, 1947), 2:111–115.

16. Rennenkampf to Zhilinskii, 26 August 1914, *Vostochno-Prusskaia operatsiia*, doc. 245, 221; doc. 246, 221–222.

17. Cuneo, *Air Weapon*, 2:116–117; Pakhaliuk, "Vostochno-prusskaia katastrofa," 12; Rostunov, *Russkii front*, 123–124; Showalter, *Tannenberg*, 190–198; N. Stone, *Eastern Front*, 61.

18. Anna von der Goltz, *Hindenburg: Power, Myth, and the Rise of the Nazis* (Oxford: Oxford University Press, 2009), 14–15; Showalter, Tannenberg, 199–205.

19. On the Second Army's invasion, see Pakhaliuk, "Vostochno-prusskaia katastrofa," 13–14; Rostunov, *Russkii front*, 120–122, Showalter, *Tannenberg*, 213–319, N. Stone, *Eastern Front*, 62–67; *Strategicheskii ocherk*, 1:77–98;*Vostochno-Prusskaia operatsiia*, 157–174, 245–322.

20. Zhilinskii to Rennenkampf, 23 August 1914, *Vostochno-Prusskaia operatsiia*, doc. 329, 263.

21. Cuneo, *Air Weapon*, 2:110–112; Lee Kennett, *The First Air War* (New York: Simon and Schuster, 1991), 27.

22. Cuneo, *Air Weapon*, 2:128; John Ferris, *The British Army and Signals Intelligence during the First World War* (Wolfeboro Falls, N.H.: Alan Sutton for the Army Records Society, 1992), 3–5; David Kahn, *The Codebreakers* (New York: Macmillan, 1967), 621–627; Showalter, *Tannenberg*, 169, 216–217.

23. Cuneo, *Air Weapon*, 2:129–130.

24. Danilov to Oranovskii, 26 August 1914, *Vostochno-Prusskaia operatsiia*, doc. 374, 280–281.

25. See Samsonov report, 27 August 1914, ibid., doc. 388, 293.

26. Oranovskii to Samsonov, 26 August 1914, ibid., doc. 367, 278.

27. Oranovskii to Rennenkampf, 29 August 1914, ibid., doc. 413, 305; Oranovskii to Rennenkampf, 29 August 1914, ibid., doc. 414, 305; Rennenkampf to corps commanders, 29 August 1914, doc. 269, 232.

28. Marshall, *World War I*, 95.

29. von der Goltz, *Hindenburg*, 16; Plessen, cited in Mombauer, "German War Plans," 72.

30. Zaionchkovskii, *Pervaia mirovaia voina*, 145, 259; Pakhaliuk, "Vostochno-prusskaia katastrofa," 12; Showalter, *Tannenberg*, 29–45.

31. Ian F. W. Beckett, *The Great War*, 2nd ed. (Harlow, UK: Pearson Longman, 2007), 76; Stanley Washburn, *On the Russian Front in World War I: Memoirs of an American War Correspondent* (New York: Speller, 1982), 29.

32. On the First Army's second clash with the Eighth Army, see *Vostochno-Prusskaia operatsiia*, 325–395; Rostunov, *Russkii front*, 126–128; N. Stone, *Eastern Front*, 67–69; *Strategicheskii ocherk*, 1:106–127.

33. Rennenkampf, First Army order # 9, 9 September 1914, *Vostochno-Prusskaia operatsiia*, doc. 536, 382.

34. *Strategicheskii ocherk*, 1:117–118; *Vostochno-Prusskaia operatsiia*, 422–424, 486.

35. *Strategicheskii ocherk*, 1:126–127; Zaionchkovskii, *Pervaia mirovaia voina*, 269.

CHAPTER 4. THE OPENING CAMPAIGNS: GALICIA, 1914

1. For the convoluted story of Austrian mobilization, see Günther Kronenbitter, "Austria-Hungary," in *War Planning 1914*, ed. Richard F. Hamilton and Holger H. Herwig (Cambridge University Press, 2010), 37–38, 45–46; Günther Rothenberg, *The Army of Francis Joseph* (West Lafayette, Ind.: Purdue University Press, 1976), 177–179; Graydon A. Tunstall, *Planning for War against Russia and Serbia: Austro-Hungarian and German Military Strategies, 1871–1914* (Boulder, Colo.: East European Monographs, 1993), 159–210; Samuel R. Williamson Jr., *Austria-Hungary and the Origins of the First World War* (London: Macmillan, 1991), 205–208.

2. On Russian plans and the advance into Galicia, see A. Beloi, *Galitsiiskaia bitva* (Moscow: Voenizdat, 1929), 62–69; Nikolai Golovin, "The Great Battle of Galicia (1914): A Study in Strategy," *Slavonic Review* 5, no. 13 (1926): 25–29; *Strategicheskii ocherk voiny 1914–1918 gg*, vol. 1 (Moscow: VVRS, 1922), 132–137.

3. On the Fourth and Fifth Armies' battles at Kraśnik and Komarów (also referred to using the nearby town of Tomashev), see Beloi, *Galitsiiskaia bitva*, 70–150; Golovin, "Great Battle," 29–33; I. I. Rostunov, *Russkii front pervoi mirovoi voiny* (Moscow: Nauka, 1976), 131–140; Norman Stone, *The Eastern Front, 1914–1917* (New York: Scribner's, 1975), 84–87; *Strategicheskii ocherk*, 1:137–159; A. M. Zaionchkovskii, *Pervaia mirovaia voina* (St. Petersburg: Poligon, 2002), 189–199.

4. Yanushkevich to Ivanov, 22 August 1914, *Strategicheskii ocherk*, 1:47.

5. On the fighting in the east, see Beloi, *Galitsiiskaia bitva*, 151–211; Rostunov, *Russkii front*, 140–145; N. Stone, *Eastern Front*, 88–90; *Strategicheskii ocherk*, 1:159–170; Zaionchkovskii, *Pervaia mirovaia voina*, 199–208.

6. *Strategicheskii ocherk*, 1:163.

7. *Strategicheskii ocherk*, 1:180.

8. On Rava-Ruska, see Beloi, *Galitsiiskaia bitva*, 212–323; Rostunov, *Russkii front*, 145–150; *Strategicheskii ocherk*, 1:171–224.

9. Southwestern Front Staff report to *Stavka*, *Strategicheskii ocherk*, 1:196.

10. Ivanov directive to Pleve, 11 September 1914: *Strategicheskii ocherk*, 1:204.

11. Stanley Washburn, *On the Russian Front in World War I: Memoirs of an American War Correspondent* (New York: Speller, 1982), 51–52.

12. On Russian pursuit, see Beloi, *Galitsiiskaia bitva*, 324–345; *Strategicheskii ocherk voiny 1914–1918 gg*, vol. 2 (Moscow: VVRS, 1923), 13–18.

13. Rostunov, *Russkii front*, 153; Beckett, *Great War*, 75.

CHAPTER 5. THE STRUGGLE FOR POLAND, AUTUMN 1914

1. A. Iu. Bakhturina, "Vozzvanie k poliakam 1 avgusta 1914g. i ego avtory," *Voprosy istorii*, no. 8 (1998): 132–136; Jeffrey Mankoff, "The Future of Poland, 1914–1917: France and Great Britain in the Triple Entente," *International History Review* 30, no. 4 (2008): 743–745.

2. *Strategicheskii ocherk voiny 1914–1918 gg*, vol. 1 (Moscow: VVRS, 1922), 127–131.

3. On preparations for offensives in central Poland and Russian reorganization, see I. I. Rostunov, *Russkii front pervoi mirovoi voiny* (Moscow: Nauka, 1976), 154–168; *Varshavsko-Ivangorodskaia operatsiia: Sbornik dokumentov* (Moscow: Voenizdat, 1938), 22–104.

4. *Varshavsko-Ivangorodskaia operatsiia*, 107–113.

5. Yanushkevich to Ivanov, 25 September 1914, *Varshavsko-Ivangorodskaia operatsiia*, doc. 7, 28.

6. Yanushkevich to Ruzskii and Ivanov, 28 September 1914, *Varshavsko-Ivangorodskaia operatsiia*, doc. 12, 33–34.

7. On Russian reorganization, see *Strategicheskii ocherk voiny 1914–1918 gg*, vol. 2 (Moscow: VVRS, 1923), 19–39; A. M. Zaionchkovskii, *Pervaia mirovaia voina* (St. Petersburg: Poligon, 2002), 288–292.

8. On the German offensive, see Rostunov, *Russkii front*, 168–175; Norman Stone, *The Eastern Front, 1914–1917* (New York: Scribner's, 1975), 97–100; *Strategicheskii ocherk*, 2:40–78; *Varshavsko-Ivangorodskaia operatsiia*, 149–265; Zaionchkovskii, *Pervaia mirovaia voina*, 292–297.

9. On the Russian counteroffensive, see *Varshavsko-Ivangorodskaia operatsiia*, 205–341.

10. Yanushkevich to Ivanov and Ruzskii, 16 October 1914, *Varshavsko-Ivangorodskaia operatsiia*, doc. 380, 255–256; Yanushkevich to Ivanov and Ruzskii, 17 October 1914: ibid., doc. 383, 257.

11. On Russian pursuit, see *Varshavsko-Ivangorodskaia operatsiia*, 369–417; *Lodzinskaia operatsiia: Sbornik dokumentov* (Moscow: Voenizdat, 1936), 25–36, 47–54; for casualties, see *Varshavsko-Ivangorodskaia operatsiia*, 504–505.

12. On the Austro-Hungarian offensive south of the Vistula, see *Strategicheskii ocherk*, 2:79–98, 118–120, 159–66; Graydon Tunstall, *Blood on the Snow: The Carpathian Winter War of 1915* (Lawrence: University Press of Kansas, 2010), 19–20.

13. On plans for the November offensives, see *Lodzinskaia operatsiia*, 15–17, 57–80, 91–114; Rostunov, *Russkii front*, 176–181; D. Rybin, *Lodzinskaia operatsiia na russkom fronte mirovoi voiny v 1914 godu* (Moscow: Voenizdat, 1938), 8–14; *Strategicheskii ocherk*, 2:108–112, 114–118, 120–124.

14. On German planning, see *Lodzinskaia operatsiia*, 14–15.

15. Yanushkevich to Ivanov and Ruzskii, 10 November 1914, *Lodzinskaia operatsiia*, doc. 50, 71–73.

16. On the course of the Łódź operation, see *Lodzinskaia operatsiia*, 115–136, 147–248, 265–324; Rybin, *Lodzinskaia operatsiia*, 15–45; N. Stone, *Eastern Front*, 105–107; *Strategicheskii ocherk*, 2:125–153; Zaionchkovskii, *Pervaia mirovaia voina*, 302.

17. Ruzskii to army commanders, 13 November 1914, *Lodzinskaia operatsiia*, doc. 149, 150–151.

18. On the Russian offensive toward Krakow, see *Strategicheskii ocherk*, 2:169–181.

19. Ruzskii-Sheideman telegraph conversation, 17 November 1914, *Lodzinskaia operatsiia*, doc. 191, 180–182; Nikolai to Ruzskii, 18 November 1914, ibid., doc. 197, 185; Nikolai to Tsar Nicholas: 21 November 1914, ibid., doc. 225, 199.

20. Ruzskii to Yanushkevich, 20 November 1914, *Lodzinskaia operatsiia*, doc. 204, 189; Sheideman to Oranovskii, 20 November 1914, ibid., doc. 256, 227.

21. *Lodzinskaia operatsiia*, 251–263, 327–344, 417–441; on manpower, see Grand Duke Nikolai to Tsar Nicholas, 30 November 1914, *Lodzinskaia operatsiia*, doc. 381, 328–329, and 13 December 1914 meeting at Brest, ibid., doc. 490, 417–419; *Strategicheskii ocherk voiny 1914–1918 gg*, vol. 3 (Moscow: VVRS, 1922), 2–5.

22. *Strategicheskii ocherk*, 3:18–24, 31–35; Tunstall, *Blood on the Snow*, 23–24.

23. *Strategicheskii ocherk*, 3:8–9, 37.

CHAPTER 6. THE MASURIAN LAKES AND THE CARPATHIANS, WINTER 1914–1915

1. I. I. Rostunov, *Russkii front pervoi mirovoi voiny* (Moscow: Nauka, 1976), 198; *Strategicheskii ocherk voiny 1914–1918 gg*, vol. 3 (Moscow: VVRS, 1922), 36.

2. A. M. Zaionchkovskii, *Pervaia mirovaia voina* (St. Petersburg: Poligon, 2002), 341–342, 347–348; Rostunov, *Russkii front*, 198–203; *Strategicheskii ocherk*, 3:35–46.

3. *Strategicheskii ocherk*, 3:47–50.

4. On the German-Austrian debates over strategy for early 1915, see Ian F. W. Beckett, *The Great War*, 2nd ed. (Harlow, UK: Pearson Longman, 2007), 160; Richard L. DiNardo, *Breakthrough: The Gorlice-Tarnow Campaign, 1915* (Santa Barbara, Calif.: Praeger, 2010), 20–23; Erich von Falkenhayn, *General Headquarters 1914–1916 and Its Critical Decisions* (London: Hutchinson, 1919), 53–59; Paul von Hindenburg, *Out of My Life* (London: Cassell, 1920), 129–135; A. V. Oleinikov, "Vymysly ob avgustovskoi operatsii 1915 goda," *Voenno-istoricheskii zhurnal*, no. 6 (2011): 7–8; Rostunov, *Russkii front*, 204–208; Graydon Tunstall, *Blood on the Snow: The Carpathian Winter War of 1915* (Lawrence: University Press of Kansas, 2010), 32–34; Zaionchkovskii, *Pervaia mirovaia voina*, 334–336, 343–349.

5. Hindenburg, *Out of My Life*, 132; Falkenhayn, *Critical Decisions*, 59.

6. *Strategicheskii ocherk voiny 1914–1918 gg*, vol. 2 (Moscow: VVRS, 1923), 29–39, 99–107, 112–114, 154–158; *Strategicheskii ocherk*, 3:26–30, 60–64.

7. Rostunov, *Russkii front*, 208–212.

8. On the Augustów operations, see Rostunov, *Russkii front*, 212–220; Norman Stone, *The Eastern Front, 1914–1917* (New York: Scribner's, 1975), 116–118; *Strategicheskii ocherk*, 3:64–76; Zaionchkovskii, *Pervaia mirovaia voina*, 349–358.

9. Rostunov, *Russkii front*, 220; N. Sakhnovskii, "Iz istorii oborony kreposti Osovets," *Voenno-istoricheskii zhurnal*, no. 11 (1984): 69–70.

10. Erich Ludendorff, *Ludendorff's Own Story, August 1914–November 1918* (New York: Harper, 1919), 156–157; Rostunov, *Russkii front*, 222; Zaionchkovskii, *Pervaia mirovaia voina* 358–359; *Strategicheskii ocherk*, 3:76–77.

11. Oleinikov, "Vymysly," 8–9, 11; Rostunov, *Russkii front*, 222–223; *Strategicheskii ocherk*, 3:77–84 (Grand Duke's order on 77); Zaionchkovskii, *Pervaia mirovaia voina*, 359–360.

12. A. V. Oleinikov, "General P. A. Pleve i boi v Pribaltike vesnoi-osen'io 1915 goda," *Voenno-istoricheskii zhurnal*, no. 4 (2009): 40–41; Zaionchkovskii, *Pervaia mirovaia voina*, 413–414.

13. Tunstall, *Blood on the Snow*, 28–31; Rostunov, *Russkii front*, 223; Zaionchkovskii, *Pervaia mirovaia voina*, 343–345.

14. Tunstall, *Blood on the Snow*, 66–81; *Strategicheskii ocherk*, 3:50–51.

15. Rostunov, *Russkii front*, 223–226; *Strategicheskii ocherk*, 3:51–52; Tunstall, *Blood on the Snow*, 81–106.

16. Tunstall, *Blood on the Snow*, 98–99; *Strategicheskii ocherk*, 3:52–54.

17. *Strategicheskii ocherk*, 3:53–58.

18. Tunstall, *Blood on the Snow*, 114–162.

19. Ianushkevich to Ruzskii and Ivanov, 19 March 1915, *Strategicheskii ocherk voiny 1914–1918 gg*, vol. 4 (Moscow: VVRS, 1922), 3–4.

20. Rostunov, *Russkii front*, 228–230; Tunstall, *Blood on the Snow*, 169–189.

21. Stanley Washburn, *On the Russian Front in World War I: Memoirs of an American War Correspondent* (New York: Speller, 1982), 89–90, 95.

22. Ivanov to Danilov, 26 March 1915, *Gorlitskaia operatsiia: Sbornik dokumentov* (Moscow: Voenizdat), doc. 3, 27–28.

23. Brusilov to Ivanov, 9 April 1915, *Gorlitskaia operatsiia*, doc. 10, 32.

24. Rostunov, *Russkii front*, 230–232; Tunstall, *Blood on the Snow*, 189–205; *Strategicheskii ocherk*, 4:9.

CHAPTER 7. THE GREAT RETREAT, 1915

1. Richard L. DiNardo, *Breakthrough: The Gorlice-Tarnow Campaign, 1915* (Santa Barbara, Calif.: Praeger, 2010), 27–30; I. I. Rostunov, *Russkii front pervoi mirovoi voiny* (Moscow: Nauka, 1976), 233–234; *Strategicheskii ocherk voiny 1914–1918 gg*, vol. 4 (Moscow: VVRS, 1922), 3–20; Erich von Falkenhayn, *General Headquarters 1914–1916 and Its Critical Decisions* (London: Hutchinson, 1919), 73–81, 86–87.

2. DiNardo, *Breakthrough*, 36–46.

3. *Strategicheskii ocherk*, 4:20–25 (quote on 24).

4. A. M. Zaionchkovskii, *Pervaia mirovaia voina* (St. Petersburg: Poligon, 2002), 404; Rostunov, *Russkii front*, 234–236; *Strategicheskii ocherk*, 4:24–28.

5. DiNardo, *Breakthrough*, 51–52. Rostunov, *Russkii front*, 236; *Gorlitskaia operatsiia*, 12–13.

6. On the initial German breakthrough at Gorlice, see DiNardo, *Breakthrough*, 53–68; *Gorlitskaia operatsiia*, 95–292; Rostunov, *Russkii front*, 238–245; *Strategicheskii ocherk*, 4:28–38; Zaionchkovskii, *Pervaia mirovaia voina*, 399–408.

7. Rerberg report, 2 May 1915: *Gorlitskaia operatsiia*, doc. 119, 98; Protopopov to Radko-Dmitriev, 2 May 1915, ibid., doc. 143, 106–107.

8. A. B. Astashov, "Russkii krest'ianin na frontakh Pervoi mirovoi voiny," *Otechestvennaia istoriia*, no. 4 (2003): 78–79.

9. Protopopov to 31st Division, 2 May 1915, *Gorlitskaia operatsiia*, doc. 122, 99.

10. Radko-Dmitriev to Ivanov, 2 May 1915, ibid., doc. 147, 108.

11. See Ivanov's comments on Dragomirov-Danilov conversation, 4 May 1915, ibid., doc. 184, 129.

12. Tsurikov to Third Army Staff, 6 May 1915: ibid., doc. 297, 178.

13. Rostunov, *Russkii front*, 246; Dragomirov to army chiefs of staff, 5 May 1915, *Gorlitskaia operatsiia*, doc. 227, 147.

14. Radko-Dmitriev to Ivanov, 8 May 1915, ibid., doc. 367, 207.

15. Nikolai Nikolaevich to Dragomirov, 9 May 1915, *Strategicheskii ocherk*, 4:33.

16. Radko-Dmitriev to *Stavka*, 10 May 1915, *Strategicheskii ocherk*, 4:34; Radko-Dmitriev to Ivanov, 10 May 1915, *Gorlitskaia operatsiia*, doc. 445, 237.

17. Falkenhayn, *General Headquarters*, 87–88, 90–91.

18. On the pursuit to Przemyśl, see DiNardo, *Breakthrough*, 72–83; Jamie H. Cockfield, "General Aleksei Brusilov and the Great Retreat, May-November 1915," *Journal of Slavic Military Studies* 26, no. 4 (2013): 658–662; *Strategicheskii ocherk*, 4:41–52; *Gorlitskaia operatsiia*, 293–353.

19. Radko-Dmitriev to corps commanders, 14 May 1915, *Gorlitskaia operatsiia*, doc. 565, 296.

20. Brusilov to Ivanov, 15 May 1915, ibid., doc. 587, 306; Lazarev report, 13 May 1915, ibid., doc. 522, 274; Shkinskii to Radko-Dmitriev, 13 May 1915, ibid., doc. 531, 277; *Strategicheskii ocherk*, 4:41.

21. R. L. DiNardo and Daniel J. Hughes, "Germany and Coalition Warfare in the World Wars: A Comparative Study," *War in History* 8, no. 2 (2001): 171; John H. Morrow, *German Air Power in World War I* (Lincoln: University of Nebraska Press, 1982), 170.

22. On the capture of L'viv, see Dinardo, *Breakthrough*, 84–101; Cockfield, "Brusilov," 663–665; *Strategicheskii ocherk*, 4:52–58. Rostunov, *Russkii front*, is uncharacteristically silent, saying nothing about these operations.

23. *Strategicheskii ocherk*, 4:65, 67; A. V. Oleinikov, "V. Bekman: 'Letnee presledovania 1915 goda bylo dlia germanskikh chastei vremenem naibolee tiazhelykh poter' za vsiu voinu," *Voenno-istoricheskii zhurnal*, no. 11 (2011): 5.

24. *Strategicheskii ocherk*, 4:55. See also Dinardo, *Breakthrough*, 139–140.

25. Dinardo, *Breakthrough*, 102–106; *Strategicheskii ocherk*, 4:75–76; Zaionchkovskii, *Pervaia mirovaia voina*, 415.

26. Dinardo, *Breakthrough*, 106–109; Rostunov, *Russkii front*, 248–252; Zaionchkovskii, *Pervaia mirovaia voina*, 417.

27. Dinardo, *Breakthrough*, 111–112; Zaionchkovskii, *Pervaia mirovaia voina*, 416–417.

28. Dinardo, *Breakthrough*, 110–113; Rostunov, *Russkii front*, 253–254.

29. Rostunov, *Russkii front*, 254–255; Zaionchkovskii, *Pervaia mirovaia voina*, 417–419; *Strategicheskii ocherk*, 4:70–71.

30. On the fighting in the north and the evacuation of Warsaw, see Iu. A. Bakhurin, "Prichiny padeniia kreposti Novogeorgievsk v 1915 godu," *Voenno-istoricheskii zhurnal*, no. 8 (2009): 71–76; Dinardo, *Breakthrough*, 119–120; Oleinikov, "Letnee presledovanie," 4; Rostunov, *Russkii front*, 257–260; *Strategicheskii ocherk*, 4:76–85; Zaionchkovskii, *Pervaia mirovaia voina*, 417–418.

31. Oleinikov, "Letnee presledovania," 6; A. V. Oleinikov, "General P. A. Pleve i boi v Pribaltike vesnoik-osen'iu 1915 goda," *Voenno-istoricheskii zhurnal*, no. 4 (2009): 40–44; Rostunov, *Russkii front*, 260–262; *Strategicheskii ocherk*, 4:80–82, 88–97; Zaionchkovskii, *Pervaia mirovaia voina*, 421.

32. On Mackensen's offensive between the Bug and the Vistula, see Dinardo, *Breakthrough*, 121–130; Rostunov, *Russkii front*, 255–257.

33. On Hindenburg's September offensive toward Vilnius, see Oleinikov, "Pleve," 44–48; Rostunov, *Russkii front*, 264; *Strategicheskii ocherk*, 4:98–122; Zaionchkovskii, *Pervaia mirovaia voina*, 422–426.

34. Dinardo, *Breakthrough*, 141 on intellectual limitations.

35. Stanley Washburn, *On the Russian Front in World War I: Memoirs of an American War Correspondent* (New York: Speller, 1982), 155–156.

36. On the Austrian fall offensive, see Cockfield, "Brusilov," 665–670; Rostunov, *Russkii front*, 273; *Strategicheskii ocherk*, 4:126–129; Zaionchkovskii, *Pervaia mirovaia voina*, 420.

37. Rostunov, *Russkii front*, 265; P. M. Portugal'skii, P. D. Alekseev, and V. A Runov, *Pervaia mirovaia v zhizneopisaniiakh russkikh voenachal'nikov* (Moscow: Elakos, 1994), 55–112.

38. William C. Fuller, *The Foe Within: Fantasies of Treason and the End of Imperial Russia* (Ithaca, N.Y.: Cornell University Press, 2006), 40–48, 104–106, 192.

39. Ibid., 11–26, 66–96, 119–126, 132–140.

40. Ibid., 193–195, 203–205, 215–256.

41. Roy A. Prete, "Mounting the Salonika Campaign, September-October 1915," *War & Society* 19, no. 1 (May 2001): 51–54, 58.

42. G. Z. Ioffe, "Vyselenie evreev," *Voprosy istorii*, no. 9 (2001): 89–90.

43. Dinardo, *Breakthrough*, 132–133; Oleinikov, "Letnee presledovanie," 6–7.

CHAPTER 8. THE CAUCASUS CAMPAIGN, 1914–1917

1. Norman Stone, *The Eastern Front, 1914–1917* (New York: Scribner's, 1975) does not discuss the Caucasus at all, but Soviet scholars and their contemporary Russian counterparts are little better. After the revolution, the new Red Army's coverage of its own history, the volumes of the *Strategicheskii ocherk*, did not include the fight against the Ottoman Empire. I. I. Rostunov, *Russkii front pervoi mirovoi voiny* (Moscow: Nauka, 1976) says nothing about the Caucasus, and today's *Istoriia voennoi strategii Rossii* (Moscow: Kuchkovo pole, 2000), a semi-official history of Russian military strategy, likewise has nothing on the Caucasus theater.

2. Mustafa Aksakal, *The Ottoman Road to War in 1914: The Ottoman Empire and the First World War* (Cambridge: Cambridge UP, 2008), 72–77; Michael A. Reynolds, *Shattering Empires: The Clash and Collapse of the Ottoman and Russian Empires, 1908–1918* (Cambridge: Cambridge UP, 2011), 41–43, 72–78.

3. Reynolds, *Shattering Empires*, 22–23, 28–29. On the Young Turks generally, see Ernest E. Ramsaur, *The Young Turks: Prelude to the Revolution of 1908* (Princeton: Princeton UP, 1957); Feroz Ahmad, *The Young Turks: The Committee of Union and Progress in Turkish Politics, 1908–1914* (Oxford: Clarendon, 1969); Aykut Kansu, *The Revolution of 1908 in Turkey* (Leiden: Brill, 1997).

4. Timothy W. Childs, *Italo-Turkish Diplomacy and the War over Libya 1911–1912* (Leiden: Brill, 1990); Richard C. Hall, *The Balkan Wars, 1912–1913: Prelude to the First World War* (New York: Routledge, 2000), 1–80; Edward J. Erickson, *Defeat in Detail: The Ottoman Army in the Balkans, 1912–1913* (Westport: Praeger, 2003), 72–250; Reynolds, *Shattering Empires* 32–33; Mesut Uyar and Edward J. Erickson, *A Military History of the Ottomans: From Osman to Atatürk* (Santa Barbara: ABC-CLIO, 2009), 219–231.

5. Hall, *Balkan Wars*, 80–129; Erickson, *Defeat in Detail*, 251–330; Robert J. Kerner, "The Mission of Liman von Sanders: I. Its Origin," *Slavonic Review* 6, no. 16 (1927): 13–14. Uyar and Erickson, *Military History*, 231–235.

6. Aksakal, *Ottoman Road*, 80–83; Erickson, *Defeat in Detail*, 340; Edward J. Erickson, *Ordered to Die: A History of the Ottoman Army in the First World War* (Westport: Greenwood, 2001), 11–13; Kerner, "Liman von Sanders: I," 12–27; Robert J. Kerner, "Liman von Sanders: II. The Crisis," *Slavonic Review* 6, no. 17 (1927): 344–363; Robert J. Kerner, "Liman von Sanders: III," *Slavonic Review* 6, no. 18 (1928): 543–560; Robert J. Kerner, "Liman von Sanders: IV. The Aftermath," *Slavonic Review* 7, no. 19 (1928): 90–112; Uyar and Erickson, *Military History*, 237–242.

7. Sean McMeekin, *The Russian Origins of the First World War* (Cambridge: Harvard UP, 2011), 102–3; Ulrich Trumpener, "The Ottoman Empire," in *The Origins of World War I*, ed. Richard F. Hamilton and Holger H. Herwig (Cambridge: Cambridge UP, 2003), 341–342, 345–346.

8. Feroz Ahmad, "Great Britain's Relations with the Young Turks, 1908–1914," *Middle Eastern Studies* 2, no. 4 (1966): 302–329; D. Iu. Kozlov, "Rossiiskie plany voiny na Chernom more i 'problema prolivov,' 1907–1914," *Voprosy istorii*, no. 8 (2007):

108; Childs, *Italo-Turkish Diplomacy*, 133–136; Ronald Bobroff, "Behind the Balkan Wars: Russian policy towards Bulgaria and the Turkish Straits, 1912–1913," *Russian Review* 59, no. 1 (2000): 76–95; Bobroff, "Roads to Glory? Sergei D. Sazonov, The Turkish Straits, and Russian Foreign Policy, 1910–1916," Ph.D. diss., Duke University, 2000, 45–46; Reynolds, *Shattering Empires*, 32–33.

9. Kozlov, "Rossiiskie plany," 100–106; Reynolds, *Shattering Empires*, 31–32, 35–36, 40–41; Kerner, "Liman von Sanders: IV," 90–95.

10. Aksakal, *Ottoman Road*, 1–56.

11. Ahmad, "Young Turks," 302–329; Aksakal, *Ottoman Road*, 58–62, 83; Chris B. Rooney, "The International Significance of the British Naval Missions to the Ottoman Empire, 1908–1914," *Middle Eastern Studies* 34, no. 1 (January 1998): 1–29; Reynolds, *Shattering Empires*, 40–45; K. Shatsillo, "Podgotovka tsarizmom vooruzhennykh sil k pervoi mirovoi voine," *Voenno-istoricheskii zhurnal*, no. 9 (1974): 94.

12. Aksakal, *Ottoman Road*, 62–72, 92–104, 120; Sean McMeekin, *The Berlin-Baghdad Express: The Ottoman Empire and Germany's Bid for World Power* (Cambridge: Harvard UP, 2010); McMeekin, *Russian Origins*, 103–109; Reynolds, *Shattering Empires* 108–112; Gerald E. Silberstein, "The Central Powers and the Second Turkish Alliance, 1915" *Slavic Review* 24, no. 1 (1965): 77–80; Trumpener, "Ottoman Empire," 345–350.

13. Aksakal, *Ottoman Road*, 91, 107–108, 137–163; S. A. Saneev, "Obstrel Novorossiisk germano-turetskimi kreiserami v 1914 godu," *Voenno-istoricheskii zhurnal*, no. 1 (2006): 40–43; Trumpener, 350–354.

14. Aksakal, *Ottoman Road*, 182–187; Bobroff, "Roads to Glory?" 197–249; Silberstein, "Central Powers," 80–89.

15. Erickson, *Defeat in Detail*, 5–15, 24–27; 328–330; Erickson, *Ordered to Die*, 1–2; Uyar and Erickson, *Military History*, 176–211.

16. Erickson, *Defeat in Detail*, 335, 341 Aksakal, *Ottoman Road*, 80–83; Uyar and Erickson, *Military History*, 237–242.

17. Erickson, *Ordered to Die*, 15–19; Uyar and Erickson, *Military History*, 243.

18. Erickson, *Ordered to Die*, 52–53; N. G. Korsun, *Pervaia mirovaia voina na kavkazskom fronte* (Moscow: Voenizdat, 1946), 11–18; Ye. V. Maslovskii, *Mirovaia voina na Kavkazskom fronte, 1914–1917 g.* (Paris: Vozrozhdenie, 1933), 22–29; Reynolds, *Shattering Empires*, 46–72, 98–102.

19. Erickson, *Defeat in Detail*, 17–18, 31, 53, 339, 343; Erickson, *Ordered to Die*, 5–11; Uyar and Erickson, *Military History*, 244–245; Zaionchkovskii, *Pervaia mirovaia voina*, 371.

20. Korsun, *Pervaia mirovaia voina*, 20–25; Maslovskii, *Mirovaia voina*, 30–42; Zaionchkovskii, *Pervaia mirovaia voina*, 372–374; P. M. Portugal'skii, P. D. Alekseev, and V. A Runov, *Pervaia mirovaia v zhizneopisaniiakh russkikh voenachal'nikov* (Moscow: Elakos, 1994).

21. On the initial Russian campaigns and Turkish response, see W. E. D. Allen and Paul Muratoff, *Caucasian Battlefields* (Cambridge: Cambridge UP, 1953), 240–248; Erickson, *Ordered to Die*, 53–54; Korsun, *Pervaia mirovaia voina*, 26–32;

Maslovskii, *Mirovaia voina*, 51–68; Uyar and Erickson, *Military History*, 245–246; A. M. Zaionchkovskii, *Pervaia mirovaia voina* (St. Petersburg: Poligon, 2002), 374–375.

22. On the Sarıkamış campaign, see Allen and Muratoff, *Caucasian Battlefields*, 249–292; Erickson, *Ordered to Die*, 54–62; Korsun, *Pervaia mirovaia voina*, 32–39; Maslovskii, *Mirovaia voina*, 68–134; Reynolds, *Shattering Empires*, 124–127; Uyar and Erickson, *Military History*, 247–248; Zaionchkovskii, *Pervaia mirovaia voina*, 375–380. For a discussion of later conflicts among the Russian generals about who could rightly claim credit for the victory, see D. G. Martirosian, "General G. E. Berkhman: 'Upravlial vsem khodom togo dela, kotoroe konchilos' bol'shim uspekhom,'" *Voenno-istoricheskii zhurnal*, no. 6 (2008): 27–30.

23. Erickson, *Ordered to Die*, 63–65; Edward J. Erickson, "The Armenians and Ottoman Military Policy, 1915," *War in History* 15, no. 2 (2008): 141–167, 145–146; Korsun, *Pervaia mirovaia voina*, 40–48; Maslovskii, *Mirovaia voina*, 137–157; Reynolds, *Shattering Empires*, 126–127; Zaionchkovskii, *Pervaia mirovaia voina*, 439.

24. The literature on the Armenian genocide is enormous and highly contentious. The Turkish government continues to insist no genocide occurred, though conceding mass killings of Armenians took place. Erickson, the leading Western authority on the Ottoman military, is agnostic on the question of genocide but details the military context and implications of the mass slaughter in *Ordered to Die*, 95–104, and especially "The Armenians and Ottoman Military Policy, 1915," 141–167. On military questions, see also S. M. Stepaniants, "Soprotivlenie armian genotsidu v gody Pervoi mirovoi voiny," *Novaia i noveishchaia istoriia*, no. 1 (2007): 218–224. For recent work on the genocide, see Taner Akçam, *From Empire to Republic: Turkish Nationalism and the Armenian Genocide* (London: Zed, 2004); Akçam, *The Young Turks' Crime Against Humanity: The Armenian Genocide and Ethnic Cleansing in the Ottoman Empire* (Princeton: Princeton UP, 2012); Donald Bloxham, *The Great Game of Genocide: Imperialism, Nationalism, and the Destruction of the Ottoman Armenians* (Oxford: Oxford UP, 2005), Ronald Grigor Suny, Fatma Müge Göçek, and Norman M. Naimark, eds., *A Question of Genocide: Armenians and Turks at the End of the Ottoman Empire* (Oxford: Oxford UP, 2011).

25. Erickson, *Ordered to Die*, 104–108; Maslovskii, *Mirovaia voina*, 157–207; Reynolds, *Shattering Empires*, 134–135; Zaionchkovskii, *Pervaia mirovaia voina*, 440–442.

26. On the Erzerum and Erzincan campaigns, see Allen and Muratoff, *Caucasian Battlefields*, 320–372; Erickson, *Ordered to Die*, 119–137; Korsun, *Pervaia mirovaia voina*, 49–77; N. Korsun, *Erzerumskaia operatsiia* (Moscow: Voenizdat, 1938); Maslovskii, *Mirovaia voina*, 207–411; V. V. Mikhailov, "Razgrom turetskoi armii i ovladenie pervoklassnoi krepost'iu," *Voenno-istoricheskii zhurnal*, no. 8 (2006): 49–53; Uyar and Erickson, *Military History*, 263–264; Zaionchkovskii, *Pervaia mirovaia voina*, 515–527.

27. On the 1917 campaigns, see Erickson, *Ordered to Die*, 159–161, 179–192; Korsun, *Pervaia mirovaia voina*, 78–85.

CHAPTER 9. RUSSIAN SOCIETY AT WAR

1. F. A. Gaida, "Politicheskaia obstanovka v Rossii nakanune Pervoi mirovoi voiny v otsenke gosudarstvennykh deiatelei i liderov partii," *Rossiiskaia istoriia*, no. 6 (2011): 123–135. There is extensive debate on the state of Russian society on the eve of war; for the key pessimistic view, see Leopold Haimson, "The Problem of Social Stability in Urban Russia, 1905–1917," pt. 1, *Slavic Review* 23, no. 4 (1964): 619–642; pt. 2, ibid., 24, no. 1 (1965): 1–22.

2. A. B. Astashov, "Russkii krestianin na frontakh pervoi mirovoi voiny," *Otechestvennaia istoriia*, no. 4 (2003): 73–75; Hubertus F. Jahn, *Patriotic Culture in Russia During World War I* (Ithaca, N.Y.: Cornell University Press, 1995): 1, 3, 8; Iu. I. Kir'ianov, "Byli li antivoennye stachki v Rossii v 1914 gody?" *Voprosy istorii*, no. 2 (1994): 43–52; Eric Lohr, *Nationalizing the Russian Empire* (Cambridge, Mass.: Harvard University Press, 2003), 11–13; O. S. Porshneva, "'Nastroenie 1914 goda' v Rossii kak fenomen istorii i istoriografii," *Rossiiskaia istoriia*, no. 2 (2010): 185–189.

3. Porshneva, "Nastroenie," 190–192.

4. M. D. Karpachev, "Dvizhenie za narodnuiu trezvost' v Voronezhskoi' gubernii v nachale XX v.," *Voprosy istorii*, no. 9 (2010): 85–96; E. V. Paskov, "Antialkogol'naia kampaniia v Rossii v gody pervoi mirovoi voiny," *Voprosy istorii*, no. 10 (2010): 80–93; V. B. Aksenov, "'Sukhoi zakon' 1914 goda: ot pridvornoi intrigi do revoliutsii," *Rossiiskaia istoriia*, no. 4 (2011): 126–139; A. S. Senin, "'Daby ogradit' viashchuiu silu': O bor'be za trezvost' v russkoi armii," *Voenno-istoricheskii zhurnal*, no. 2 (1992): 59–61.

5. Aksenov, "'Sukhoi zakon,'" 133–134; Anton V. Posadskii, "World War I: A Russian National Perspective July 1914 to February 1917 (Materials from Saratov Province)," *Journal of Slavic Military Studies* 15, no. 1 (March 2002): 74–75.

6. Thomas Earl Porter, "The Emergence of Civil Society in Late Imperial Russia: The Impact of the Russo-Japanese and First World Wars on Russian Social and Political Life, 1904–1917," *War & Society* 23, no. 1 (May 2005): 49–51; Posadskii, "Saratov," 70–71.

7. A. A. Budko et al., "Preodolevaia strakh i opasnost', rossiiskie mediki s chest'iu vypolniali svoi dolg," *Voenno-istoricheskii zhurnal*, no. 9 (2004): 42–44; A. A. Budko et al., "V izvestnye momenty na voine, ne meditsina, ne nauka, ne operatsiia igraiut samuiu vazhnuiu rol', a organizatsiia raboty," *Voenno-istoricheskii zhurnal*, no. 8 (2004): 58, 61.

8. S. V. Kazakovtsev, "Organizatsiia gospitalei i lazaretov v Viatskoi gubernii vo vremia Pervoi mirovoi voiny," *Voprosy istorii*, no. 9 (2007): 137, 140; V. Iu. Kuz'min, "Zemskaia meditsina na voennoi sluzhbe," *Voenno-istoricheskii zhurnal*, no. 3 (2004): 59–60; Budko, "Preodolevaia," 47.

9. Budko, "Preodolevaia," 42; Budko, "V izvestnye momenty," 58–60; A. Kavtaradze, "Iz istorii russkogo general'nogo shtaba," *Voenno-istoricheskii zhurnal*, no. 3 (1976): 104.

10. Budko, "V izvestnye momenty," 61; Budko, "Preodolevaia," 48.

11. William C. Fuller, *The Foe Within: Fantasies of Treason and the End of Imperial Russia* (Ithaca, N.Y.: Cornell University Press, 2006); Lohr, *Nationalizing*, 13–17, 31–54.

12. Fuller, *Foe Within*, 172–175; Lohr, *Nationalizing*, 3, 55–120; David Rempel, "The Expropriation of the German Colonists in South Russia During the Great War," *Journal of Modern History* 4, no. 1 (1932): 49–67.

13. Posadskii, "Saratov," 58–62.

14. Peter Gatrell, *A Whole Empire Walking: Refugees in Russia during World War I* (Bloomington: Indiana University Press, 1999); A. N. Kurtsev, "Bezhentsy pervoi mirovoi voiny v Rossii (1914–1917)," *Voprosy istorii*, no. 8 (1999): 98–113.

15. Iu. A. Bakhurin, "Prichiny padeniia kreposti Novogeorgievsk v 1915 godu," *Voenno-istoricheskii zhurnal*, no. 8 (2009): 74; Fuller, *Foe Within*, 175–180; G. Z. Ioffe, "Vyselenie evreev iz profrontovoi polosy v 1915 godu," *Voprosy istorii*, no. 9 (2001): 85–97; Lohr, *Nationalizing*, 121–165; Victor B. Shklovsky, "At the Front—Summer 1917," trans. Richard Sheldon, *Russian Review* 26, no. 3 (1967): 224.

16. Astashov, "Russkii krest'ianin," 74, 81; Posadskii, "Saratov," 63–64. I. V. Narskii, "Frontovoi opyt russkikh soldat, 1914–1916 gody," *Novaia i noveishchaia istoriia*, no. 2 (2005): 202.

17. Iu. A. Bakhurin, "O pervykh brataniiakh s protivnikom v gody pervoi mirovoi voiny," *Voprosy istorii*, no. 12 (2010): 167–168; S. N. Bazanov, "'Nemetskie soldaty stali . . . perepolzat' k russkim "tovarishcham' i bratat'sia s nimi,'" *Voenno-istoricheskii zhurnal*, no. 6 (2002): 43–45.

18. A. B. Astashov, "Dezertirstvo i bor'ba s nim v tsarskoi armii v gody Pervoi mirovoi voiny," *Rossiiskaia istoriia*, no. 4 (2011): 44, 47–48.

19. Astashov, "Dezertirstvo," 45; Astashov, "Russkii krest'ianin," 80.

20. Dominic Lieven, *Nicholas II: Emperor of All the Russias* (London: Pimlico, 1993), 210–216; Richard Pipes, *The Russian Revolution* (New York: Vintage, 1990), 223–228.

21. John R. Schindler, "Disaster on the Dvina: The Austro-Hungarian Army in Serbia, 1914," *War in History* 9, no. 2 (2002): 188.

22. S. Kliatskin, "O sisteme komplektovaniia staroi armii," *Voenno-istoricheskii zhurnal*, no. 1 (1966): 108; A. Iu. Bezugol'nyi, "Voenno-okruzhnaia sistema v Rossii v period Pervoi mirovoi voiny i revoliutsionnykh sobytii 1917 goda," *Voenno-istoricheskii zhurnal*, no. 10 (2008): 25; I. I. Rostunov, *Russkii front pervoi mirovoi voiny* (Moscow: Nauka, 1976), 276. For older but roughly comparable figures, see Nicholas N. Golovine, *The Russian Army in the World War* (New Haven, Conn.: Yale University Press, 1931), 44–50.

23. Kliatskin, "O sisteme komplektovanie," 109; Bezugol'nyi, "Voenno-okruzhnaia sistema," 25; M. V. Os'kin, "Problema rezerva dlia general'nogo nastupleniia russkoi armii v 1917 g.," *VI* #8 (2011): 145; Rostunov, *Russkii front*, 276; Joshua Sanborn, *Drafting the Russian Nation: Military Conscription, Total War, and Mass Politics, 1905–1925* (Dekalb: Northern Illinois University Press, 2003), 35–36, 79–81; *Strategicheskii ocherk voiny 1914–1918 gg*, vol. 7 (Moscow: VVRS, 1922), 16, 27–28.

24. I. N. Grebenkin, "Ofitserstvo rossiiskoi armii v gody pervoi mirovoi voiny," *Voprosy istorii*, no. 2 (2010): 54.

25. Grebenkin, "Ofitserstvo," 57; David R. Jones, "The Imperial Russian Life Guards Grenadier Regiment, 1906–1917: The Disintegration of an Elite Unit," *Military Affairs* 33, no. 2 (1969): 292–296; S. V. Konstantinov and M. V. Os'kin, "Russkie ofitsery voennogo vremeni. 1914–1917 gg," *Voprosy istorii*, no. 8 (2009): 100, 107–108; S. A. Solntseva, "1917: Kadrovaia politika revoliutsiia v rossiiskoi armii," *Otechestvennaia istoriia*, no. 6 (2004): 109.

26. Peter Kenez, "Changes in the Social Composition of the Officer Corps during World War I," *Russian Review* 31, no. 4 (1972): 369–370; V. M. Korovin and V. A. Sviridov, "Narodnyi uchitelia, melkie sluzhashchie, nebogatye torgorvtsy, zazhitochnye krest'iane . . . poluchali status 'Vashe blagorodie,'" *Voenno-istoricheskii zhurnal*, no. 2 (2004): 34–36; Grebenkin, "Ofitserstvo," 52–53.

27. Kenez, "Changes," 372–373; Konstantinov and Os'kin, "Russkie ofitsery," 107–108.

28. Grebenkin, "Ofitserstvo," 56; Kenez, "Changes," 374; Konstantinov and Os-'kin, "Russkie ofitsery," *Voprosy istorii*, no. 8 (2009): 110.

29. Ian F. W. Beckett, *The Great War*, 2nd ed. (Harlow, UK: Pearson Longman, 2007), 60–61; Graydon Tunstall, *Blood on the Snow: The Carpathian Winter War of 1915* (Lawrence: University Press of Kansas, 2010), 13; Martin van Creveld, "World War I and the Revolution in Logistics," in *Great War, Total War: Combat and Mobilization on the Western Front, 1914–1918*, ed. Roger Chickering and Stig Förster (Cambridge: Cambridge University Press, 2000), 66.

30. Budko, "V izvestnye momenty," 58–59; Peter Gatrell, *Government, Industry, and Rearmament in Russia, 1900–1914: The Last Argument of Tsarism* (Cambridge: Cambridge University Press, 1994).

31. Rostunov, *Russkii front*, 194–195; Tunstall, *Blood on the Snow*, 37–38; A. M. Zaionchkovskii, *Pervaia mirovaia voina* (St. Petersburg: Poligon, 2002), 341. For rewards for recovered equipment, see Alfred Knox, *With the Russian Army, 1914–1917* (London: Hutchinson, 1921), 196, 217.

32. Gerd Hardach, *The First World War, 1914–1918* (Berkeley: University of California Press, 1981), 92–94; Rostunov, *Russkii front*, 195–196; Lewis H. Siegelbaum, *The Politics of Industrial Mobilization in Russia, 1914–1917: A Study of the War Industries Committees* (London: Macmillan, 1983).

33. Roger Chickering, *The Great War and Urban Life in Germany* (Cambridge: Cambridge University Press, 2007), 146–149, 165–166, 241–242, 447; Ivor L. Evans, "Economic Aspects of Dualism in Austria-Hungary," *Slavonic and East European Review* 6, no. 18 (1928): 529–542; S. L. A. Marshall, *World War I* (New York: Random House, 1965), 314–316; David Stevenson, *Cataclysm: The First World War as Political Tragedy* (New York: Basic, 2004), 280–281.

34. Hardach, *First World War*, 108, 111, 134.

35. Ibid., 134; Peter Holquist, *Making War, Forging Revolution: Russia's Continuum*

of Crisis, 1914–1921 (Cambridge, Mass.: Harvard University Press, 2002), 26–46, 94–110; M. D. Karpachev, "Krizis prodovol'stvennogo snabzheniia v gody Pervoi mirovoi voiny (po materialam Voronezhskoi gubernii)," *Rossiiskaia istoriia*, no. 3 (2011): 66–81; M. V. Os'kin, "Prodovol'stvennaia politika Rossii nakanune fevralia 1917 goda: poisk vykhoda iz krizisa," *Rossiiskaia istoriia*, no. 3 (2011): 53–66; Posadskii, "Saratov," 80–81.

36. Os'kin, "Rezervy," 146–147; J. N. Westwood, *A History of Russian Railways* (London: Allen & Unwin, 1964), 172–177.

37. Tsuyoshi Hasegawa, *The February Revolution: Petrograd, 1917* (Seattle: University of Washington Press), 73–103, 198–211.

CHAPTER 10. THE BRUSILOV OFFENSIVE, 1916

1. On the offensive on the Strypa, see *Strategicheskii ocherk voiny 1914–1918 gg*, vol. 5 (Moscow: VVRS, 1920), 10–15; A. M. Zaionchkovskii, *Pervaia mirovaia voina* (St. Petersburg: Poligon, 2002), 460–461. For discussion of the potential amphibious attack on Bulgaria, see V. B. Kashirin, "Nesostoiavshaiasia ekspeditsiia russikh vooruzhennykh sil na Balkany osen'iu 1915 goda," *Novaia i noveishchaia istoriia*, no. 6 (2004): 175–203; *Strategicheskii ocherk*, 5:8–9.

2. Jehuda L. Wallach, *Uneasy Coalition: The Entente Experience in World War I* (Westport, Conn.: Greenwood, 1993), 78–79; A. Iu. Pavlov, "Rossiia na mezhsoiuznicheskikh konferentsiiakh v gody Pervoi mirovoi voiny," *Voenno-istoricheskii zhurnal*, no. 2 (2010): 25–31; A. Iu. Pavlov, "Russkii ekspeditsionnyi korpus v Salonikakh," *Voenno-istoricheskii zhurnal*, no. 9 (2001): 56–61; I. I. Rostunov, *Russkii front pervoi mirovoi voiny* (Moscow: Nauka, 1976), 279–282; Zaionchkovskii, *Pervaia mirovaia voina*, 489–491. On the Russian expeditionary force, see Jamie Cockfield, *With Snow on Their Boots: The Tragic Odyssey of the Russian Expeditionary Force in France during World War I* (New York: St. Martin's, 1998).

3. Rostunov, *Russkii front*, 276; *Strategicheskii ocherk voiny 1914–1918 gg*, vol. 6 (Moscow: VVRS, 1923), 12.

4. *Strategicheskii ocherk*, 5:15–17 and 6:12–17; Rostunov, *Russkii front*, 282–284, 287–289; Wallach, *Uneasy Coalition*, 81–82; Pavlov, "Rossiia na mezhsoiuznicheskikh konferentsiiakh," 27–28.

5. On the Lake Naroch offensive, see Rostunov, *Russkii front*, 284–286; Norman Stone, *The Eastern Front, 1914–1917* (New York: Scribner's, 1975), 227–231; *Strategicheskii ocherk*, 5:17–26; Zaionchkovskii, *Pervaia mirovaia voina*, 509–512. N. Ye. Podorozhnyi, *Narochskaia operatsiia v marte 1916 g.* (Moscow: Voenizdat, 1938), is an extraordinarily detailed dissection.

6. A. A. Brusilov, *Moi vospominaniia* (Minsk: Kharvest, 2003), 214–218; Timothy C. Dowling, *The Brusilov Offensive* (Bloomington: Indiana University Press, 2008), 1–3; S. G. Nelipovich, "Tsena pobedy: General'noe nastuplenie rossiiskoi armii letom–osen'iu 1916 goda: postavlennye zadachi i dostignutye tseli," *Voenno-*

istoricheskii zhurnal, no. 10 (2011): 4; Rostunov, *Russkii front*, 289–294; *Strategicheskii ocherk*, 5:26–29, 111–112; Zaionchkovskii, *Pervaia mirovaia voina*, 534–537.

7. Brusilov, *Vospominaniia*, 232.

8. Rostunov, *Russkii front*, 305.

9. On Brusilov and the Southwestern Front's preparations, see Brusilov, *Vospominaniia*, 214–230; Dowling, *Brusilov*, 42–47; Rostunov, *Russkii front*, 294–307; I. I. Rostunov, *General Brusilov* (Moscow: Voenizdat, 1964), 118–139; N. Stone, *Eastern Front*, 237–240; *Strategicheskii ocherk*, 5:31–33, 36–41, 113; *Strategicheskii ocherk*, 6:1–27; Zaionchkovskii, *Pervaia mirovaia voina*, 538–540. The Brusilov offensive, unusually, is covered by two volumes of the *Strategicheskii ocherk* series, which describe the same events from two points of view. Volume 5 was written by Klembovskii, who fought under Brusilov in 1916 and blames the limited success of the offensive on *Stavka* interference and the cowardice of Evert at the Western Front as well as Brusilov's subordinates. Zaionchkovskii, author of volume 6, is much more critical of Brusilov's failures of imagination.

10. S. V. Averchenko and A. Iu. Lashkov, "Deistviia aviatsii i zenitnoi artillerii v khode Brusilovskogo proryva letom 1916 goda," *Voenno-istoricheskii zhurnal*, no. 6 (2011): 12–13; Averchenko, "Brusilovskii proryv, bor'ba v vozdukhe: chast' 1—podgotovka," *Voenno-istoricheskii zhurnal*, no. 10 (2011): 11–15; V. A. Kirillov and V. P. Zhuravel', "Radioelektronnoe protivoborstvo vlialo na khod operatsii Pervoi mirovoi voiny," *Voenno-istoricheskii zhurnal*, no. 8 (2004): 48.

11. Brusilov, *Vospominaniia*, 221.

12. For an impressive example, see map of XL Corps sector, 28 April 1916, RGVIA f. 2134, op. 1, d. 60, l. 121; for the 30th Corps, see ibid., l. 124.

13. See map of trench system, c. late April 1916, RGVIA f. 2134, op. 1, d. 60, ll. 160–161.

14. 39th Corps to Kaledin and accompanying map, 28 April 1916, RGVIA f. 2134, op. 1, d. 60, l. 126.

15. Brusilov, *Vospominaniia*, 230–231; Rostunov, *Russkii front*, 307–311; *Strategicheskii ocherk*, 6:20–21; for Alekseev's order, see *Strategicheskii ocherk*, 5:114.

16. On Brusilov's initial breakthroughs, see Brusilov, *Vospominaniia*, 234–237; Dowling, *Brusilov*, 62–87; Rostunov, *Russkii front*, 311–312; N. Stone, *Eastern Front*, 247–254; *Strategicheskii ocherk*, 5:41–44; *Strategicheskii ocherk*, 6:28; Zaionchkovskii, *Pervaia mirovaia voina*, 540–548. The Ninth Army is particularly well covered in A. I. Litvinov, *Maiskii proryv IX armii v 1916 godu* (Petrograd: Voenizdat, 1923), and A. Bazarevskii, *Nastupatel'naia operatsiia 9-i russkoi armii: iiun' 1916 goda* (Moscow: Voenizdat, 1937).

17. John Schindler, "Steamrollered in Galicia: The Austro-Hungarian Army and the Brusilov Offensive, 1916," *War in History* 23, no. 1 (2003): 38–39, 43–44; Dowling, *Brusilov*, 88–90.

18. On the consolidation of gains and rejection of deeper attacks, see Dowling, *Brusilov*, 92–93; Rostunov, *Russkii front*, 312–317; *Strategicheskii ocherk*, 5:44–46;

Strategicheskii ocherk, 6:28–31, 35–40; Zaionchkovskii, *Pervaia mirovaia voina*, 548–553.

19. Kaledin to corps and division commanders, telegram 01997, 8 June 1916, *Nastuplenie Iugo-zapadnogo fronta: Sbornik dokumentov* (Moscow: Voenizdat, 1940), doc. 174, 243–244; Brusilov to army commanders, directive 1594, 8 June 1916, ibid., doc. 171, 242.

20. Brusilov, *Vospominaniia*, 237–239.

21. Rostunov, *Russkii front*, 317–320; *Strategicheskii ocherk*, 5:29–58, 61. *Strategicheskii ocherk*, 6:31–35.

22. Makhrov intelligence summary 6542, 31 July 1916, RGVIA f. 2134, op. 1, d. 95, l. 239; 8th Army Intelligence summary, 25 June 1916, RGVIA f. 2134, op. 1, d. 95, l. 22.

23. Brusilov, 239; Makhrov intelligence summary, 2 June through 21 July 1916, RGVIA f. 2134, op. 1, d. 95, ll. 236ob–237.

24. Nelipovich, "Tsena pobedy," 5–6.

25. Brusilov, *Vospominaniia*, 240–248; Dowling, *Brusilov*, 95–150; Rostunov, *Russkii front*, 320–325; *Strategicheskii ocherk*, 5:59–102; *Strategicheskii ocherk*, 6:41–56, 59–62; Zaionchkovskii, *Pervaia mirovaia voina*, 554–563.

26. Averchenko and Lashkov, "Deistviia aviatsii," 14–15; Averchenko, "Brusilovskii proryv, bor'ba v vozdukhe: chast' 2—nastuplenie," *Voenno-istoricheskii zhurnal*, no. 12 (2011): 11–19.

27. Brusilov to army commanders, 3 August 1916, *Strategicheskii ocherk*, 5:118.

28. *Strategicheskii ocherk*, 5:102–108, on Nicholas, see 107; *Strategicheskii ocherk*, 6:84–91, 98–110. Zaionchkovskii, *Pervaia mirovaia voina*, 606.

29. Ian F. W. Beckett, *The Great War*, 2nd ed. (Harlow, UK: Pearson Longman, 2007), 160–163; Dowling, *Brusilov*, 122–126; Alistair Horne, *The Price of Glory: Verdun, 1916* (London: Penguin, 1964); Rostunov, *Russkii front*, 326. Zaionchkovskii, *Pervaia mirovaia voina*, 552; *Istoriia voennoi strategii Rossii* (Moscow: Kuchkovo pole, 2000), 114.

30. Dowling, *Brusilov*, 168; Nicholas Golovin, "Brusilov's Offensive: The Galician Battle of 1916," *Slavonic and East European Review*, no. 39 (1935): 588; S. G. Nelipovich, "Tsena pobedy," *Voenno-istoricheskii zhurnal*, no. 10 (2011): 3, 7; Os'kin, "Russkaia loshad'," 43; *Strategicheskii ocherk*, 5:73, 108; Zaionchkovskii, *Pervaia mirovaia voina*, 563–564. A Soviet-era source claimed 1.5 million casualties among the Central Powers and 500,000 for the Russians: Rostunov, *Russkii front*, 325.

31. *Strategicheskii ocherk*, 6:25, 110, 134.

32. Golovin, "Brusilov's Offensive," 578, 587; *Strategicheskii ocherk*, 6:25, 110, 134.

CHAPTER 11. THE ROMANIAN DISTRACTION, 1916

1. Samuel R. Williamson Jr., *Austria-Hungary and the Origins of the First World War* (London: Macmillan, 1991), 209; Catherine Durandin, "Rumania, the War and the Army, 1914–1930," *War & Society* 3, no. 2 (September 1985): 45–54; S. L. A. Marshall,

World War I (New York: Random House, 1965), 262; V. N. Vinogradov, *Rumyniia v gody Pervoi mirovoi voiny* (Moscow: Nauka, 1969), 121–148.

2. "Hungary and Roumania in 1916," *Slavonic Review* 6, no. 17 (1927): 441–443; Ian F. W. Beckett, *The Great War*, 2nd ed. (Harlow, UK: Pearson Longman, 2007), 171; Glenn Torrey, *The Romanian Battlefront in World War I* (Lawrence: University Press of Kansas, 2011), 10–13; Vinogradov, *Rumyniia*, 148–163.

3. William J. Astore and Dennis E. Showalter, *Hindenburg: Icon of German Militarism* (Washington, D.C.: Potomac Books, 2005), 36–38; Michael B. Barrett, *Prelude to Blitzkrieg: The 1916 Austro-German Campaign in Romania* (Bloomington: Indiana University Press, 2013), 32–39; Anna von der Goltz, *Hindenburg: Power, Myth, and the Rise of the Nazis* (Oxford: Oxford University Press, 2009), 34–36; S. L. A. Marshall, *World War I* (New York: Random House, 1965), 277. Torrey, "Campaign of 1916," 27–29; Vinogradov, 164–169.

4. A. M. Zaionchkovskii, *Pervaia mirovaia voina* (St. Petersburg: Poligon, 2002), 598; Barrett, *Prelude*, 15–20; Torrey, *Romanian Battlefront*, 14–21; Glenn Torrey, "The Romanian Campaign of 1916: Its Impact on the Belligerents," *Slavic Review* 39, no. 1 (1980): 26–28; Vinogradov, *Rumyniia*, 173–177.

5. Torrey, *Romanian Battlefront*, 21–29; *Strategicheskii ocherk voiny 1914–1918 gg*, vol. 6 (Moscow: VVRS, 1923), 57–58; Zaionchkovskii, *Pervaia mirovaia voina*, 597.

6. Barrett, *Prelude*, 7–15; Torrey, *Romanian Battlefront*, 30–33.

7. Zaionchkovskii, *Pervaia mirovaia voina*, 559–560; Barrett, *Prelude*, 20–29, 50–59; Torrey, *Romanian Battlefront*, 42–60; Vinogradov, *Rumyniia*, 177–179.

8. For Zaionchkovskii's memoirs of his experience, see "Zapiski gen. A. M. Zaionchkovskogo o Dobrudzhanskoi operatsii 1916 g.," *Krasnyi arkhiv*, no. 3 (1933): 24–45; quotation on 30. For Alekseev's accusation, see Alfred Knox, *With the Russian Army, 1914–1917* (London: Hutchinson, 1921), 484. See also Barrett, *Prelude*, 68–71.

9. On Mackensen's offensive in the south, see Brusilov, *Vospominaniia*, 254–256; Barrett, *Prelude*, 60–68, 71–92; Vinogradov, *Rumyniia*, 179–181; *Strategicheskii ocherk*, 6:112–114; Torrey, *Romanian Battlefront*, 61–90.

10. On the Flămânda crossing see Barrett, *Prelude*, 127–144; Torrey, *Romanian Battlefront*, 80–90; Vinogradov, *Rumyniia*, 181–182. For Alekseev's telegram, see Vinogradov, *Rumyniia*, 181.

11. For the Central Powers' counteroffensive in the Carpathians, see Barrett, *Prelude*, 93–126; Torrey, 93–109, 116–133; Vinogradov, *Rumyniia*, 182–184.

12. On Romanian collapse, see Barrett, *Prelude*, 144–184, 238–280; Torrey, *Romanian Battlefront* 115–116, 128–153; Vinogradov, 184–190.

13. Brusilov, 256–258; Barrett, *Prelude*, 280–289; Torrey, *Romanian Battlefront* 154–158; for Zaionchkovskii quote, see *Strategicheskii ocherk*, 6:97.

14. Barrett, *Prelude*, 289–297; Torrey, *Romanian Battlefront*, 158–170; Zaionchkovskii, *Pervaia mirovaia voina*, 606.

CHAPTER 12. THE COLLAPSE, 1917

1. *Strategicheskii ocherk voiny 1914–1918 gg*, vol. 7 (Moscow: VVRS, 1923), 16–17.

2. Louise Erwin Heenan, *Russian Democracy's Fatal Blunder: The Summer Offensive of 1917* (New York: Praeger, 1987), 11–15; I. I. Rostunov, *Russkii front pervoi mirovoi voiny* (Moscow: Nauka, 1975), 331–333; Jehuda L. Wallach, *Uneasy Coalition: The Entente Experience in World War I* (Westport, Conn.: Greenwood, 1993): 83–85; A. Iu. Pavlov, "Rossiia na mezhsoiuznicheskikh konferentsiiakh v gody Pervoi mirovoi voiny," *Voenno-istoricheskii zhurnal*, no. 2 (2010): 28–30; *Strategicheskii ocherk*, 7:12–15; A. Zhilin, "Nastuplenie russkoi armii letom 1917 goda v voenno-politicheskikh planakh antanty," *Voenno-istoricheskii zhurnal*, no. 3 (1982): 59–60.

3. A. Kavtaradze, "Iiun'skoe nastuplenie russkoi armii v 1917 godu," *Voenno-istoricheskii zhurnal*, no. 5 (1967): 111; Heenan, *Fatal Blunder*, 15–18; Rostunov, *Russkii front*, 333–337; *Strategicheskii ocherk*, 7:17–31.

4. Heenan, *Fatal Blunder*, 23–33; L. P. Morris, "The Russians, the Allies and the War, February–July 1917," *SEER* 50, no. 118 (1972): 34; Pavlov, "Rossiia na mezhsoiuznicheskikh konferentsiiakh," 30–31; Zhilin, "Nastuplenie," 60–61.

5. On the Jelgava operation, see Rostunov, *Russkii front*, 338–341; *Strategicheskii ocherk*, 6:121–129; Zaionchkovskii, *Pervaia mirovaia voina*, 622–626; Allan K. Wildman, *The End of the Russian Imperial Army*, vol. 1 (Princeton, N.J.: Princeton University Press, 1980), 116–117.

6. F. Akimov, "Bolsheviki v bor'be za soldatskie massy Iugo-Zapadnogo fronta (1914-fevral' 1917 g.)," *Voenno-istoricheskii zhurnal*, no. 2 (1977): 87–88; Wildman, *End of the Russian Imperial Army*, 1:75–120.

7. Tsuyoshi Hasegawa, *The February Revolution: Petrograd, 1917* (Seattle: University of Washington Press), 215–310; Rex Wade, *The Russian Revolution, 1917* (Cambridge: Cambridge University Press, 2000), 29–42; Wildman, *End of the Russian Imperial Army*, 1:121–158.

8. Hasegawa, *February Revolution*, 313–390; Alexander Rabinowitch, *Prelude to Revolution: The Petrograd Bolsheviks and the July 1917 Uprising* (Bloomington: Indiana University Press, 1968), 32–53; Wade, *Russian Revolution*, 42–52.

9. Hasegawa, *February Revolution*, 431–515.

10. John R. Boyd, "The Origins of Order No. 1," *Soviet Studies* 19, no. 3 (1968): 359–372; Hasegawa, *February Revolution*, 390–404; Wildman, *End of the Russian Imperial Army*, 1:182–190; *Strategicheskii ocherk*, 7:40–42; Guchkov to Alekseev, 22 March 1917, *Strategicheskii ocherk*, 7:121–129.

11. Rostunov, *Russkii front*, 346–349; S. A. Solntseva, "1917: Kadrovaia politika revoliutsiia v rossiiskoi armii," *Otechestvennaia istoriia*, no. 6 (2004): 102–116 (for total of dismissed officers, see 104); *Strategicheskii ocherk*, 7:40, 122–123; Wildman, *End of the Russian Imperial Army*, 1:214.

12. Keith E. Neilson, "The Breakup of the Anglo-Russian Alliance: The Question of Supply in 1917," *International History Review* 3, no. 1 (1981): 62–75; Charles J.

Weeks Jr. and Joseph O. Baylen, "Admiral Kolchak's Mission to the United States, 10 September–9 November 1917," *Military Affairs* 40, no. 2 (1976): 64–66.

13. Paul von Hindenburg, *Out of My Life* (London: Cassell, 1920), 270; Erich Ludendorff, *Ludendorff's Own Story, August 1914–November 1918* (New York: Harper, 1919), 2:13–14.

14. V. N. Bogatyrev, "Organizatsiia politicheskoi raboty v Vooruzhennykh silakh Rossii v marte-oktiabre 1917 goda," *Voenno-istoricheskii zhurnal*, no. 10 (2005): 51–52; Marc Ferro, "The Russian Soldier in 1917: Undisciplined, Patriotic, and Revolutionary," *Slavic Review* 30, no. 3 (1971): 483–512.

15. M. A. Babkina, "'My, voennyi sviashchenniki, vsem serdtsem provetstvuem obnovlenie rodiny nashei na nachalakh politicheskoi, grazhdanskoi, i religioznoi svobody," *Voenno-istoricheskii zhurnal*, no. 2 (2006): 37–41; Bogatyrev, "Organizatsiia politicheskoi raboty," 52.

16. V. L. Kozhevin, "Deiatel'nost' soiuza ofitserov armii i flota (mai–avgust 1917 g.), *Voprosy istorii*, no. 9 (2005): 137–142; Matthew Rendle, "Forging a Revolutionary Army: The All-Russian Military Union in 1917," *War in History* 19, no. 1 (2012): 49–71.

17. Bogatyrev, "Organizatsiia politicheskoi raboty," 53–54; A. A. Budarin, "Spetsial'nye predstaviteli novoi vlasti: Materialy po istorii voennykh komissarov 1917 goda," *Voenno-istoricheskii zhurnal*, no. 12 (2003): 33–34.

18. Robert S. Feldman, "The Russian General Staff and the June 1917 Offensive," *Soviet Studies* 19, no. 4 (April 1968): 535; Richard Abraham, *Alexander Kerenskii: The First Love of the Revolution* (New York: Columbia University Press, 1987), 201–202; Wildman, *End of the Russian Imperial Army*, 2:18–24.

19. A. S. Senin, "Zhenskie batal'ony i voennye komandy v 1917 godu," *Voprosy istorii*, no. 10 (1987): 176–182; Laurie S. Stoff, *They Fought for the Motherland: Russia's Women Soldiers in World War I and Revolution* (Lawrence: University Press of Kansas, 2006), 53–103, 114–139; Melissa Stockdale, "'My Death for the Motherland Is Happiness': Women, Patriotism, and Soldiering in Russia's Great War, 1914–1917," *American Historical Review* 109, no. 1 (2004): 78–116.

20. F. Akimov, "Bolsheviki v bor'be za soldatskie massy Iugo-Zapadnogo fronta (1914–fevral' 1917 g.)," *Voenno-istoricheskii zhurnal*, no. 2 (1977): 84; Feldman, "General Staff and 1917," 527–528; Kavtaradze, "Iiun'skoe nastuplenie," 112–113; M. V. Os'kin, "Problema rezerva dlia general'nogo nastupleniia russkoi armii v 1917 g.," *Voprosy istorii*, no. 8 (2011): 144–145.

21. Rostunov, *Russkii front*, 353–354.

22. *Strategicheskii ocherk*, 7:44–45, 58, 130–133; Feldman, "General Staff and 1917," 529–532; Rex Wade, *The Russian Search for Peace, February–October 1917* (Stanford, Calif.: Stanford University Press, 1969), 51–73.

23. *Strategicheskii ocherk*, 7:48–53.

24. Abraham, *First Love*, 198–201.

25. On the Kerenskii offensive in general, see Feldman, "General Staff and 1917,"

537–539; Kavtaradze, "Iiun'skoe nastuplenie," 111–117; Zaionchkovskii, *Pervaia mirovaia voina*, 656–659; A. V. Oleinikov, "Udarnye batal'ony russkoi armii: Organizatsiia, taktika, i podgotovka shturmovykh chastei v Pervuiu mirovuiu voinu," *Voenno-istoricheskii zhurnal*, no. 8 (2010): 13–14; Rostunov, *Russkii front*, 358–359; *Strategicheskii ocherk*, 7:64–74.

26. *Strategicheskii ocherk*, 7:72.

27. On Kornilov, see P. M. Portugal'skii, P. D. Alekseev, and V. A Runov, *Pervaia mirovaia v zhizneopisaniiakh russkikh voenachal'nikov* (Moscow: Elakos, 1994), 159–208.

28. On the Austro-German counteroffensive, see Rostunov, *Russkii front*, 359–361; *Strategicheskii ocherk*, 7:78–84, 88–92.

29. Rostunov, *Russkii front*, 362–363.

30. Stoff, *They Fought for the Motherland*, 103–113.

31. Abraham, *First Love*, 231–234; *Strategicheskii ocherk*, 7:75–76, 85–88.

32. On the July Days, see Rabinowitch, *Prelude to Revolution*.

33. Michael B. Barrett, *Operation Albion: The German Conquest of the Baltic Islands* (Bloomington: Indiana University Press, 2008), 33–42.

34. On background and preparations for the Riga Offensive, see Bruce I. Gudmundsson, *Stormtroop Tactics: Innovation in the German Army, 1914–1918* (Westport, Conn.: Greenwood, 1995), 114–117; Zaionchkovskii, *Pervaia mirovaia voina*, 668–670; Rostunov, *Russkii front*, 366–369; *Strategicheskii ocherk*, 7:95–97.

35. On the Riga campaign, see Gudmundsson, *Stormtroop Tactics*, 117–118; Zaionchkovskii, *Pervaia mirovaia voina*, 670–676; Rostunov, *Russkii front*, 369–371; *Strategicheskii ocherk*, 7:97–102.

36. Klembovskii to Danilov, 4 September 1917, *Strategicheskii ocherk*, 7:104.

37. Richard Pipes, *The Russian Revolution* (New York: Knopf, 1990), 446–447; Wildman, *End of the Russian Imperial Army*, 2:184–191.

38. On the Kornilov Mutiny, see Wildman, *End of the Russian Imperial Army*, 2:191–223. For Kornilov as eager to seize power, see Alexander Rabinowitch, *The Bolsheviks Come to Power: The Revolution of 1917 in Petrograd* (New York: Norton, 1976), 94–150; for Kornilov as the dupe of the manipulative Kerenskii, see George Katkov, *Russia, 1917: The Kornilov Affair—Kerenskii and the Break-up of the Russian Army* (London: Longman, 1980), and Pipes, *Russian Revolution*, 451–464; for an effort at a compromise, see James D. White, "The Kornilov Affair—A Study in Counter-Revolution," *Soviet Studies* 20, no. 2 (1968): 187–205.

39. Alekseev to Dukhonin, 15 September 1917, *Strategicheskii ocherk*, 7:106–107.

40. Richard L. DiNardo, "Huns with Web-Feet: Operation Albion, 1917," *War in History* 12, no. 4 (2005): 396–417; A. Harding Ganz, "'Albion'—The Baltic Islands Operation," *Military Affairs* 42, no. 2 (April 1978): 91–97; Barrett, *Albion*, 42–55, 61–64; *Strategicheskii ocherk*, 7:92–94, 107–110.

41. Ganz, "Albion," 93–94; O. Kuvaldin, "Moonzund: 1917 god," *Morskoi sbornik*, no. 11 (1987): 16–18; Barrett, *Albion*, 63–72, 83–84, 101–108, 122–124; Zaionchkovskii, *Pervaia mirovaia voina*, 677.

42. Ganz, "Albion," 94–95; Kuvaldin, "Moonzund," 18–19; Barrett, *Albion*, 94–96, 116–128; *Strategicheskii ocherk*, 7:111–112.

43. Kuvaldin, "Moonzund," 19–20; Barrett, *Albion*, 101–103, 128–152.

44. Kuvaldin, "Moonzund," 19; Barrett, *Albion*, 152–164.

45. Barrett, *Albion*, 165–186.

46. Ibid., 199–200; Kuvaldin, "Moonzund," 19–22; S. D. Lappo, "Moonzund i tserel'," *Morskoi sbornik*, no. 12 (1998): 69.

CONCLUSION

1. Giordan Fong, "The Movement of German Divisions to the Western Front, Winter 1917–1918," *War in History* 7, no. 2 (2000): 225–229; I. I. Rostunov, *Russkii front pervoi mirovoi voiny* (Moscow: Nauka, 1976), 373.

2. A. Kavtaradze, "Oktiabr' i likvidatsiia kontrrevoliutsionnoi Stavki," *VIZh* #4 (1968): 113–115; S. N. Bazanov, "Poslednye dni general-leitenanta N. N. Dukhonina v Stavke," *VIZh* #11 (2001): 54–55.

3. Kavtaradze, "Oktiabr','" 116–120; Bazanov, "Poslednye dni," 55–60.

4. M. V. Frunze, "Edinaia voennaia doktrina," in *Izbrannye proizvedeniia* (Moscow: Voenizdat, 1940), 28.

5. On the general issues of Russia's limited historical memory of World War I, see Karen Petrone, *The Great War in Russian Memory* (Bloomington: Indiana University Press, 2011).

6. David L. Hoffman and Yanni Kotsonis, *Russian Modernity: Politics, Knowledge, Practices* (New York: St. Martin's, 2000); Peter Holquist, "Information Is the Alpha and Omega of Our Work: Bolshevik Surveillance in its Pan-European Context," *Journal of Modern History* 69, no. 3 (1997), 415–450; Holquist, *Making War: Forging Revolution: Russia's Continuum of Crisis, 1914–1921* (Cambridge, Mass.: Harvard University Press, 2003); Joshua A. Sanborn, *Drafting the Russian Nation: Military Conscription, Total War, and Mass Politics, 1905–1925* (Dekalb: Northern Illinois University Press, 2003).

7. Compare the picture of Western Europe in Jonathan House, *Combined Arms Warfare in the 20th Century* (Lawrence: University Press of Kansas, 2001), 64; Brian Bond, *War and Society in Europe, 1870–1970* (Leicester: Fontana, 1983), 139–141; Alvin D. Coox, "Military Effectiveness of Armed Forces in the Interwar Period, 1919–41: A Review," in *Military Effectiveness*, ed. Allan Millett and Williamson Murray (Boston: Allen & Unwin, 1988), 2:257–258; with the Russian-Soviet experience in Bruce Menning, *Bayonets before Bullets* (Bloomington: Indiana University Press, 1992), 123–129, 211–217, and Richard Harrison, *The Russian Way of War: Operational Art, 1904–1940* (Lawrence: University Press of Kansas, 2001).

8. A. G. Kavtaradze, *Voennye spetsialisty na sluzbe Respubliki Sovetov, 1917–1920* (Moscow: Nauka, 1988), 222–224; John Erickson, *The Soviet High Command* (New York: St. Martin's, 1962), 318.

9. Iosif Stalin, *Sochineniia* (Moscow: Partizdat, 1946), 4:148–151.

10. Mikhail Frunze, "Front i tyl v voine budushchego," in *Izbrannye proizvedeniia* (Moscow: Voenizdat, 1940), 69.

11. N. A. Danilov, *Ekonomika i podgotovka k voine* (Moscow: Voenizdat, 1926), 190; David R. Stone, *Hammer and Rifle: The Militarization of the Soviet Union, 1926–1933* (Lawrence: University Press of Kansas, 2000), 52, 57–58. There are obvious parallels here to Hitler's reluctance to fully mobilize the German economy for war. For the shell shortage as myth, see Norman Stone, *The Eastern Front*, 144–164.

12. I. Korotkov, "Obobshchenie opyta voin v mezhvoennyi period," *VIZh* #6 (1976): 95–100; T. A. Baraksina, "'Staraia russkaia armiia v etoi voine dala ves'ma mnogo pouchitel'nogo . . .'" *Voenno-istoricheskii zhurnal* #7 (2002): 78–80; Revolutionary Military Council order #355, 10 December 1918, Russian State Military Archive, f. 4, op. 3, d. 48, l. 220ob; Petrone, *Great War*, 205–208, 214–220; *Strategicheskii ocherk voiny 1914–1918 gg*, 7 vols. (Moscow: Vysshii voennyi redaktsionnyi sovet, 1920–1922).

13. See for example, M. A. Rozhdestvenskii, *Lutskii proryv* (Moscow: Voenizdat, 1938); V. Betoshnikov, *Brusilovskii proryv: Operativno-strategicheskii ocherk* (Moscow: Voenizdat, 1940); *Nastuplenie Iugo-zapadnogo fronta: Sbornik dokumentov* (Moscow: Voenizdat, 1940).

14. Vejas Gabriel Liulevicius, *War Land on the Eastern Front* (Cambridge: Cambridge University Press, 2005).

A Note on Sources

The Russian Revolution and subsequent Civil War imposed a split on available sources and, as a result, in the literature on the Eastern Front. Histories of the war written and published in the west relied on German and Austrian sources, supplemented by the writings of Russian exiles. The key figures on the Eastern Front were quick to write memoirs: notably Falkenhayn and Ludendorff in 1919, Hindenburg in 1920. In addition, the new Austrian state published a voluminous official history, *Austria-Hungary's Last War (Österreich-Ungarns letzter Krieg) 1914–1918*, published 1930–1939. Its German equivalent was *The World War (Der Weltkrieg) 1914–1918*, published from 1925 through 1944. Memoirs on the Russian side were thinner for the high command: Tsar Nicholas kept a fairly pedestrian diary. He and both of his wartime chiefs of staff—Yanushkevich and Alekseev—died in 1918 without leaving memoirs. Grand Duke Nikolai, the first commander in chief, survived to escape into exile, but likewise did not write memoirs. Many émigrés did recount their experiences, of course, though they lacked access to documentary sources. Quartermaster-General Danilov published his account of the war in 1924, and Nikolai Golovin's 1931 *The Russian Army in World War I* was particularly influential. Anton Kersnovskii, a young émigré, wrote a lengthy history of the Russian army that included a great deal on the First World War. Brusilov's memoirs were published in 1929 in the Soviet Union and abroad, and quickly translated into English. British military attaché Alfred Knox also published his account of his time in Russia in 1921 as *With the Russian Army: 1914–1917*. Winston Churchill's *The Unknown War*, published in 1931, used these sources extensively. A generation of English-language history, as a result, was written by eyewitnesses or based on eyewitness accounts, but without access to Russian archives.

In Soviet Russia, by contrast, memoirs were much less prominent as tsarist officers who remained in the country were circumspect about their experiences. Though the new Soviet Russia that emerged from World War I saw itself as distinct from the tsarist regime that fought the war, the Red Army recognized the need to understand military history in order to prepare for the next war. It systematically gathered materials in order to write the history of the Eastern Front. The result was the *Strategic Outline of the War* [*Strategicheskii ocherk voiny*], *1914–1918*, published in seven volumes from 1920 to 1923. Relentlessly operational in its focus, the quality of the work is uniformly high, though it does not discuss the Caucasus Front. A. M. Zaionchkovskii, author of parts of the *Strategic Outline*, in 1923 also published *The World War* [*Mirovaia voina*], *1914–1918*, a quite good stand-alone history of the war covering all combatants and all fronts. The authors of these works, generally high-ranking tsarist veterans of the war, enjoyed extensive access to original documents. While they were not averse to settling personal scores, the collective nature of the project and the Red Army's urgent need for an objective evaluation of the war prevented the worst excesses of individual bias and political correctness. While Soviet accounts included boiler-plate commentary on the failings of the tsarist regime, they were quite accurate on the operational history of the war.

This pattern continued into the 1930s. The Soviet military published a series of document collections, each hundreds of pages long and containing hundreds of documents, on key operations. These included major collections on the 1914 invasion of East Prussia (*Vostochno-Prusskaia operatsiia*, 1939), the battles in Central Poland (*Varshavsko-Ivangorodskaia operatsiia*, 1938), the fighting around Łódź (*Lodzinskaia operatsiia*, 1936), the 1915 Austro-German breakthrough at Gorlice-Tarnów (*Gorlitskaia operatsiia*, 1938), and the 1916 Brusilov offensive (*Nastuplenie Iugozapadnogo fronta*, 1940). This scholarly raw material was accompanied by dozens of narrower monographs on particular battles and campaigns, many of high quality, as the Red Army prepared for renewed war against Germany on the plains of Eastern Europe.

After World War II, Russia's experience in the First World War was generally a low priority for Soviet scholars. Certainly good work was done: K. F. Shatsillo and A. G. Kavtaradze wrote extensively about imperial Russian defense policy and the Russian army's central organization. I. I. Rostunov, relying heavily on the *Strategic Outline*, wrote the standard Soviet history of the Eastern Front and a biography of Brusilov. Nonetheless, there was comparatively little effort to update prewar Soviet literature on operational history 1914–1917, as the military history profession emphasized the experience of the Second World War.

The basis for a renewed examination of the war in the east certainly existed. The Russian State Military-Historical Archive, located in Moscow, collects documents relating to Russia's military past through the end of World War I, and contains well over 3 million files, each of which can contain hundreds of pages of documents. The available source material on World War I, as a result, is enormous. In recent years, the history of the Eastern Front has drawn renewed interest from scholars in Russia and abroad. For Russians, the end of a Soviet-centered narrative of the past has refocused attention on aspects of history that had been systematically neglected before the fall of communism. In the West, an excessive focus among historians on

1917 and the Russian Revolution as a complete and total break with the past has given way to an effort to look for continuities from the tsarist into the Soviet period, and that naturally requires a closer look at Russia's wartime experience. Russian and Western scholars have thus begun the process of systematically mining those documents to expand our insights into Russia's experience of the First World War, but that is still at a relatively early stage. A number of excellent monographs have expanded our understanding of the Russian home front, but there is much less in English on specifically military questions.

Otherwise excellent surveys of operations from the German and Austrian point of view by Richard DiNardo and Dennis Showalter do not take advantage of Russian sources. A number of Russian scholars such as Oleg Airapetov, A. B. Astashov, A. V. Oleinikov, and Maksim Os'kin have tapped into newly available sources to produce a range of books and articles, but little of that has made its way into English-language literature on the war. There are some exceptions: Bruce Menning has begun to clarify the nature of prewar Russian planning, for example. Russian experience on the battlefield, however, has remained opaque to an English-speaking audience. The goal of this book is to bring that research to the attention of a broader reading public.

Index